Politics, Murder and Love in an Italian Family

What did it mean to live with fascism, communism and totalitarianism in modern Italy? And what should we learn from the experiences of a martyred liberal democrat father and his communist son? Through the prism of a single, exceptional family, the Amendolas, R. J. B. Bosworth reveals the heart of twentieth-century Italian politics. Giovanni and Giorgio Amendola, father and son, were both highly capable and dedicated Anti-Fascists. Each failed to make it to the top of the Italian political pyramid but nevertheless played a major part in Italy's history. Both also had rich but contrasting private lives. Each married a foreign and accomplished woman: Giovanni, a woman from a distinguished German-Russian intellectual family; Giorgio, a Parisian working-class girl, who, to him, embodied revolution. This vivid and engaging biographical study explores the highs and lows of a family that was at the centre of Italian politics over several generations. Tracing the complex relationship between Anti-Fascist politics and the private lives of individuals and of the family, *Politics, Murder and Love in an Italian Family* offers a profound portrait of a century of Italian life.

R. J. B. Bosworth is one of the world's leading historians of modern Italy. He is an Emeritus Professor at Jesus College, Oxford, and the author or editor of thirty-one books and many chapters and articles. He published his first book with Cambridge University Press, *Italy, the Least of the Great Powers: Italian Foreign Policy before the First World War*, and was co-editor, with Joseph Maiolo, of the second volume of *The Cambridge History of the Second World War*. His numerous prize-winning publications include the definitive biography of Mussolini in English.

Figure 0.1 Giovanni and Giorgio, staring at different futures (1911).

Politics, Murder and Love
in an Italian Family

The Amendolas in the Age of Totalitarianisms

R. J. B. Bosworth

University of Oxford

CAMBRIDGE
UNIVERSITY PRESS

Shaftesbury Road, Cambridge CB2 8EA, United Kingdom

One Liberty Plaza, 20th Floor, New York, NY 10006, USA

477 Williamstown Road, Port Melbourne, VIC 3207, Australia

314–321, 3rd Floor, Plot 3, Splendor Forum, Jasola District Centre,
New Delhi – 110025, India

103 Penang Road, #05–06/07, Visioncrest Commercial, Singapore 238467

Cambridge University Press is part of Cambridge University Press & Assessment,
a department of the University of Cambridge.

We share the University's mission to contribute to society through the pursuit of
education, learning and research at the highest international levels of excellence.

www.cambridge.org
Information on this title: www.cambridge.org/9781009280174

DOI: 10.1017/9781009280167

First published 2023

Printed in the United Kingdom by TJ Books Limited, Padstow Cornwall

A catalogue record for this publication is available from the British Library.

Library of Congress Cataloging-in-Publication Data
Names: Bosworth, R. J. B., author.
Title: Politics, murder and love in an Italian family : the Amendolas in the age of
    totalitarianisms / R.J.B. Bosworth.
Other titles: Amendolas in the age of totalitarianisms
Description: Cambridge, United Kingdom ; New York, NY : Cambridge
    University Press, [2023] | Includes bibliographical references and index.
Identifiers: LCCN 2022033343 (print) | LCCN 2022033344 (ebook) |
    ISBN 9781009280174 (hardback) | ISBN 9781009280211 (paperback) |
    ISBN 9781009280167 (epub)
Subjects: LCSH: Politicians–Italy–Biography. | Amendola family. | Amendola,
    Giovanni, 1882-1926. | Amendola, Giorgio. | Anti-fascist movements–Italy–
    History–20th century. | Italy–Politics and government–20th century.
Classification: LCC DG574 .B67 2023 (print) | LCC DG574 (ebook) |
    DDC 945.09092/2–dc23/eng/20220928
LC record available at https://lccn.loc.gov/2022033343
LC ebook record available at https://lccn.loc.gov/2022033344

ISBN 978-1-009-28017-4 Hardback

For David Laven and his love for a myriad of Italies

Contents

Figures

Preface

'What a fine fellow you are!' she would say. 'How fine and fat!' In these parts [the Basilicata] ... fatness is a mark of beauty; perhaps because the underfed peasants can never hope to attain it and it remains the prerogative of the well-to-do.*

Carlo Levi, *Christ Stopped at Eboli: The Story of a Year*
(New York: Farrar, Straus and Giroux, 1947), p. 154

I have written my Covid book. It displays what happens when an old historian is locked down, the Bodleian is to most intents and purposes closed, but trade with Italian second-hand bookshops is open. A pandemic may have been the initial trigger of *Politics, Murder and Love in an Italian Family: The Amendolas in an Age of Totalitarianisms,* but its other origins lie well in the past and in my own '*lungo viaggio*' (long journey) into being the historian I am of modern Italy. My first memory date is 1976. Then, having departed from Australia just before the disastrous election of 13 December 1975, when a benighted popular vote supported vice-regal intervention and sent the enlightened Labor government of Gough Whitlam packing, my wife, Michal, our two small children and I lived in Rome through the next twelve months. I spent most days trekking across town to the diplomatic archives held at the Farnesina, planned to be the headquarters of the Fascist Party but finished after 1944 and converted into the ministry of foreign affairs. I was then an 'old fashioned[ish] diplomatic historian', starting to write *Italy, the Least of the Great Powers: Italian Foreign Policy before the First World War* (Cambridge, 1979). The archives were only open from 9 a.m. till 1 p.m.; in reality, given the surly habits of the lady keeper there, from *c.* 9.30 a.m. to *c.* 12.15 p.m. During those hours she spent most of her time in the consultation room talking loudly on the phone. It was a relief

---

*Carlo Levi's 1935–6 record of peasant thought far from Gramscian theoretics or 'democracy', but perhaps an unspoken assumption of the large presence of the Amendolas, father and son, in Italy's South.

to turn over the last ambassadorial telegram of the day. I knew that I had a whole afternoon to Romanise.

This year – 1976 – turns up in Chapter 6 in my story of the Amendolas. In the national elections held on 20 June, the Italian Communist Party almost achieved a *sorpasso* (an overtaking) of the Christian Democrats who had ruled since 1946 – that is, even longer than the Liberal Country Party had dominated Australia before Whitlam. Such a gain might have entailed a *compromesso storico* (historic compromise) in a Eurocommunist manner with global effect. For an '*indipendente di sinistra*' (independent leftist) like myself, at least for part of 1976 I could boast to depressed friends enduring reactionary 'Liberal Country Party' restoration in Australia that Italy might be different.[1]

Before and after the elections, Mike, I and the children could happily go to such local leftist consciousness-raising events as a *Festa dell'Unità* (punning on unity and the name of the communist daily paper, *L'Unità*) beside, say, gorgeous Castel San Angelo. At the cinema, we could view the first (162 minutes) and second (154 minutes) parts of Bernardo Bertolucci's *1900*, with its allegedly definitive peasant history and what now seems its cor blimey Anti-Fascist message on the imminent triumph of the Resistance. Why else did (Marx's) old mole of revolution turn up (for the second time in the movie) in the last scene? We could pack into the Teatro Eliseo on the Via Nazionale and hear Oxbridgean, radical, 'milord' Denis Mack Smith address a vast audience about his new book on Mussolini, *Le guerre del Duce*.[2] It offered a rival, less polite, view of the Duce from that being ponderously advanced by Renzo De Felice, the ultimate 'archive rat' in his endless 'biography' (minus the human side) of Mussolini.[3] A major contributor to this debate was none other than Giorgio Amendola. In 1976, he gave an interview about Anti-Fascism in what was then a modish publishing activity. More about that work can be found in Chapter 6.[4] But, better than observing historiographical wrangles, I could read – and did read – another new book, Giorgio Amendola's *Una scelta di vita*, and enjoy its mixture of party and family, politics and sex. Readers of *Politics, murder and love in an Italian family* will find a similar amalgam in the pages that follow.

In 1977, my family and I returned to Australia, to stay there most of the time for the next three decades, if with annual trips to Italian libraries and archives. At the University of Sydney, there had been a major development with the arrival of a new Professor of Italian, the globalised Venetian Gino Rizzo. He could tell a good story about how, when an ordinary Fascist soldier, he had somehow lost his rifle but managed to hide the fact from his officers for over a year. Rizzo presided over a foundation named after his very English predecessor, Freddy May.

From the History Department I was invited to be the Frederick May Foundation's (FMF's) deputy director. Before too long, Whitlam accepted a role as the FMF's honorary governor and became an active participant in its events. That European winter, I travelled to Rome together with Rizzo and Gianfranco Cresciani, a Triestine immigrant to Australia and 'my first student', although he knew far more about Italy than I did, and was, and is, the only serious historian of Italians in Australia. We were a little astonished to be greeted with largesse at the Ministeri dei Beni Culturali and degli Affari Esteri (Ministries of Culture and of Foreign Affairs). It seemed that Italian government circles had decided that the 1976 crisis in Australia meant that it was an interesting country, even though the sizeable post-1945 emigration from Italy there had ceased a decade earlier.

So, every four years, while Gino and I stayed in post, in 1978, 1982 and 1986, the FMF could stage grandiose, interdisciplinary conferences. We could welcome the greatest figures in contemporary Italian culture – Umberto Eco,[5] La Gaia Scienza,[6] Adriano Spatola,[7] Giulia Niccolai, Alberto Asor Rosa, Francesco Alberoni, Giuseppe Bertolucci, Franco Ferraresi, Marina Zancan, Laura Balbo, Dacia Maraini, Paolo Valesio, Luigi Ballerini, Paolo Sylos-Labini, Marcello Colitti – and a parade of major historians – De Felice, Enrico Serra,[8] Emilio Gentile, Giovanni Sabbatucci, Ettore Sori, Gianfausto Rosoli, Franco Venturi, Sergio Bertelli, Sergio Romano,[9] Giorgio Spini,[10] Giuliano Procacci[11] and Rudolph Vecoli.[12] I have fond memories of Procacci (who was an Italian Communist Party senator) and Spini (the Waldensian leftist father of Valdo Spini, a sometime mayor of Florence destined to play a considerable part in what might be termed 'the strange death of Italian socialism') sitting on the lounge floor of our Sydney terrace in August 1978. They were helping us to a better knowledge of the words and tunes of such wartime songs as *Fischia al vento* (PCI) and *Bella ciao* (more generic). The flag of the 'Myth of the Resistance' had been planted in Australia (where the majority of immigrants, poor and rich, actually retained a nostalgia for Mussolini).

During its halcyon days, the FMF aspired to high cultural contact with Italy at its most contemporary, defying the immigrant world whose cautious and self-appointed leadership had been accustomed to represent itself cosily in meetings of Dante Alighieri societies. There, the deepest hope might be that, after listening to some talk or other, an Australian could peer knowledgeably at a Michelangelo (or was it a Botticelli?) and, more usefully, distinguish pappardelle from fettuccine on their next visit to Rome, Florence or Venice. By contrast, the FMF, steering away from 'pretty history' (as I, for one, disdainfully called it), published an academic yearbook, entitled *Altro polo* (Gino Rizzo assured us that the words appeared somewhere in Dante and so might have prefigured the religious poet's discovery of the Antipodes). I co-edited two of these,[13] but there were others on topics far from my own interests and knowledge.[14] All tried to be serious and to blend Italian and Australian expertise.

I had come back from Cambridge to Sydney in 1969 wearing a Harris tweed sports coat and a St John's College tie, still in quite a few senses a child of an Australo-British Empire (even if I had long supported Pakistan at cricket). But the FMF and its friendly and fascinating visitors were immersing me in an Italy that I could scarcely otherwise have known. I discarded the tie and doffed the coat. My path to being a historian of modern Italy was opening. And somewhere there was Giorgio Amendola's last autobiographical volume, *Un'isola*, with its artful mixture of Fascist tyranny and corruption, Giorgio's romantic love at first sight in Paris for Germaine, his working-class lifetime partner and wife, and their marriage on the prison island of Ponza. When I came to write a great deal about what I always call 'the Italian dictatorship', I was conditioned by Giorgio's image of totalitarianism, Italian-style. In his portrayal, it may have been intrusive and murderous but it always offered the chance of a special case. In other words, it was always potentially corrupt, Italian-style.

In Giorgio's account, Fascism, however bloody, never overwhelmed the family, the Italian family (and, hence, the Italian communist family). I have spent my lifetime exploring the nature of Mussolini's Italian dictatorship. In this, very likely, my last book, readers will find that I continue to avoid cosy moralising about absolute evil, even when Giovanni Amendola probably invented the word '*totalitatario*' and then sacrificed his life to the Italian dictatorship's bloody violence. Father and son were very different men. But each saw his own truth through a glass darkly, as all of us do or ought to admit to doing.

Abbreviations

ANC	Associazione Nazionale dei Combattenti e Reduci
ANI	Associazione Nazionalista Italiana
BANU	Bulgarian Agrarian National Union
BR	Brigate Rosse
CLN	Comitato di Liberazione Nazionale
EEC	European Economic Community
FMF	Frederick May Foundation
GAP	Gruppi di Azione Patriottica
GDP	gross domestic product
IMRO	Internal Macedonian Revolutionary Organisation
M5S	Movimento Cinque Stelle
MSI	Movimento Sociale Italiano
MVSN	Milizia Volontaria per la Sicurezza Nazionale
PCdI	Partito Comunista d'Italia
PCI	Partito Comunista Italiano
PDS	Partito Democratico della Sinistra
PFR	Partito Fascista Repubblicano
PNF	Partito Nazionale Fascista
PPI	Partito Popolare Italiano
PSI	Partito Socialista Italiano
RSI	Repubblica Sociale Italiana
SAP	Sezione Alleati del Proletariato
SPQR	Senatus Populusque Romanus

Introduction

When I told Clare Alexander, my splendid agent for over two decades, that I wanted to write a book about the Amendolas, father and son, she replied sceptically: 'Who has ever heard of the Amendolas?' In Italy, as noted in my Conclusion, Giovanni, the Anti-Fascist, is commemorated in almost every town and city; Giorgio less so, but he does have an active foundation named in his honour. But, outside Italy, Clare was right.

My initial response was to compose my first chapter. My purpose in Chapter 1 is to highlight through 'thick description' three drastically violent episodes in the Amendolas' story. Two were pitiless Fascist bashings of Giovanni, the first in Rome on *Santo Stefano* (Boxing Day), 1923; the second in Tuscany on the night of 20–21 July 1925. Giovanni died in Cannes on 7 April 1926, very much as a result of the violence inflicted on him.

His eldest son, the teenage Giorgio, watched the mayhem happen and was there at Giovanni's bedside when he died in agony. From then on, and following his father's testament, Giorgio found himself automatically burdened with becoming the new 'head' of the Amendola family. Before too long, he grew disgusted by the pessimistic inaction of Giovanni's Anti-Fascist friends and, for example, the closure into pure scholarship of the liberal historian and philosopher Benedetto Croce. In reaction, in November 1929, he made what he called his 'life choice' for communism as the only serious way to oppose Mussolini's dictatorship. Two years later he departed for Paris and began work for the Partito Comunista d'Italia (PCdI or Communist Party of Italy) under its canny leader, Palmiro Togliatti.[1]

Over the next decade Giorgio was a loyal communist, and thus an obedient Stalinist, even if Togliatti and some other PCdI chiefs may have secretly retained in their hearts Italian comprehensions of how the world worked best. In any case, throughout the 1930s, Giorgio spent quite a bit of his time in Fascist gaols. During this time – first in Paris, then in Italy, and then back in France – he pursued in his personal life a love story with a young woman named Germaine Lecocq from Paris. She was young,

1

beautiful and loving, and she also came from what Giorgio romantically thought was the real City of Revolution. Meanwhile, the Party leadership always knew that Giorgio was an Amendola and craftily sought to harness both his commitment and the prestige of his name to their cause.

In 1943 came new opportunity. In April, Giorgio secretly crossed the Italian border and became part of the communist effort to organise armed resistance to Mussolini and, from September, to the Nazi Germans who had occupied much of the country. The symbolic act occurred on 23 March 1944, when, under Giorgio's command, young partisans organised an assault on Nazi soldiers, killing thirty-three of them. In response, the Nazis massacred 335 'Anti-Fascists' of various political and religious stances at the Ardeatine Caves, just outside Rome. Chapter 1 ends with a thick description of this still deeply controversial event – part Amendola family vengeance, part communist terrorism, part heroic resistance against alien tyranny.

Inevitably, my first chapter does something to introduce readers at some speed to Giovanni and Giorgio in between the three violent incidents. However, the rest of the book fills in the detail with greater calm and decorum. Giovanni's rise and fall are narrated in Chapters 2 and 3, while Chapter 4 is specifically devoted to recording what we know – which is not everything – about Nelia Pavlova, a woman whose part in Giovanni's life has been strangely blotted out in Italian scholarship. Chapters 5 and 6 then tell Giorgio's story to his death and that of Germaine. The Conclusion reviews the more recent fate of their reputations, with Giovanni's on the rise and Giorgio's diminishing given the global collapse of communism.

The book thus recounts the lives of a father and son, each of whom can be imagined happily occupying the highest political power in Italy, but each destined to fail in such ambition. Throughout the two decades of Mussolini's dictatorship, and then in the Republic after 1946, each man confronted what we call totalitarianism. The term was invented in Italy and then taken up by Mussolini's regime (and not disdained by the Vatican as a description of itself). During the Cold War after 1945, totalitarianism was widely accepted as describing the cruel oppression that occurred in the Stalinist and post-Stalinist USSR. In critical eyes, the Partito Comunista Italiano (PCI or Italian Communist Party) was therefore an organisation aiming to create a totalitarian Italy. The Party's leadership – and Giorgio Amendola – preferred to argue that they favoured 'an Italian road to socialism', and Giorgio often paraded his father's devotion to liberty (however defined) as proof of the PCI's Italian character. It may well be that Mussolinian Fascism and Togliattian communism were always totalitarianisms, Italian-style, never quite a mimicking of Hitler's or Stalin's 'total' tyrannies. Tracking Giovanni's and Giorgio's paths through the perils of twentieth-century politics will cast light on Italian and European history, on their individual lives, and on all of us who still endeavour to avoid the absolute.

Enough of this introduction. Now readers may start my first chapter, with extra assistance from my list of the key dramatis personae of the book. Here, then, follows a study that I trust will demonstrate that, for many reasons, it is worthwhile hearing of the lives of the Amendolas – even outside Italy – and why Clare Alexander's critical question can be given a positive response.

Dramatis Personae

Giovanni Amendola (1882–1926): Liberal democrat 'martyr' to Fascism.

Eva Kühn (1880–1961): Giovanni's wife, Baltic German within the Romanov empire, new woman, proto-feminist, sometime Futurist.

Nelia (Cornelia) Pavlova (1895–1940?): Giovanni's Bulgarian-French liberal democrat lover during the last years of his life.

Salvatore Mario Amendola (1884–1954): 'Uncle Mario' in this story and a key figure in his generation of the family, alternative 'head' of the family to Giorgio.

Giorgio Amendola (1907–80): Giovanni and Eva's eldest son, communist, never quite PCI leader.

Germaine Lecocq (1909–80): Parisian working-class woman who joined Giorgio in their Love Story, painter.

Ada (Adelaide) Amendola (1910–80): Giovanni and Eva's daughter, apolitical doctor, pursued her professional life without caring much who ruled in Rome.

Antonio Amendola (1916–53): Giovanni and Eva's second son, independent communist.

Pietro Amendola (1918–2007): Giovanni and Eva's third son, orthodox communist.

Maria Antonietta Macciocchi (1922–2007): Pietro's wartime wife, marriage dissolved in 1948, European New Leftist.

Quite a few other Amendolas turn up in my story, but these are the most significant ones.

1 Political Violence and the Amendolas, Father and Son

It was the *Giorno di Santo Stefano* (St Stephen's day), 1923, the day after Christmas but a time of normal work in an Italy where family presents were exchanged on Befana (Epiphany, 6 January); Santo Stefano did not become a holiday until 1947. Early that cold morning, Giovanni Battista Ernesto Amendola left his apartment at Via di Porta Pinciana 6. He was a member of the Chamber of Deputies and a journalist, the leading figure on the editorial board of *Il Mondo* (*The World*). This afternoon newspaper had been founded only in January 1922 but had acquired a circulation of 100,000 copies in a country still not fond of mass media. By late 1923, *Il Mondo* had grown ever more hostile to Fascism – which had been in power in Italy over the last year – with Amendola, in his past positioned on the conservative wing of Liberal politicians, by now a combative Anti-Fascist.

Amendola trudged down six floors to reach the street. Palazzi on the Via di Porta Pinciana stood along its east side, 'modernised' a few decades earlier in the Umbertine style of many sectors of the post-Risorgimento city. To the west it skirted the beautiful Pincio, which led into the celebrated Borghese gardens. Modernity went only so far; the Amendola family's rented flat was not serviced by a lift (nor did it possess a bath – Giorgio, the eldest of four children, recalled that the whole family relied on a weekly clean at the public washing facilities of the Albergo Diurno Cobianchi, situated quite a traipse across town). Giovanni and his wife, Eva, had on occasion talked of the quintessentially bourgeois act of home purchase but somehow they were always too busy, cash-strapped, intellectual or bohemian to get around to it.[1]

The family had been given to sudden and frequent changes of housing. They had moved to their current flat late in 1917 when Giovanni had returned from the front, as he had done on a number of occasions since his call-up in March 1915. During his war service, he had been promoted to the rank of captain, awarded a medal and wounded; he also caught potentially debilitating malaria.[2] In today's Rome, no memorial recalls the presence of the Amendola family at number 6, but a blue plaque does note that Ida Luzzatti (born 1881) and Elena Segrè (born 1910) were rounded up from there on 16 October 1943, the day when Pope Pius XII failed to protest against Nazi/Fascist racial swoops 'under the very windows' of the Vatican and a thousand Jewish victims were sent to their deaths at Auschwitz.[3] The story of the Amendola family is scoured by murder but not directly by the Holocaust, as this memory site tells us.

Giovanni had been born in Naples on 15 April 1882. His family had roots in the town of Sarno, an agricultural centre that, for five centuries after 1000 CE, boasted its own bishop. Since the fall of the Kingdom of the Two Sicilies, Sarno had increased its dependence on the port city of Salerno, thirty kilometres to its south. In recent decades, the sculptor Giovanni Battista Amendola (1848–87), uncle to our Giovanni, had won local, national and even some international fame; a statue in his honour was erected in his home town in 1922.[4] In Sarno, Amendolas mattered.

Figure 1.1 Giovanni Amendola, young, determined, beautiful and 'like an Indian god'.

Giovanni Amendola had grown into a giant by local standards, six feet tall (1.83 metres), and, as middle age began to arrive, he was a strapping figure. One historian says that he resembled a 'wrestler', given his 'massive' body, large head, deep-set eyes and a 'virile dominating expression' – all in all, a man born to command.[5] His voice, contemporaries reported, was 'warm and full throated'.[6] He had thick, dark, lustrous hair and olive skin. Photographs show that, when slimmer in his youth, he was notably handsome – to an admirer, the 'incarnation of an Indian god'.[7] One image in 1911 has him cuddled by his toddler, Giorgio (born 21 November 1907). On the edge of his thirties, Giovanni had grown a moustache; but it is his shining dark eyes surveying the world that demand an onlooker's attention. They do not focus on his son.

If any beauty contest can be imagined in the Italian political world of 1923, neither Il Duce nor the king could compete – Benito Mussolini, prime minister and leader of the Fascist movement, born 29 July 1883 and so just Giovanni's junior, but by now balding and, at 1.69 metres, much shorter than Amendola; Victor Emanuele III (king from 1900 to 1946), tiny (1.53 metres), with a face that seemed wizened from his birth (11 November 1869). Everyone in the know accepted that the king was a '*mezza cartuccia*' (half-pint), with implications that went beyond height. Before too long Mussolini's hair turned white, prompting him to adopt a shaven pate. Propaganda in the 1930s suggested that this revised version expressed his militant and martial side; it also concealed his ageing. Certainly, Giovanni towered over both his nation's 'leaders' physically and, history has concluded, morally. The king, as it shall soon become clear, was coldly to betray Giovanni, while Mussolini would bear heavy responsibility for his painful death.

Although Amendola had gloried in the character and lifestyle of a free intellectual, and although his family was always short of ready money, he was a fastidious dresser. In a photograph he has donned a winged collar, a fob watch and a natty waistcoat, which did not hide his expanding girth. His elegance contrasted with the *arriviste* Mussolini, who had scrambled upwards as a journalist and politician from quite a few rungs below Amendola on the class ladder. In office, the Duce required training from his rich, older, Jewish lover, Margherita Sarfatti, and from a worldly-wise retired ambassador, on how to avoid solecism in his attire. Giovanni had no such need, even if a family report says that his fondness for books curtailed lavish expense on his wardrobe.

When he stepped onto the Via di Porta Pinciana, Giovanni was headed for the office of *Il Mondo*, situated in the Via della Mercede, below the Spanish Steps. The Chamber of Deputies or Montecitorio was a way further, standing nearer the Tiber River, across the Via del Corso and abutting the Piazza Colonna, boosted by the column of the 'philosophical emperor' Marcus Aurelius (161–80 CE). Did Giovanni, like many Italians, ruminate on *romanità*, the heritage from classical Rome that lay all around the city that had become the capital of the new nation of Italy only in 1870? Fascists were already making much of their determination to build 'Mussolini's Roman Empire'. But Liberals had also been conscious of the need to find greatness for what they had called 'the Third Italy', despite their country's actual novelty. Maybe, like the stoic Marcus Aurelius, Giovanni, too, imagined a future where he could apply philosophy to the virtuous exercise of power.

Giovanni had left his four children in his apartment in the charge of a couple who acted as the family housekeepers: the man, Beppe Pietrangeli, a Roman, had worked in Lisbon, allegedly for the king of Portugal, before being expelled by the republican revolution of 1910; his Portuguese wife, Maria, did the cooking.[8] They took everyday responsibility for the home life of Giorgio, a helter-skelter, sports-loving,[9] sixteen-year-old, presently a less than distinguished pupil at the elite Ennio Quirino Visconti Liceo, and his teenage sister Adelaide (always called Ada), born on 30 January 1910. Considerably younger were two other brothers, the grandly named Antonio Lucinio Maria, born 28 February 1916, and Pietro, born on 26 October 1918 (Giovanni rejecting the temptation of the patriotic name Vittorio).[10] Their mother was Eva Oscarovna Kühn, born in Vilnius in the Russian empire on 21 January 1880. Her background, like that of many intellectuals from the Baltic region, was culturally and linguistically German. She was Giovanni's senior by two years. They had married in January 1907.

But on Boxing Day 1923, Eva was with neither her children nor her husband. Even before marriage, she had suffered from what contemporaries coyly called a 'nervous condition' and historians of the Amendolas have not explained further. 'Relapses' could come upon her at any time and in any place – in 1922, for example, when she went back to see her family in Vilnius in an independent Lithuania, with its members divided by their rival experiences of the Bolshevik revolution.[11] She spent time in clinics in Naples and then Viterbo. But, by late 1923, after she had briefly returned home, she could not cope with the Fascist violence whirling around her husband and children, nor with Pietro's scarlet fever and kidney trouble.[12] In response, she was put into the hands of a specialist called Dr Mendicini and the nuns of the Sorelle Ancelle della Carità order[13] at the Villa Giuseppina on the Via Nomentana, at number 154 (from 1929, the Mussolini family, with its five legitimate children, would be installed in the Villa Torlonia at number 70, closer to the Porta Pia).[14] Eva remained under medical and Catholic care until rescued by her daughter in 1933.[15] Once removed from tutelage, she lived a normal enough life until her death on 28 November 1961.

Mussolini's Fascist movement had 'marched on Rome' late in October 1922; his regime made the official date of their 'revolution' 28 October. However, in December 1923 it was still not totally clear how long the Duce might rule Italy. He headed a coalition government, of which only thirty-five deputies belonged to his Partito Nazionale Fascista (PNF, National Fascist Party), although it seemed certain that, in the planned coming elections, actually to be held on 6 April 1924, his power would be reinforced. One reason was that the violence of black-shirted, paramilitary, Fascist squads had not been subdued. Indeed, one of Mussolini's early acts as prime minister was to establish by decree on 14 January 1923 the Milizia Volontaria per la Sicurezza Nazionale (MVSN, Voluntary Militia for National Security) as a formal Fascist Party armed force, an implicit rival to the royal army of the Italian nation state.

A year later, Rome was much subject to squadrist forays. On the evening of 29 November, the villa owned by ex-prime minister Francesco Saverio Nitti (1868–1953) on the Via Alessandro Farnese, not far from the Vatican, was invaded by armed Fascists. Nitti, a Liberal, had been prime minister between June 1919 and June 1920 and was hated by rightists for failing to make sufficient post-war territorial gains. A fellow southerner, he was Giovanni Amendola's major patron. Amendola had been elected to parliament as a 'Democratic Liberal' in November 1919. Nitti quickly but briefly promoted him to the undersecretaryship of finance (May–June 1920).

In his movingly humane memoirs, Giorgio Amendola recalled in the summer of 1923 being sent to another Nitti family house at Acquafredda di Maratea on the Tyrrhenian coast in the region of Basilicata for school holidays.[16] There, he found rich and toothsome food cooked under the supervision of 'Donna Antonia', Nitti's wife (Giorgio was a fast-growing boy and, when she was around in their home life, Eva hated cooking), a 'magnificent' and unpolluted beach, an extensive library holding the most recent national and international journals and papers, and intelligent conversation. Augmenting such delights was the friendship of Filomena Nitti (born 10 January 1909), a good friend of his sister Ada; family elders thought the teenagers should be 'fidanzati' (committed girl- and boyfriend).[17] But that prospect of easy, politically inflected joy soon faded.

In autumnal Rome, the Fascists devastated the ground floor of the Via Farnese villa, taking special gratification in wrecking the library. Nitti avoided physical harm by staying concealed on an upper floor. Shortly afterwards, Giorgio was visited by a 'courageous, offended, indignant'

Filomena. When the adults began to talk over what had happened, Giorgio recollected being astounded and dismayed by the refusal of Nitti to make the house invasion an object of official parliamentary complaint. 'My words were received with embarrassment and smiles of indulgence' as springing from 'the inexperience of my sixteen years', he wrote. Even his father remained 'silent and thoughtful'. The Nitti family read the message of the times and went into exile, first in Switzerland and later in Paris, where the ex-prime minister continued an obsessive (and racist)[18] campaign against what he judged the French mistreatment of the Germans at the peace-making of Versailles and subsequently.

Nor was there any special reaction when, almost immediately afterwards, the apartment in the Via di Porta Pinciana was twice the object of loud squadrist incursions, with the Amendola family protected by the fact that the Fascists found climbing the narrow staircase up six floors off-putting. Can Mussolini's men, somewhere beneath the bluster, have retained a timid (and unathletic) side?[19] Both the Nitti villa and the Amendola apartment had theoretically been guarded by the Carabinieri or state police. But, when the squads moved in, the Carabinieri made no effort to stop them.

At least as menacing as the failed raids on the Via Pinciana apartment was the way in which, on 15 December, furious Fascist demonstrators prevented Giovanni, despite his being a local member of parliament, from joining the king in a patriotic ceremony at Salerno.[20] The local paper, La Riscossa Fascista, promised that 'we shall shortly liquidate him', while Il Popolo d'Italia, Mussolini's own daily, stressed that Giovanni's 'crimes' (that is, his temerity in opposing Fascism) 'will not be forgotten'.[21] When, that 26 December morning, he strode down the steepish hill into the Via Crispi, named after the Sicilian Liberal prime minister and imperialist, now being depicted a 'precursor' of Fascism despite his policies in Ethiopia leading to the disastrous defeat at Adwa in 1896, Amendola had reason to be wary.[22] But he was a brave man, intransigent in his commitment to justice. He was not given to turning back and, in Giorgio's vivid account, he sternly rejected any suggestion that his bold and combative son, who had added boxing to his other sporting skills and was himself almost as tall and broad as his father, should accompany and guard him.

Amendola grew aware that a car was slowly following his path. The squadrists had been gearing themselves up to assail him for three days without much attempt at concealment. Just as the Via di Porta Pinciana morphed into the Via Crispi, with a route to Il Mondo via either the Spanish Steps or the Piazza Barberini beckoning, the assault came. Three or four squadrists stormed out of the car and, pell-mell, battered

Amendola with their 'holy cudgels' (*santi manganelli*), as they dubbed their treasured offensive weapons in their slogans. They struck their target viciously on the shoulders, neck and head, bundling him to the ground where they continued their beating, brutally kicking him in the genitals. However, this was central Rome and the assault was in public gaze. From apartment windows or from the street, people cried out in alarm. The assailants jumped back into their car, where a driver had kept the engine running, and drove off at speed. Typical of the times, despite the open nature of the criminal violence, the police soon suspended their investigation 'for lack of proof'.[23]

Giorgio, who had disobeyed his father and had tagged along after him some minutes later down towards the city, had bumped into a school friend, Fabrizio Sarazani. He lived in an apartment looking out over the Via Crispi and had watched everything that went on. The two boys learned that some first aid had been provided for Giovanni's bleeding, badly gashed head. He had been charitably carried to the Ospedale San Giacomo degli Incurabili, down near the Tiber and ironically close to the mausoleum of the Emperor Augustus. At the hospital, the doctors reported at 10 a.m. that Giovanni had wounds and lacerations on the right side of his head and the base of his skull and further scratches across his face. They judged him in their formulaic phrasing, despite the sinister name of their workplace, as 'recoverable in a fortnight (so long as no complications ensued)'.[24]

The details of the onslaught on the opposition politician soon spread. One onlooker had scrupulously recorded the number plate of the Fascist thugs' car. Then, Ludovico Perroni Paladini, one of Amendola's assailants, quarrelled with his *camerati* (the Fascist term for comrades, as distinct from the Marxist *compagni*) and, in the second half of 1924, fled to France to tell all.[25] The squadrists came from a militia cell in the Via Magnanapoli near Trajan's column. They were under the discipline of a sort of PNF secret police, taking orders from Emilio De Bono, general and Fascist quadrumvir in October 1922, who was presently acting as commander of the MVSN. On 20 December 1923, he had formally taken office as chief of police.[26] The activities of Perroni and his friends were well known to Fascism's political leadership; it is said that, when Mussolini heard of Amendola's fate – while with his family in Milan for Christmas – he remarked that now he would have a keener appetite at dinner.[27]

One later commentator, Giuseppe Prezzolini, an archetypal collaborator with Fascism who had been an intellectual patron of Giovanni before 1914, claimed that members of an extremist faction had clubbed Giovanni on their own initiative. Their exploit blocked a possible compromise that the Duce was brooding over with Amendola. Mussolini, Prezzolini maintained, on 27 December, acknowledged that Giovanni was his 'most redoubtable adversary' but too 'heroic' for give-and-take negotiation.[28] However, the party newspaper, *Il Popolo d'Italia*, which since Mussolini's appointment as prime minister had transferred to the editorship of his younger brother Arnaldo, was swift and unrepentant in blaming hostile opposition speeches as having caused the violence and not its actual perpetrators.[29] There was no admission of a frustrated deal there.

For the moment, the effect on Italian opinion of such open violence against a respectable critic of the government was uncertain. Quite a number of important figures sent their best wishes to Giovanni, when in hospital or after he returned home, where he was still bedridden.[30] One well-wisher was celebrated Neapolitan Liberal philosopher and historian Benedetto Croce, an Anti-Fascist of a kind with whom the Amendolas, father and son, had complex relationships. On 27 December, Croce wrote of his regret at the news of the 'sad aggression'. But perhaps it could have a good effect, he added hopefully, in fostering 'repugnance towards things of that kind'.[31] Another person to state how 'moved' he had been by the beating, and how admiring of Amendola's political courage, was Luigi Albertini, long Giovanni's boss at *Il Corriere della Sera* and still editor of that distinguished paper. He did not remain so much longer.[32]

Lingering hope for the survival of humane values was soon out of place in Italy. In the April elections, Mussolini, head of what was called the '*listone*' (big list) of candidates, many of whom were recent converts to Fascism (somehow understood), won 374 of the 535 seats available. Giovanni Amendola, despite recurrent Fascist ferocity towards him and his supporters, held on in his home region of Campania with what was called the 'constitutional opposition' – in his case banded into a Unione Meridionale (Southern Bloc). It retained eight seats across the South of Italy from just over 1 per cent of the vote.

Undaunted in his conclusion about the moral intolerability of Mussolini's government, Amendola stiffened his challenge to Fascism. Notably he did so when parliament reconvened on 6 June 1924 in a speech that was interrupted by the Duce on twenty occasions with louring hostility. The election results, Amendola maintained, were wholly illegitimate and, in claiming a parliamentary majority, Fascism was demanding that Italians sell their souls for a mess of pottage. He, like all men of decency and honour, was not thus tempted.[33]

An earlier speech by the wealthy reformist socialist Giacomo Matteotti had similarly deplored the violence that had scoured the elections and hinted further that corruption in the framing of government oil contracts might reach as far as Arnaldo Mussolini. His oration had elicited five angry objections from Mussolini. Young Giorgio remembered listening to the socialist and his milling Fascists enemies from a balcony where deputies' family members could watch proceedings in the Chamber of Deputies.[34] In reaction to Matteotti's weighty oration, retribution was planned. Amerigo Dumini, who, in January 1924, had accepted command of a Fascist hit squad that would be better organised than the MVSN men who had acted on 26 December 1923, took charge of punishing Mussolini's critics. Dumini was American-born (in St Louis in 1894); in his own definition a patriot, he had returned to Italy in 1913. He volunteered to serve in the First World War, was wounded, and won a silver medal for his courage. From 1919 he became associated with the infant Fascist movement in Tuscany, a region where it was at its most bloody. Thereafter, he served on various secret missions abroad, returning to Italy just before Christmas 1923.[35] Now, in June 1924, he planned to exact revenge on either Amendola or Matteotti.[36]

Fate decreed that the victim was Matteotti. On the afternoon of 10 June, Dumini and four or five *camerati* grabbed Matteotti when he was walking along the Lungotevere Arnaldo da Brescia, where he had his flat. They shoved him into the back of their large car, which had been parked overnight in the *cortile* (courtyard) of the ministry of the interior. They then drove into the countryside and continued their beating until Matteotti died, although it is not totally clear whether the assailants' intention had been to kill him. Certainly, they reacted to murder in an amateurish fashion, driving around until they almost ran out of petrol. Eventually they scrabbled a shallow grave just off the Via Cassia, a major road out of Rome. As with the violence inflicted on Amendola on 26 December, someone had spotted the car, which was quickly identified, and had observed the kidnapping. At least until after 1945, when Giovanni Amendola replaced him in some circles, Matteotti was destined to be the archetypal martyr of Fascism, a sort of lay saint remembered by Anti-Fascist ordinary Italians, as well as by such distinguished foreigners as Arthur Henderson, Léon Blum and Sylvia Pankhurst, his murder the key proof that Benito Mussolini was a brutal tyrant and a serial killer and Fascism the most evil of ideologies.[37]

During the late summer of 1924, political Italy sank into crisis over the 'disappeared' deputy; his stinking, mouldering corpse was not discovered until 16 August.[38] The question became whether a prime minister, who at a minimum tolerated murderers within his entourage, could stay in office. Amendola knew the just answer and it did not take him long to rally opposition and to become its leader, at least among people who still thought of themselves as Liberal. On 13 June, Mussolini had denied in parliament any involvement in Matteotti's disappearance; a few days later, he ordered the resignation of those of his staff rumoured to be most involved. Such a lame attempt at virtue lacked conviction. On 26 June, a majority of opposition politicians from across the party spectrum, but without full non-Fascist unanimity, met in Montecitorio's Sala della Lupa (Room of the She Wolf, which had nurtured Romulus and Remus) and decided to boycott a parliament that, it was said, lay under siege from vicious Fascist militia. The chief spokesman of what came to be known as the 'Aventine Secession' – taking its name, with Anti-Fascist *romanità*, from events between 495 and 493 BCE described by Livy – was Giovanni Amendola.

A tumultuous year followed both for Amendola and for Italy. For a time, it seemed that Mussolini could not survive as prime minister. Yet, the greatest powers in the country – the monarchy, the Vatican, the army, big business – fearing civil war or a Russian-style revolution, havered, each reckoning that the Duce's retention of office was the least worst alternative. Giovanni may well have thought that, before long, Victor Emmanuel III would summon him as the new generation Liberal politician of the greatest stature, a patriot and a loyal monarchist, pledged to assert Italy's post-Risorgimento constitution against Fascist infringement, and charge him with framing a non-Fascist government. While he waited, on 8 November, Amendola set up a new group, the Unione Nazionale delle Forze Liberali e Democratiche (National Union of Liberals and Democrats), which was constitutionalist in its essence. It was still fluid in the non-organised traditions of Italian liberalism, but with the potential to become a governing force, even a governing liberal party. But the king did not send for Amendola or his followers.

In the very days of the formation of the Unione Nazionale, Victor Emmanuel was shown two crucial statements demonstrating without question the involvement of the highest Fascist circles in Matteotti's murder. He ignored them. He was similarly silent when, on 27 December, *Il Mondo* published crucial confirmatory evidence, the devastating Rossi memorandum.[39] With the king passive and what had once been the Liberal establishment unable or unwilling to counter Fascism in an effective manner, Mussolini's greatest threat now came from extremists within his own party, who were swaggeringly making plain their fear that the Duce was no leader. On 3 January, Mussolini half timorously took the decisive step of declaring to the Chamber of Deputies that he assumed full 'political, moral and historic' responsibility for violence associated with his movement and party. His particular care was to damn the Aventine, which, in any case, had begun to splinter. The communists had deserted the cause on 26 November; back in August, their chief ideologue, Antonio Gramsci, no proto-Liberal, had accused Amendola of 'semifascism'.[40]

Amendola had always maintained his opposition to any form of socialist revolution and his deep distaste for Marxist materialism. That stance did not stop Mussolini declaring that the leader of the Unione Nazionale and the whole Aventine crew were no better than Bolsheviks, plotting 'against the constitution, sharply revolutionary'. 'Force,' the Duce bellowed to the Chamber of Deputies in conclusion to his speech, was the 'only solution' in a battle between Fascist good and its foes' evil.[41] Henceforth, Mussolini was no longer to be merely a prime minister. He became instead dictator, the charismatic chief of a regime, not the head of government. As the propaganda message put it, now '*Mussolini ha sempre ragione*' (Mussolini is always right). Liberalism (Italian-style) had had its day; Fascism must rule for the foreseeable future.

Intrepidly, Giovanni tried to counter this development, while again displaying misguided loyalty to the king and to the Savoy dynasty. After spending the night of 2–3 January at a friend's house for fear of a new savage raid on him and his family's apartment, he was relieved to learn that, on the day of Mussolini's speech, Giorgio had managed to walk away from a band of thugs surging balefully around him in the Rome Galleria, across the road from Montecitorio. The next day, Giovanni sought urgent communication with Victor Emmanuel through his aide-de-camp, General Arturo Cittadini. He virtuously evoked the Risorgimento to claim that he and the rest of the Aventine were being treated worse that their grandparents had been by Habsburg Austria. The press had lost its freedom of expression. The police did nothing. 'Bloody anarchy' threatened. Firm action could resolve the problem in forty-eight hours. If not, the country's institutions, which Giovanni and his friends so revered, would fail, and Victor Emmanuel would face the choice of total withdrawal into private life or exile. The king must act to defend 'the great patrimony of honour and hope' that constituted the kingdom of Italy, and unfurl 'the pure flag of the Risorgimento'.[42]

Victor Emmanuel did not reply, either then or during the next six months while Mussolini's regime erected its so-called totalitarian state;[43] Giovanni sadly wrote that the king had abandoned him and his colleagues.[44] On 23 April 1925, intellectuals supporting the regime, led by philosopher Giovanni Gentile, published a manifesto praising Mussolini and Fascist ideas. In response, a week later, on May Day, a day that he would have once rejected as corrupted by socialism, Amendola managed to organise and release in *Il Mondo* a 'manifesto of Anti-Fascist intellectuals'; among the signatories was Croce, for once stirred from his usual stance that scholarship must continue whatever the disgrace of short-term politics. Nitti, typically, had earlier and unhelpfully written from Paris that he deplored what was going on in Italy but had to finish yet another book on the state of international relations as disturbed by the injustices of Versailles, and the effort was tiring him out.[45]

But words, critical or not, could not turn back the tide of Fascist aggression. Instead, a 'second wave' of squadrism washed violently across the country, notably in Tuscany. In Rome, on 5 April, Fascist bruisers again attacked Amendola while he was walking down the Via dei Serpenti, not far from the royal Quirinale palace, but he managed to take refuge before suffering severe injury.[46] His mood began to vary between his accustomed ebullience and deepening depression. In April, he wondered in a letter to Albertini whether exile was the only choice, as it had been for Risorgimento heroes Giuseppe Mazzini and Giuseppe Garibaldi.[47] On 3 June, he told such Aventine colleagues as later Christian Democrat prime minister Alcide De Gasperi and moderate socialist Filippo Turati that he must give up the leadership of the Anti-Fascist group, which was becoming 'a hodgepodge of the homeless'. In a week's time, he stated, he would commemorate the anniversary of Matteotti's kidnapping and then retire.[48]

But he did not. On 10 June, he was granted a last interview with the king, without much sign of improvement in their relations; Amendola did now seem to accept that he would have to become a republican, although, on 22 June, Cittadini forwarded him a polite note in which Victor Emmanuel thanked him for sending congratulations to his daughter, Princess Mafalda, on her engagement. In contrast to his depressed talk about vacating the scene, Amendola, three days earlier, had been revived by what he thought was a promising first congress of the UN, which he claimed could yet, with 'tenacious work', overcome our 'months of hard prison'.[49]

It was summer and time for a break. On 7 July, Mussolini informed his ambassadors that Amendola had requested and been granted a passport. The Duce judged Giovanni his greatest enemy and instructed his diplomats to pay close attention to whatever he might do abroad.[50] In fact, Amendola did not depart into exile but instead planned a refreshing stay at the spa of Montecatini in Tuscany. He had booked himself in to the upmarket Grand Hotel e La Pace, a jewel of Liberty architecture.[51] On the morning of Monday 20 July, using Chamber of Deputies' notepaper, he dashed off a letter to the fifteen-year-old Ada, whom he had sent on holiday to the beach, telling her that he was off to the spa until 1 or 2 August. He had seen Eva (who was 'not too bad') at the clinic, but adjured Ada to take on the responsibility of being a little mother to her two younger brothers in regard to their behaviour and their health; Antonio should not get too excited and Pietro's physique might still be a worry.[52] Giorgio, meanwhile, had been sent by himself to stay with rich cousins at Baronissi in the hills behind Salerno. Friends also arranged an excursion for him around the gorgeous Amalfi coast. In his memoirs, Giorgio recalled his tryst with a tall blonde American from Cleveland named 'Elen' (Giorgio never did master English); her kisses lived on in his mind, as did a photograph with 'for ever' scribbled on it.[53]

With his private world apparently in order, Giovanni tried to manage his public life. He had taken care to pass the detail of his trip to Giovanni Capasso-Torre, head of the government press office, and so, he believed, to Mussolini. In response he was advised that he could go ahead with the journey into Tuscany 'without danger'. Around 3 p.m., accompanied by his faithful secretary, Federico Donnarumma, Amendola, with what must have been relief and pleasure, strode through the entrance of the Grand Hotel.[54] But optimism was misplaced; death, not relaxation, awaited.

Montecatini lay in the province of Lucca (in 1928 it was moved to the newly established province of Pistoia, a nearer *città*). Over the preceding years, this part of Tuscany had come to be dominated by the violent extremist 'ras' (squadrist boss) Carlo Scorza, and his elder brother, the corrupt banker Giuseppe.[55] Carlo had been born at Paola in Calabria in June 1897, tenth in a family of twelve children. He moved to Lucca in 1912. He was therefore a southerner who was finding an identity in the nation of Italy, an ambitious member of the 'emerging middle classes', according to historian Renzo De Felice, the staunchest backers of Fascism. Maybe he and his brother also knew something of the habits of the 'Ndrangheta, Calabria's durable association of organised crime (and murder). In different vein, the brothers' hometown of Paola boasted as its most celebrated son the austere San Francesco da Paola (1416–1507), whose sanctuary is located there. Carlo's cousin, Alighiero, was a member of the Minim order, resident in the Paola monastery. In 1945, he would connive to conceal Carlo in difficult times.[56]

When Carlo Scorza was charged with murder, he produced a specious and mendacious argument claiming, at the hour of Giovanni reaching Montecatini, to have been absent from the town until the last moment. He alleged that the hostile demonstrators who greeted Giovanni on his arrival and grew noisier and less controlled as the hours passed were expressing spontaneous, chronic, local contempt for Anti-Fascism. Then, Scorza was assisted in such a claim by a *raccomandazione* (letters or other methods of recommendation) from Giovanni Battista

Montini,[57] Pope Pius XII's Substitute Secretary of State and later Pope Paul VI, who had presumably been approached by Alighiero Scorza. Fascists often found value in a family member from some religious order or other.

Scorza may have enjoyed his post-war claim to innocence and remained a Catholic of a kind. But more convincing is the detailed account of events, bolstered by archival documents, made by the historian Umberto Sereni to a conference commemorating Giovanni held at the Grand Hotel e La Pace, and then at the Palazzo dei Congressi in Montecatini in October 1996. Sereni noted that Lucca's prefect on 2 July had reported to Rome that Carlo Scorza was in complete charge of political events in the province. He was especially close to the new and extremist PNF secretary, Roberto Farinacci, who, in March 1926, was to act as the legal defender of Dumini when he had to face a court for the Matteotti murder. Farinacci was self-consciously the squadrist of the squadrists, the most violent (and corrupt) of the violent (and corrupt). On 31 May he had visited Lucca for a ceremony inaugurating a monument to Fascists killed during the movements' rise to power, and he took the occasion to justify vicious payback. Before and after Farinacci's visit, Scorza's paper, *L'Intrepido* (The Intrepid), demonised Giovanni Amendola as a 'sinister' figure. Editorials urged the 'necessary suppression of all those who out of cowardice or Jewish-Masonic-internationalist calculation' plotted against the nation and the regime's values. On 16 July, Scorza condemned any who wrote for *Il Mondo* as 'people who want to create the Anti-Italy, the Anti-State and the Anti-Nation'.[58]

There were quite a few reasons to judge that the rowdy, jeering, Fascist throng in the streets of Montecatini on 20 July had been 'in every detail' stage-managed from Rome, certainly by Farinacci and perhaps by Mussolini, with Scorza as their trusty agent.[59] When evening drew on, seething, cudgel-wielding young men, driven on by Guido Guidi, Scorza's brutal deputy at Montecatini, broke into the Grand Hotel in an angry search for the 'traitor' Amendola, scandalising wealthy clients after they rudely broke open bathroom and toilet doors. Old-fashioned Liberal gentleman as in some ways he was, Amendola grew especially disturbed by his genteel fellow guests' inconvenience in this regard and what it would entail for Italy's reputation in the best foreign circles. However, the local police did nothing; indeed, their local chief, Alberto Trezza, who had himself been a squadrist in 1921, spurred on the demonstrators.

The first prefectural reports from Lucca to Rome maintained that Scorza had calmed matters in a judicious speech, while only 'three windows' in the hotel had been broken and the police had stemmed the tumult, with Amendola and Donnarumma allowed to leave Montecatini.[60] The reverse was true. Scorza, from the hotel balcony, had bawled his regret that Amendola had not been beaten, while back-handedly adding that the squadrists should be generous 'towards the traitor, the renegade, the head of the opposition'. An anonymous bystander reported that it had all been disgracefully similar to 'what the Arabs do in Libya when they have a chance to ambush an Italian soldier'. Changing his metaphor to a more general view of barbarism, he added that, around midnight, a 'cannibal-style departure' had been imposed on Amendola and his secretary, in theory towards the railway station at Pistoia, where an early morning train was scheduled to leave for Rome. Back at Montecatini, each had been pushed into a separate car after making their way on foot through a screaming mob whose members landed blows on their enemies and broke at least one car window. Initially, some Carabinieri guaranteed safe passage, but, at the first junction out of the town, they turned aside, as did the car in which Donnarumma was travelling.[61] Amendola was left alone with his Fascist captors (three or four of them were in the car), just as Matteotti had been in June 1924.

Giovanni's suffering was to be more prolonged than that of the socialist. Amendola had initially tried to persuade Scorza to allow him to pass the night at the hotel, since he wisely feared what might happen under cover of darkness. In response, Scorza pledged his 'protection'. Giovanni was right to be afraid. Not far along the road, at the small settlement of Ponte a Nievole, between the towns of Monsummano and Serravalle, the car stopped, blocked by a log lying conveniently across its path. It was a trap. Giovanni was pushed outside to be beaten and beaten some more by fifteen Fascists, at least one of whom had added a large nail to his *manganello* (cudgel). The Fascist bully boys may have killed him but for the fact that their assault was suddenly lit up by the headlights of another car coming from the direction of Pistoia. It is said that, in tourist Tuscany, it had a foreign number plate. In alarm, the Fascists scattered, leaving Giovanni, bleeding, broken and inert.[62] It took the Italian Republic until 1965 to place a small memorial plaque at Ponte a Nievole to record the Fascist savagery.[63] A classicist might conclude that, just as the last philosopher of the Roman empire, Boethius, died beneath 'barbarian' Gothic clubs in 524 CE, so now the last active philosopher-liberal of Risorgimento Italy was being beaten to his death by Fascist barbarism.

An unnamed saviour rushed Amendola to hospital at Pistoia for treatment of 'multiple contusions on the forehead, face, knee and right arm, cuts to his lower lip and left hand, deep bruising around his eye sockets with sub-corneal haemorrhage'. In the dry formal formula of emergency departments, he could be cured 'in three weeks, if there were no complications'. Presumably doubting whether a provincial hospital was medically advanced, Donnarumma, who had got to Pistoia, found a place for his boss on the 4.15 a.m. train, and, the next day, Giovanni was back in his bed at the flat on the Via di Porta Pinciana. On his return to Rome, the *questore* (police commissioner), alert to Anti-Fascists and their misbehaviour, reported that his head was 'almost completely *fasciata*' (that is, not Fascist-ised but bandaged up).[64] Giorgio rushed back from his holiday, aware of an eldest son's responsibilities. He recalled that his father lay in bed for many days, scarcely able to read the telegrams of sympathy that arrived – though not, Giorgio noticed, in the same number as in December 1923.[65] Giovanni, his son wrote sadly, was damaged both physically and morally; over the next days, according to one contemporary account, three of his ribs were surgically removed. His lungs and thorax had been permanently damaged.[66] Amendola had every reason now to conclude that he had lost the battle against Mussolini's dictatorship.[67]

Naturally, there was no serious effort to prosecute the squadrists. In a flaunting of his Fascist virtue and local power at Lucca, Scorza married his Calabrian childhood sweetheart, Maria Cerchiara, in a civil rite on the Saturday and in church on the Sunday morning after the mauling of Amendola. The local archbishop, charitable towards Fascist murderers, officiated. Cabinet members Costanzo Ciano and Giacomo Suardo acted as witnesses and Mussolini sent 'cordial wishes to an old camerata'.[68] None blanched at his savagery. To be sure, in 1931–2, Scorza's career took a turn for the worse when he picked a quarrel with new PNF secretary, Achille Starace (another southerner, but from Lecce). As a result, Carlo and his brother lost authority in Lucca, although Scorza, ever more a Mussolini loyalist,[69] re-emerged in desperate circumstances from April to July 1943 to become the last secretary of the PNF.

Following the war and the fall of Fascism, the soon to be fatal attack of 20–21 July was finally investigated and a guilty verdict brought in against Scorza, Guidi and six others. However, Scorza appealed and, in 1949, a court in Perugia decided that Amendola's death had not been fully planned and, anyway, the accused had to be amnestied under the provisions of a presidential decree of 22 June 1946;[70] this generous and forgiving legislation is generally known as the 'Togliatti Amnesty', after the PCI chief Palmiro Togliatti, then serving as minister of justice. In any case, Scorza had secretly departed to Argentina, a reliable sanctuary under its Mussolini-admiring dictator, Juan Perón. He stayed there until 1962, working in 'publicity' for the ex-Fascist industrialist Vittorio

Valdani. Thereafter, he returned to a comfortable life in Italy, finally dying in a Tuscan villa on 23 December 1989 aged ninety-one.[71]

Amendola never recovered from his battering in Tuscany. He soon went into exile in France, although he did come back to Rome at Christmas 1925 for a last meeting with Eva at her clinic (no one had yet told her of the assault on her husband, nor would she hear of his death for some years).[72] Two operations in Paris failed to restore Amendola's health and, on 7 April 1926,[73] he died at a clinic in Cannes, not far from the Italian border. He was forty-three. Doctors blamed an incurable lesion and growth in his lungs and throat passage. Presumably hoping that his family would not remain a target of Fascist violence, Giovanni, at least according to press sympathetic to the regime, stated from his last bedside that 'his death is not due to the violence inflicted on his person and should not be exploited as was that on the Hon. Matteotti'.[74] But such a noble pledge to forgive and forget did not stop Fascists, with evident police approval, demonstrating outside the flat in the Via di Porta Pinciana as soon as the news came through from Cannes. Shortly afterwards, they finally entered and sacked the Amendola flat, albeit in the absence of Giorgio and the other children.[75] By contrast, and perhaps with unwonted honesty and even half-admiration, Mussolini wrote to the king about the death, admitting that Amendola was 'better than the others'.[76]

It is time in this introductory chapter to shift attention to Giorgio, his envelopment by his father's death and his eventual presiding over what can be read as his Anti-Fascist vengeance. Again an event, in this case occurring on 23–24 March 1944, requires description. But first, let me return to Giovanni's deathbed in April 1926. A younger brother, the Neapolitan jeweller Salvatore (generally called Mario), and a number of his political friends and associates, including Albertini, did make it to Cannes before Giorgio died. But his last breath was taken in the company of his eldest son, Giorgio; Meuccio Ruini (1877–1970), a radical patriot whose political course had been similar to Amendola's and who remained a staunch Anti-Fascist; and Nelia Pavlova,[77] a Bulgarian journalist who had become Giovanni's partner over the preceding months and, at an unknown time, may have borne him a son.

Giovanni wrote his last will and testament in Paris in February, telling his children that he now accepted his destiny and hoping that they would forgive his mistakes but also stay loyal to his 'elevated idea of life'. He was not rich – he had been one liberal who paid little attention to prospering through capitalist deals – but he believed that his friends would relieve his children's worst poverty. They did. He gave special thanks to his brother, Mario, who had come to see him in Paris, to Pavlova and Donnarumma (his lasting tie to Sarno), while devoting a long paragraph to Eva, begging her pardon for his sins in their relationship and pledging that he would carry the debt of her great love with him into eternity. He thanked and blessed her, and hoped her health could revive so that she could take pleasure in their children's company. He had one other piece of advice to his sons and daughter, but undoubtedly aimed mainly at his eldest son, Giorgio, now on the edge of manhood and about to become head of the Amendola family. They must be less adventurous and bohemian than he had been. They must ensure that, before venturing far 'into any other activity, public or private', they built for themselves 'a solid base of economic independence'.[78] Giovanni went to his grave patriarchally convinced that the family was the prime place of definition and loyalty for all Amendolas.

Class also mattered. Whatever else he was, as the counsel to become wealthy indicated, Giovanni Amendola died a bourgeois. On the day after the death, the much richer Liberal and patriot, Albertini, took pains to walk around the garden of the refined Hotel Carlton with Giorgio and offer sage advice. Giorgio should enrol in a serious university course, study hard and accept that he bore major responsibility for his siblings. When, a week later, Nitti came from Paris to Rome for a discreet funeral ceremony held in the capital, he said the same, adding sententiously that the best subject for study was his own, economics. But Giorgio was reluctant to obey his seniors, if it meant going into political deep freeze. In any case, to Giorgio's remembered adolescent disgust, Nitti had unfeelingly left his charming daughter Filomena behind in Paris.[79]

Certainly, there were changes to be absorbed, although the Amendola children's path was smoothed financially by Albertini, Giustino Fortunato and other well-off Liberals. They had known, liked and respected Giovanni, and they now collected ample funds for his family, at least in the short term. For all the razzamatazz of Fascist totalitarianism, the regime did very little to diminish Italians' longstanding commitment to their families (and class). Throughout the dictatorship, the Amendolas remained the Amendolas. Now Uncle Mario made available the second floor of his newly built, elegant residence on the Vomero, with beautiful views over the city and the Bay of Naples, as residence for his own and his brother's children – seven in all in what was a crowded house. As a way of relieving the situation, Alfredo Frassati, who had just been dropped through Fascist pressure from the editorship of the Turin paper *La Stampa*, and whose son, Pier Giorgio (beatified by John Paul II in 1990), had died tragically of meningitis in June 1925, offered to adopt Antonio. The often rebellious second Amendola boy was despatched to Turin and enrolled at school with the Salesian order. Antonio, however, found his new family's piety intolerable, preferring the freewheeling, secular household of the Amendolas. Soon, he was expelled by his Catholic teachers and, in 1931, aged fifteen, fled the Frassatis and the Salesian priests to re-join his uncle in Naples.[80] But he, like Giorgio, was not to be content with life on the Vomero.

When Giovanni's tomb had been finished at Cannes in 1928, it was inscribed with a liberal democratic, Anti-Fascist message: 'Here lies Giovanni Amendola waiting.'[81] On a number of occasions in his later life, Giovanni had prophesised that a whole generation, twenty years, would be needed to rid Italy of Fascism and dictatorship. Each of his sons, but especially Giorgio, worked to that end. Each was a patriot. But each also became a communist (of somewhat varying kinds). None was a liberal democrat. Within his family, Giovanni's soul was not destined to march on unrevised.

Giorgio, the oldest by a decade, led the way. His path through adolescence was certainly rendered harsher by watching his father's unyielding struggle and violent death. Well-meaning old men with some sort of commitment to liberalism may have been telling him to calm down. But Giorgio knew that he had every reason not to listen to them. His father had died heroically fighting Fascism. His heir must not forgo an active struggle against tyranny and murderers.

In 1928, Giorgio went twice to Cannes, as the building of his father's tomb moved towards completion. On the second occasion in October, he saw Nelia Pavlova for the last time.[82] Of more immediate significance for Giorgio was a trip in May, when he also travelled to Paris. In his later life, he recalled over and over again that he sought out Claudio Treves, a reformist socialist friend of Matteotti, whose intellect he believed to be 'severe' and enlightened.[83] Giorgio met Treves holed up in a poor hotel and expectantly thrust into his hands a memorandum that he had prepared on continuing Anti-Fascist resistance. Treves' response was dismaying:

Dear Giorgio, I admire your sentiments very much. I see with pleasure that, in Italy, there are some young Anti-Fascists who wish to set out on the road and continue the struggle. But let me tell you frankly, don't look to us. We are the defeated, those who have failed. There is no point in seeking help from us. Find your own path.

Then he burst into tears and hugged Giorgio, who was 'moved by his sincerity but extremely demoralised by this confession of impotence'.[84] It was almost as though, from beyond the grave, his father was again telling him to behave like a good bourgeois, safeguard his younger siblings, grow rich and respectable, and wait out Mussolini's regime until it was his turn to reach middle age.

Giorgio, tall, strong and determined, preferred to fight. While still at the Liceo Visconti, he had joined the Unione Goliardica per la Libertà (Student Freedom Union), a grouping of Anti-Fascist university students, and, despite his youth, acquired a senior role. He maintained this connection after he moved to Naples in October 1926, enrolling at the local university, first in law and then in political economy. By definition, as an Amendola, he rejoiced in excellent contacts with the leading intellectuals of the city, at least as long as they had not gone wholly over to Fascism.

Trying to be a good son, Giorgio did his best to read widely, mixing political texts, some now by Marx, amplified by Proust, Rolland and Gide, and Filomena Nitti's regular letters.[85] He was given access to the vast library kept in the Neapolitan villa of Benedetto Croce, the Liberal who rigidly defended the view that scholarship must place itself above political struggle, more and more to Giorgio's disgust. Paradoxically, Giorgio also met Amadeo Bordiga, who had lost the leadership of the PCdI in 1926 (he was formally expelled in March 1930), been arrested by the Fascists, sent for a while into *confine* (internal exile) and, in 1928, formed a dissident group apart from the party. Bordiga had an upper-class family background and a degree in engineering; his company built Uncle Mario's new house, where he became the first significant communist of Giorgio's acquaintance. But Bordiga, too, told him to get on with studying and could not comprehend Giorgio's dislike of the strict bourgeois regulations for dinner time and dress of the Neapolitan Amendolas.[86]

From Paris, Filomena was still writing, but Giorgio feared that their love could not blossom; in any case, when they met in Paris, she told him she must not desert her father. For each of them, political activism had to be privileged over everything else. Especially when the collapse of Wall Street in October 1929 seemed to demonstrate that capitalism was dying, there was only one place to go: communism. Some of Giorgio's university friends had already joined the party. Most had only a slight connection to the PCdI in exile in Paris, led by Togliatti (the anti-Bordiga intellectual chief of the movement, Antonio Gramsci, had been imprisoned in 1927). Not yet attracting severe attention from the Fascist secret police, the young Anti-Fascists in Naples read, debated, lent each other books and disdained Mussolini. The most influential among them was the Jewish agronomy graduate Emilio Sereni, whom Giorgio had known from high school days in Rome. Sereni had joined the party in 1926.

For Giorgio Amendola, talk must lead to action. Symbolically, perhaps romantically, Giorgio chose 7 November 1929, the twelfth anniversary of

the Bolshevik seizure of power in Russia, to sign his membership of the
PCdI. Still only twenty-one, he had made his 'life choice' and defined his
Anti-Fascism.[87]

For the moment, Giorgio hid his conversion from his family, as well as
from the Fascist secret police. In the summer of 1930, seemingly dutifully, he finished his *laurea* long essay and was awarded the top grade in
his degree.[88] Sereni and Manlio Rossi-Doria, another bright young
friend from Rome now based in Naples, had been trying to make proper
communication with party headquarters in Paris. But their activity
alerted the Fascists, and they were arrested and sentenced to fifteen years
in gaol. Naples could not stay safe for Giorgio for much longer.

So, in early 1931, the Neapolitan group decided that Giorgio should
leave for Paris. Throwing off the pursuit of the far from alert Fascist
police, Giorgio set out from Milan for Bern on the 10 p.m. train on 1
April. He shared his compartment with a 'beautiful Swiss girl' and was
soon chatting deeply with her. Seeming young love could be useful.
'When we were going across the border, I handed over our passports
together [his was false]. They [the border guards] looked at them with
scarce attention and stamped them as was needed.' Giorgio reached
Paris late the next evening, briefly putting up at a hotel that he quickly
realised doubled as a brothel.[89] However, the next day, he went to meet
the party leadership; he was greeted by the welcoming, motherly, Teresa
Noce and the 'cold and aloof' Luigi Longo, party husband and wife.

For many years, a number of comrades, especially if they came from
the working class, retained suspicions of Giorgio, '*il figlio di un ministro*'
(the Cabinet minister's son; in 1922, Giovanni had been minister for
colonies) as they denominated him, half in friendship, half not.[90] After
all, Giorgio's class background was anything but orthodox, at least in
theory (many PCdI leaders in reality came from society's upper ranks),
and communism was not given to friendly unanimity. Giorgio reached
Paris just as Togliatti and Longo decided to expel four of their leading
associates, 'the three' – Alfonso Leonetti, Pietro Tresso and Paolo
Ravazzoli (each ironically risen from a poor background) – and, separ-
ately, Angelo Tasca. They were punished for being too critical of the
(Stalinist) line of no alliances and for refusing to disdain social democrats
as 'social fascists'. Each was not fully committed to the Comintern's
brutal and simplistic line of class against class.

Throughout the devil's decade of the 1930s, Giorgio loyally worked for
the PCdI, with its Machiavellian leader Togliatti (born 1893) perhaps
acting as a surrogate father for him.[91] Togliatti's realism, which allowed
him to survive Stalin's purges, even though, from 1934 to 1938, he
served as a key member of the Comintern in Moscow, was certainly in

striking contrast with Giovanni's purism. During these years, Amendola did conventional enough party duty in France, Germany, Switzerland, Britain and back in Italy, where he was gaoled from 1932 to 1937. Throughout this party apprenticeship, Togliatti treated him as a junior of promise and significance; Giorgio Amendola, on occasion to his embarrassment, was never a simple party cadre.

There was one notable absence in Giorgio's curriculum vitae: he did not go to the USSR. Until after 1945, he did not see the 'home of the Revolution' up close. Nor did he serve in Spain. When the bloody civil war broke out in July 1936, he was still confined on Ponza, a prison island in the Tyrrhenian sea off Naples. Longo, by contrast, acted as communist agent to the International Brigades from December 1936 to the defeat of the Republic in 1939, accepting the job of spymaster (on other Republicans) and military officer.

When Giorgio came back to France in October 1937 while the purges reached their height in the USSR, the party seemed uncertain about his best role. Ruggero Grieco (born 1893), the lieutenant of Togliatti and the person to whom Giorgio was closest, was under dangerous charge from the Comintern of 'opportunism'. As Amendola recalled, 'the comrades seemed to me distracted, preoccupied, nervous'.[92] After what sounds like a set of odd jobs and, whether fortuitously or not, avoiding what had seemed an imminent transfer to Moscow, in February 1939 Giorgio was posted to Tunis. His job there was to open a pro-communist, 'Anti-Fascist' newspaper, *Il Giornale degli Italiani di Tunisia*, well financed by the local Jewish community.[93]

Giorgio was therefore heavily, if locally, engaged, when, in August 1939, the startling news came through of the Ribbentrop–Molotov Pact. However, a loyal communist must do what a loyal communist must. On 24 August, Giorgio wrote obediently in *Il Giornale* that the Soviet step was fully justified. The immediate consequence was the destruction of Giorgio's work over the last months. The French imperial authorities seized copies of *Il Giornale* and local Jewish funding ceased.[94] Weeks of confusion followed. They were complicated further by Mussolini's ambiguous choice of 'non-belligerency' in regard to the world war. His regime was not yet the fighting ally of either Hitler or Stalin, although its verbal anti-communism did not cease. The French government now knew that communists were its enemies, driving Giorgio into clandestinity. It was not until January 1940 that he could tell his family in Italy that he had reached Paris. In his memoirs he recalled a rough winter passage to Marseille, complicated by the 'voluminous baggage' assembled by his working-class French wife, Germaine, little daughter, Ada, and mother-in-law, Hélène Augustine Lecocq.[95] In

Paris, few comrades remained active and, in the summer of 1940, he and his family moved back to Marseille and began a party life.

Giorgio's wartime allegiances remained complicated until the Nazi invasion of the USSR on 22 June 1941 – and, with family ties never completely sutured, even after that. Perhaps Giorgio, traversing some sort of Italian path to socialism, could draw comfort in a name change. From May 1943, whether approved by the Comintern and the Soviet dictator or not, the Partito Comunista d'Italia became the Partito Comunista Italiano (PCI) – and the implication grew over the years that it might find its own national way forward. Back in April, Giorgio had crossed into Italy, leaving his family in Provence. He would not see them again until the war had ended in Allied and Soviet victory. His task was to help organise armed opposition to the Fascist regime from an initial base in Milan, where, shortly after his arrival, he could celebrate the outbreak of worker strikes (even though they were more spontaneous than PCI inspired). His experience of war may have been belated and slanted by his loyalty to Stalin in Moscow; he later remembered crying in relief when the BBC reported Stalin's declaration in November 1941 that Moscow had repelled the Nazis.[96] However, now in Italy, he confronted the dilemma of bloody death on a much greater scale than the individual suffering of his father.

During that year, momentous events succeeded each other. The Allied invasion of Sicily began in the early morning of 10 July 1943; by 17 August, the island had been entirely 'liberated'. Back in Rome, on the night of 24–25 July, the Fascist grand council voted that Mussolini pass military governance back to King Victor Emmanuel. Scorza, Giovanni's murderer, was one of seven to remain committed to the dictator and so opposed the motion. On the following afternoon, when the Duce went to his usual biweekly royal interview, he was arrested on the king's orders, and Pietro Badoglio, ex-chief of general staff, accepted nomination as prime minister. There followed forty-five days of confusion until, on 8 September, Badoglio and the king made public the fact that they had signed an armistice with the Allies. As they did so, German troops flooded south into the country. In craven reaction, the king and prime minister fled to Brindisi in the far south to seek refuge with Allied forces. Italy became split into a 'Kingdom of the South', subservient to the Allies, and, as formally consti-tuted in November, the Italian Social Republic (RSI, Repubblica Sociale Italiana), Fascist *camerati* with the Nazis in the North.

The Allied armies made slow progress up the mountainous peninsula. On 22 January 1944, a landing at Anzio on the coast fifty kilometres south of Rome, designed to speed the advance, failed to prove decisive. Rome remained under German occupation with assistance from *repubblichini*,

Italians who remained loyal to the Fascist cause for reasons of ideology, misplaced patriotism or opportunism. Mussolini had been rescued from imprisonment at an Apennine resort on 12 September 1943, and thereafter was restored to head the RSI from ministries scattered around the North of Italy; he took residence at a villa on Lago di Garda, leading to talk about the RSI as the Republic of Salò, a small nearby town. Pope Pius XII stayed at the Vatican and proclaimed Rome an 'open city', endeavouring thereby to save it, the Romans, the church and himself from bombing and actual battle. However, neither the Nazis/Fascists nor the Americans approved the principle that they should avoid action in the city and its surroundings. Over the next months, Rome's Second World War grew bloodier and the Resistance there grew – despite it being split between factions and however much the more independent members were resentful of the communists' slavish devotion to Moscow.

Already in 1941–3, the party had used Giorgio's family contacts to add to its credibility in negotiations with non-communist Italian Anti-Fascists in exile. In October 1941, Giorgio supported Giuseppe Dozza and Emilio Sereni in greeting the socialists Pietro Nenni and Giuseppe Saragat and *Giustizia e Libertà* (Justice and Liberty) liberal democrats Silvio Trentin and Francesco Fausto Nitti (Filomena's cousin) at Toulouse to frame an 'action committee' of Anti-Fascist unity. In March 1943, again as Dozza's subordinate, he met Saragat and the Sardinian Emilio Lussu, this time at Lyons to agree on a leftist programme for resistance and after the war. Every Italian was now charged with actively resisting Mussolini and Hitler. Together in victory, the partially united Left promised that they would build a state based on work and severely confiscate 'exploiters and war profiteers'.[97]

Back in Italy from April 1943, Giorgio, despite his relative youth, readily assumed a leadership role. On 30 August, this time with Longo and Mauro Scoccimarro (born 1895), he again attended a formal meeting with Nenni, Saragat and Lussu to establish a 'tripartite military junta' committed to fight Nazism/Fascism to the bitter end.[98] By the end of October, the PCI had created Gruppi di Azione Patriottica (GAP) or *gappisti* as their own partisan fighting force, pledged to strike against the RSI and its German masters by whatever method and on whatever occasion possible. Antonio Trombadori took GAP command in Rome and its province, with Giorgio Amendola as his supervisor. As Giorgio remembered, 'the training was tough, essentially political and moral'; as he did not add, his was a staff officer's role and not that of a humble soldier.[99] The men and women under his command, most young and few working class, were determined to act soon and often. They were ready to defy cautious words that dribbled through from Togliatti in

Moscow, while also having to fob off criticism from Longo, Pietro Secchia and other chiefs based in Milan.[100] The party did, of course, remember to recall their debt to the 'heroic Soviet people ... workers, peasants and intellectuals, fused into a single block of energy and will ... under the genial guide of Stalin'.[101]

The most dramatic and bloody action occurred on the Via Rasella, a street not far from where Giovanni had been assaulted in December 1923 or from the Quirinale royal palace. Again, I shall narrate events in detail.

Perhaps no one remembered, but the Via Rasella was where Benito Mussolini had lived a promiscuous bachelor life at an apartment in the Palazzo Tittoni during his early years in office. The attack was scheduled for 23 March, twenty-fifth anniversary of the foundation of the Fasci di Combattimento, the first Fascist movement in Milan, and, from its name, a returned soldiers' league.[102] On that afternoon, Giorgio, who was living in disguise in a flat looking out over the Piazza di Spagna, was due to meet Sergio Fenoaltea, a liberal democrat friend first known in his Roman elementary school days, outside the church of Sant'Andrea delle Fratte. At 4 p.m., they strolled up to find the Christian Democrat Anti-Fascist, Alcide De Gasperi, once a colleague of Giovanni Amendola on the Aventine and destined to be eight times prime minister between 1945 and 1953.[103] De Gasperi lived in the missionary Palazzo di Propaganda Fide, a building that belonged to the Vatican state and so gave security from Fascist intrusion.[104] Sandro Pertini, the socialist who would become Italy's president in 1978–85, Riccardo Bauer of the liberal democrat Partito d'Azione and De Gasperi, as local leaders of the Comitato di Liberazione Nazionale (CLN, National Liberation Committee), had approved partisan action, without knowing the detail of what had just occurred in the Via Rasella. When, after the event, he was told about the attack, Pertini, for one, gave his 'total approval'.[105]

It was a beautiful warm, sunny day – as the song went, *a Roma è sempre primavera* (in Rome, it's always springtime) – even if locals sardonically greeted such weather as a '*giornata da B-17*' (a time for American bombers).[106] Not that day and not for the *gappisti*. Their target, largely by chance, was to be the Eleventh Company of the Polizeiregiment Bozen (police regiment from Bolzano), 'neither select not very fresh troops' who had come to the city in February to assist the brutal Nazi administration. There were 156 of them. What provoked major controversy after the event was that they might be defined as 'Italians', since they were German speakers from the province of Bolzano in Italy's Alto Adige (Süd Tirol), which had been placed under direct Nazi control after 8 September. Their German officers and non-commissioned officers

(NCOs) were reported with (racial) contempt to rate the men as south-ern peasants lacking martial spirit. When they turned into the Via Rasella on 23 March, late, they were ordered by their commander, Major Helmuth Dobbrick, to sing loudly in German, despite the fact that more careful officials had recommended that such affront to the Romans should be avoided on a dangerous anniversary day.[107]

On that street near the Palazzo Tittoni and the corner of the narrow Via del Boccaccio, which offered an escape route to the Piazza Barberini, Largo del Tritone and the rest of the city, twelve *gappisti* impatiently awaited them. There were seventeen young partisans in the group in total, four of them women, who had together planned what was to come.[108] Over the last few days they had assembled twelve kilograms of TNT placed in a steel container, and next to it six more kilograms of explosive and iron shards to act as lethal shells. They reckoned that, in fifty seconds between the fuse being lit and the explosion, they could disappear, although it was also intended that, in the resulting confusion, three of them could fire four 45 millimetre mortars at the heavily armed troops, calculating that they were likely to be wounded or bewildered, unable to resist such attack.[109]

Dressed in a Roman street cleaner's uniform of dark blue canvas with peaked caps, two of their number, Rosario Bentivegna and Carla Capponi, collected the heavy metal double-barrelled garbage receptacle, stamped SPQR (Senatus Populusque Romanus) with a *romanità* that survives in contemporary Rome, from a comrade's cellar not far from the Colosseum. The back segment contained the bombs. Bentivegna bumped it down the path towards the Via Rasella, worried that the shaking prompted by the uneven surface could set something off. Capponi carried the mortars in her shopping bag, which sprouted vege-table tops. Near the Quirinale, they met two actual street cleaners, who asked in local dialect where Rosario came from and what he was pushing, unconvinced when told it was a load of cement. Laughing, they moved to lift the lid and look inside but thought better of it, assuming that the fake street cleaner was actually transporting something to be sold on the black market. Was it prosciutto, they joked?

A step down the Via del Quirinale, a turn to the right and the bomb was in place in the Via Rasella, outside the Palazzo Tittoni. It was 2 p.m., the beginning of siesta, an ideal hour to minimise civilian casualties from the coming explosion. Other armed partisans took up stations along the street, pretending to be busy with various tasks. Time ticked by. Nerves tightened. Bentivegna, whose charge it was to set off the explosion, swept the street ever cleaner, pausing to light and relight his pipe. On two occasions there was a false alarm. Siesta was coming to an end, and, after 4 p.m., the street might get crowded. At 3.45, Pasquale Balsamo meandered past Bentivegna to say that their immediate commander, Carlo Salinari (fighting name Spartacus – *romanità* again impossible to avoid), advised that, if no Germans appeared in the next fifteen minutes, they should take the lethal rubbish cart away and scatter.

At 3.50 p.m. came the sound of German singing. Polizeiregiment Bozen marched up the Via Rasella. Franco Calamandrei, a *gappista* who was the son of one of Italy's leading jurists, in 1924–5 a member of Giovanni's Unione Nazionale, gave the signal.[110] Bentivegna put his pipe to the fuse, for a moment without effect. But then he smelled it smouldering; he had fifty seconds to escape and rushed down the Via del Boccaccio. At the corner of the Via delle Quattro Fontane, Carla Capponi handed him a raincoat to cover his street cleaner's garb, not worrying that it might be out of place in Roman sunshine. In the Via Rasella, a *portiere* who emerged with bad timing from the Palazzo Tittoni was told in an urgent whisper to retreat indoors; three building workers were informed that they should scarper given that the Germans were coming. Earlier, some boys who wanted to play football had had their ball kicked away, much to their annoyance.

Then came the massive explosion, followed by confused firing and counter-firing. Those partisans who had been waiting to do so threw their bombs. In the Propaganda Fide, De Gasperi felt the building shake, asking Amendola and Fenoaltea what had happened before they proceeded contentedly to their high tactical discussions, all self-consciously behaving as the officer class and not more humble soldiery.[111] According to the partisan count, only two civilian bystanders, one never identified and the other a thirteen-year-old boy, Pietro Zuccheretti, were killed, and one was wounded by the blast. Zuccheretti came out of the Via del Boccaccio at the wrong moment and was blown apart; his feet were never found. Twenty-eight soldiers died from the bomb and five more shortly afterwards. A hundred were wounded.[112] The Via Rasella attack had proved to be what Anti-Fascist Italians claim was the biggest partisan assault on Nazi occupiers in any European city. In planning it and bearing party responsibility for the resulting deaths, Giorgio Amendola had demonstrated that he was a fighting communist and Anti-Fascist, and, in his mind, nineteen years after the terrible assault at Ponte a Nievole, Giovanni Amendola's demand for justice was fulfilled.

The events on the Via Rasella were met by the Nazis with vicious reprisal. Hitler, when informed, ordered the destruction of the entire neighbouring zone of the city and the execution of fifty Italians for every dead soldier. In the end, he settled for a ten to one ratio. On the afternoon of 24 March, the Germans, with *repubblichini* police as their

auxiliaries, seized 335 Italians – some from gaol, many from the SS
torture chambers on the Via Tasso, and others simply rounded up from
the streets of Rome. As soon as possible after being collected, they were
shot at the Ardeatine Caves just outside the city. Nazi arithmetic was
flawed but the five extra Italians, as a Nazi officer remarked, were there
by accident but had to die nonetheless.

Figure 1.2 Giorgio and Sergio Fenoaltea, arm in arm across the
political divide in (liberated) Rome (1944).

The events of 23–24 March remain 'an open wound in the memory and feelings of Rome' and Italy. The Ardeatine Caves mausoleum is the most obvious site to hallow Italians as 'victims' of the Second World War.[113] However, already on 25 March, from the Vatican, *L'Osservatore Romano* treated the Nazis and the partisans as sinners equally worthy of rebuke, urging them to realise their 'responsibility towards themselves, towards the lives they are to safeguard, and towards history and civilization'.[114] Roman opinion, on the whole, probably agreed.[115]

Two days later, Togliatti arrived back in Italy from Moscow with a message that came to be called the *svolta di Salerno* (U-turn at Salerno), ordering communists to go on fighting but also to seek alliances wherever they might – with the monarchy, with the Vatican and with the other residues of Liberal Italy. Stalin stood behind the latest abrupt communist revision. However, once the war was over, and after 1953 when Stalin was safely dead, Togliatti slowly and carefully adopted the line of 'an Italian road to socialism'.[116] When that happened, Giorgio, the son of Giovanni, the grandchild of a Garibaldian and great-grandchild of a Mazzinian, was delighted to find his party embodying the 'good' traditions of national history that looked back to the Risorgimento.[117]

Down the decades, in law cases and histories, questions have continued to be asked about whether the Via Rasella was a 'terrorist' act, whether Amendola and the other communists knowingly provoked Nazi reprisals, and whether the partisan chiefs and *gappisti* should have turned themselves in before the murders at the Ardeatine Caves. But at no time did Giorgio resile from the attack. With an intransigence and severity that his father's ghost may have admired, until his dying day he was certain that, against Nazism/Fascism (and the invaders of your nation), you struck whenever and however you could. He also always maintained that the 'people' agreed with that policy.[118] If he was then a terrorist, a terrorist he had to be, a communist fighter and his father's son.

Throughout the Fascist years, blood and history ran together for the Amendolas and for Italy. Now it is time to examine in more detail how the public and private lives of a liberal democrat saint and martyr father and a communist partisan (or 'terrorist') son meshed, and, in so doing, to vividly explore lights and shadows in Italian history over the century from 1880 to 1980.

2 The Rise of Giovanni Amendola, 1882–1919
Man of Liberal Democratic Ambition

Through his first four decades, Giovanni Amendola strode energetically down the Italian road to liberalism. From his origins in an uncelebrated part of Campania, from a family clinging to the lowest rungs of the middle class, he moved determinedly up and up. En route, there were numerous staging posts: moderate socialism, religion of great variety (but never Catholicism), marriage to a 'new woman' from the Romanov empire, pure philosophy, political philosophy, academic life, political journalism, war service with promotion in his country's officer corps, and then, in November 1919, election to the Chamber of Deputies for one of the seats in the College of Salerno. That first direct step towards political power was followed speedily by appointment to what was the outer cabinet, but with the crucial post-war task of helping to manage Italy's finances. Within the framework of Italian liberalism, as set in place by the Risorgimento, other young men also emerged into political prominence. But few ranged quite was widely as young Giovanni Amendola.

Within his own generation, Giovanni Amendola stood tall in what had been the world of Italian politics since the Risorgimento, when the nation state of Italy had been invented. During the subsequent so-called Liberal era, some Italians learned slowly and often reluctantly, if sometimes aggressively, to base their identities in the nation and its institutions. Their version of liberalism doubtless accepted parliament as the final guarantor of law, constitutional monarchy and the local version of capitalism. But it remained tinctured with its own special features. Amendola, therefore, did not belong to, let alone lead, a modern mass political party; he was no Italian W. E. Gladstone. Successive prime ministers were similarly their own men. They entered office because they were estimated to have special competence among the crew of politicians in the Chamber of Deputies; to be possessed of a strong local base and a growing set of loyal(ish) clients, mostly accumulated through the process of '*trasformismo*' (adaptability in ideology and action); and to have ownership of, or have worked as a journalist on, a

33

newspaper that would make their case more loudly than that of others. In 1919, Amendola already had each of these qualifications or was giving every sign of developing them. He was the favoured underling of Prime Minister Francesco Saverio Nitti and a well-regarded journalist working for the great Milan Liberal newspaper *Il Corriere della Sera* and its celebrated editor, Luigi Albertini. He had secured twin bases of great potential promise. To most observers, Amendola seemed to stand on the threshold of a brilliant political career, a future prime minister in waiting.

No doubt he must wait, a contemporary might have added, since the Liberal system was gerontocratic. In January 1919, Amendola was only thirty-six. Of those who had recently held the highest office or who were to do so over the next three years, Paolo Boselli had been born in 1838, Luigi Luzzatti in 1841, Giovanni Giolitti in 1842, Sidney Sonnino in 1847, Antonio Salandra in 1853, Vittorio Emanuele Orlando in 1860, Luigi Facta in 1861, Nitti in 1868 and Ivanoe Bonomi in 1873. Amendola was their junior by one to four decades. History therefore taught that, although his allegiance in 1919 was to a group calling itself Democrazia Liberale (Liberal Democracy) – not a party, just a band of associates – his turn at the highest level lay far in the future. Maybe his rise could accelerate, given the apparent promise that, following the widening of the suffrage in 1913 and what was being claimed as a 'people's war', Liberal Italy was moving towards a more genuine democracy and a shake-up of the old order. Yet, his most obvious path still lay in serving under some older man in this or that Liberal government, and in a variety of ministries. Only when freighted by that sum of experience might King Victor Emmanuel III summon him to the Quirinale palace. Amendola was a member of the 'emerging middle classes', bourgeois enough to be taken seriously and with fresh appeal as a new man, a candidate for office who could no longer be ignored. But, on his country's past record, emergence to actual power was unlikely to be precipitate.

In the event, Amendola did not triumph. Benito Mussolini stood in his way. In January 1919, the Duce was only thirty-five, Amendola's junior by a year. From March 1919, Mussolini was leader of a political movement, not a party, called the Fasci Italiani di Combattimento. Since November 1915, he had been owner-editor of a national paper, *Il Popolo d'Italia*, its foundation dismissed by Amendola as a news-sheet seeking to be moral but succeeding only in being wordy.[1] In November 1919, when Giovanni entered the Chamber of Deputies, Mussolini humiliatingly failed to be elected in a Milan seat. But in the contest between the two, he was not the inferior for long. His rise to the prime ministership by 1922, and to dictatorship by 1925, was astonishingly rapid, and, to Amendola and his friends, entailed the ruin of the country's Liberal values. Mussolini was to preside not merely over a variation in the Liberal system, but over what he boasted was a revolution and the replacement of the old Liberal state with a new 'totalitarian' one. In so doing, he not only defeated Giovanni Amendola, but allowed or encouraged his killing.

Giovanni Amendola was born in Naples on 15 April 1882. He was the son and first child of Pietro Paolo Amendola and Adelaide Bianchi. Pietro Paolo served in the Carabinieri (the nation's gendarmerie, a militarised force that played a prominent part in policing Liberal Italy). Much of Pietro Paolo's deployment was in the long 'war' after 1861 against brigands – that is, rebellious southern peasants unattracted to, and ignorant of, the new nation.[2] There were eventually six children: three brothers (Giovanni, Salvatore ('Mario') and Vincenzo) and three daughters (Letizia, Luisa and Maria). Giovanni – in full, Giovanni Battista Ernesto – was often called by his second name in his family, especially by his pious Catholic mother.[3] Over previous decades the family had been based at Sarno, a town a little south of Naples, where Pietro Paolo's father, Michele, had been a miller and then had run a small grocery store. Pietro Paolo had seven brothers and sisters in what was quite an Amendola clan.

The Amendolas were not peasants and knew that a deep gap separated them from such lesser beings. They were literate town dwellers who did not draw their living from the land. During the Risorgimento, Pietro Paolo had sought to push himself forwards. Family legend claimed that, when he was a boy of only ten or eleven,[4] he volunteered for Garibaldi's *Mille* in 1860. He was too young to join in the taking into Italian hands of Sicily and then the rest of the Bourbon Kingdom of the Two Sicilies. But he stayed loyal to Garibaldi, who soon gauged the first governments of the new nation too lacklustre and timid for his tastes and who, in 1867, launched an attack on papal power. In Garibaldi's opinion, Pius IX was keeping Rome from its natural role as the country's historic capital (and model of revived imperial grandeur). At the small town of Mentana, not far outside the city, on 3 November 1867 a motley crew of 5,000, calling themselves with inevitable classical reference the Legione Garibaldina (Garibaldi Legion), were beaten back by papal forces, stiffened by support from Emperor Napoleon III's France. The Legione suffered 150 dead and 220 wounded, among the latter Pietro Paolo, with 1,700 taken prisoner.

It was a temporary defeat. Within three years, Napoleon III and Pius IX had lost political authority. On 20 September 1870, Italian troops stormed the Porta Pia to make Rome Italy's capital. Thereafter, Pietro Paolo retained contact with the 'Hero of Two Worlds', acting as secretary of the Società Reduci Patrie Battaglie (Association of Returned Soldiers in Battles for the Fatherland). Slowly, he moved upwards socially, leaving behind those family members who stayed at Sarno. After Carabinieri service in Naples and then, for two years (1884–6), in Florence, he took his growing family to Rome. In the nation's capital, he swapped police service for a lowly post in the ministry of education as a 'category C' clerk. He successfully secured employment for his younger brother, Liberato, within the ministry. To achieve these transfers, he used the contacts and *raccomandazioni* that were a habitual part of client–patron (and family) life in Liberal Italy. One credible story is that Pietro Paolo persuaded his cousin, Giovanni Battista, the sculptor, to give two eminent Liberals, Giustino Fortunato and Ferdinando Martini, a bronze and a marble head that he had fashioned. Such obsequious generosity ensured that they became reliable patrons of the Amendolas; Fortunato remained such until his death in 1932.[5]

Yet Pietro Paolo's success should not be exaggerated since the cushy but scarcely overpaid post that he obtained in the education ministry was as a museum guard at the Galleria Corsini beside the Tiber and next to the Regina Coeli gaol, destined for a time to hold his grandson, Giorgio. In his autobiography, Giorgio claimed that Giovanni had on occasion talked of the poverty of his household in his youth. They had made it to Rome but scarcely joined the beautiful people. A hard-boiled egg might have to be shared between four of the children and any oil used to dress a salad was measured drop by drop. Of Pietro Paolo's six children, only Giovanni was permitted to engage in something approaching a modern education, and even he left his technical school at fifteen.[6]

Adelaide Bianchi's family had stronger roots in the middle class. Her father, Marco, was a builder who helped construct the Rome–Cassino railway in the papal state. He was also a Mazzinian. In 1867, his wife informed on him to her priest over a planned Mazzinian action; that year Giuseppe Mazzini disdainfully refused to take a seat in the Chamber of Deputies, pronouncing that he was still the foe of the established order. As a result of his wife's denunciation, Marco was gaoled until the fall of Pius IX's Rome in 1870. Restored to freedom, he rejected further contact with her and his children. Family legend claimed that he died rich and alone. He had wanted to see his children on one last occasion. However, Pietro Paolo refused to allow his brothers- and sisters-in-law to attend his deathbed unless their mother accompanied them. Marco angrily rejected such an idea and, in response, cut off any inheritance.[7]

Other, vaguer, family stories alleged that 'Saracens' (who played a significant part in Emperor Frederick II's domination of the South and who for centuries raided Italian coasts) had somehow found a place in the Amendola bloodstock, which was why Giovanni had such sallow skin. A rival claim was that a Spanish soldier stood in the family line. Family believers in the black legend of Spain muttered that it explained the religiosity, which for a time would enchant young Giovanni. Still less specific was the idea that the move to Sarno had come from the surrounding hills or the nearby coastline.[8] No one wanted to explore whether there had been any peasants in the family line but neither did any of the Amendolas flirt with malign northern European ideas about racial purity.

What is striking in Giovanni Amendola's life story is how promptly and completely he broke away from this commonplace background. His sturdy journey upwards began in his teens. In 1897, taking advantage of another family contact, he was employed by Edoardo Arbib as an assistant on his radical paper, *La Capitale* (The Capital). Arbib, a patriot of Jewish heritage, had been a Garibaldian in his youth and by now was a Freemason (membership was in many ways the ticket of entry into Liberal politics and high society)[9] and a respectable journalist, commenting from somewhere towards the left of the amorphous Liberal system. He also served first as a parliamentary deputy and then as a senator. Arbib was open-minded enough not to blanch when Giovanni joined the Gioventù Socialista (Socialist Youth) of his San Eustachio quarter in Rome. Although there is no hard evidence on the matter, Giovanni may have been arrested there in 1898, when an authoritarian government, headed by a general, Luigi Pelloux, tried to repress growing socialist (and Catholic) dissidence in the country.[10]

In any case, Amendola's flirtation with socialism was short-lived. He scorned Marxist materialism for the rest of his life. In his mind, the spiritual must always trump ordinary needs. Man's identity must be mystical, not merely practical. In 1899, he experienced some sort of spiritual crisis, writing almost a dozen articles on religious themes for *La Capitale*. He penned poetry, as any thinking seventeen-year-old might do, but, more unusually, he managed to get it published under the title *Urne, storia naturale di un'adolescenza* (Urns, the Natural History of an Adolescence), sententiously mixing death and life but insistent that his own past was null and void.[11] His future was as yet shrouded. But Amendola wanted to move as far as possible from humdrum Roman family life.

Could his destiny lie in the East? The wife of his first patron, Arbib, was interested in theosophy. An Italian branch of Annie Besant's world-ranging movement had opened in January 1897. Besant herself came on a lecture tour two months later but subsequently left her Italian followers mostly under the supervision of Isabel Cooper-Oakley, another woman with wide contacts in British India. Besant did, however, reappear in October 1904 to address the new Roman branch of the Società Teosofica (Theosophical Society).[12] Cooper-Oakley was a Freemason and enrolled the promising and handsome Giovanni Amendola in her *Dio e Popolo* (God and the People) lodge. In September 1901 she wrote personally to him as 'My dear son and pupil', intimating that he might think about joining the Italian emigrants then flooding into the USA. In that New World, she maintained, 'there is an intense desire for psychic powers' and little 'culture' opposing it.[13]

Amendola did not pursue that proposition. But he was deciding that mysticism could explain the meaning of life, bring him to a knowledge of God and disclose 'some hidden thing, some hidden power'[14] in a fashion that neither Marxism nor his family's hackneyed patriotism did. Pietro Paolo was an admirer of the Sicilian Francesco Crispi, the ex-Garibaldian, and, in 1887–91 and 1893–6, prime minister. A convinced imperialist, Crispi launched the African adventure that tumbled to disastrous defeat at Adwa in Ethiopia in March 1896.[15] Giovanni was impatient at nationalist muddle, even if he never forgot the patriotic lesson that the African defeat had amounted to a 'national bereavement'.[16] Therefore, he paid no attention when, in September 1899, his father wrote to reprimand his son against 'fuming like a steam furnace' and offered paternal counsel that he calm himself down with 'a good dose of Ice [sic]'. Giovanni, Pietro Paolo warned, was losing time focusing on things that did not matter. He must learn to face life more realistically and tranquilly.[17]

Mutinously, Giovanni did not listen. Rather than behaving like a good petit bourgeois and accepting that, as the eldest son, he should acquire a store of wealth and status to safeguard his siblings when it was his turn to become head of the family, Amendola threw himself into theosophy. Again defying familial orthodoxy and propriety (which, on his own deathbed, with some hypocrisy, he would preach to his eldest son), he soon relied on subsidies from his youngest brother, Vincenzo, four years his junior, who had joined the army.[18] Throughout the next decade, Giovanni remained given to seeking loans from rich and accommodating friends.[19] In every aspect of his life, he was relinquishing his parents' norms and habits. A serious young man of determined principle, while he sought deep understanding of theosophy and its connections to

Buddhism and other Eastern religions, Giovanni swore off meat, wine, tobacco and sex.[20]

Although unable to settle down to complete a university degree – he began one at Rome in mathematics, a subject in which he had starred at school,[21] but dropped out, stating that he preferred literature – he read widely, noting his admiration for the utopian thoughts or deeds of such famous but varying authors as John Ruskin and Leo Tolstoy. He set himself to learn languages: English, German and even Sanskrit were added to Italian and his fluent French. He tried yoga and speculated about Neoplatonism, as well as seeking to achieve *karma* through his good intents and deeds.[22] He published a romantic article about Luigi Lucheni, the Italian anarchist who, in 1898, assassinated Empress Elisabeth of Austria, taking the chance to condemn anarchism.[23] He expanded the borders of his mind as widely as possible, earnestly undertaking that he would plumb 'the renewal of the ethical and political consciousness of western nations in harmony with their most elevated spiritual and cultural traditions'.[24] 'I have always sensed in the depths of my soul a religious and priestly mission,' he assured himself. His vow could not be satisfied within the Catholic Church, which had opposed the Risorgimento and was still locked in a Cold War with the Italian state but nonetheless provided faith for the overwhelming majority of Italians.[25]

He was so vocal and passionate that the theosophists thought him their coming man. But maybe theosophy was not offering ultimate meaning? Maybe theosophists did not come up to his standards? By January 1902, he began to express doubts, worrying in an article that he wrote for the journal *Teosofia* of a dim dilettantism among members of the Società Teosofica. They were not serious and stern enough in helping him to find 'a doctrine and a method that could resolve scientifically the religious needs of human society'.[26] Maybe he must move from religion to politics and help convert all Italians to a mystical sense of their national belonging.

Such grandiose ambition long survived in his mind. But, at twenty-one, he faced another issue: love. In December 1903, at a theosophist lecture, he met a young woman called Eva Kühn, who, for a Giovanni gazing at new worlds beyond boring little Rome, must have seemed fascinatingly global. She had been brought up in Vilnius, now the capital of Lithuania but then ruled by the Romanov empire. Napoleon had called it 'the Jerusalem of the North'; 40 per cent of the population of 150,000 in 1900 were Jewish. The umlaut in the Kühn name, however, separated Eva's family from that heritage. Their language and culture were Baltic German, their religion Protestant and evangelical. Vilnius boasted the oldest university in the region; it had been founded in 1579. The Kühns were intellectuals, 'erudite, well off and united' (and numerous – Eva had six siblings). The family knew Tolstoy and may have been his distant relations. Eva's mother, Emma, had been trained at one of the most aristocratic girls' schools in Moscow, while Eva's father, Oscar, taught literature at a local technical high school, wrote poetry and articles of literary criticism, loved music with a passion and especially devoted himself to the romantic thought of Heinrich Heine. Sadly for his daughter, Oscar had died in his forties when Eva was in her early teens.[27] In her old age, however, she remembered to a granddaughter the thrill and delight of a Russian Christmas when her parents had decorated their tree with real, juicy, bright orange-coloured mandarins.[28]

Figure 2.1 Eva Kühn, young, confident, beautiful and foreign, a new woman in Vilnius (1906).

Young Eva grew up polyglot and self-consciously intellectual, a new woman of a kind as yet scarcely imaginable in Italy and certainly not in the Amendola family with its patriarchal gender relations. Tolstoy, whom she read and later translated, had many complex thoughts on love and nature, God, men and women; she brooded over his lessons. When Eva was seventeen in 1897, she was sent to England to perfect her English and then on to university at Zurich, where she read philosophy, winning a prize for an essay on the American transcendentalist Henry Thoreau (1817–62). In order to add Italian to her other languages, with the aim of completing a degree in comparative literature, in September 1903 she came south to Rome. There she was drawn into the Società Teosofica, to whose members, in March 1904, she gave a lecture on Schopenhauer (1788–1860), a philosopher whom she was studying hard and deeply admired.[29] Schopenhauer had tried to probe the nature of 'metaphysical will' and, like the theosophists, consulted Eastern religions to do so.[30]

A couple of months later Eva met Amendola through a mutual friend from her home country. The first correspondence between the couple-to-be, then in French (as it remained), had Giovanni, although her junior chronologically (by two years) and in much cultural experience, promising, as one who knew the theosophical world better than she did, to give her an unnamed book that could help her.[31] Another letter the next day was more ardent. Giovanni evoked their souls, musing how they could connect more deeply, while promising to bring her Annie Besant's *Autobiography* 'on Tuesday'. 'I must get to know you better,' he added.[32]

Two weeks later they were in love. Now adopting the intimate *tu*, he addressed her as 'My sweet little Eva' in a lengthy letter, and he was sure that his 'love' coincided with the tender nature of her person and soul. Sex was a little way off, however, since he stressed: 'I have for you the same respect that I hold for my innocent little five-year-old sister.' He was a virgin; 'never have I seen *loving* [he wrote the word in English] eyes cast on me' by a female. He was delighted to know that her beauty mirrored her soul and was in harmony with her physicality. He ended: 'accept a kiss on your dear childlike cheeks'.[33]

A few weeks later there was another epistle in which Giovanni was less clumsy in his meditation on their relationship. The two, he said, should work together. He must learn Russian, while he hoped that she could 'develop for herself the spiritual elements of theosophy as an intimate thing in your life'. Then the new religion could have 'value for yourself, independent of me and my person'. In their loving, he wanted to open a place for their souls that could allow the 'most perfect evolution of her nature'. The same day he complained that 'my poor parents know nothing of my real life'. He had family duties but she was more important. 'My ties with you begin to weave themselves into my spiritual life.'[34] They were so engrossed with each other's deep conversation that, one evening, they were locked into the Borghese gardens when they did not notice closing time.[35]

Can Eva have sometimes wondered whether this handsome, young, southern Italian actually understood her proto-feminism or her wide-ranging high culture? And was he quite as pure in eliminating self-interest as he swore he was? His words often sounded masculine. She could reply girlishly. As she informed him almost gaily, she had been 'good' and had risen at 7 a.m. each morning to read Annie Besant's *Thought Power* (at twenty-eight pages not the longest of religious texts, but it was in English).[36] He might have distanced himself from his family. But not too far, it seemed. So Eva assured him that she had taken pains to introduce herself to his three sisters, signing off this confession of conventional virtue with a kiss on each of his 'dear eyes'.[37] In another letter she declared that, endeavouring to please an Italian son, she already really loved his mother.[38]

Soon, Giovanni had to move away from Rome since he had been summoned to compulsory military service. From Bracciano, he warned Eva, in a manner that might be read as ominous, not to get overexcited, while promising that he was planning his 'material independence' from his family after his training was over.[39] In June, he added, whether as a warning or an allurement in what sounds more like callow self-absorption than love, 'I am the most complicated intellectual organism whom I have ever known.' His interests, he explained gravely, stretched across art, science, poetry and philosophy. Theosophy allowed him to unite his 'intellectual, emotional and moral consciousness and affirm the life of the soul'. Yet he often felt terribly alone. Drifting far from theosophy, he could dream of becoming pope and ending all religious wars and divisions.[40]

That ambition was a little unrealistic. Now, instead, the two began to discuss whether they should marry in autumn or summer 1905. Giovanni, for once letting her teach him, remarked that, on her recommendation, he had read *The Brothers Karamazov*. In doing so, he had not escaped his self, however. Scanning the book's pages, he had been convinced that he resembled all the brothers, but especially Alyosha (the most religious and 'virtuous' one). Dostoevsky, he told her (a woman who spent much of her life translating Russian) with a glib assumption about the breadth of his own culture, was the equal of Shakespeare.[41]

Amendola was set on a marriage that could carry him up and away from his family, and, as he wrote in July from Padua, where he was still in army training, far from the disorder and brutishness of Italy.[42] Plainly he had found no human contact with what must have been his peasant ordinary soldiers. Amendola may have been a southerner but his self-image as a questing man of culture was cut off from the frequently illiterate majority of the population there. How different from that tedious, murky world was Eva, he must have thought, the woman able to read almost every European language, the friend or relation of Tolstoy, a thinker of great thoughts, the partner with whom his soul could explore and master the world and beyond. When she visited him in Padua for three days, they may have each lost their virginity and were troubled by the emotional cost.[43]

For Eva and Giovanni, true love had another downside. The practical checked the philosophical. On 5 August, Giovanni informed her in a short note that his father had refused permission for them to marry,[44] as he was entitled to do in Liberal Italy until Giovanni turned twenty-five. Marriage must wait until April 1907, two long years into the future. Soon the family situation deteriorated further and Eva may have been the prime cause. Giovanni explained in a longer communication that his father was worried that his son did not have enough funds or settled work for marriage, and both Pietro Paolo and Giovanni were alarmed by Eva's emotionality. She had composed an 'awful' letter to Pietro Paolo, which, it turned out, had fallen into Giovanni's hands. He told her sharply, with no apology for his interference, that it amounted to a 'crime'. Luckily, Giovanni and his mother had opened the letter before it reached his father's desk and decided not to pass on her words. She should write again '*sweetly and charitably*', Giovanni, very much the patriarch, instructed her, and without expressing too much '*passion*' for him, stressing that she was a 'balanced and reasonable' girl.[45]

As he added a week later, with sentiments that sounded scarcely well directed to a 'new woman': 'you are really my child, my dear child, whose naivety I find so ravishing'. As far as their love was concerned, Giovanni added, not quite forgetting their religious and philosophical excursions together, '*I want to develop your spiritual individuality*'. A delayed wedding was a good idea. When marriage did happen, she could look forward to reaching the 'full maturity of her feminine organism and of your whole being through *being a mother*'. His earlier words about profound philosophical labour together now perhaps rang hollow; they certainly needed amendment. By the time he was forty-five, he foresaw in a way that he must have thought comforting, he would have earned a pension, their children would have grown up, and he and she could combine in 'a work for humanity and the soul' – true happiness, however postponed.[46] It was a promise that events were to thwart. He was dead just before his forty-fourth birthday.

Their relationship had further contradictions. In unalloyed patriarchal mode, Giovanni assured her that he was like a father to her even though he also planned to have children with her, eliciting in response another girlish note back signed 'your little frog' and recording her weight as 54.5 kilograms.[47] She lacked Giovanni's classical beauty, being much shorter than he was, with a high forehead, thick lips, a mass of curly black hair and liquid dark eyes. However, she was still a physically attractive young woman, albeit inclined to melancholy and little fond of laughter.[48]

Beyond broils with her intended in-laws and simmering doubts about Giovanni's interpretation of being an equal intellectual partner, Eva drifted into another crisis shortly afterwards, although it is not recorded in correspondence between the two, which is lacking for this period. Eva reacted badly to Annie Besant's lecture in October 1904, a confrontation between the two provoking outright collapse. She then returned to Vilnius for psychiatric treatment, oppressed by severe headaches and what was feared to be 'cerebral congestion'.[49] She did not go back to Rome for more than a year. Eva's mother, another who disliked the relationship that had begun in a foreign place, cautioned her that Giovanni was a 'bear' who had kept her in chains.[50] Despite family disapproval on both sides, the two stayed in contact, with Giovanni, in October 1905, declaring amorously that he had kept her every letter under his pillow while she had been away. Typically, he added the news that brooding on Wagner's *Parsifal* could prepare a man for sacrifice. But he did express pleasure at reports that she was cured and happy.[51]

During their time apart, Giovanni changed direction. He had abandoned theosophy and left Cooper-Oakley's Masonic lodge to join one attached to the mainstream Grande Oriente. He lasted there until 1908, after which he sometimes attacked the Masons but without ever concluding that they were the Liberal system's main problem.[52] More significantly, he had put himself in touch with Giuseppe Prezzolini and Giovanni Papini, two men who had daringly established themselves at the cultural summit of Liberal Italy. Their quest for 'modernisation' has sparked wide examination of the problem of whether pre-1914 European intellectuals were preparing their societies for the Great War or for the totalitarian and authoritarian regimes that spread across the continent from the 'revolutions' in Russia in 1917 and Italy in 1922. Prezzolini, the son of a prefect, came from a social rank well above Amendola, but Papini's family had a similar Garibaldian, petit bourgeois background.

Each was almost the same age as Amendola and neither had completed a university degree. Rather, in 1903, they had burst into cultural journalism together, editing a monthly 'literary review' entitled *Leonardo*; it lasted until August 1907. Simultaneously, they wrote copiously for the weekly *Il Regno*, founded by the nationalist Enrico Corradini, also in 1903. It stopped circulation in 1906. Two years later, Prezzolini and Papini replaced these journals with *La Voce*, a weekly that, until the outbreak of world war, occupied a central role in national intellectual life.[53] As an admiring American historian has put it, the two aimed through their publication to 'build the civil society and culture' that could permit 'a genuine mass politics' to emerge in Liberal Italy, even if, when being more modest, they saw themselves and their friends as constituting a 'party of intellectuals'.[54]

In 1905, Amendola made contact with, first, Papini and, later, Prezzolini, publishing religious, literary and theoretical commentary in *Leonardo* and earning a congratulatory note from American philosopher William James, who, along with Friedrich Nietzsche, was much admired by Prezzolini's and Papini's circle.[55] James told Amendola that, in these writings, he was making himself into a 'champion of intellectualism'.[56] It was a heady advance from the obscurity of theosophy. In November, Giovanni promised Eva that he had opted for 'the practical life, seeking to curb egoism, that is my centre today', although he rather undermined his claim by proceeding to say patronisingly that 'a certain round head belonging to a sweet little girl called Eva Kühn' might not be fully ready for Nietzsche.[57]

Eva dutifully replied that she was proud of his success in his new field and volunteered that, if he sent her his articles, she could translate them; after all, no less a man than William James had congratulated her from Stanford on her ability to convert his prose into Russian.[58] Soon she added news of the political instability of Russia in revolution; its threat was driving her rich and aristocratic friends away from Vilnius and making it hard for her to concentrate, although she was tempted by the idea of supporting a worker–soldier revolutionary alliance. Her fear of 'boiling over' lingered, however, and so she avoided demonstrations. Instead, she was reading as much as she could of Greek philosophy. Her mastery of that language was improving. She did find space to warn him that Besant and Cooper-Oakley were 'self-conscious liars', whose thought was sham. She was sure, she said, by contrast, that his and her love rippled with 'poetry and strength'.[59]

Giovanni did half-apologetically worry lest his 'egoism and inexperience' had worsened her mental troubles, while recalling how her 'feminine innocence' had attracted him and warning that her 'metaphysical preoccupations can either be an instrument favouring a more elevated life or a danger'. He was reading *War and Peace* to get to know her better and had actually met William James. Giovanni agreed that his and her souls were intertwined and, in more quotidian vein, reported that his parents were now glad that the young people had resumed correspondence.[60] In January 1906, he disclosed that he was coming to Vilnius to find her. He was, he said, not like other men; he would fall on his knees before a woman only once. That woman was Eva, even if he was still capable of complaining bossily that 'naivety is the predominant characteristic of all your letters'.[61]

As intellectually venturesome as ever, he had criticised Croce, the Neapolitan who had established himself as the leading idealist philosopher in Italy, because Croce had a low opinion of Schopenhauer.[62] Giovanni's travel arrangements therefore were partly quickened by love and the revived prospect of marriage, and partly by his intense intellectual ambition. Over the summer and autumn of 1906, he visited Vilnius, Moscow, Berlin and Leipzig, everywhere hunting out intellectual links and aspiring to weighty thought. Eva had promised him that she would organise a stay with Tolstoy and he does seem to have briefly visited the celebrated estate at Yasnaya Polyana.[63] In July he dashed off a note to Prezzolini to say that, in a Lithuanian forest, his mind had meditated about 'the whole weight of our history and our centuries-old culture'. He found Russia to be a country of deep pain, 'with Will lost in the ocean of emotions'.[64] Not altogether detached from practicality, in Moscow he offered Croce a connection with a Russian journal interested in his works. In return, having reached Berlin, he sought and received a *raccomandazione* to local professors and was not put off when Croce warned him that Germans usually 'knew nothing of Italian or *italianità*' (the Italian spirit).[65] William James also wrote in his favour and sent details on Harvard in case Amendola decided to transfer there. Giovanni confessed to Prezzolini that he had not taken to Berlin and could not understand how anyone could spend his life in such a place. He exchanged letters with the Spanish writer and philosopher Miguel de Unamuno, another liberal of sorts, mentioning that he could read Spanish but not yet write it.[66]

Suddenly, in mid-December, he told the Spaniard that he had not mastered the book that Unamuno had sent him since he had urgently to return home.[67] His marriage to Eva was planned for 25 January 1907 at the Valdese (Waldensian) Protestant church in Rome, despite some surviving reservations from Pietro Paolo.[68] The choice of the Valdesi was not a religious one but a compromise between Eva's Russian Protestantism and Giovanni's inchoate non-Catholic Catholicism. The couple had signed at a civil ceremony a week or two earlier.

Giovanni's belief that motherhood was the summit of female life was soon put to the test. Ten months after the wedding, and after a tough twelve hours in labour, Eva was delivered of Giorgio, their first child. Despite the Waldensian wedding, the family heir was baptised by Pope Pius X in St Peter's, striking and even remarkable proof of the Amendola family's enhanced status.[69] Their daughter, Adelaide (Ada), followed in January 1910, prompting a philosophical disquisition from Giovanni a few weeks before the birth about how they had only met six years ago but had almost immediately bonded their souls and bodies. Their life together, he wrote, meant the opening of their hearts to a 'poetry that was a little sad and a little tragic' but deeply meaningful. These ruminations arrived by letter because Giovanni was absent at work in Florence, where, for a time, he held a modest secretarial position to a society favouring the fine arts; like a good eldest son, he was sending a third of his meagre salary back to his mother in Rome; her health had taken a turn for the worse.[70] He remained unsure whether he could get back to Rome and see his mother, Eva and Giorgio for Christmas.[71]

Figure 2.2 Eva, with her mother-in-law at her shoulder, uneasily nursing baby Giorgio among Amendola family members (1908).

With his private life apparently settled, although it was soon to have more ups and downs, the years from 1907 to 1914 were, in many ways, halcyon ones for Giovanni Amendola. To be sure, from time to time he joined in the squabbling that was always likely to erupt among Italy's Liberal intelligentsia. As early as January 1907, he had written to Croce lamenting Papini's 'charlatanism', while later in the year he switched to assure Papini that he had 'one of the best minds of our generation'.[72] However, in 1913, Giovanni informed Papini that, as a rigorously 'classical and past-oriented (*"passatista"*) thinker', he had no time for his sometime associate's self-indulgent game playing.[73] Soon after the war, Amendola firmly dismissed Papini as 'an abject personality whom I have disdained profoundly and publicly for years'.[74] In his old age, Prezzolini remembered for his part that Giovanni had 'irrevocably' broken with him on four occasions, and all but the last in 1925 had proved short-lived.[75]

Typical was an angry letter that Amendola wrote to Papini on 6 July 1911 declaring that he was ending his collaboration with *La Voce* because Prezzolini was so irritating, 'overbearing', 'unbending', 'ridiculous', 'not a friend'. Ten days later, he told Prezzolini that he had changed his mind and was resuming their work together.[76] In March–April 1912, he again expostulated that he was finished with *La Voce* and Prezzolini for ever; he felt as though a brother had stabbed him in the back in a dispute that they were having over correspondence with Croce. On this occasion, it was Prezzolini who apologised, appeasing Amendola with a pledge that he had never been rancorous towards him.[77]

Obsessively hard-working, Giovanni often burst out with more generalised anger at the Italy of his times. On frequent occasions he damned Giolitti, who was the dominant politician of the era leading up to the First World War and five times prime minister. Giolitti had told his daughter that he was a tailor who could not 'succeed in dressing a hunchback if he does not take the hump into account'.[78] To some this was sensible realism; to the purist Amendola, Giolitti's rule bore the gross stain of corruption and cynicism. Amendola's prime slogan and that of his fellows on *La Voce* was and remained: 'Italy, as it is today, does not please us.'[79] In such circumstances, his generation of intellectuals must deny any approval of Giolitti's 'regime', his 'false dictatorship'.[80] Forgetting his adolescent quarrel with his father, Amendola had decided that Crispi pursued an ethical line far superior to the behaviour of Cavour or Giolitti.[81]

It was not just the Liberal leader who aroused Giovanni's disdain. In October 1910, Amendola told readers of *La Voce* that Italy was 'composed in nine-tenths of a flock of slaves without any ideals (the ruled) and of a tenth that is a nauseating jumble of the inept, the sceptical and the fixers without faith or conscience (those who rule)'.[82] Italy, he contended sombrely, was a country of 'small shopkeepers, hoteliers and slaves'.[83] Nor were those who might be modernising the national economy any better. 'Lombard industrialists, Genoese shipping magnates, the businessmen and bankers of northern Italy' possessed no real answers to the country's economic and cultural problems. At its root, the matter was ideological. 'In Italy, it is the national question, not the social one, that we must resolve.' Italians must be persuaded to believe in their nation and themselves and to do so in their deepest hearts, with religious dedication.[84]

For the present, he complained, ordinary men, workers and peasants (women were beyond his ken) were no better than the bourgeoisie. As Prezzolini recalled, Amendola remained unsmiling when he wrote off the people as a 'blind giant'. Sicilian peasants, he added, were a nasty combination of egoism and timorousness. As *furbi* (cunning operators), their perpetual ambition was to secure advantage for their family and *paese* (home village or town), even at the cost of their neighbours, other workers or the nation.[85] All in all, he wrote in 1909, the 'plebs' were 'illiterate, sensual and sceptical' – in every attitude, the reader might conclude, the opposite of Amendola or his self-image.[86] Socialists jabbered beyond the pale. In June 1914, just before Archduke Franz Ferdinand went to Sarajevo, Amendola disparaged Benito Mussolini, once a young man who had ambitiously tried to attract the attention of *La Voce* and its circle but who had become the editor of the Socialist Party's daily, *Avanti!* In the pages of the paper *Il Resto del Carlino*, where he was now employed, Amendola denounced in lordly manner the 'overactive and delirious brain of the aesthete of politics who goes by the name of Benito Mussolini', a swaggering journalist who could be ignored by his betters.[87]

A month later, Amendola flirted with the idea that a genuine liberal party should be established in Italy, with him likely in the leading role.[88] But July 1914 was not the time for such bright ideas. In any case, his public life had for some time been troubled by his private. So obsessive and implacable was his determination to work that his role as father of a family was often annoying. As he told Eva in February 1910, when he was back in Florence and she, the very new baby and Giorgio stayed in Rome, he was unavailingly wrestling with a theory of knowledge. Although he was separate from his wife and children (blessedly, he implied), he could not concentrate or find enough time to think and write properly. There were too many meetings and discussions in his diary, he whinged.[89]

His worthy aim remained to convert Italy into 'a real religious national democracy'. In undertaking such a task, he needed to be both philosopher and activist (unlike Croce).[90] In Amendola's opinion, the country desperately needed a 'vital and lasting' state, based on 'the ethical and religious idealism of our generation'.[91] Given such duty, he could scarcely lavish attention on Eva and the children. When, in April 1910, Giorgio suffered from a toddler's illness, Giovanni assured Eva that he had written urgently to get his mother or one of his sisters to help. When, in November, Giorgio was turning three, Giovanni apologised for not writing much and not getting back to Rome for the birthday but promised that he had put a present in the mail.[92]

Eva might have been a mother but she, too, mixed complaint at life's little irritations with deep ponderings, some of which accorded with Giovanni's and some did not. In October 1912, she wrote in annoyance about what she viewed as Uncle Mario's greed after the death of his and Giovanni's mother; he, not they, had taken over the family house on the Aventine. A woman, she stated on a different theme, blessed naturally with more 'vital forces' than a man, needed to have a new child every two years. She was happy to become pregnant again but wanted simultaneously to get on with a massive work. She planned to start with Christ, and then explore Dostoevsky,[93] Tolstoy, Carlyle, Schopenhauer, Henry George, Raphael, Bach, Beethoven and others to achieve a synthesis of what a modern religious life should be. It could occupy her for a decade. He could play a part (perhaps a minor part) in the work as a significant contemporary philosopher.[94]

With Eva still working on her own account, while her husband held his precarious and poorly paid job as director of the small Biblioteca Filosofica in Florence from October 1909 to September 1912, the conception of further children was postponed. Before Giovanni left Rome, Eva had been earning twice as much as he did and had made a positive impression in educational circles with an essay on the modern teaching of languages.[95] In 1912, with what might be read as a more practical observation of the needs of the Italian people than Giovanni had reached in his lucubrations on crafting a national political religion, she wrote an essay on the American political economist Henry George (1839–97). His views on taxing the rich to foster greater egalitarianism, she knew, had won favour with Tolstoy. Eva was impressed and wanted to convey his ideas to a broader audience. Eventually, she did publish her piece, but not until after the war, and then in Marinetti's *Roma Futurista*, not an ideal place to investigate political economy.[96]

The post at the Biblioteca Filosofica now lapsed and Giovanni returned from Florence. He made little attempt to hide an affair with the Italian poet, novelist and feminist Sibilla Aleramo, whom little Giorgio dreamily registered as his first ideal of feminine beauty, despite remembering his parents' loud nightly arguments over her. (By the time he was recording this first crush, Giorgio knew that Aleramo was a signatory of the *Manifesto of Anti-Fascists* and a communist sympathiser.[97]) Whether in reaction to her experience of the 'double burden' or in irritation at Giovanni's automatic assumption of the superiority of his thought over hers, in 1913–14 Eva began her own passionate affair with another Italian philosopher, Giovanni Boine, a friend and associate of her husband. He died of tuberculosis in 1917, four months short of his thirtieth birthday. Five years younger than Giovanni, he, too, was a member of the *La Voce* circle and had lived for a time in exhilarating Paris. He was another intellectual searching for a religion that could absorb the people, but pessimistically more certain than Amendola that the world around them was collapsing. Together the two men debated the work of Søren Kierkegaard (1813–55), yet another intellectual who had strained to renew religion.[98]

On a summer day in 1914, Eva caught the train to Genoa with the intention of running away with the younger man, but, put off by last-minute second thoughts, she did not alight as scheduled and went on to Turin. A mutual friend, Emilio Cecchi, who took pains to assure her that her husband had no intention of locking her in a madhouse, offered mediation. Amendola did complain resentfully that she had displayed 'complete insanity' but, stiffly, he offered her his 'charity and pardon'. Whether or not fully won over by such cold words, she agreed to go back to Rome and her children.[99] In autumn that year, despite Cecchi's promise, she was again despatched to a 'clinic' for three months to calm her 'state of agitation'; she was told that she must regain her 'sanity and self-control'. Giovanni explained to a friend that Eva 'was suffering from a physiological illness provoked by the over-elation and exhaustion of her nervous system'.[100] When quizzed about the affair with Boine late in his life, eldest son Giorgio reckoned, with what may have been a hollow chuckle, that his mother had 'fallen in love with all his father's friends'.[101]

While Giovanni and Eva wrestled over how their different obsessions could coexist in marriage, Amendola had made a number of further and what he hoped were deeper excursions into philosophy, always with the ambition of detecting how to remake the Italian future through a new form of civic religion. In 1908, he reviewed his nation's philosophers for a French journal, maintaining that contemporary Italy was opening up intellectually in a fashion that it had not done for two centuries. Croce, he agreed, held the palm for the present. But there was the chance to go further among contributors to *Leonardo* and those who were delving into

William James and contemporary German and other European work.[102] Amendola also decided that a re-reading of the mystical Frenchman Maine de Biran (1766–1824) could allow him to find a synthesis that went beyond what he had now decided was Besant's superficial theosophy.[103] Religion, he still stipulated, lay at the base of 'all the highest manifestations of the human spirit'.[104]

But, he contended, a man's Will was what most needed comprehension. It must work for good – not, as German theoreticians of the Superman argued, out of sheer power, but somehow to spread freedom to all. Properly speaking, Will was the opposite of Evil, possessed of a fundamentally religious nature. Its purpose was 'to block man's savagery ... to discipline and inhibit' extreme emotions.[105] In 1911, Amendola published a long essay entitled *La Volontà è il bene* (The Will Is the Good) in the hope that he was charting a gospel through which 'a spiritual reality could be constructed for all Italy'.[106]

In this regard, 'philosophy', he wrote, 'always has liberty as its supreme object' while it searched out 'the most perfect form of the soul' in realms well beyond materialism.[107] In 1911, he did briefly establish his own journal, entitled *L'Anima* (The Spirit), in association with Papini. It soon collapsed, but not before devoting a thirty-page issue to Boine's meditations on 'religious experience'.[108] That year Amendola also graduated in philosophy from Rome University with a thesis that examined criticism over the years of Immanuel Kant. His work won praise and he hoped it could result in a position as an academic philosopher. But no university summoned him to a permanent place on their staff, Milan and Padua both rejecting him, the latter in disparaging phrases.[109] He had to digest the discouraging terms of that failure but presumably did not know that Croce had dismissed him as more of a dilettante than a serious academic philosopher.[110] The nearest he got to a teaching life was from April to September 1914, when he filled in at Pisa[111] until the chair was taken over by Giovanni Gentile, an 'actualist'[112] who became the best-known intellectual supporter of Fascism and was killed by communist partisans on 15 April 1944 near his Florence villa.[113] With a neophyte's innocence, he wrote to Eva in April 1914 about how much pleasure he had gained from giving his first university class.[114]

Reluctantly, however, Amendola was shifting to a path that ensured his thoughts were not to be reserved for an ivory tower but preached to a wider audience. He still rejected Croce, repeating that an individual must remain active and could not merely lock himself away in his study.[115] The Neapolitan philosopher-historian, he decided in 1915, stood out as a lonely stone 'spire' but one that did not stir a modern nation. Croce's prose – which was 'somewhat false and artificial' anyway – meant that, in reality, he was 'a master of the late baroque', an era destined to end. Amendola mused that Croce lacked 'profound human inspiration' (unlike him).[116]

In August 1912, he had written to his close, lifetime friend Alessandro Casati, a general's son and Conte di Soncino, perhaps the wealthiest of the group around *La Voce*,[117] with a query about another career direction. The Bolognese newspaper *Il Resto del Carlino*, an organ with national ambitions that had been taken over by landowner interests in 1909 and was determinedly anti-socialist,[118] had offered to appoint him the paper's editorial assistant in Rome. The salary was high enough to make his family life much easier. But, he asked, 'Will journalism not push me to lowering the intellectual and moral tone of my life? That I absolutely do not want.' Perhaps, therefore, he at first mused primly, he could take on a more junior and less onerous position.[119]

Yet, maybe day-to-day journalism better matched his intellect and moral purpose? He half-knew, as Prezzolini put it critically, that his articles in *La Voce* were fluent but scarcely brilliant or incisive; they were neither delineating a new philosophy nor truly reforming Italy and the world. Prezzolini later recorded Amendola's efforts to dominate their circle, but then put him in the second rank of his collaborators.[120] For a man who had risen quickly and, for all his pledge of austerity and unsmiling seriousness, was highly ambitious, was it time to get closer to the world of politics? With every year, his fascination with formal religions had diminished. The modernist movement, he feared, had not brought a new reformation to the Catholic Church, nor had it persuaded Italians actually to read the New Testament.[121] What they rather needed was a political religion of the nation. They must be converted into true believers fully convinced that their identity sprang from the (Liberal) nation created during the Risorgimento and especially by the wise governments of the *Destra* (Right) during the first decade and a half after 1860. Maybe a high-quality journalist and not too deep a philosopher could best assist that process.

So, in September 1912, Amendola took up a post in *Il Resto del Carlino*'s editorial office in the national capital. The issue of the moment was the colonial war in Tripoli now moving to its conclusion, following Italy's attack on its Ottoman rulers in September 1911. The Italian government had not bothered with a formal declaration of war and Italy's army soon engaged in savage battle against the few Turkish troops and the more numerous, mainly Arab, men, women and children who lived in the territory. After conquest, the land was to be named Libya, as it had been when it was the greatest grain-producing province of Imperial Rome, a deserved trophy for a Third Italy.[122]

Prime Minister Giolitti had tightly controlled the national and international context of colonial war making. The invasion had been preceded and was accompanied by noisy propaganda from a group of writers who in 1910 had joined in the Associazione Nazionalista Italiana (ANI, Italian Nationalist Association). From 1 March 1911 (the fifteenth anniversary of the defeat at Adwa), they published a weekly entitled *L'Idea nazionale* (The National Idea). In 1914 it became a daily. The two most important men on its editorial board were the nationalist philosopher Enrico Corradini (celebrated for turning Marxism on its head by arguing that Italy was a proletarian nation, needing to overthrow the power of old bourgeois empires such as Britain and France) and the journalist Luigi Federzoni. The latter was destined to replace Amendola as minister of colonies when Mussolini became prime minister and to become minister of the interior when Scorza and his squads beat Amendola to the edge of death in July 1925.[123] In the summer of 1913, however, an affable Federzoni had written to tell Amendola that he was 'a highly original type for a journalist, a gentleman'.[124]

Almost all Amendola's writing about philosophy had been based on a quest for a national identity that went beyond material wealth or poverty, eschewed Marxism but might entail war. The Bosnia and Herzegovina crisis of 1908 convinced him that Austria-Hungary was an irreconcilable enemy; as he complained in January 1909, 'We are not a nation and, until we are, we cannot seriously discuss our social order.'[125] That year, he joined the Associazione Trento e Trieste (Trent and Trieste Association), an irredentist group certain that Italy remained incomplete until it had 'regained' from Austria-Hungary ownership of lands running up to the Brenner Pass and at the head of the Adriatic, where Italian was overall the language of the majority. Amendola similarly campaigned that the University of Trieste should remain an 'Italian' institution, despite being located in the Habsburg empire. He condemned the pacifist writings of the English journalist Norman Angell, urging that his country's diplomats actively oppose any advance by Austria-Hungary in the Balkans.[126]

Amendola declared that Italy must affirm its power over its weaker neighbours to the east. Facing the massive emigration to the New World – by 1913 almost a million per annum, the great majority from southern regions – he demanded that the nation find a way to deploy emigrants for 'the supreme needs of the national stock' (*razza*).[127] He recalled in horror the 'bestial cowardice' that Liberal leaders – apart from Crispi – and the people, pullulating on the 'piazza', had displayed after the Adwa defeat.[128] Since Italy's chief enemy was Austria-Hungary, the country's highest ambition should be to 'regain' 'the Trentino, Istria and some islands [in the Adriatic]', he maintained, a future that could be satisfactorily negotiated with the 'South Slavs'. Those aims had a greater centrality than anything to be done in Libya after its conquest. An Austro-Italian battle was therefore inevitable and demanded urgent prep-aration 'with vulpine care'. Such a conflict, he added overconfidently, need not provoke full-scale European war.[129]

When the October–November 1913 elections were being contested, he wrote in *Il Resto del Carlino* in favour of Federzoni's successful candidacy for one of the seats in the Chamber of Deputies for the constituency of Roma I and openly called him a 'friend'.[130] In 1911, he also published a small edition of the poetry of Michelangelo (perhaps spurred by Eva's planned examination of Raphael). His introduction contains a medley of what soon was swelled in Fascist rhetoric, in which Michelangelo (and Dante, on whom Amendola also commented effusively) was a great man of the past to be invoked in making Italy great again, and Amendola's personal emphasis on austere liberty. He summed up Michelangelo as a 'fighter' who expressed an 'infinite' and global need with 'his passionate and always renewed invocations of freedom, which passed through every grade of sadness and emotion in order to revive the human voice in every heart'.[131] Giovanni was clearly hoping that his readers could identify him with the great artist, architect and poet.

Yet Amendola did not unite with the ANI, opposing too rude a nationalism. He had never been a fan of Corradini, viewing his version of imperialism as far too cynical. War for war's sake, he insisted, was a desperately destructive formula and must always be opposed on ethical grounds. In 1913, he expressed dismay when Federzoni beefed up his campaign in Rome with a crew of 'pugilists', young men who, a historian might conclude, were squadrists in the making when they filed through poor quarters of the capital belligerently singing the *Marcia Reale* (Royal March).[132]

In regard to the colonial venture in Libya, Amendola was far more discreet in response than were the Nationalists. While the latter talked elatedly about 'the promised land', most of Amendola's colleagues on *La Voce* similarly approved an 'Italy on the march'. In his decade of philoso-phising, Amendola, despite his past flirtation with Indian religions, had displayed little interest in the world beyond Europe. When Tripoli first became a topic of keen journalistic discussion, Amendola was inclined to think that action there was too expensive and could only play to the advantage of the real national enemy, Austria-Hungary. Among his friends, the historian Gaetano Salvemini, a fellow southerner from Molfetta and stern critic of Giolitti as 'the minister of crime', as well as a man who wanted Italian democratisation and wanted it now, strongly opposed the war. Libya, Salvemini memorably wrote, amounted to no more than a *scatola di sabbia* (a sandpit).[133]

From December 1911, Salvemini switched his writings from *La Voce* to a new weekly that he edited called *L'Unità* (Unity). However, by then, Amendola judged that the colonial campaign must be supported. In his eyes, it amounted to a test of loyalty to the nation and to Risorgimento liberalism. Writers and philosophers must rally behind the flag when 'an area of current affairs' transmuted into 'history'. They must obey soldiers and diplomats, since 'our sense of duty [*serietà*] forces us to recognise our incompetence' in grand policy.[134] The team at *La Voce* stood for their country's 'moral renewal', not for this or that foreign policy. By late October, Amendola was trying to persuade Salvemini that Italy was not waging war because of Corradini's and other nationalists' 'chatter' but out of 'necessity'. If Italy had not moved, another power – Germany perhaps – would have seized Libya.[135] 'National discipline' was of crucial significance at such times. It was perfectly possible to retain reservations about the campaign, and there was no need to mimic the ANI's 'cheap adventurism' and its supporters' ludicrous talk of the territory as an 'Eldorado'; their rhetorical excesses carried them far from the world of ordinary Italians.[136] But war was war. It should be fought neither sentimentally nor in some humanitarian manner but to victory. Italy must surmount its colonial test and teach the world about its 'tenacious will to rise in power'.[137]

The conflict in Libya was, in very many ways, a prelude to the First World War. By August 1914, when all the European Great Powers, except Italy, were locked in battle, Amendola had risen further in his nation's journalistic world. On 15 March that year, Luigi Albertini, editor of *Il Corriere della Sera*, widely regarded as the Italian equivalent of *The Times* and the country's most prestigious and authoritative newspaper,[138] asked him whether he might leave *Il Resto del Carlino*. Might he agree to be one of *Il Corriere*'s lead correspondents in Rome, in an office headed by Andrea Torre, a Freemason and a distinguished liberal journalist (from 1916 to 1920 he was president of the Federazione Italiana della Stampa, the journalists' union)? Torre was sixteen years older than Amendola and from his home province of Salerno; the two were to have a fluctuating relationship after 1919.[139] Initially, Amendola again tried to retain space for his teaching commitments at Pisa and not altogether sacrifice 'scientific and intellectual activity for journalism'.[140] But he was soon very much a *Corriere della Sera* man.

Il Corriere della Sera was owned by the Crespi family, rich textile manufacturers. The paper's main base was in Milan, city of the Italian stock market and the country's business capital. But the paper's reputation spread across the Italian establishment and, outside the country, it was read as the best press source on Italy. Its line was patriotic and anti-socialist, proud of the Risorgimento and therefore Liberal and modernising, critical of Giolittian fudging and *trasformismo* but unlikely to applaud radical action. In almost every particle Amendola shared its credo; he had been delighted in March 1914 when Giolitti was ousted as prime minister by the more conservative southerner Antonio Salandra. The new leader, he wrote, stood for the better side of liberalism and a proper state.[141] Amendola had expressed this view in *Il Resto del Carlino*, but he was to become a closer friend of Albertini than he had ever been of Prezzolini and his other acquaintances among the intelligentsia. According to one contemporary, Albertini and Amendola, in their quiet seriousness, were like two English gentlemen, odd residents of Italy.[142] Still rejecting what Giovanni in June 1914 had deplored as the freedom-hating 'demagoguery' of the ANI,[143] Albertini, Torre and Amendola, together from August 1914 to May 1915, endeavoured to pilot Italy virtuously into world war. As the paper proclaimed in September 1914, a neutral Italy meant 'an Italy, less than it is today, less not so much territorially, as economically, militarily, politically; less also morally'.[144] Victory would bring greater happiness to all Italians and finally fully instruct them about their national identity.

Just into his thirties, Giovanni Amendola had not won every battle in his life as he marched from religion to philosophy to political journalism. But he had a good war.[145] From August 1914 to Italy's entry into the conflict on 24 May 1915, the *bien pensant* sector of the country strongly favoured intervention. Almost universally, intellectuals asserted that Italy could now show itself as a genuine Great Power, a modernised or modernising country that no longer required the demeaning care of a 'hunchback's tailor'. Those who believed that they could see the future may have disagreed about much but they were certain that war offered opportunity. So Amendola found himself in the same camp as the ANI (once the Nationalists had renounced their initial idea in the July crisis that Italy should fight for the Triple Alliance against Britain, France and Russia). *La Voce* may have been trickling to its end in 1916, abandoned by Prezzolini and Papini in late 1914, but they, too, spoke up for war. So, from a position as a more advanced democrat, did Salvemini. And, from October 1914, so did Mussolini, who converted himself from a revolutionary socialist to a revolutionary interventionist and walked out of the editorship of *Avanti!* Undoubtedly, the greatest celebrity among pro-war intellectuals was the ornate, self-indulgent poet Gabriele D'Annunzio; blessed with a strange friendship with the puritan Albertini, he was one of the few bold enough to address *Il Corriere*'s editor as '*tu*'.

In this coterie of intellectuals and journalists ambitiously seeking their own enhanced influence and virtuously proclaiming their desire to preach a new national gospel to the people, Amendola stood in the mainstream, well placed to advance towards political authority. No doubt, he still addressed Albertini as *Lei* (the third person form of 'you') and as *Direttore* (Chief). But he put into words as well as anyone in Albertini's circle what liberal conservative Italy wanted from the war. A contemporary mourning Amendola's death in 1926 emphasised that he and Albertini had swiftly developed a 'perfect spiritual communion', each being 'composed and ordered, serious and methodical' in life and thought.[146] Under their aegis, they believed, Italy could be great again, both ethically and in power politics, as it had never managed to be since the Risorgimento or, perhaps, since the fall of Rome.

In August 1914, Amendola had already concluded that the acquisition of Libya and a planned assertion of predominant influence in Albania meant that, with naval control along a line from Tobruk (طبرق) to Valona (Vlorë), Italy could supervise 'one of the great highways of the world' while also securing domination of the Adriatic.[147] In June 1915, having already departed as a lieutenant to the front, Amendola told Albertini that Italy must look to a 'long war'. Extended time in battle could allow it to occupy the full extent of its wanted territory. It must fight for genuine and complete victory and not accept limits, as had occurred in 1859 and 1866 during the Risorgimento. The holy process of constructing a nation meant that this war, too, like those of Garibaldi, Cavour and Mazzini, was fought for 'independence'. But, he stressed: 'I hope this can be the last and not the penultimate war of independence.'[148]

Military service in the patriotic cause of 'Risorgimento II' further bolstered Amendola's curriculum vitae. It added practical experience of soldiering to his certainty that he was reaching a pinnacle in his fevered pursuit of his 'moral duty' to foster a 'true national consciousness' in every Italian.[149] To a considerable degree, Giovanni's was a cushy war. It began at Bassano in May 1915 and the Alpine front, where Amendola served as an artillery officer. However, Giovanni never withdrew from all journalistic work – or its accompanying politicking. By Christmas of that year he was back in Rome, afflicted by malaria that he had caught behind the lines at Monfalcone.[150] In February 1916, he was expecting an urgent recall to the front (and he would therefore miss the coming birth of his third child, Antonio) but, in fact, he stayed on and on.[151]

When he did finally return, he mainly acted as liaison between the fighting forces and the general staff, still with time to tell Eva that thinking about philosophy was his key activity. 'Work', he added, was what mattered most to a man, although he was glad to have children and sure that he would be closer to them as they grew up.[152] It was now, on 13 May 1917, east of Gorizia, that he was wounded in the face by an exploding shell, with its shards hitting him 'only millimetres from an eye without damaging it'; he had been on a tour of inspection to the trenches.[153] The injury was serious enough to confine him to bed for ten days and to allow another extended stay in Rome. He also won a bronze medal for whatever heroism had been involved (he was disappointed that it had not earned him silver).[154]

Giovanni was, in sum, an able enough officer, if very much a bourgeois one who served in the corridors of parliamentary power more assiduously than in the Alps or on the Isonzo. It might be that, on occasion, he thought ordinary peasant soldiers were like 'donkeys' in their ignorance and unpreparedness to fight.[155] But, he reckoned, such feebleness in battle was as much the fault of the old and new negative political forces in Liberal Italy: the corruption sponsored by Giolitti, the continued efforts by some wayward politicians merely to fight a 'little war', the dangers of socialism and Catholicism on the home front, and the decision to camp timidly on the Isonzo River and not, for example, to launch more imaginatively into Albania.[156]

During his war service, there may have been a significant development in Amendola's private life. While recovering either from his wound or malaria, sometime late in 1916 or in spring of the next year, Giovanni met a 'tall, blonde, blue-eyed' nurse called Cornelia Pavlova (usually known as Nelia).[157] She was a Bulgarian, the daughter of Mladen Pavlov (1848–1935), once the close companion of Hristo Botev (1848–76), the poet hero martyr of the first awakening of Bulgarian nationalism. Pavlov remains an important enough figure in national history to have a street named after him in central Sofia; his flat in the city bears a memorial plaque.[158]

Pavlov did not favour the country as forged in 1876 by his comrade Stefan Stambolov, the so-called 'Bismarck of Bulgaria'. Pavlov, a judge and a lawyer, and remaining proud to be thought an educationalist, retreated in dudgeon to a private life, with first a Turkish and later a French wife.[159] Pavlova was born in 1895 to his second marriage, in the commune of Oryahovo on 29 July, a birthday she shared with none other than Benito Mussolini (she was twelve years younger than the Duce). Pavlova was therefore twenty-one when her life first mingled with Amendola's. As will be explained further in Chapter 4, she was to be the mother of a son who was probably theirs.

Mladen Pavlov, by the twentieth century, disapproved of his country's move towards Germany and away from Russia, while also preaching the need for greater equality and for restricting the power of the church, ideals that he passed on to his daughter.[160] He became a supporter of Aleksandar Stamboliyski, head of the Agrarian Union, a peasant party propagandising the slogan 'Down with Monarchy, Long Live Democracy'.[161] Stamboliyski opposed Bulgarian King Ferdinand's rash decision to enter the war on the German side on 14 October 1915. Pavlov and his daughter fled to France. Pavlova later claimed (as a daring young woman) to have sent King Ferdinand a stiff note warning him that his choice for Germany meant that he would be damned by all Bulgarians and indeed by other members of the royal family through the ages.[162]

In Paris, where she seems already to have received part of her education, Nelia enrolled as a nurse in the Red Cross. Between 1914 and 1921 she found time to write quite a bit of poetry in Bulgarian, often consulting the lyrical poet Kiril Hristov, now recognised as a 'builder of Bulgarian literature', about its worth.[163] As the war continued, she switched to the Italian front, where she won a *Medaglia Croce Rossa Italiana* (Italian Red Cross Medal) for her service. Writing in *Paris Soir* after Amendola's death, she recalled 'forming a deep attachment' with the 'grand patriot' Giovanni at the hospital in Monfalcone.[164] Eventually they certainly became lovers. It is not clear whether their relationship went that far in 1916–17, whether Nelia was more smitten than Amendola, or whether Nelia fantasised to some degree about Giovanni's devotion to her.

The war certainly did not resolve all the complications in Amendola's legitimate marriage. Italian involvement in the conflict expanded Eva's career as a Futurist writer, despite her more orthodox female bourgeois service from time to time nursing wounded combatants. Already in 1912, she had begun writing under the pseudonym 'Magamal' (a male character in Futurist chief Filippo Tommaso Marinetti's violent, racist and imperialist novel *Mafarka le futuriste: romain africain* – as with the *Manifesto*, first published in French in 1909). In more scientific frame of mind, albeit driven by her own experiences, she prepared but did not publish a study on 'Madness and reform of clinics for the insane'. Yet, following her own retreat to the Rome clinic in autumn 1914, the war seemed in some ways to resolidify her marriage to Giovanni, who did not fail to keep her informed about developments on the Russian front relevant to her family in Vilnius.[165]

When he was called up in March 1915, two months before Italian entry into combat, Eva, her children and the rest of the Amendolas patriotically saw Giovanni off towards war training from Livorno. In May, husband and wife had time to get together in Padua and it was there that their second son, Antonio, was conceived. Reflecting on that meeting five months later, Giovanni ponderously but well-meaningly philosophised that their relationship lacked any 'trace of hypocrisy' in a way that could frequently be found between man and man but was 'rare between a man and a woman'.[166] In 1916–17, he often declared himself especially close to Antonio, to whom he wrote personal messages rather beyond an infant's comprehension.[167] As he confessed in April 1917, 'I am terribly in agreement with you in that dreadfully bourgeois conviction that our children are the most sympathetic beings whom I know' – although that did not stop him from criticising Giorgio (that 'fat undisciplined animal') for modest academic performance, suggesting that Eva should slap him down.[168]

Yet Eva still liked to be defined as a Futurist, even though, in July 1917, shortly after being wounded, Giovanni told her that he preferred 'concentration, reflection, examining oneself' to Futurist fancy.[169] In the previous year, following their new son's birth in February, Eva had published in Marinetti's *L'Italia Futurista* a poem entitled 'Velocità' (Speed), combining the Futurist fascination with rapid momentum with an endorsement of female independence and autoeroticism. During the war she began composing a long novel, *Eva la futurista*. Eventually she sent the manuscript to Marinetti, but she did not persuade him to publish it.[170] Soon after the war ended, she took her family to Milan and became an active participant in the social activities of the Futurists and the infant Fascist movement there.

Figure 2.3 Eva and her three children (1916).

In his public life, the last twelve months of the war and the first months of peace saw other developments that threatened Amendola's positioning in his nation's mainstream. Late in 1917, the military catastrophe at Caporetto, which Amendola, recalled to his officer duties, experienced directly,[171] fretted Italian claims to be a Great Power, while the Bolshevik revolution in Russia carried menacing appeal in Italy, where socialists began to sing '*E noi faremo come la Russia, chi non lavora, non mangierà*' (We'll do what they do in Russia: whoever doesn't work, won't eat).[172] With regard to the Bolshevik peril, in May 1918 Amendola wrote in *Il Corriere della Sera* about 'the huge danger rising in the East', made all the worse by the Treaty of Brest-Litovsk between the new Soviet regime and imperial Germany. Policymakers of good will on the Allied side, he argued, should urgently seek to foster a '*fascio* [sic] of the best people in Russia' to stem Bolshevism.[173] The word *fascio* had not yet acquired its later meaning; after all, the more patriotic members of the Chamber of Deputies after Caporetto were arrayed in what they called the *fascio parlamentare per la difesa nazionale* (the parliamentary union for national defence). Amendola was happy in May 1918 to think that he had stopped the crumbling of its membership.[174]

The flight in the north-east from Caporetto, after which Italian forces only rallied on the Piave River, fifty kilometres from Venice, was blamed by Amendola on the men. Peasant soldiers, he complained, displayed the self-interested cowardice of 'the savage and the ignorant' when they ran away crying, 'Hooray for peace, for the pope, for Giolitti or for the socialists.'[175] But officers, including the most senior ones, had committed dire errors, too, and the army chief of staff, Luigi Cadorna, long admired by Albertini,[176] had behaved no better than a 'Don Quixote'.[177] According to Amendola – his view might have been predicted by those who knew him – the real problem was spiritual. Cadorna might be a nice man, but those who had so far led the war militarily and politically had not comprehended that the first requirement of the mass age now upon them was to make Italians know that they were Italian. The Germanic enemy was barbarous. Italy's unreliable Allies in Britain and France were merchants and shopkeepers who grossly underestimated the Italian war effort and should not be trusted. The bourgeoisie (and its men of culture) must stand firm for Italy and guide the people to victory.[178]

The arena of national policy, where in 1917–19 Amendola took a position that separated him from other, more authoritarian and soon to be Fascist nationalists, had its individual cast. He may have condemned the racist pan-Germanism of William II's imperial regime on more than one occasion.[179] He did repeat the cliché of wartime nationalism, extending back into classical times, that Italy must be ready to repel a barbarous northern threat to its '*civiltà*' (cultural civilisation).[180] But, to Giovanni's mind, the chief foe was not imperial Germany but Austria-Hungary, the power that, in 1914–15, in 1859–60 and in 1866, had proved itself the 'hereditary enemy' of the Italian nation state.[181]

In deciding that a multinational empire was out of place in a modern-ised and what he now sometimes called a democratic – despite his haziness about the adjective's meaning – world, Amendola became con-vinced that the Habsburg empire must be replaced. Could it finally be the time of a Mazzinian 'Europe of the peoples' (led morally by Italy)? At the beginning of 1918, he admonished British Prime Minister David Lloyd George and US President Woodrow Wilson for favouring Habsburg survival in some form and for never rejecting out of hand talk of a separate peace with the new Emperor Karl. The worst fate for Italy, Amendola insisted, was to have 'fought a huge war to end it with a military defeat [Caporetto] and an Austrophile peace'.[182]

Amendola had found an enemy at home in Sidney Sonnino, the minister of foreign affairs throughout the war. Superficially, he might seem to have had much in common with his senior, Sonnino, an oppon-ent of Giolitti of puritanical sentiment, based on the conservative wing of Italian liberalism. It was Sonnino who, confronting the crises of 1898–9, had urged the country to 'go back to the constitution' created in the Risorgimento, that era much admired by Amendola.[183] During the war, Sonnino set out a policy of '*sacro egoismo*' (holy egoism), one that dis-dained any idea of 'principle' surpassing self-interest, in the manner favoured by Woodrow Wilson. Sonnino thought that his task was not to make the world safe for democracy but to continue and enhance Italy's shaky role as a Great Power. In such a process he saw no particular reason to campaign for the death of Austria-Hungary.[184]

But, in 1917–18, in the pages of *Il Corriere della Sera* and elsewhere, Amendola proclaimed loudly that Sonnino must go.[185] Sonnino, he lamented to another journalist, totally failed to plumb the meaning of Caporetto and the Russian Revolution. Blindly pursuing the exact terms of the Treaty of London that had formally brought Italy into the war in 1915, he was useless in a new world that required a new international morality and a new line on the 'suppressed nationalities' of Central and Eastern Europe, and, in special regard to Italy, of the Balkans.[186] As a man by now with many contacts, in July 1918 Amendola wrote to Albertini in what proved to be false triumph, saying that, in a number of person-to-person conversations, he had persuaded Prime Minister Vittorio Emanuele Orlando to remove Sonnino from office.[187]

In the Balkans, the greatest issue was what, in 1914, had been the small and, in gentlemanly diplomats' eyes, erratic, almost savage, nation of

Serbia,[188] a place easily enough labelled 'barbarous' by classically trained Italians and by overexuberant fans of the ANI. But, by 1917, there was talk of a new expanded state on Italy's post-war north-eastern border, where the South Slav peoples could unite into a country eventually called Yugoslavia in a fashion that some saw bore parallels with the way in which, during the Risorgimento, Piedmont had led Italians to unity. If nationality, measured by language and culture, was to become the best yardstick for defining what were, perforce, to be new borders, then there might need to be some adjustment of the hopes to make territorial gains in Dalmatia and the upper Adriatic. In Amendola's mind, somewhat diverse from Woodrow Wilson's, every (European) people was now to have its own Risorgimento and, ideally, bless Italy as providing the first model of a happy new world.

In the early months of 1918, Amendola therefore became the key publicist for a congress called to Rome from 8 to 10 April. Attending were Serbs and other South Slav delegates and what was a roll call of the Italian public intelligentsia; Amendola termed it 'the top grade of Italian political opinion'.[189] It embraced Albertini, Federzoni, Prezzolini, Salvemini, Torre and many others. Squeezed in was Benito Mussolini, who had also been wounded at the front and had returned to his paper, *Il Popolo d'Italia*, through which he was seeking to make an indelible mark; he was flattered to join so many famous names.[190] After three days of talks, the delegates inscribed what they called the 'Rome Pact', pledging to peaceful collaboration and the resolution of any disputes between Italy and what was shortly to be heralded as the Kingdom of Serbs, Croats and Slovenes.

It all came to nothing, as Amendola lamented only a few months later in four long articles in *Il Corriere della Sera*. Sonnino, he charged, was mainly to blame by squandering what could have been immense gains for Italy and European peace in the new era of 'self-determination'. The foreign minister had thrown away Italy's chance to exert 'a politically and economically leading role in the Eastern Danube Basin and the Balkans': in other words, to be the prime and pre-eminent new 'democratic' nation.[191] Sonnino had failed to seize the opportunity to be Wilson's key collaborator in the new Europe and left Italy unable to compete against the unrepentant imperialism and greedy power politics of Britain and France, where the prime minister, Georges Clemenceau, was only too ready to become the cynical patron of the Kingdom of Serbs, Croats and Slovenes. Sonnino had done nothing to assist the national claim to '*Fiume italianissima*', the port now called Rijeka in Croatia. It was to be the epicentre of nationalist excitation for Italians in 1919–20, the venue of what many see as D'Annunzio's trial run of Fascist propaganda in his 'poetic dictatorship' there.[192]

Amendola's attempt to modernise Italian policy on its north-eastern border was a failure. Moreover, it stained him with the mark of Cain for those in his country determined to assert national greatness by whatever means. He had become one, perhaps the worst, of the '*rinunciatori*' (those guilty of turning their back on the Italian nation by renouncing territorial gain). Nationalists and Fascists were ruthlessly to make him pay, dismissing with contempt his own certainty that he remained a patriot among patriots.[193]

Such battles remained for the future. However, when, following its final victory over Austria-Hungary at Vittorio Veneto on 4 November 1918, Italy entered the months of peace, and when, in April 1919, Giovanni Amendola celebrated his thirty-seventh birthday, he seemed to have secured a high place among the new generation of intellectuals, journalists and politicians in his country. Since 1917, if not before, he was in regular contact with voters in the family home town of Sarno, preparing the way for his entry into the Chamber of Deputies in the next election. Warned that, in Sarno as elsewhere, 'appetites came with eating', he replied that he was sure that he could resist and contain 'local chatter', accustomed as he was to 'steer a line past shoals rather greater than were to be found in the seas of Sarno'.[194]

His greatest, perhaps unexpressed, ambitions for political power appeared near fruition. Perhaps he could teach Italians to believe that they were Italian in a modern and democratic fashion, their minds shaped by the high ideals of Mazzini, Garibaldi and the other heroes of the Risorgimento, adepts of a positive civic religion of the nation. As he had written in *Il Corriere della Sera* on 21 November 1918, Italy had won the war, its 'last war for independence'. The nation was finally composed territorially and now could be made spiritually as well. At home, it needed order and discipline (and government provision of such basic needs as safe drinking water and roads in the South). Abroad, it should have no truck with 'imperialist policies'.[195] Italians had genuinely fought a war to end war, and thus for the cause of humanity as well as the nation (but they should not abandon their own small empire).[196] Perhaps inconsistently, Amendola was convinced that the state was what mattered – not the growing but, in his eyes, deceitful and marauding mass parties. He was ready to stand firm on every front, an intransigent soldier for his version of virtue and morality. He might or might not have located the key to the future. But, from his relatively lowly origins in the middle classes and his family's regional background in the South, Amendola had become a man with whom his contemporaries had to reckon.

As yet, however, he was not a saint and martyr. His destiny over the next seven years was to become one.

3   Giovanni Amendola

A Condottiere *of Pure Anti-Fascism?*

Leone Cattani, a schoolboy friend of Giorgio, his fellow on the Unione Goliardica per la Libertà, believed that Giovanni Amendola was a charismatic chief. He was, he wrote, like a *'condottiere* of the sixteenth century'.[1] This parallel from the past was destined to become a cliché during the Fascist regime, where the new *condottiere* was not an Anti-Fascist but rather the Duce, Benito Mussolini, and the charisma was his alone. So unstinted was the praise showered on him during his dictatorship that any figure from the past on the Italian peninsula who had won historical standing was depicted as the dictator's predecessor. Even St Francis of Assisi was dragged from his historical context and elevated into an honorary Fascist before his time.[2] Especially in its second decade after 1932, the regime became ever more dependent on populist charisma politics. By then, in winning consent for the regime, 'Mussolini' (somehow defined) mattered more than did the fine print of Fascist philosophy. His myth lingered. Even after the calamities of the Second World War, the collapse of Fascism and the end of post-Risorgimento Italian pretentions to be a Great Power, Mussolini's name held – and still holds – purchase for many Italians.[3]

Maybe the labelling of Amendola as another *condottiere* is merely proof of the poverty of historical reference for commentators in a country, which, after all, never existed before 1860. Yet it is worth pausing, doing what previous historians have not done and ponder parallels that exist in the lives of Giovanni Amendola and Benito Mussolini. The two men were foes until the death of Amendola and their ghosts were still foes in the construction of memory after 1945. Yet, somewhere in the fine print of their lives and ideas, lay intriguing overlap.

In 1919, it seemed that, to use the parlance of the boxing ring, to which he was oddly attracted, Amendola stood as the probable heavyweight champion of the new generation for a Liberal nation and state being re-visioned into some sort of mass society, to be guided by a new, reformed, ruling class. Mussolini looked a lightweight by comparison, overactive, overexcited, playing outside the established rules and picking up a word, *fascio*, that had often appeared in the country's political vocabulary but had never acquired a fixed meaning. Such might have been the appearance. But, in Italy, fretted by its own version of the First World War, time was to be out of joint and the past a false guide to the present.

In the six years from 1919 to 1925, Mussolini moved speedily upwards from being head of a movement (the Fasci di Combattimento) to leader of a party (Partito Nazionale Fascista or PNF (National Fascist Party), founded on 9 November 1921). This party was fortified with a militia, to be formalised as the MVSN in January 1923, a body that the national army did not oppose (and that King Victor Emmanuel was unwilling to have tested in Anti-Fascist combat on 27–28 October 1922).[4] Mussolini, the Duce, was leader of the MVSN too. Backed by a combination of political artifice and pitiless savagery, Mussolini became prime minister of the nation state at the head of a coalition government on 31 October 1922. Thereafter, from 3 January 1925, he transmogrified into dictator for life, commanding a permanent regime. In such a position, he rapidly reworked the Liberal state into a totalitarian, Fascist, one. Judging Amendola as his most serious surviving opponent – *the* Anti-Fascist, *the* Anti-Mussolini, *the* last champion of the Liberal state – he drove him to his death.

Amendola, by contrast, had focused on that state, hoping to reform it, never in a drastically radical, 'revolutionary' manner but always loyal to what he deemed the beneficent part of the Liberal Risorgimento. In that task, he remained chary of modern mass parties. In his view, still to be sturdily opposed was the old Socialist Party, which he had rejected before 1914. The Partito Socialista Italiano (PSI, Italian Socialist Party) had been established on 15 August 1892; the Partito Comunista d'Italia (Communist Party of Italy) split from it on 21 January 1921. Equally alien to a Liberal state in Amendola's mind was the new Catholic party (Partito Popolare Italiano or PPI, Italian Popular Party), founded on 18 January 1919. Over the subsequent years, Amendola on more than one occasion brooded over a liberal party to be organised in some sort of modern manner. He did so especially in his last months of life with the Unione Nazionale delle Forze Liberali e Democratiche. But, in reality, this body, like its predecessors, was a movement not a party, little more than another Liberal grouplet. Its members owed allegiance to its chief, Amendola, but their association was never disciplined with the forms and processes of modern times. Amendola, last defender of the Liberal state, never fully accepted that a mass age required a mass party. Instead, in his mind, the country needed a new ruling class, expressed in a government of the Centre, attracting reformist socialists, tolerable Catholics and sensible, well-behaved conservatives.[5] In a curious manner, Amendola was imagining what he could never call a renewed, moral and spiritual Giolittism. As he contended in a speech at Salerno in May 1922, parties such as the PPI and the PSI did not really have deep roots in the 'masses'. 'The real masses,' he maintained, 'lived exclusively private lives.'[6]

His ideas were virtuous and, at least in his mind, 'democratic'. He wanted them to become the credo, the lay religion, of every (male) Italian whose identity was fused with the nation. But he did not see that such a mystical process needed an organised base, party branches in every *paese*, formal membership lists, daily activity. Through such blindness, the heavyweight of 1919 over the following years faded into a featherweight to be brushed aside by bloody Fascist power, which had its own claim to have converted Italians to its religion of the nation.

This result could scarcely have been predicted when the war came to an end. At that stage in Italian history, Mussolini's life and that of Amendola had moved in some harness, but with Mussolini always trapped in the inferior role. Both can be defined as members of the emerging middle classes. Both thought of themselves as intellectuals; the story goes that Mussolini's legitimate wife, Rachele, was expected to address him as *professore* until after the birth of their fourth child in 1927.[7] Similarly, when, in 1919, Nitti was in the process of forming his government, he whetted Amendola's vanity by writing to him as 'Dear Professor' (with implied acknowledgement of his pre-war academic career as a philosopher).[8] Professor Amendola and Professor Mussolini both reckoned philosophy to be the senior discipline in the human search for meaning. Each wanted to be recognised as a man of ideas. While Amendola was losing out to Giovanni Gentile in obtaining a chair at Pisa, Mussolini, from November 1913 to December 1914, edited a 'revolutionary socialist fortnightly', pretentiously entitled *Utopia*, hoping to find new solutions for old Italy.[9] Yet, were words or philosophical profundity really enough? In reality, both men were intensely ambitious, ready to experiment with a range of ideas but always anxious to carve out a personal path to greater power or respect. Mussolini was prepared to do so cynically; Amendola was not.

There were other major differences. Even though he came from the North (the 'rebellious' and idiosyncratic Romagna) and not the South, Mussolini was always located a step or two down the class ladder from Amendola. Moreover, in following his father, Alessandro, into the socialist movement, Benito Mussolini seemingly locked himself into being obliged to speak up for the working class in a country and society where they had yet to win political respectability or authority. Mussolini did try to break into the self-consciously elite circle of *La Voce* but without major success, while Amendola simply behaved as though it was automatic that he could compete with, or surpass, the perspicacity of Prezzolini and Papini. Where Amendola married up and out to a fiercely intellectual woman of high Russo-German culture, two years his senior, Mussolini married down into the peasantry. His wife, Rachele, seven years his junior, had scant education and, in a curious family compact, was the daughter of Alessandro's lover in his final days.

One man automatically knew about the wider world at least in Europe; the other may have aspired to do so, but was rooted deep in the provinces. Amendola readily assumed that he would find audiences wherever 'civilisation' flourished. He believed that he could converse with men of his type, the best people, the great and the good, in every European country and in the USA. When Mussolini experienced Switzerland and the Austrian Trentino, it was as a poor immigrant badgered by the police. He talked as a young man of migrating to the USA. Had he gone, he would have arrived as just another of the millions of poor, unregarded Italians.

When there was military training or war service, Mussolini could not expect to be promoted above the rank of non-commissioned officer; he was made a corporal in March 1916 and a sergeant in February 1917.[10] By contrast, his younger brother, Arnaldo (born 1885), who had qualifications sufficient to be a petty bureaucrat and therefore to be accepted by the authorities as lettered in a way that Benito, despite his marked journalistic abilities, was not, automatically entered officers' school when he was conscripted in 1917. Both Mussolini and Amendola were wounded (Mussolini during exercises behind the front) and then permitted to resume their careers as journalists. But only Captain Amendola was accorded a medal for valour. Amendola did talk about catching at a 'spiritual unity' as an Italian with his peasant soldiers at the front, but without engaging in genuine intimacy with them. As for the organised working class and trade unions behind the front, he deemed them as any conservative nationalist might – as *imboscati* (shirkers and draft dodgers), men unwilling to do their national duty.[11] Mussolini, by contrast, wrote a war diary, which, early in his time of political power, was propagandised as the definitive statement of the war experience of the 'ordinary Italian soldier'.[12] When memory was marshalled in the mass age of a new post-war world, there were vast advantages in not having been an officer.

Both were capable, hard-working and even ruthless journalists. But, in 1919, Amendola wrote for his country's most celebrated Liberal newspaper, *Il Corriere della Sera*; in 1913 it claimed a print run of 350,000 copies. Mussolini edited his own *Il Popolo d'Italia*, but as yet with limited circulation and span, and no reputation outside Italy. By 1919, Amendola had pushed into the ruling class of Liberal Italy as if it were

his right, proclaiming that, for him, service to the nation was an obliga-
tion and he awaited his call to higher office. Mussolini, by contrast, was
an outlandish figure, a loud-mouthed troublemaker and little more
than that.

The balance between the two did not change much during 1919, the
year that ended with Amendola triumphantly elected to the Chamber as
one of the deputies for Salerno. Members of his Democrazia Liberale
grouping were the pledged loyalists of F. S. Nitti, the radical who had
become prime minister in June 1919; Nitti lasted in office until June
1920. Amendola's chief local opponent was Giovanni Carnera, a
Freemason; he was a client of Giolitti and the 'system' that had dominated Italian politics for the decade before the war. Carnera may have been
the object of withering moral disdain from Amendola, but he retained a
seat until 1924.

Amendola was an important enough journalist to spend much of the
first half of 1919 in Paris, commenting worthily for *Il Corriere della Sera*
on the peace-making and maintaining his vendetta against Sonnino, who
left office for the last time following Nitti's appointment as prime minister. When released from work at Versailles, on 20 May, Amendola gave a
three-hour speech at a town in his electorate excoriating the errors of the
foreign minister,[13] who had made plain his pleasure that Orlando had not
included Nitti (Treasurer in the government formed after Caporetto) in
the Italian delegation serving in Paris.[14] Just what the audience comprehended of the detail of his oration must be left to the imagination.

In regard to politics more generally, Amendola was active as a critical
commentator on the peace-making. He was so busy at Versailles that, on
24 January, Albertini doubled his pay, congratulating him for his vast
array of 'contacts'.[15] In regard to domestic affairs, Amendola did not
forget to keep in touch with his local agents, '*capi elettori*' (electoral
chiefs), men who, in the manner of Liberal Italy but not of a mass society,
provided accurate guidance to how many votes were to be found in this
paese or that and who could spread helpful news that the state was to
finance this or that road or railway construction and so prove its benefi-
cence, however far off and alien its capital Rome remained in local
minds.[16]

When the mayor of Mercato San Severino – a man who, in Giolittian
view, was a client of Amendola – was forced to resign by Carnera's
faction, Giovanni quickly rallied to the mayor's defence as a good patron
should. A bonny fighter, he emphasised that, as long as he had 'local
strength and friends', he was 'never so happy as when I have to
struggle'.[17] He told Albertini that he was unsure about talk of electoral
reform; a *scrutinio di lista* (parliamentarians grouped into rival lists), in his

opinion, played into the hands of Giolittian traditions of 'corruption' in the South. It was also likely to hand the Italian state over to a 'red–black' (Socialist–Catholic) bloc and thus betray 'the Liberal Party which has made and developed the Italian state'. The problem, he argued, was deepened by universal (male) suffrage.[18] While campaigning continued, he reported drily that he had managed to despatch some hundred of the thousands of *raccomandazioni* begged from him; morally, he added with doubtful apology, he did not want to foster too many local illusions about himself as a patron.[19] He told another follower that the South needed 'revolution', a term that in his mind meant the creation of a 'modern culture' and the efficient organisation of the 'productive bourgeoisie';[20] about the complex traditional reality of southern peasants, still far from nationalised into Italians,[21] he stayed largely silent. He did like to claim that the poor quality of infrastructure, not the nature of landownership, caused the backwardness, but he avoided the word '*miseria*' (desperate poverty) when talking about the South.[22] Amendola might have run as a 'liberal democrat'. However, his liberalism was still that established in Liberal Italy – that is, where the state expressed itself in parliament and where there was no need for modern mass parties, loyal to mass ideologies and selling their programmes to the electorate every four or five years. Equally, Amendola's definition of democracy scarcely entailed mass political participation and his comprehension of 'corruption' usually meant the behaviour of networks of friends hostile to his own.

Amendola remained a patriot who wanted Italy to be an assertive Great Power. He did not, however, waste sympathy on the post-war flourishing of extremist nationalism. So, on 15 January, he reported to Albertini that Woodrow Wilson opposed Italy obtaining Istria and Fiume. The American, however, might well approve Fiume being made into a free city, while Dalmatia could be neutralised and the new Kingdom of Serbs, Croats and Slovenes with it. The Yugoslav nation could therefore be as Belgium had been meant to be after its foundation in 1830. It could become a loyal Italian client and not dally with expansionist dreaming. In a postscript, Amendola advised that it was time for his boss, who had long subsidised the spendthrift poet and called him a 'friend',[23] to 'put D'Annunzio out the door', not merely for his 'rhetorical imperialism' nor even because of the fact that he had disgracefully plotted his way to a gold medal for his phoney war service. D'Annunzio's contact with the equally deplorable Mussolini in Milan (as Amendola viewed him by now) was another disgrace.[24] But worst was his endeavouring to become the 'Grand Chastiser' of the Liberal state and system.[25] What a sad joke, he implied, to be rebuked by the country's most selfish immoralist!

On every imaginable issue, Amendola was far too serious and pure a personality to be attracted by the poseur D'Annunzio. In June, he wrote sarcastically (and without reply) to him as 'Dear Friend', querying if the poet had been behind libellous claims in the right-wing press that he and Albertini had pocketed 'ten million to betray our country in regard to the north-eastern border'.[26] D'Annunzio's melodramatic seizure of Fiume on 12 September 1919, Amendola told Albertini four days later, meant that the state was being haunted by a combined 'threat' of mad, meretricious patriots and Bolsheviks. In *Il Corriere della Sera*, he bitterly attacked the numerous strikes that were occurring in 1919–20, claiming that 'Moscow' regarded Italy as 'the most promising garden' for its poisonous plants. Gun-toting socialists needed to be put down firmly by the 'state's armed forces'.[27] Nonetheless, he warned, 'all things considered, the first [the delusional patriots] are more dangerous than the second [the leftist revolutionaries]'.[28] D'Annunzio's stupid romp in Fiume led nowhere positive, he insisted. It only deepened the socialist threat to Italian well-being at home and therefore tipped the country into the dismal fate of the *biennio rosso*.[29]

Amendola, in his own mind, was and remained a patriot to his bootstraps. But his cognisance of an able and sensible foreign policy was far from the one being enunciated by D'Annunzio or the Nationalist Association. As Amendola told the Chamber in 1921, by contrast with the puerile grandstanding of Federzoni and his friends, the country could best recover its strength through 'a policy of peace', one that would 'restore freedom of action to Italy in the international arena'. If Europe was re-forming itself into blocs, then Italy should stand apart from them (a policy to be favoured by Foreign Minister Dino Grandi under Fascism).[30] Italy, in Amendola's mind, faced no contradictions in aiming to be the most moral, and therefore the most authoritative, of the Great Powers.

While the issues of the great world preoccupied him on many fronts, Amendola was again failing to settle his private life. From Paris, he wrote briefly to his wife Eva, apologising for being too busy to have been in contact.[31] Amendola may not have known that Eva, who had moved her own and their children's lives to Milan and its environs, had volunteered D'Annunzio her support over Fiume and was flirting with the radical rightists whom her husband despised.[32] In her absence, Amendola did turn up at their Rome apartment and remembered to send her a small subsidy for household expenses. But he was soon again regretting his failures as a family correspondent since he had become preoccupied with his electoral campaign at Sarno.[33] Early in 1920, by now a member of the Chamber of Deputies, he worried that he had not heard from Eva and asked her to send news by telegraph. People were accusing him of being homosexual, he was half amused to recount, so irregular had been his meetings with his wife. Still, they had finally come together again at Porto Ceresio on Lake Lugano over Christmas and New Year 1919–20. Reflecting on their relationship, a month later, Amendola wrote to say how sure he was that their marriage was 'indissoluble'. He had been 'sweetly and purely' uplifted by observing his children's innocence (even if Giorgio – nicknamed 'Todo' – was eating too much).[34] In orthodox paternal vein, he had earlier warned his eldest son, in a letter dashed off on Chamber of Deputies' notepaper, that he must study harder and speed through exams rather than stumbling over them.[35]

But public affairs were what really counted. So, in a speech on 1 November 1919, to be republished after 1945 in a series entitled 'The new democracy', Amendola pronounced that 'Italian national democracy faces a historic crisis'. Either Italy, as 'born in the war', must 'realise itself completely in spirit, institutions, economics and culture' or it must 'hand over direction of the state ... to other political philosophies, other methods and other men' (by that he meant the Socialists or the Catholic PPI). A new ruling class was desperately needed. Yet the country must do its best to resist the 'fanciful and wordy sentimentalism of the masses'. The war had been entirely justified. Had Italy avoided it, the country would have surrendered to 'historic decadence'. It had beaten and destroyed Austria-Hungary, won sensible borders in the north-east, and, in so far as foreign policy was concerned, given Italy greater space and security. There was no doubt that the war had been both righteous and advantageous.

But the nation must renounce 'strike mania' and stop running into debt. 'The basic problem in today's Italy,' Amendola stated with a hint of his pre-war philosophising, was 'a matter of Will' – that is, 'a moral problem'. The budget needed balancing. Men must get back to work. 'Italy must base itself politically and economically on agriculture,' he counselled. It could thus be 'a great peasant democracy', even if attention needed to be paid to the desire for trade protection among businessmen and landowners. The state must build schools and renew the army. It must conquer illiteracy, overcome southern backwardness through state intervention and thereby raise peasants to the same level as other citizens. 'At any cost, we must maintain public order,' he concluded.[36]

It was a massive agenda and one with evident contradictions in its understanding whether Italy was already a democracy (surely it was not) or still had to travel a long and expensive road to reach such happiness. How was all the state intervention that Amendola advocated to be paid for? He did not ask – but he continued to conventionally oppose spendthrift policies. Amendola's answers and his questions were too complex for the times. Soon, it became clear that the rival politics of Mussolinian

Fascism, with its own version of a new ruling class, offered simpler, if not entirely different, solutions, except that they were to be ruthlessly imposed by violence, the drastic cancellation of liberal debate, the suppression of rival parties, and the forging of a new state rather than the reform of the old one.

Throughout 1919, Amendola solidified his friendship with Nitti, who had his own accountant's recipe for Italy. The new prime minister proclaimed that the country must 'produce more and consume less', a dismal formula in troubled times.[37] In the last four weeks of his government, Nitti promoted the new deputy, Amendola, to government office as his under-secretary for finance. It might be thought an odd role, given Amendola's perennial difficulties with his family budget and his lack of training in economics. His ten-year-old daughter Ada ('Jaja' within the family) sent him sweet congratulations from her (expensive) boarding school in Milan, where, she added innocently, they were busy collecting funds for the children ruled by D'Annunzio in Fiume (presumably to her mother's pleasure).[38]

After he became an under-secretary, Amendola wrote piously to Eva claiming that he had never been at all driven by ambition but merely by the desire to do something positive. 'If I have to leave my office tomorrow,' he stated, 'not only shall I not regret it, but I shall be very happy.' In regard to the family budget, he added the warning that his pay as an under-secretary was substantially less than he received from *Il Corriere della Sera*.[39] The Amendola household, it seemed, might well have to produce more and consume less.

Just before he reached office, Amendola had told his wealthy friend Alessandro Casati, with whom he had been close during their experience as officers in the Great War (although Casati was more often at the front than he was),[40] that he and others wanted to call a national congress of those loyal to *democrazia liberale* (liberal democracy). What was being contemplated, he explained, had 'a certain grandeur about it'. Was Casati interested in linking himself to what was to be 'for the first time since the existence of the Italian state, an attempt to organise a liberal party'? Such an organisation, Amendola argued, must be 'useful for our country'. It could have been. However, the new party of those emerging middle classes in Italy, those who might have been thought likely to become liberal in a modern manner, was to be the PNF. Casati himself was destined briefly to accept office as minister of education in succession to Giovanni Gentile in Mussolini's coalition government in 1924–5.

Four weeks were scarcely time enough for Amendola to master the nation's finances. Nitti's fall on 15 June did not offer a prospect that this patron could soon return to office; in fact, Nitti was soon devoting himself to composing a long series of works hostile to the Paris peace-making and objecting to what he saw as the unjustified persecution of the permanent Great Power, Germany.[41] Amendola, the client, was left to fend for himself (or, potentially, to make himself the new patron of the causes that Nitti had represented). In November 1921, Amendola again expressed hope in the better organisation of a wider group of liberal democrats in the Chamber, and he tried to persuade a reluctant Nitti to adhere to them.[42] The PNF had been formally established a fortnight earlier (on 9 November), when Mussolini, who had adroitly made a tactical withdrawal from Fascist infighting, was restored as the all-powerful Duce of his growing followers.[43]

In the short term, Amendola had to protect his home base not so much from Mussolini as from the vengeful Giolitti. On 20 June, he wrote to Eva sarcastically about the arrival in power of a new man who was eighty years old (Prime Minister Giolitti was in fact seventy-seven).[44] Somewhere between the lines, Amendola was viewing himself as a – or even *the* – leading figure of a new Liberal generation whose time must come. But Mussolini's own advance, he did not yet acknowledge, was making that prospect less likely.

When Giolitti endeavoured to organise an election, as he had been accustomed to do before 1914, and, with Machiavellian intent, took on Mussolini as a short-term ally, Amendola wrote indignantly to Albertini that the Liberal prime minister was 'a shameful liar, with something devilish, a taste for brigandage, about him'.[45] Holding the election was 'insane'.[46] Around Sarno, Giolitti's client Carnera was encouraging local Fascists violently to break up Amendola's electoral meetings, riots approved at the highest level.[47] What Amendola justly wanted by contrast was the urgent restoration of public and economic order and a tough response both to Fascists and Bolsheviks – a key peasant supporter of his was murdered by local communists at an electoral meeting in October 1920.[48] A month later, he expressed doubt at Albertini's view that the socialists were fully to blame for the present woes. But he did hope that contacts with the Nationalists and Fascists could assist in 'restoring order' and he was sure that maximalist socialists needed to be opposed everywhere.[49] In his view, the new Catholic Populist Party, led in an unseemly manner by a priest, Luigi Sturzo, and, like the socialists, flirting with the universal and the internationalist to the damage of the nation, also bore much responsibility for the travails of post-war Italy.[50] In other words, Amendola's policy was an assertion of the authority of the post-Risorgimento state, with – or, most likely without – an organised Liberal party to sustain it.[51] Amendola was still positioned on the conservative edge of Italian Liberal politics.

Amendola's private life lent little comfort. Hopes of a holiday together with Eva in the summer of 1920 were not realised. On 2 July, he wrote to his wife about his deep desire 'finally to reunite the family, and I hope that this revival of our family life in Rome will occur under a good star'. In that regard, he wanted her to be 'a good and honest companion through the life which is left to us after our youth'. She must accept him for what he was, 'with all my faults'.[52] Alas for such optimism (with its renewed unconscious sexism). In early September, Eva, still in the North, collapsed with 'grave nervous exhaustion' and was hospitalised. In response, Amendola was forced urgently to take Antonio and Pietro, little more than toddlers, back to Rome, with the Portuguese housekeeper as his assistant. That sacrifice did not stop him quickly heading for Sarno and his electorate, where Giolitti was plotting his removal from parliament as the most annoying and least 'transformable' of his foes.[53] A fortnight later, Eva was better. But Amendola still feared for her future. The intellectual burden that she sought to carry (as a free-thinking woman), he told her patriarchally, was too much for 'a mother of four children'.[54] Her mental health continued to fluctuate. In early 1922, she was back in care,[55] and a trip to Vilnius later that year did not improve her condition. Amendola had to confront the key moments of the Fascist rise to power as a single father, at least in regard to his legitimate marriage.

Figure 3.1 Pietro, Antonio and Ada, semi-orphans of Anti-Fascism (1922).

Amendola held his seat in the May 1921 elections that brought Mussolini and thirty-five Fascists into the Chamber of Deputies. Giolitti's cunning electoral ploy was a failure. His government soon fell. On 4 July, he was replaced by weak administrations led by Ivanoe Bonomi, and, then, from 26 February 1922, by Luigi Facta, a modestly mutinous client of Giolitti. In the spirit of the moment, during the 1921 elections and their aftermath, Amendola had been pleased at the local formation of a Legione Amendola (Amendola Legion), comprising mostly ex-soldiers patriotically glad to back the be-medalled Amendola's candidature.[56] A few months later, with different phrasing but similar intent, he urged an important local agent of his to ensure that his men were like 'lions' not 'rabbits'. When it came to dealing with the 'antediluvian' Giolitti and his friends, he argued, 'you cannot make war without getting wounded'.[57]

But his men were not Fascists; they did not wear military shirts, travel armed, kindle terror or rely on national organisation. They did not constitute a militia. They were not a challenge to a Liberal state. Amendola did insist that he stood for a complete 'moral unity' among the bourgeoisie and for the use of 'the firmest hand against the Bolsheviks and the Fascists'.[58] In 1921–2, he wanted to command a 'Liberal battle' against 'Bolshevik madness' and the Fascist refusal to bow to legal order.[59] But his war must be honourable, aiming perhaps to update but never to discountenance the established practice of the Liberal state. It must never infringe the law or the constitution.

Exactly where his ideas were taking him remained clouded. In November 1921, Amendola, as a good client might, could still assure Nitti, who was given to grumbling that he was the prime object of unreasonable Nationalist attack while continuing obsessively to write his books,[60] that, 'in my soul, I am unshakeable in my faithful friendship for you'.[61] But maybe Amendola was realising that, when it came to policy, Nitti was better at moaning about the country's collapse into being like a Balkan state and predicting that the whole country would 'dissolve' in a few months time than at diagnosing some more positive way of dealing with the deepening social and constitutional crisis.[62] It is therefore understandable that, in February 1922, Amendola accepted an appointment as minister of colonies in the new Facta government, despite its Giolittian colour. Rumour added that Captain Amendola had been considered as minister of war in charge of the nation's armed forces. He was equipped for that office through his war experience and deep patriotism – and, even more so, given his stalwart temperament and rigorous determination to impose order on the opponents of the Liberal system, whether on the Left or the Right. On Befana (6 January) 1922, as if in preparation for such a ministry, Amendola presided over a highly patriotic ceremony at Sarno where he inaugurated a display of the flags of returned and wounded soldiers by kneeling before them. He spoke of how moved his soul was in recalling 'the great war of Italian and human redemption'. His belief was limitless in the 'certain future of the Italian nation' – his and all Italians' 'immortal *Patria*', he pronounced. In battle, Italy had contributed the most out of all the warring powers and now was rightly possessed of its 'holy borders'.[63]

In practice, Facta was dissuaded from making Amendola army minister when Fascists, Nationalists and others on the Right, backed by some in the officer corps, spoke up against such an appointment.[64] The offer, which Amendola accepted, was therefore the colonies. It seemed a strange ministerial placement, except as another staging post on Amendola's hoped-for path to the prime ministership (as at least one contemporary observer saw).[65] His two predecessors in the post, Luigi Rossi and Giuseppe Girardini, were minor figures in the political firmament. Given Italy's post-war domestic traumas, what has been called Italy's 'tatterdemalion empire'[66] was scarcely a burning political issue.

The place of greatest focus was Libya, where, during the First World War, the bloody conquest of 1911–12 had proved fragile. In 1918–19 there had been talk of the creation of a 'Tripolitan' republic in the west of Libya and de facto rule by the Muslim Sanusi order in the Cyrenaican east, with Italy left in direct command only of its coastal forts.[67] Some rhetoric painted national policy there with a coating of Wilsonian liberalism; Nitti seemed the senior political figure favouring a generous policy towards the indigenous inhabitants of the land.[68]

On occasion, Amendola sounded as though he, too, might back a deal with the local Arabs and Berbers, as marshalled by their 'chiefs'.[69] Not for long, however. In his own intellectual journey, Amendola had stuck to a rigorously Eurocentric and high cultural itinerary. Similarly, although a man of the 'South', Amendola had paid little attention to the flood of emigrants who left Italy in the decade before 1914, hundreds of thousands through the port of Naples. He gave no endorsement to the statement of the aristocratic Sicilian Antonino di San Giuliano, Italian foreign minister from the attack on Libya to the outbreak of the First World War, that such departures amounted to a 'haemorrhage' of Italy's best blood and by implication needed to be channelled to colonies under Italian rule.[70] Despite his philosophical flourishes about liberal democracy, Amendola still viewed emigrants as far beyond his ken, just as peasants (and women) were.

By the time Amendola entered his ministry, a key appointment had been made in Tripoli, when, on 16 July 1921, the sinuous Venetian entrepreneur Giuseppe Volpi accepted office from Girardini as governor of the colony.[71] Volpi had been Giolitti's agent in the negotiations with

Turkey that produced the peace of Ouchy in October 1912. But now he preferred war, already in 1921 ordering troops ruthlessly to take control of Misrata (and soon gladly accepting from the king the title of Count of Misurata, with the Italian spelling of the name). Volpi may have acted largely on his own initiative. But he returned to Rome just as Amendola took office, Volpi harbouring a suspicion that the new minister might be 'anti-colonialist' and the knowledge that he was definitely anti-Giolittian. Amendola had, after all, been only a lukewarm supporter of the invasion in 1911–12. However, in a meeting between the two on 4 March, Amendola approved the governor's tougher line.[72] He thereby helped launch the career of Rodolfo Graziani, destined to be the most Fascist of Italian soldiers and the general who imposed a lethal 'Roman peace' on Libya. While Amendola was minister, Graziani's campaigns were already producing indigenous casualty rates at ten times and more of Italian losses. It may be true that, early in his term of office, Amendola, with what might sound like sweet reason, told Nitti that he was endeavouring to acquire a detailed understanding of Libya. But, he added, his first aim remained to convince the Arabs that Italy would never accept 'humiliation' in what he thought must remain its colony.[73]

Before Amendola visited Libya in late June, he stated roundly to the Chamber of Deputies that allowing autonomy to Arabs in either half of the territory held no advantage. Rather, if Italy made such concessions, the country would give place to 'an advanced sentinel of Islamic revolt against European occupation in North Africa for which we would be granted the honour of paying the expenses. We would have to cover with our flag the reaffirmation in the Mediterranean of a principle of anti-Western and anti-Christian conquest.'[74] Although Amendola could intimate that to some degree he admired Muslim civilisation as it had been expressed in Sicily around 1000 CE,[75] even in 1925 he still applauded the harsh French suppression of Abd el-Krim's independence revolt in Morocco.[76]

A full assessment of the colonialist Amendola is impossible because his term as minister was cut short by the Fascist March on Rome and his resultant departure from office.[77] His administration was attacked by the small Fascist movement in the colony as being too kind to the indigenous population.[78] He was certainly more reluctant than Volpi to add squadrist forces to the colonial army. He preferred *ascari* (native troops) from Eritrea and Somalia, claiming that this choice followed the pattern of France and other European empires (a decade and a half later, Mussolini, after the bloody conquest of Ethiopia, happily envisaged an Italian 'black' army of 500,000 men).[79]

But it is hard to read Amendola as discarding the imperialism of the least of the Great Powers. Rather, despite some emollient words about achieving 'peace and conciliation' in the territory, Amendola envisaged a future in which Libya could become the site of major agricultural development. The colony could be made to flourish through the labour of the working classes who could convert the territory into 'a genuine Italian province'.[80] In July, he told the Senate that millions of emigrants could not be settled there; but, in time, tens of thousands could.[81] On 12 September, in Trieste, Amendola sounded decidedly nationalist when he preached that Italy's 'lack of primary resources', apart from its exuberant population growth, gave it a 'right of expansion'. He did not mention *romanità*, which was hard to keep out of Fascist and ANI rhetoric on the subject. But he did maintain that 'the Mediterranean is the natural historical and geographical environment' for Italian growth and prevalence. Italy, he argued, must be both a Christian and a Muslim power.[82]

Such attitudes should not come as a surprise. Plenty of other Europeans who thought of themselves as liberal democrats approved of their countries' empires, while Wilson himself was deeply racist in his views of non-whites in his own country, and of Japanese or Latin Americans in the world beyond. Similarly, Nitti, Amendola's patron and friend but an unrepentant European imperialist in his assumptions, was convinced that 'barbarous', 'black', French colonial troops, when they occupied the Rhineland, 'murdered women, assaulted and raped children and old women' in a fashion that made any wartime brutality committed by the 'civilised' Germans pale into insignificance.[83]

In any case, it is doubtful whether Amendola gave more than half his attention to his ministerial brief on distant empire, even if he did nobly claim to have laboured to develop a full understanding of what was best for Italian Libya.[84] He had many pressing domestic issues to confront. One major focus of his mind was a new daily paper, *Il Mondo*, launched on 26 January 1922 in combination with Giovanni Ciraolo (acting for Nitti) and Amendola's old friend and rival from *Il Corriere della Sera* Andrea Torre, with helpful finance from the Neapolitan industrialist Francesco Matarazzo, whose family origins, like Amendola's, lay in the province of Salerno.

It might seem that, in concentrating on this new paper as an enlightened organ of 'liberal opinion', Amendola was constructing for himself a base to challenge Mussolini's *Il Popolo d'Italia*. But in its preference for high culture and its openness to debate, *Il Mondo* was at once more sophisticated and less effective than its Fascist rival. It did nothing in charisma invention, a publicity line in which *Il Popolo d'Italia* was becoming the foremost influence in proclaiming that Mussolini was his country's natural Duce.

In June, Nitti and Amendola tried for a time to set up a Partito Democratico (Democratic Party), prompting Torre's departure from the editorial board of *Il Mondo*, which was now to be headed by Alberto Cianca.[85] The most eager advocate of this new party was Meuccio

Ruini, a Romagnole whose career had parallels with that of Amendola. He, too, had served as an under-secretary under Nitti. The Democratic Party was designed to unite forces at the centre of the national political spectrum, and thus opposed to Fascists and Nationalists on the Right and socialists and communists on the Left. Its success was, Ruini declared, a 'matter of life and death' for the Liberal state.[86] A deep friendship was now welded between Ruini and Amendola. However, like its liberal predecessors and successors, the Democratic Party gave few signs of possessing the discipline and concentration of a mass party. The PNF was scoured by factional and personal divisions, but the propaganda of *Il Popolo d'Italia* could hide or downplay them. By contrast, *Il Mondo* and the Democratic Party were too high-minded and elitist to give precise definition to liberal democracy and provide sufficient organisation to become an effective shield against Fascist advance.

Through the summer and early autumn of 1922, the Fascists were violently taking over much of the communal life of northern Italy, affirming that they were saving their country from Bolshevism. They were even growing in the South, to the unhelpful disgust of Nitti, who lamented in letters to Amendola in August and September that the country had become 'a madhouse', while 'the healthy element' was utterly disorganised and unable to counter Fascist violence.[87] By then, the most curious stratagem of the moment had failed. In late July and the first half of August, there were preliminary soundings, led by Nitti and supported by Amendola, for a scheme aimed at recruiting Gabriele D'Annunzio to the Liberal state. The expectation was that 'Il Comandante' could soar above Il Duce. As with much to do with the political D'Annunzio, a historian is boggled by what might have been the implications. A critic might conclude that their willingness to talk to the nationalist poet indicated that Nitti and Amendola belonged to the conservative side of Italian politics, backers no doubt of 'liberty' but scarcely fans of equality or social democracy. However, just as a final meeting was planned on 14 August, D'Annunzio, for reasons that remain obscure, fell out of his villa's window and rendered himself hors de combat in any subtle negotiations through the next crucial weeks of the Fascist rise to power.[88]

Despite this failure, Amendola continued to urge that the state must be defended against the Fascist threat. In July 1922, he wrote in *Il Mondo* that what the country required was a reworking of the Facta government, perhaps with a new man in charge (he was too modest to advance his own name), and certainly with more 'vital' policies and notably the severe application of the law. What was wanted was a government of the 'best people'.[89] In the South, an alliance of landowners with positive ideas, the bourgeoisie, intellectuals, clerks and returned soldiers united in the

Associazione Nazionale dei Combattenti e Reduci (ANC, the National Returned Soldiers League, still independent from Fascism) could represent the new world created by the First World War and compose a fresh ruling class.[90] Amendola still ignored the majority peasants, remaining opposed to leftist demands for land distribution. He had no apparent understanding that 'the people' – 'grocers, shopkeepers, pensioners, journalists and government employees' – whose views meant something in Rome and who could be influenced by government policy or ideology had nothing to do with those, especially day labourers, who precariously eked out a living from the land, eternally conditioned by *miseria*.

Figure 3.2 Giorgio and Giovanni, stalwart Anti-Fascists (March 1924).

Amendola similarly kept up a historical and philosophical barrage against the faults and inadequacies of Fascism, often summoning his pre-1914 expertise. The exponent of the 'Will for good' was appalled to think that an Italian party might be importing Nietzschean ideas. What malign idiocy was there in Mussolini's casting himself as a German Superman, with its 'smell of Walhalla', he asked dryly? Italy's Latin rationality could not be seduced in that way.[91] Nor were the pathetic lies of a new Napoleon III and a parody of dictatorship beguiling.[92] In sum, Amendola declared on 13 October, in phrases that still convince some but not all historians[93] and that were in contradiction to his past musings about a national religion, that 'the Fascist state is a mystical state; the Liberal state is a state based on reason'.[94]

On 24 October, the Fascists met at Naples and, to all intents and purposes, announced that they were about to mount a coup by 'marching on Rome'. Mussolini retained a Plan B by retreating to his home base in Milan, negotiating there with many figures among the old Liberal leadership. When Facta talked of resigning his prime ministership, four of his ministers – Giulio Alessio (minister of justice), Paolino Taddei (minister of the interior), Marcello Soleri (minister of war) and Amendola – tried to ginger resistance to the Fascist offensive. On the evening of 27 October, they believed that the king, who had just returned to Rome from his estates, had signed an order for a state of siege, meaning that he committed the army to oppose any Fascist 'march'.[95] Earlier that day, Amendola had written in *Il Mondo*, blaming Fascist adventurism for a slide in the value of the *lira* and asserting that 'the state still has the strength and capacity to defend itself if it is really being threatened and assaulted'.[96] On the next day, he boldly urged 'each man to his post, each to his set of responsibilities'. The army was loyal. The glorious *mutilati* (those wounded in the war) stood behind the state. Italy and its (Liberal) state must emerge stronger from its current travails.[97]

By then, however, the die had been cast in another way. The state of siege had been revoked at 9 a.m. on the morning of 28 October, the king refusing to endorse it and Facta's cabinet, which had been meeting since dawn, split. Giorgio Amendola remembered late-night phone calls on the 27th, his father's departure to the Palazzo del Viminale for urgent talks, his return, and then a further phone call when it was already day with the grim news that the March was not to be opposed. Around midday, the placards that had been pasted up in Rome advertising the state of siege were covered over; by the late afternoon, some squads had victoriously reached the city streets.[98] On the evening of the 29th, charged with forming a coalition government, Mussolini took an overnight sleeper train from Milan. On the morning of the 30th, he saluted the king as his prime minister, bearing in his knapsack, he pronounced, in words that must have appalled Amendola, the 'Italy of Vittorio Veneto', the nation that had won the war.

Amendola's nightmare seemed a reality. However, his patriotism, his idea of duty and his conservative dedication to the Liberal state meant that he could not yet head intransigent opposition to the new government. As he remarked to a friend on 7 November, it might seem that legality had suffered an 'irreparable blow'. But his 'sense of responsibility' told him that he must extend 'a veil of forgetfulness' over the events of 28–29 October and allow Mussolini and his ministers, a number of whom had once been his friends, to get on with the tasks required to solve the country's problems. The parliament could restore constitutionality by voting in the new government. Then everyone could wait and see.[99] On 19 November, Amendola complained in *Il Mondo* that Mussolini's first speech had sounded lamentably like the rant of a dictator. But, since then, the Duce may have begun to show 'loyalty to the constitution'. Maybe he genuinely wanted to plant the new regime 'in the "humus" of national consciousness'. Maybe he did bear an inheritance from the spiritual nationalism of Mazzini and the good Risorgimento. Maybe his ideas had something 'democratic' about them and could unite 'producers and intellectuals', as well as restoring national order and discipline.[100] Maybe the Liberal state was not yet vanquished.[101]

Amendola remained well aware of the ferocious challenge that freshly black-shirted Fascists were launching against him in the province of Salerno. 'Giolittians' in the past might not have been squeamish about their dealings with opponents, but Fascist squads had violence as their watchword, daily activity and menace. On 15 December, Amendola protested directly to Mussolini about the matter, without satisfactory reply.[102] On Christmas Day, he reflected to a friend that the prospect of reviving his 'devastated private life, whether spiritual or familial', was a positive but could not proceed while he had to defend his seat and those friends who sustained him in it.[103] Around Salerno, it was becoming obvious, Mussolini was worse for Amendola and his clients than Giolitti had been.

Insofar as national politics were concerned, until the early summer of 1923, Amendola, like Nitti, Albertini and others in his circle, tried hard not to denounce the government too irrevocably. In *Il Mondo* in March, Amendola did highlight what he viewed as Mussolini's jagged switches in policy and reminded his readers that a single party could never be permitted absolute rule in an Italy loyal to the Liberal Risorgimento.[104] A party must not transmute into a state.[105] Yet, since it was obvious that the PNF was riddled by indiscipline, he could still imagine Mussolini breaking from his cruder associates and opting to restore legality and order. Despite its rhetorical claims to be a political army, the PNF could in no way compare with the 'grey-green' men of the royal army with their utter dedication to 'the immortal soul of the *Patria*'.[106]

In May, Amendola grew less forgiving, complaining about the 'totalitarian system' being utilised against his friends at Sarno (apparently then inventing the term without as yet its full meaning). He justified his neologism, with its implication of something that had surpassed totality, by describing how, in local elections, violent squads, in combination with such key government officials as the local prefect and the police, were operating against him. Maybe such behaviour was novel, maybe not. His foes were composed of 'old elements more or less varied, and new elements, more or less mature'. Maybe, on the popular level, it was something of a re-run of deplorable socialist behaviour during the *biennio rosso*, he mused?[107] Or was it just Giolittismo redivivus? A month later, Amendola was still worrying that Mussolini was 'a strange mixture of intransigence and astuteness, romantic improvisation and niggling practical calculation'. The Duce could boastfully assume an 'extreme personal role' and yet be in blatant disagreement with PNF members, dominating one day, caving in the next.[108]

In *Il Mondo*, Amendola, as though waiting for clarification, focused on foreign policy more than in the past. Intimating that he could be a statesman if summoned by the king, he joined Nitti in disparaging the French occupation of the Ruhr,[109] suggesting that Britain should be more respectful of Italian interests,[110] and, in November, deriding Hitler's attempted Beer Hall Putsch and intended dictatorship.[111] On a couple of occasions he underlined the natural connections between Italy and Germany – Bismarck and Cavour had treasured them – and objected to French crudity over reparations from the war.[112] Even in April 1924, he still found time to urge accommodation between the nations that had won and those that had lost the war, firmly rejecting any idea of splitting Germany into more than one state.[113] He drew relief from the victory of moderate leftists in the French elections late that month; liberal democracy and decent international relations were confirmed there, he told himself. It was foolish to think that any European state could fend for itself alone.[114]

Still sounding elitist and conservative, he had more than once impugned Mussolini for being unable to pursue a consistent line internationally, reminding him that the Great Man, Cavour, had never succumbed to over-vivid dreams.[115] When the Duce plunged into a crisis with Greece over Corfu at the end of August 1923, Amendola had little sympathy for the Greeks, approving the Italian use of force. Soon, however, he was complaining that Mussolini was not skilful enough best to advance the national cause. The Duce's errors, and his movement's fatuous xenophobia, were pushing Italy down to a 'lower rank' as a power. The nation would pay the cost of their ignorance and incompetence, he advised.[116]

As far as the Italian parliament was concerned, Amendola naturally rejected the electoral reform, made in the name of moderate Fascist Giacomo Acerbo;[117] it aimed at rewarding the party that, in the next election, won the most votes with 65 per cent of the seats. In the Chamber on 12 July, he condemned the scheme as unconstitutional and as breaking from the Risorgimento, earning menacing shouted interruptions from such brutal Fascists as Francesco Giunta and Cesare Maria De Vecchi, as well as from the more moderate Acerbo and the Nationalist Ezio Maria Gray.[118] His opposition, judged critically by the later Marxist historian Giampiero Carocci as 'bitter, pessimistic, morally intransigent and politically abstentionist', did not prevent the passage of the bill.[119] But Amendola had clearly become the leader of liberal Anti-Fascists. The socialists and communists had also harshly attacked the Acerbo law but Amendola was not yet ready for a grand alliance with them. The maximalist mainstream Marxists, he reiterated in August 1923, had no serious programme and, at base, lacked 'reason'; they were footling revolutionaries.[120]

The Fascists took note of Amendola's potential as a rival national leader in reserve. For Mussolini, in what should be read as intimidating words, Amendola was 'an intelligent enemy' (a rephrasing of 'intelligent canaille', an expression that had prompted Amendola unavailingly to challenge the Duce to a duel).[121] Such half-praise, of course, carried the threat of violence.

In autumn 1923, Amendola's chiding of Mussolini became sharper. Contemplating what had been learned from the year of Fascist rule, Amendola damned the government's '"*totalitarian*" spirit'; now, the word meant rule that imposed control over the future and preached a single 'credo'. His use of it had expanded to more like what has become its modern meaning, with a bleak estimation of Mussolini's tyranny. Fascism was not so much offering a faith, Amendola argued, as 'denying the right of any to have a conscience'.[122] He clung to his own deep spiritual belief in the nation, proclaiming on the anniversary of victory that the war had forged the 'spiritual unity of Italians … for ever'.[123] By the end of the year, he had come up with a formula that was destined to last into the Cold War when he stated roundly that 'Bolshevism', as purveyed by Lenin or his Italian communist mimics, had an 'identical mentality' with Fascism. 'Democracy,' he wrote, 'rejects any type of dictatorship whether it be proletarian or fascist or military.'[124] When Lenin died on 21 January 1924, Amendola sardonically noted that this 'bitter enemy of intelligence and the bourgeoisie was an intellectual and a bourgeois'. His Bolshevism was 'romantic' and 'messianic', horrid in being doctrinaire, an 'extreme negation' of the 'West', mystical, irrational and false.[125]

Through these difficult months, Amendola's legitimate married life brought little private relief. In mid-1923, Eva was confined at Viterbo and medical reports on her nervous condition flicked up and down. In July, she was well enough to be sent a subscription to *Il Mondo*, and, in what might be thought a predictable sweetener, a box of expensive Talmone chocolates. She learned from her husband that her children were well and frequently asked after her, always expecting her to reappear at the family flat on the Via di Porta Pinciana.[126] In November, a fleeting return home triggered a further collapse and Eva was transferred to the Roman clinic where she would stay for the next decade, unable to play the woman's part, soon to be enthused over by sexist Fascist propaganda, of the 'exemplary wife' of Giovanni and mother of their four children.[127]

By the end of 1923, Amendola was being balefully singled out by Mussolini and his squads as a major enemy, the more 'intelligent the more needing to be silenced'. When his patron, Nitti, had his Rome villa assaulted, the ex-prime minister and his family quickly went into exile, first in Switzerland, then in Paris, further exposing Amendola to Fascist attack. As Amendola lamented in a short article in *Il Mondo*, in his speeches Mussolini was becoming steadily more intolerant of press criticism.[128] Now came police intervention on the side of local squads to stop Amendola attending a patriotic ceremony in Naples, despite his being a distinguished local member of parliament, and then the squadrist beating on 26 December. Ten days after that attack, Amendola was still confined to bed by his injuries, with his wounds seeping pus. He was slow to resume a full workload at *Il Mondo*.[129] Yet he rebuffed any idea that he timidly follow Nitti into exile. As he proudly told a friend on 12 January: '[T]here are times in one's life when one has only one thing to defend, one's honour. In such defence, one must by absolute necessity be intransigent.'[130]

The prime focus of Amendola's life during the first months of 1924 was the election held on 6 April. The Acerbo law was not needed since Mussolini's *listone* won more than 60 per cent of the vote and a vast majority of seats. (Amendola's old colleague, Andrea Torre, splitting the Liberal vote at Salerno, stood on the list and thereafter became a Fascist.[131]) Amendola found that his home *comune* of Sarno now voted 4,400 for the *listone* and 27 for him.[132] But he did hang onto his seat on one of the competing Liberal lists; still no liberal party had been organised.

The *listone* had won over a great majority of emerging middle-class voters, men who, in ordinary circumstances, might be thought of as the electoral base of liberal democracy. Was it now at last time for Anti-Fascist liberals to get around to fully organising a modern party? Amendola was again half converted to the idea, setting up a Unione Meridionale in May. In November, it was expanded to become the Unione Nazionale delle Forze Liberali e Democratiche to afford better coordination of Anti-Fascism than in the past. It could, however, only count among its members eleven deputies, eleven senators and sixteen ex-members of parliament. The Unione Nazionale might have been, as Amendola put it, 'the organisation of the powers of the opposition under the constitution'. But its writ did not run far beyond parliament.[133]

Back on 6 June 1924, Amendola had taken the lead in moving a motion in the Chamber that it should not approve the government's official statement to the crown. In a lengthy speech he vigorously attacked the Fascist conduct of the elections, ignoring repeated rancorous challenges from Mussolini.[134] Four days later, Dumini's gangster squad kidnapped and murdered not Amendola but the reformist socialist Matteotti. In response, on 26 June, Amendola and 125 other Anti-Fascist deputies withdrew to what they called their Aventine Secession. For a brief moment, Amendola could almost cry victory, if in phrases that still do not seem completely democratic: 'I do of course know that Italians are cowardly deal-makers. But things are so terrible and grave that not even Africans could swallow them without choking. Now, in reality, Fascism no longer exists to those whose eyes are open; it does not dare to speak.'[135] Might Mussolini fall?

The answer was no. It was high summer and, from 9 July, Amendola retreated alone for ten days and more to the gentlemen's spa at Salsomaggiore; he had been visibly acquiring a middle-class paunch now that he had passed into his forties. Perhaps, too, the beating that had been inflicted on him in December 1923 had left lasting bodily effects; certainly, he complained that health worries curtailed his independent action.[136] In October 1924, he grumbled to his old journalist associate Ugo Ojetti, now compromising with Fascism, that he felt fifty, not forty.[137] Whatever the case, he sipped the waters and did little more to prompt a government collapse, perhaps assuming that, as in the Liberal past, negotiations would begin between leading figures to replace the Duce. Did not King Victor Emmanuel III still command the state, as the constitution decreed?

Summer was the vacation season, Amendola had told a friend, when a man 'reflects, studies the ground, looks for a way forward and prepares his strength'.[138] He did make some half-hearted attempt, through

Albertini, to rally Italian business interests against a government involved in murder.[139] On 26 August, the rich entrepreneur Giacinto Motta, who had accepted a place on the *listone* in the elections, expressed his 'disgust' at recent events. However, he added dispiritingly that industrialists could not allow themselves to play at politics. Given what had happened in the *biennio rosso*, 'the productive class can only praise the Mussolini government', he argued. He was 'still full of horror and disgust at the horrible end of Matteotti'. However, the 'Bolsheviks and socialists' had opened the path to murder. Any rebuke from Amendola to the business world was therefore unjustified, whether to him or to other industrialists. They just wanted to be able to 'work in peace' and prosper the bottom line.[140]

By the time summer came to an end, it was clear that the Aventine could not expect sufficient business or other old ruling-class support. Should he take a step back, Amendola asked himself? In September, he denied to Aldo Rossini, one of the founders of the ANC, in his time to be a senator (with a new noble title) under Fascism, that he had any arrogant belief that 'only the Aventine works for Italy'. He was happy, he added, always to stare over its borders for evidence of greater initiative from someone else to reunite Italians. He was pleased not to be central to any such plan and to 'wait, hoping' that another force or another person could 'expel the madness that is beating at our doors'.[141]

Yet he still could not reconcile himself with moving too far to the Left. As far as he was concerned, the three Marxist political groupings may have been Anti-Fascist but they were scarcely reliable friends and allies. Maybe he could talk with such reformists as Filippo Turati and Claudio Treves. But the maximalists and the communists were impossible. Among the PCdI leadership, Ruggero Grieco, a southerner born in Foggia, and later to be Giorgio Amendola's generous Communist Party patron, damned the Unione Meridionale in August 1924 as 'a monstrous and vain manoeuvre by losers', 'a *fascio* of landowners, their lawyers and money men, the people who had enslaved the South'.[142] In December, Camillo Bellieni, another be-medalled volunteer officer from the war and active in returned soldier politics in his home island of Sardinia, acknowledged that Amendola was 'a gentleman and an intellectual'. However, he complained in a letter to the 'liberal socialist' Piero Gobetti that the Unione Nazionale leadership in the South needed to amount to more than a collection of 'Masonic cliques'. It 'must get down into the masses and talk to the peasants'. The Unione Nazionale, as constituted, was, he feared, feebly adapted to that task.[143]

The youthful Gobetti (born 1901), who was to die prematurely in Paris on 15 February 1926 of tuberculosis, his health undermined by more than one Fascist beating, had often been in contact with Amendola about the Anti-Fascist cause, without the two ever solidifying their relationship. The passionate Gobetti found his elder 'solitary, uncomprehending, severe, austere and unpopular'.[144] Apart from personal reservations, Gobetti regretted that the Aventine Secession did not propose a sufficiently radical break with a past, which, in a phrase that resounded down the years, had led Fascism into being 'the autobiography of the nation'.[145] He and Amendola each campaigned against the drift to open dictatorship but without finding intellectual accord.

In the more sentimental Anti-Fascist, post-1945 historiography, the Aventine is depicted as a heroic last throw of democracy before the imposition of totalitarian tyranny. As Elio D'Auria, Amendola's most faithful chronicler, has argued, the Aventine could have produced a 'profound modernisation of Italian society' under its 'unopposed leader', potential prime minister, Amendola.[146] Perhaps there is a case to be made in that regard. However, the Aventine was never sustained by a modern organised party with a mass base. Rather, it was an opposition Liberal government in internal exile, waiting for King Victor Emmanuel to do what Amendola and his closest friends thought was his constitutional duty and sack the current murderous prime minister, even if that step might have to entail (temporary) military rule. While its members waited for the royal Godot, the Aventine remained an uneasy coalition. It bore some resemblance to the Christian Democrat-led Italy that came into existence after 1946, with its own version of parliamentarism and legal process, and thus 'democracy', but with an idiosyncratic understanding of liberty and equality. Prezzolini was not being totally cynical when he maintained that Amendola won the meagre popular support that he received more because the Fascists singled him out as their enemy than from his ability to convince Italians about his narrow version of democracy.[147]

An ex-Fascist minister, notorious for his corruption, had enough temerity after Mussolini's fall to claim that it was the Aventine Secession that prodded Mussolini into becoming a dictator rather than some sort of 'democrat'.[148] It is an absurd claim. Yet, Mussolini's assumption of open dictatorship on 3 January 1925 did demonstrate that the efforts of the Aventine's supporters to remain constitutional, monarchist and Liberal were fading – or, to be more honest, had failed. Alfredo Capone's defence that Amendola, in remaining monarchist, was prompted by his knowledge that, in the final analysis, Victor Emmanuel III commanded the armed forces, needed in any crisis, and so embodied the state, fails to convince.[149] From 1922, Mussolini had won the loyalty of Armando Diaz and Paolo Thaon di Revel, heads of the army and navy at the end of the war. At the Aventine, the last warriors for the constitution and state achieved in the Risorgimento had been unable to enrol behind their cause the army officer corps, the king, or any serious element of the old ruling class, Vatican, industrialists or large landowners.

Amendola was honest enough to half-admit this situation. At the end of February 1925, he wrote to a fellow journalist to indicate that, even if the task was thankless, he had no intention of abandoning the field. But, he added, rather belatedly, 'to win we have to *mobilise* the spirit of our people. A few gagged papers and a few politicians cannot achieve a miracle for all. Therefore we must feverishly dedicate ourselves to organisation.' His friends must expand the presence of the Unione Nazionale throughout the country. 'It is the only fresh force,' he maintained hopefully, 'that exists across the Left.'[150]

Such hope was barren. Among those who might have been thought to be Amendola's natural friends, the proponents of high culture were ready, in great majority, to accommodate themselves to Mussolini's dictatorship. On 21 April (the date said to mark the foundation of Rome in 753 BCE), Giovanni Gentile assembled 250 signatories to approve a 'Manifesto of Fascist intellectuals'. Those signing were such men from Amendola's past life as Acerbo, Bottai, Corradini, D'Annunzio, Federzoni, Marinetti, Ferdinando Martini, Ojetti and Luigi Pirandello (with whom Amendola had quarrelled clamorously in September 1924).[151] They proclaimed that, following the victory in the First World War, individual Italians must find their souls and minds, their 'reasons for living, their freedom and their rights' in the *Patria* – that is, in the Fascist *Patria*. The feeble freedoms of Liberal Italy had had their day. Anti-Fascists who yearned for them were opposing the laws of history.

Amendola was appalled at least about the latter plans. He at once began to organise a reply from 'Anti-Fascist intellectuals', their rival credo being published in *Il Mondo* on 1 May.[152] He judged, together with Neapolitan intellectual Arturo Labriola (another of the Aventine Secessionists), that Gentile's manifesto was 'ridiculous'. There might be some intellectuals reconciled to the regime, he conceded, but they had to accept that it was a fundamentally 'irrational phenomenon, born from chaos and aggravating that chaos'.[153] Labriola was among the signatories to the rival manifesto, as were Albertini, Sibilla Aleramo (once Giovanni's lover), Luigi Einaudi and Gaetano Salvemini, along with fifty others. Croce, who had turned unreservedly against Mussolini and Fascism only after the speech of 3 January,[154] accepted being recorded as a 'promoter' and wrote much of the text.

Such a proclamation could not alter the steady toughening of the dictatorship and its construction of a 'totalitarian state', which was meant to prove that the old Liberal constitution had been replaced by the new

Fascist one, just as Gentile had said.[155] Was there a half-flattering of Amendola in the fashion in which Mussolini and Fascism took over his neologism for themselves?

What could be done? Nothing much except words, words, words. Amendola might proudly declare on 18 June: 'The Aventine has shown no intention to withdraw. It will not retreat and above all it will not flee. It is always at its post.'[156] Such rectitude was all very well, as was a complimentary letter from the young Sicilian Ugo La Malfa, destined to lead the Republican Party in post-1946 Italy. The young man expressed his thanks and admiration for the way in which Amendola had led 'openly and without hesitation and uncertainty' those who viewed Fascism as a combination of 'hatred and violence'.[157]

It was deserved praise, at least among non-Marxist Anti-Fascists. Yet Amendola was not a flawless hero. Although there is no written trace of it, in these months his affair with Nelia Pavlova must have continued. Nor did other male behaviour vanish. In late June, Amendola, acting as Italian journalists – including Mussolini – had long done, fought a morning sabre duel with Tullio Giordana, the editor of *La Tribuna*, whom he wounded on the forehead on the ninth pass. The two hugged manfully afterwards in the Italian and bourgeois manner. Giordana's career had had plenty of parallels with Amendola until, in 1923, he had rallied to Mussolini and proceeded to lambast *Il Mondo* for lack of patriotism. Not long after his duel, he reversed this line and, in his turn, fell victim to Fascist beating and an armed invasion of his flat.[158] In retrospect, the 1925 duel seems a petty quarrel. A historian might conclude that the two men's fierce confrontation was a last gesture of a disappearing Liberal, male and bourgeois journalists' world. It was to be followed soon afterwards by the murderous attack on Amendola, commanded by the less than gentlemanly Scorza at Montecatini and its environs. The two parties did not hug after that event.

Amendola had been severely injured and, for some weeks, took refuge at another spa, the French one at Vichy. From there, on 13 September, he wrote to Albertini with his reiterated message that 'I shall never give up the fight while breath remains in me'.[159] He was not always so positive. On 1 October, he reported at greater length from the small town of Nérac in the Garonne, where he had been staying with Luigi Campolonghi, a journalist associate who had gone into exile. His letter, lamenting in detail the damage done to his physical and psychological health, was addressed to a military friend (and member of the Unione Nazionale), ex-General Roberto Bencivenga, who was soon to be sentenced to five years *confino* on Ponza. Amendola told him sadly: 'I am a man who in forty years has spent the capital of sixty.' His troubles, he thought, dated from 1914 but had deteriorated once he became a member of parliament. So much of the struggle there and nationally against Fascism had been left to him. He now battled mentally against demoralisation. Physically, he had not recovered from his beatings. Two months after the assault in Tuscany, he could scarcely move his arm and needed twelve hours or more in bed each day. 'In such a state,' he vowed, 'I shall not run away nor desert' the struggle. But his friends must recognise how battered he was and furnish extra assistance. When he came back to Rome, he did not want to admit his weakness publicly. But others must be ready to cover for him. In the interim, he was off to Paris for more medical treatment and then planned to stay somewhere on the Riviera for a while.[160]

In fact, he did not find time to relax; by early November, he was back in Rome, perturbed to hear from Giorgio that Eva was no better.[161] Albertini, Fortunato and Salvemini were among those to send him best wishes.[162] Croce over-readily believed that he was almost fully recovered, adding the unhelpful advice that he should give up the Aventine Secession and return to the Chamber of Deputies.[163] In Rome, the dictatorship was even more aggressive than it had been; from the day before his return, the censors seized every issue of *Il Mondo*. The paper and the ideas it reflected, Amendola told Campolonghi, were 'being condemned to die strangled into silence'. Socialists and Republicans, he complained, retained some space for their preaching. But not 'democrats in opposition'.[164]

At Christmas he was left to inform a cousin dolefully that he had 'based my life and activities on God'. Now, at a moment of almost total adversity, he must contemplate the 'millennial experience of man and not despair'.[165] To the reformist socialist Turati (another associate of the Aventine), he added that they must be proud that, although 'having tenaciously preferred the side of the defeated, they had not lost their souls'. One day, he prophesied, the 'cause of the defeated' must become the 'cause of the victors'. The sun would shine through, however dark the night might seem at present. To another friend he underlined his certainty that 'our children and our grandchildren will bless the memory of those who never despaired'.[166] His most regular correspondent in these weeks was his old boss, Albertini, who had been sacked from the editorship of *Il Corriere della Sera*, for which he wrote a last editorial on 25 November.[167] Amendola took time to see Eva at her clinic one last time, where she did not recognise how physically damaged he had been by Scorza and his men.[168]

Giovanni was making his farewells. In early February, he left for Paris and another, unavailing, operation; on 9 February, he told Giorgio that surgery had been delayed because his high temperature was refusing to go down. Writing from his bed was arduous, he stated, but Giorgio should admit such travails only to the family's *'intimate* friends'.[169] In response, in successive letters, Giorgio tried to cheer him up with bright family news: Antonio and Pietro were doing well at school. Ada did not eat enough, hoping to become slimmer and more attractive. He, by contrast, was always hungry and had put on still more weight. But he was trying to study better and was 'completely immersed in Greek philosophy and reading the *Inferno* [of Dante]'.[170] Ada, when she wrote, perhaps less encouragingly, called Antonio a *'boia'* (literally an executioner, but here a troublemaker). She promised to crack down on him and his school scores were going up.[171] Whether or not cheered by such reports, on 19 March Giovanni sent his children one final message, typically urging them, and especially Giorgio, to work hard.[172]

Before retreating to France, Amendola had made one last brave public statement against the dictatorship's open persecution of the Aventine deputies. It did not save them from Fascist totalitarianism; they were finally banned from parliament on 9 November 1926, 123 deputies then losing their seats. By that time, Amendola was dead. So, to all intents and purposes, was his version of Italian liberalism. He had no immediate heirs. Some observers saw the Rosselli brothers, Carlo and Nello, victims in June 1937 of the most notorious Fascist murder of the regime's political opponents during that decade, as preserving his heritage. The *Giustizia e Libertà* movement, which Carlo led, did campaign for liberties that Amendola approved and for which he went to his death.[173] Yet Arturo Labriola was near the truth when, in 1928, he had regretted that Amendola had never found 'either success or following among our middle class or in the grand bourgeoisie of big landowners and industrialists'; Amendola, like Croce and Fortunato, Labriola added sadly, had stood for 'a dictatorship of cultured men' and eschewed the masses.[174]

It might, therefore, not be a surprise to find that, when, in 1943–5, active resistance was drawing at least some Italians into armed battle against the Nazi-fascism of the Repubblica Sociale Italiana, a suggestion that a partisan band should take Amendola's name was rejected. Northerner resistance fighters recalled him vaguely as a man from Naples, the detail of whose ideas was 'unknown' to them.[175] Only some time following the end of the Second World War could the claim be made that all non-communist resistance had borne a heritage with his blessing.[176] As late as June 1946, Croce, with the intellectual arrogance sadly typical of him, damned his sometime friend and colleague in philosophy with faint praise. 'With his fine death,' the rich Neapolitan, dependent for his cultured lifestyle on his landowner family, remarked, 'he rescued a life not unstained by error and intellectual mediocrity hidden by his political stance.'[177] At that time, with his own blindness (and racism), Croce was calling the removal of Liberal Italy's empire from national rule a British '*Diktat*', ignoring the appalling connotations of the word and his country's savage imperial record. Croce's comprehension of liberal democracy had stricter limits than did Amendola's.[178]

Despite Croce's lordly snub, Giovanni Amendola's reputation revived as life under the Republic wore on, and, with the centenary of his murder approaching in 2026, his stoic fight against Fascism is remembered with advantages. In the present world, his version of liberal democracy may have antique aspects, but it can be read as nourishing much politics in the West.

However, insofar as the historical record is concerned, when it came to active resistance from 1926 to 1945, it was not Amendola's liberal ideas but rather his family that kept a struggle against Fascist dictatorship going. There was some irony in this situation. His sons – especially the eldest, Giorgio, but also Antonio and Pietro – actively opposed Mussolini. They did so while well aware of their father's heroic sacrifice. Yet, their Anti-Fascism was based not on liberal ideals but instead on (some form of) communism.

Nonetheless, it is right to conclude that Giovanni Amendola was the prime liberal democratic victim of Italian Fascism. Cianca, his colleague at *Il Mondo*, thought that his was a martyrdom endured with 'sublime resignation'.[179] After the battering in Rome on 26 December 1923, Amendola knew that he was a marked man for a political movement that viewed the murder of its opponents as wholly acceptable. In walking proudly to the second and worse attack on the night of 20–21 July 1925, Amendola displayed his 'intransigent will'. He was properly viewed by the regime as their most dangerous opponent, maybe the 'only serious candidate in succession' to Mussolini, had King Victor Emmanuel been braver and more charismatic than he was.[180]

Was he a saint? As shall be demonstrated in the next chapter, Nelia Pavlova thought so. Deserving that title is always difficult. Amendola was not always admirable in his private life or in the evident limitations of his comprehension of democracy where colonised peoples, women, communists and southern peasants were concerned (in 1925, however, he did for the first time, while condemning the 'wastefulness' of strikes, agree that socialist unions could be a positive force in a modern society).[181] But his defence of parliament, a free press, legal process and open and intelligent debate and his refusal to tolerate an armed party militia or overt political violence were consistent and unqualified. Although always to some extent a Risorgimento Liberal, his mind bound into the Italian nation state with its many limitations before 1914, Amendola did fight the good fight. To a large degree, therefore, Giovanni Amendola and his ghost helped steer his country towards a richer democracy after 1945, however much currently threatened by the rise of populism and the social media triumph of the opinionated over the expert.

Nelia Pavlova
Giovanni's Last Lover, Convinced Admirer and Liberal Democrat Partisan

In April 1924, at a moment when Amendola was feverishly concentrating on preserving a seat in the Chamber at the elections, the Bulgarian journalist, Nelia Pavlova, now in her late twenties, was back in Rome, having fled from the nationalist coup in Sofia via Paris. Whatever had happened when she had nursed Amendola at Monfalcone in 1916–17, or in the interim, when her professional labours or tourist pleasures had brought her to Italy on more than one occasion, now she approached *Il Mondo* on a formal-sounding basis as a contributor to the paper. She contacted Alberto Cianca, who, since August 1922, had been the paper's editor, enquiring whether he could find space for her reflections on the Great War in her native Bulgaria.[1] When she failed to receive a reply, she wrote instead to Giovanni, addressing him respectfully as '*Egregio onorevole e ammirevole amico*' (Dear MP and admired friend); the rest of the letter was in French. Could he cajole Cianca to favour her work as a journalist, she asked, all the more since she had now decided to make Italy her adopted '*patrie*'?[2]

Amendola must have reacted positively to her plea. In its issue of 24 May, the ninth anniversary of Italian entry into the war, *Il Mondo* printed her piece, granting it prominence.[3] Perhaps coincidentally, ten days before Pavlova's appeal to him, Amendola had lamented to a friend that Eva's condition grew steadily worse. For two taxing years he had been living with his housekeepers and his four children. 'My private life is tough soldiering' (ironically, the word that he used was '*milizia*'). 'No less hard than my public life,' he complained. 'But I force myself to do my duty, both in the one and the other.'[4] Was Pavlova going to relieve, or had she already partially relieved, the worst of his isolation and sense of failure? After his death, Pavlova certainly treasured her memory of him as an Anti-Fascist saint and martyr; now, during the months left to him, she offered a simpler form of physical and personal relief.

Figure 4.1 Nelia Pavlova, young, confident, beautiful and a foreign new woman.

Although she remains in some ways a tantalisingly shadowy figure, Pavlova had experienced tumultuous times since her wartime service in the Italian Red Cross. In Bulgaria, the decision of King Ferdinand to fight the war to a bitter end on the German side had proved a catastrophic mistake for the country and for himself. In 1918, Agrarian leader Aleksandar Stamboliyski, who had been gaoled three years earlier just before Bulgaria entered the war (Italy declared war on Bulgaria on 19 October 1915), emerged from prison. His Bulgarian Agrarian National Union (BANU) won the highest vote in the country in the August 1919 elections, a figure that increased in a fresh ballot held in March 1920.[5] Ferdinand had already been forced to abdicate (he lived until 1947), on 3 October 1918, having been replaced by his eldest son, Boris (born 1894), who took the grandiose title of Tsar Boris III. On 25 October 1930 at Assisi, Boris was destined to marry Giovanna, one of Victor Emmanuel III's daughters; Mussolini acted as state registrar for the event.

That chapter in the story of the Bulgarian dynasty lay ahead. But once the war was over, Mladen Pavlov and his daughter seem to have returned to Bulgaria, although Nelia readily travelled to other places. Father and daughter must have applauded their friend and patron Stamboliyski's time in office from 1919 to June 1923. There is some suggestion that Nelia acted as Stamboliyski's 'secretary' for part of the time, but just what that position entailed is hard to determine.[6] Fluent in a number of languages, she certainly worked as a journalist under Bulgarian government aegis, whether at home or abroad. Photographic evidence places her in Italy in December 1920, when she visited Pompei, but, earlier in that year, she was in Sofia.

She reported from the Genoa conference on reparations from April to May 1922, taking her place as part of the Bulgarian delegation, an elevated role for a young journalist.[7] After it was over, she interviewed Prince Livio Borghese[8] about the League of Nations' Inter-Allied Commission assessing reparations on Bulgaria. They met in Rome, with some controversy resulting. Borghese contested her account of their exchange, vehemently denying that he had captiously suggested that the Bulgarian government had done 'absolutely nothing' to pay its debts from the war. In response, he was bitterly attacked in the Sofia press.[9] *L'Epoca*, a rival radical paper to *Il Mondo*, had carried the interview; the paper had been founded in 1917 by Tullio Giordana, ironically Amendola's unreliably Anti-Fascist opponent in the duel of June 1925.

Bulgaria was a more uniformly peasant country than Italy but its political life had an idiosyncratic cast.[10] If parallels were sought with Italy, then some of Stamboliyski's and BANU's behaviour might bear comparison with Fascism. Certainly BANU's power was reinforced by a paramilitary 'Orange Guard', with its own version of *manganelli* as its favoured weapon against enemies. Chief among its foes were Bulgaria's socialists and communists, engrossed by what was occurring in the country's traditional Big Brother, Russia.[11] At the same time, BANU disdained too much urban development, defining itself as the party of the peasantry and for the peasantry. Equally, Stamboliyski made plain his mistrust of intellectuals, especially bohemian intellectuals of the sort that Giovanni Amendola and Eva Kühn were. Both Stamboliyski and Amendola may have desired their people's identity to be perfectly nationalised. But the happy future Bulgarian society imagined by Stamboliyski was scarcely the same as Amendola's hope in a strong liberal democratic Italian nation state.

BANU and Stamboliyski were doubtless staunchly anti-communist, but they also faced enemies on their right, notably among the remorseless irredentist Internal Macedonian Revolutionary Organisation (IMRO) and its military backers. After BANU won another election on 22 April 1923, IMRO determined on a coup to be rid of Stamboliyski. They began, on 9 June, by seizing Sofia. Five days later, the BANU leader was captured while hiding in the countryside, tortured, murdered and dismembered. His head was sent back to Sofia in a cake box. Nelia and her father fled to Paris and what seems to have been a flat they owned there. Given that her father was in his seventies, there may have been pressing reasons for Nelia to broaden her professional activity.

Until she stopped publishing with the onset of the Second World War, Pavlova matured into a highly capable journalist; by the 1930s, she was an expert on the Balkans and beyond. When in Paris, she lived in the Rue de la Félicité in the prestigious seventh arrondissement, near the parliament and the Eiffel Tower, was a member of the national journalists' union, and was known for her broad expertise across Eastern Europe.[12] In Romania, Turkey, Bulgaria (once its politics calmed following the 1923 coup), Czechoslovakia, Hungary and Yugoslavia,[13] she nourished excellent contacts, which she was willing to use boldly and well from what became her normal base in Paris. Why, then, did she show up in Rome in April 1924, when Italian politics were, after all, still in turmoil, and talk about making her permanent base there?

There is no direct evidence to answer this question. What is clear from a scattering of letters that have been preserved in the Amendola archive and published by Elio D'Auria as a supplement to his sixth and final volume of such correspondence is that a deep relationship swiftly developed between Giovanni and Nelia. It was so sudden that it may suggest that the pair had been more than nurse and patient at Monfalcone during the war, or, more likely, that there had been intimate post-war contact given opportunity and cover through Pavlova's journalistic work and justification for Giovanni from Eva's recurrent nervous illness. Certainly, by 26 June (a fortnight after the Matteotti murder and the very day of the Aventine Secession), Pavlova was sending Amendola a (typed) love letter. She signed it 'Chiffon' (your little darling) and addressed him as 'Mon John'.

She wanted to cry and laugh at the same time, she confided. 'How much I need your kisses at this moment more than ever and all the more when I am separated from you,' she disclosed passionately. But she was robust and resilient and could always be consoled by thinking about his admirable integrity. Suffering, for her, was 'a secret joy'. 'My John, my dear, my all, my good, I adore you, do you understand?' she rhapsodised. 'I love you to the depth of my secret soul.' She had been worried to hear that another woman had booked an appointment to see him at *Il Mondo*. But she was sure that she could have complete faith in 'his love and his heart'. 'Don't laugh at me,' she confided artlessly, 'for I am feeling small at the moment but, as you know, I am a woman, and so I need to be spoiled.'[14]

Love letters should perhaps be best left in the privacy of their composition. But Nelia's rhetoric bore parallels with Eva's during the early years of her relationship with Giovanni. Pavlova, fifteen years Eva's junior, replicated some of the character of Amendola's wife. Both were foreign. Both had seen something of the world. Both knew a number of languages. Both normally communicated in French. Both were capable writers and women of ideas. Both could fend for themselves and win an adequate place in the cultural world. But, in their correspondence, both fell automatically into the verbiage of Italian patriarchy in expressing their love for Giovanni in submissive terms. Neither had what we would today reckon was a democratic relationship with him. At least in their dealings with him, neither conducted herself as a new woman.

In August 1924, Pavlova wrote again, this time from Frascati, hoping that Giovanni was enjoying time with his children further to the south. She was sad, she remarked, that she had not received any news from him on that day, with the implication that, usually, they were in daily contact. He must tell her when he planned to be back in Rome.

By the time of their next preserved communication, on the afternoon of 26 September, she had moved to Paris, where she was endeavouring to sublet her flat. Amendola, by then, was labouring to solidify Aventine opposition to Fascism. 'You will laugh at me to see a businesswoman rather than a woman of easy virtue,' she wrote. Parisian life was all hard work. Unlike in Rome, in the French capital she had to get up at 7 a.m. each morning and, by evening, she just collapsed into bed. She had taken time to visit the Italian embassy and gained the impression that the ambassador, Baron Romano Avezzana, was not thrilled with political events in Rome but thought that they must be endured. She also met Italian press officers in Paris; their group was headed by Emanuele Ceria from the still independent *La Stampa*.

The last paragraphs of her letter switched to more private matters. That evening she was going out with a relative of hers; the woman had a car and so she would not get too tired. 'Write to me,' she urged. 'Think about your little darling and don't try to cheat on me. As for me, I love you, united as we are by [our] baby.'[15] If her words are to be read literally, Giovanni had made his new partner pregnant with the same speed that he and Eva had conceived Giorgio following their wedding.[16] Or was the baby already born?

Later that day, she wrote again. She had received a letter from him sent from Rome two days earlier and had more to report. 'As you can see I work even in my profession of woman of easy virtue,' she stated in what was an edgy running gag in their relationship. She had met Louis Charles de Chambrun, the *chef de cabinet* of the French ministry of foreign affairs, and, through him, had booked an interview with Édouard Herriot, the Radical prime minister. Had her articles on 'the troubled Balkans' and on Anatole France yet come out in Rome? *Il Mondo* should leave three columns free for her to report on her talk with Herriot. 'Do you understand, dear leader of the opposition?' she asked. In signing off, she sent him a warm embrace and told him again, 'I love you.'[17]

In her next letter, on 29 September, Pavlova was delighted to have heard from him. 'Everything that I see, that I have to face and that I do is with you, for you and always,' she began ardently. Again she painted her busy hours as a journalist. She repeated the news about Chambrun, whom she now described as the press officer at the ministry, and her approaching 'friendly talk' with Herriot. Chambrun, who was to become French ambassador in Rome in 1933–5, had been 'charming', she said. He took her to a lavish lunch in the Bois de Boulogne and an afternoon at the racetrack, where she admitted to dropping 200 francs. 'A woman as serious as I am … can still commit little follies,' she confessed girlishly. In the evening she had retreated to her small hotel. She added: 'I think of you and my infant, for whom I've bought some baby clothes.' She was sure that Amendola would develop a love of such things. For the moment she was pleased that he had his two younger sons with him and 'you retain your family duties'. 'Poor dear John, how your life is mine.' He must write again if he was going into the countryside. He must think of her and metaphorically she enclosed for that day 'lots of my kisses on your lovely mouth'.[18]

The next afternoon she wrote again, imagining that he had gone out of the city. Not with another woman, she enquired? (However, in October she sent a stunningly beautiful photograph of herself to her poet mentor, Kiril Hristov, with whom she remained in regular contact about literary issues.) 'Not being a big traitor. Be sure that I shall never pardon you if that is so, and our baby will never love you,' she added. 'You must not make me afraid. He [her infant son] is so good with me. Do you understand? … As for me, I love you constantly and now more than ever. Being apart attaches me to you all the more,' she swore, even if she still worried sometimes. 'I have suffered so much in my life that I really want peace and serious love with their pains and joys.' She was very fond of Paris but was about to return to Italy. She planned to do so after she had spoken to Herriot and written up her account for *Il Mondo*. Meanwhile, she was to dine with Ricciotti Garibaldi, grandson of Giuseppe and, unknown to her, an agent of the Fascist secret police.[19] She rounded off the letter with the thought that she was providing news as though he were a member of her family. But, in fact, he was something dearer than that. 'You comprise my whole existence,' she avowed, and so again she gave him 'a big kiss on his big mouth'.[20]

On 1 October her news was that she had to delay her departure from Paris for business reasons. Garibaldi had given her a contact with socialist chief Léon Blum; an interview should follow. The letter ended with an unusual burst of Italian, in which she complained about feeling exhausted by all that she had to do – whether with work or motherhood, she did not say. She signed off 'with a big, big kiss; believe me love that I love you just so very much'.[21]

In D'Auria's collection, two shorter letters follow. They are undated but seem to have been written around the same time. In one, Pavlova reported that she was to speak to French leftist foreign minister Aristide Briand the next day. She believed that Briand wanted to meet Amendola and she could smooth that contact. In the immediate term, she could ask him questions that Amendola transmitted to her.[22] She signed off 'Nellinke', a Slavic pet name that might remind Giovanni of his and Eva's use of similar words for each other and their children.

The other letter, probably written in Rome after she had returned there, grumbled that Amendola's preoccupation with the Unione Nazionale was preventing them from meeting. 'But henceforth one must take second place even when the heart bleeds,' she told herself with her sense of duty struggling against her physical longing. 'See the mystical and passionate sentiments of love sometimes turning into sharp arrows, which bury themselves in our hearts.'[23] On 11 November, she again swapped French for Italian and wrote as a fellow journalist and a lover. She begged that he publish her article on Herriot as soon as possible. She knew that he was busy. But 'even the great Napoleon liked to relax some time ... after the sun set,' she added seductively. She did not send him any kisses since she was waiting to give them 'when you come to take them'.[24]

In the published Amendola correspondence, there is a final letter, dated 14 December 1924 and written in French, but from Rome. Part of it again focused on work. Pavlova had been compiling a piece for the Paris press about Italian policy towards the League of Nations. She had interviewed Briand, who was visiting Rome, and had another meeting booked with him. She had lots to tell her Giovanni, and, she noted, she was happy about the high prestige that he held in French political circles. Could he come to her apartment, either in the afternoon or in the evening after 9 p.m.? She hoped to see him 'in good health, with a smile on your lips and joy in your heart'. And she embraced him 'very tenderly'.[25]

Sadly, evidence in the Amendola correspondence about Nelia's and Giovanni's relationship during the rest of his life ends here. Yet there are

some significant glimmerings from other sources. Most intriguing are the
Bulgarian archives, where quite a number of letters between Nelia and
the poet Hristov are preserved. The most significant is dated 24 June
1930 and directed to Hristov, who then held a post at Prague University.
Her life overflowed with deep sadness, Nelia divulged. 'As you [*vous*]
know, I lost my husband [sic], murdered by the Fascists.'[26] Then, 'eight
months ago, I lost *my only son*. I have been really unhappy in my affec-
tions. My son, who was seven years old, died in four days from a terrible
attack of meningitis.' Her father, she added, was bearing up well despite
his eighty-three years. Her sister and brother in Bulgaria kept her regularly informed about him. Much unhappiness and worry, then, but she
was publishing and she had a flight to Eastern Europe booked, leaving
Paris on 15 July.[27]

Nelia's son is not named but it is now clear how and when he died at
'*sept ans*' or in his seventh year (European counting for what in English is
six). But that places the child's birth in 1923 and her pregnancy back to
1922. Her claim that Giovanni was her 'husband' might be explained
away as her argument to herself about the importance of their relationship (and a denial that she was a loose woman). However, it does seem
that her talk of her 'baby' in the letters of 1924 referred to an infant, who
was presumably being looked after much of the time by another relative,
whether in Paris (perhaps by her 'French' mother) or in Bulgaria, where
her siblings lived. If Giovanni Amendola was the child's father (and given
the present state of the evidence doubts must remain), their love affair
had been sexual for some time, during the political crises between the
Fascist rise to power and the Aventine Secession, making the formal
phrasing of her initial approach to Giovanni at *Il Mondo* all the odder.

There is another important letter in the Hristov files. Nelia wrote it
from Paris on 22 August 1928. She began by saying chattily that she had
had to extract his address from a friend, since, when she was expelled
from Italy early in 1926, the Fascists, who had sacked her flat, had stolen
all her papers, letters and address book. Then, without anyone knowing
about it, she had languished in prison in Trieste for a fortnight, before
being forced across the border. 'I was married with the martyr Amendola
who was murdered two months after our marriage. I have a six-year-old
[five-year-old] son, a little orphan,' she confided with a timetable that did
not make sense.

She had not lost courage, however. Summoning all her strength,
energy and soul, she had forged a career as a journalist and had won
recognition in Bulgaria, Italy and also France, 'where the going is really
tough'. After the Stamboliyski business, she had hesitated about going
back to Bulgaria. But, recently she implied, worried by her son's health,

she had returned home and allowed him to breathe 'Balkan air'. The trip sparked him up. She stayed three months, travelling across the country, and, on one occasion at least, dining out in Sofia with her father. She had more articles in the process of publication, she was pleased to report, and she thought that the situation in Bulgaria was improving. She was now widely loved there. Hristov could make a similar return to his home country and his many local admirers, she counselled.[28]

Again, then, this letter suggests a son born in 1923, and again the claim, surely false, that she had somehow wed Giovanni in 1926 (while he was married to someone else). Are there Italian sources, we must now ask, that can cast light on Nelia's life between 1922 and Giovanni Amendola's death in April 1926?

Regrettably, there is nothing to show exactly when or where her son was born. Nor does Giovanni ever positively admit to being the father, let alone to marrying Nelia. In the current scanty state of the evidence, nor do we know how Nelia reacted to Mussolini's pronouncement of his dictatorship in January 1925, to the vicious beating of Amendola in Tuscany in July, or to the first weeks of his slow and doubtful recovery.

It is clear, however, that, late in 1925, Pavlova was again living in a flat in Rome, seemingly without her son. She resided in the city most of the time from when Amendola returned there from France in November 1925 until February 1926, when he left for his second unsuccessful operation in Paris. The usual sentimental emphasis in the existing Italian literature is that Giovanni held a last Christmas meeting with Eva at her clinic, her 'nervous condition' ensuring that she did not realise how ill he was. Locatelli claims that he generously took her roses, chocolates and an array of reading matter (with little effect).[29] What Pavlova thought about Amendola's wife and such a meeting is a question no one has asked.

What is plain, however, is that the regime grew irritated that Pavlova was giving comfort to Amendola and spitefully determined to stop her. At 3 o'clock on the morning of 19 January 1926, the flat she rented in Rome was invaded and she was arrested. She was interrogated for hours; at 5 p.m. she was taken home and told she had ten minutes to pack her bags. She had 300 lire in her pocket. That night she was dragged across Italy as a prisoner and, soon after, expelled from the country at Postumia (a dating that makes her later claim of 'two weeks' in Trieste gaol into an exaggeration, another of the falsehoods in her correspondence with Hristov that deserve pondering). There is no mention of a small child; he must have been living with another member of the Pavlov family elsewhere. Amendola managed to send her 2,000 lire, but, as always, short of cash himself, he appealed to Albertini to provide more. Giovanni maintained standoffishly that 'Signora Pavlova' had never really done politics and was being punished unfairly: 'her only wrong being that she belonged in our family and shared our sentiments'. She had been attacked 'in the most cowardly manner imaginable', he protested.[30]

By 3 February 1926, Pavlova was recovering from her experience of Fascist aggression in an Austrian clinic, the Sanatorium A. Woolf. Amendola told Albertini, with cold or careful phrasing, that no money had got through to 'that person in Vienna'.[31] Could he check what had happened?

Pavlova did not take long to recover from the physical and moral outrage of the attack on her flat and her expulsion from Italy. She promptly resumed contact with Giovanni once he was in Paris. Now Giorgio met his father's lover seemingly for the first time and was pleased, he recalled, to find a woman who could give his father renewed 'force and courage'.[32] The eldest son was not alone in accepting Giovanni's second relationship. On 5 March, a letter from his brother Salvatore ('Uncle Mario'), who had travelled back from Paris to Rome, told him that his 'family' was doing reasonably there. In closing, Salvatore passed on 'the most affectionate greetings' to Pavlova (he called her 'Madame'). Among the family, at this stage Pavlova's role in Giovanni's life was not much of a secret.

It was in these weeks that Amendola wrote his last will and testament. It was dated 21 February 1926 and composed from his bed at the Clinique Médicale, Rue Piccinni 6, in the fifteenth arrondissement. Some of its contents have been reported in Chapter 1, and it was as much the work of a dying bourgeois family man as of an Anti-Fascist saint and martyr.

Quite a long paragraph testified to his debt to Eva's 'great love' for him, her time as 'the courageous and hard-working companion of my difficult youth' and her role as the mother of his children, as well as apologising for being unable to render her life happy – without the slightest hint that his own patriarchalism may have hindered their marriage. The fault lay not in her 'good and honest nature' but in her 'unhappy nervous system', he wrote half-forgivingly. When it came to Nelia, she earned a one-sentence paragraph and there was no reference to a son or acknowledgement that he was the boy's father. 'I beg my children to pass on my personal memory to Signora Nelia Pavlova to whom I am grateful and obliged for devoted friendship and assistance lavished on me in the saddest moments of my life, at cost to herself' was how Amendola awkwardly phrased their tie. At the end of the document, he did ask that the letters that he and Nelia had exchanged should be returned to her, while the rest he wanted destroyed. He signed off with 'a long and tender hug to Eva, Giorgio, Ada, Antonio and Pietro', but not to Nelia.[33]

Yet, through these last weeks of his life, Pavlova stayed devotedly by Giovanni's side. When Giorgio Amendola reached Cannes in time to salute his dying father and be anointed head of the Amendola family, it was Pavlova who told him that death was inevitable given the damage done to Giovanni's lungs.[34] She was one of the three people who stood beside his hospital bed when he died. Giorgio recalled Giovanni's last moment, with his own self-obsession: 'His cough became more and more heart-breaking. Then he pulled himself up, looked around, raised his hand to give me a caress and fell back. That was all.'[35]

Pavlova did not merit further mention; she must have been left to trudge sadly back to Paris and resume her work as a journalist. There, on 14 June, she gave an extended interview to *Paris Soir*, a moderate rightist paper edited by Eugène Merle, with sales of up to 100,000 copies. The paper hailed her as 'a notably eloquent conference speaker and well-informed literary critic' who had secured 'a place of the highest merit in Italian journalism'. She had been brutally driven out of Italy, 'without any regard for her wartime service, her talent as a writer and her gender', and had taken refuge in France. There, she fully deserved to be treated as a 'Latin sister who was suffering for *la liberté*'. In her complex identity, France was now (again) her *patrie* – or one of them, along with Bulgaria.

In her article for *Paris Soir*, Pavlova sketched her background in more detail, noting that she was the daughter of Mladen Pavlov, the Bulgarian patriot, and a French mother. She had spent much of her youth in France. However, after family protests against King Ferdinand banned them from Bulgaria, she and her mother had moved to Italy with the onset of war. There, she began to work for the Italian Red Cross. She had met Amendola at Monfalcone, formed a 'deep attachment' with him, she added without chronological specificity, and was still championing his work and ideas. He had tragically 'died on the field of honour of *liberté*'.

Beyond such personal matters, Pavlova must have persuaded Merle to let her write an editorial, which used the anniversary of the death of Matteotti on 10 June to mount a stinging attack on the Italian dictatorship. Fascism, she stated, was the 'most dramatic and lamentable' political phenomenon of the time. It had killed Amendola. Sounding almost Marxist, she maintained that it marshalled 'a great army of the Italian reactionary classes [allied] against the economic evolution of the working classes'. Fascists were the hirelings of Big Business and large landowners. Mussolini was another king of Prussia, a bloody tyrant, happy to replicate the aggressive policies of imperial Germany before 1914, but given to chopping and changing his friends from one day to the next. His intimate ties with the USSR deserved notice to persuade possible rightist friends that he should not be trusted. Since 1922, Mussolini had overturned Liberal Italy's record of progress since the Risorgimento, and the Savoy dynasty had proved completely ineffective at thwarting him.[36]

Later that year, Pavlova repeated her story to an audience at the internationalist Club du Faubourg, with the discussion reported this time in the left-leaning *La Lanterne*.[37] She similarly won attention in *Le Rappel*, a radical republican paper, originally owned by the sons of Victor Hugo.[38] Pavlova, in other words, with some ideological flexibility, was trying to preach to France the lessons that Giovanni Amendola had taught her about Mussolini's dictatorship, international fascism and the progressive side of Italian liberalism since the Risorgimento. Despite Amendola's condescending remark that she did not really understand politics, she had adopted a left-leaning but anti-communist, republican and liberal democratic stance to which she stuck over the next decade. Her comprehension of democracy might trouble a severe later critic but she was not alone in that regard.

Her life did take some months to settle down into prosperity and purpose, although, in June 1927, she wrote a eulogy for the Radical Cartel des Gauches daily *Le Quotidien* for Arturo Labriola, an independent Naples intellectual with whom Giovanni had enjoyed friendly relations during his last years.[39] By then, Labriola had diluted his initial syndicalism into a vaguer, left-leaning republicanism. But her career as a journalist still stuttered. Despite being able to find some niches for her work in the Paris press, on 27 July Pavlova wrote a long letter to Luigi Albertini worrying about her fate. Time passes after great unhappiness, she philosophised in opening, and your mind 'instinctively takes flight towards the future'. But the past could not be dislodged so easily. 'In the eyes of his child,' she reported, Giovanni Amendola 'still lives'. The boy is 'all mine', she added. 'With his innocent smile, he is always serious. He [Amendola] is still alive.' What, she wondered in continuing emotional vein, might her time with his father signify about life after death and the chance finally to locate justice and charity in the world?

[margin handwritten note: martyr]

Becoming more practical after such unsettled musing, she remembered that she had not been in contact with Albertini since the two had cried together at Cannes immediately after Giovanni's death. When she had gone back to view her Rome apartment following the Fascist attack on it, she found it 'shattered, broken, burnt, including my books'. Now, in Paris, she was garnering a little money from her work as a journalist, while her sister sent her extra relief from their property in Bulgaria. She therefore had enough for herself. But what about the child, who was 'a consolation but ... also a deep anxiety'? She could retreat to her small

[bottom margin handwritten note: Not a radical ... Small, establishment GA]

apartment but presently owed a debt of 7,000 francs at the *pension* where she had been staying. She had appealed to friends in Italy but without reply. The 'concentration' of (non-communist) Anti-Fascist exiles in Paris were hopelessly disorganised and divided, Turati, Treves and the rest being reduced to a sad state. So could he 'do some little thing in my regard?' she asked, reaching the nub of her letter. In compensation, she added '*with complete discretion*', she could pass on information. In that regard, her knowledge went beyond the Italians, where, she confessed, 'I only see the *elite* among the emigrants,' but, by now, she had realised that Ricciotti Garibaldi was an enemy. In September, she planned to bring out a book in Paris on 'our dear Departed'. She was sure, she concluded winsomely, that her son would have a hug ready for Albertini should he ever visit Paris.[40]

No eulogistic book on Giovanni appeared. However, maybe she did intend to write it. In the frontispiece of *Au Pays du Ghazi*, a study of Atatürk's Turkey (1930), Pavlova listed her past works[41] and books that she was planning. Among these was a study to be entitled *Le Christ de l'Italie*. It was never to appear. But can she have intended it to be a holy portrait of Giovanni Amendola?

The Albertini papers have no record of a reply or of Pavlova and her son receiving financial assistance from the 'super-tutor' in the generous way that Amendola's legitimate children did, or of him taking up her curious offer to be his spy in Paris. But Pavlova was again in Cannes when Giorgio revisited his father's tomb in October 1927. She was, he recorded, 'battered and tormented', upset when Anti-Fascist exiles accused her of trying to pass herself off as Giovanni's widow (no insinuation of 'marriage' now).[42] Pavlova and Giorgio met again in Cannes for the second anniversary of Giovanni's death in April 1928. Now she rejected a generous offer of financial assistance from 'Uncle Mario'. Giorgio noted that he never saw her (nor the unmentioned half-brother) again.[43] Perhaps disingenuously, he maintained in his memoirs that he had been unable to trace her in later years,[44] although they both lived for a time in Paris, after his arrival there in 1931, and she must have been easily contactable. He did not give space to the possibility that their failure to communicate may have been enhanced by the clash between her democratic leftism and his communism. After all, it was in 1928 that the Comintern imposed on the party the line that social democrats and their friends, people with ideas like those of Pavlova (and of the dead Giovanni Amendola), were 'social fascists', just as much the 'white guard of capitalism' as were outright fascists.

Back in Paris, just after the meeting in Cannes, Pavlova was prominent in favouring the foundation of a liberal democratic Ligue

International Antifasciste, winning the backing of such celebrities as Albert Einstein, George Bernard Shaw, H. G. Wells, Henri Barbusse, Mihály Károlyi, Georges Duhamel and Ilya Ehrenburg (this last a somewhat surprising figure on the list). Fascism, she contended, was at its worst in Italy but it was international in nature, aiming to block legal process and social development and, in a nutshell, undermine civilisation.[45] Over the next few years, there were a number of other such groupings but there is no further evidence of Pavlova finding a leading post in their cause.

In terms of day-to-day living, Pavlova had remade a professional life for herself as a journalist of distinction. Fobbed off as it seemed by the Amendola family and the rich 'super-tutors', Pavlova built an identity as a woman with excellent connections in the Balkans and beyond. She crafted a role in Paris cultural life as a left-leaning but patriotic observer of Eastern European affairs. In August 1928, she made something of a splash in *Le Petit Parisien*, a populist Paris paper aiming more at sales than at austere accuracy, with articles on Bulgaria. She romantically represented it as 'the country of red roses'; she had been touring around Bulgaria (she did not mention that it was with her son) and gleefully painted a positive version of the 'splendour of religious buildings in Sofia'.[46] Her family connection with BANU meant that she had obtained a lengthy interview with Atanas Burov, the Bulgarian minister of foreign affairs from 1926 to 1931, a banker with close ties to the League of Nations. Burov, she reported, appreciated French foreign policy and was a Francophile sympathiser with the Little Entente.[47] Most of the Eastern European leaders whom Pavlova interviewed over the next decade were, she said to the presumed pleasure of her readership, of the same persuasion.

In March 1929, Pavlova gave a lecture at the Hautes Études Commerciales on Macedonia and its prospects, again assuring her audience of the natural Francophilia of the locals, while retaining her family Bulgarian nationalist line that the territory was terra irredenta for Sofia, its people oppressed by cruel Yugoslav rule.[48] A few months later, she could boast a scoop in a meeting with King Michael of Romania, whom she labelled 'the youngest monarch in the world'. In 1927 he had succeeded his grandfather, temporarily blocking his disgraced father, the later King Carol, from the throne. Michael was only seven years old and the more important connection was his mother, Princess Hélène, with whom Pavlova talked woman to woman. But she did find room to report that the young king was being given a severe education. Already he could ride well and had won the 'universal sympathy' of the Romanian people, her readers may have been cheered to learn.[49]

Over the next decade, Pavlova continued to confer with major politicians across the region, a somewhat anomalous example being the authoritarian and Italophile Hungarian prime minister, Gyula Gömbös, in April 1934; later that year he tried to nominate Mussolini for the Nobel Peace Prize.[50] In July 1936, she gave *Le Quotidien* a detailed assessment of Czechoslovakia, where, typically, she had travelled widely. It was, in her view, a praiseworthy Francophile liberal democracy, serenely enjoying its membership of the Little Entente. Its worst threat came from Konrad Henlein and the pro-Nazis of the Sudetenland – soon, indeed, to push inter-war Czechoslovakia towards its ruin.[51]

In April 1933, Pavlova spoke at a ceremony recording the life of postwar French foreign minister Aristide Briand, whom she hailed as an apostle of international peace.[52] In May 1937, she reviewed the overall political situation of France for *Le Populaire*, organ of the socialist prime minister, Léon Blum, at that time head of a popular front working in uneasy association with French communists (their deputies gave Blum external support in parliament).[53] Even on the subject of French domestic affairs, Nelia Pavlova had gained a serious place in Parisian journalism.

Back in 1930, Pavlova had travelled further afield, journeying in the most modern fashion by air, as she had informed Hristov that she would do. The popular illustrated weekly *L'Oeil de Paris* celebrated her as a female intrepid enough to fly to Ankara via Budapest, Belgrade, Sofia and Istanbul and back through Prague and Warsaw.[54] A photograph of her from this time survives. She is bare-shouldered, dressed in what looks like an evening gown. Her hair, which may have darkened over the years, is set in a fashionable bob with a parting down the middle. She has quite a prominent nose and a wide mouth set into an ambiguous half-smile. Her eyes look tensely into the middle distance.[55]

The prime purpose of this journey was for her to collect material for a book about the regime headed by the Ghazi (Warrior Chief) in Turkey. Otherwise known as Field Marshal Mustafa Kemal, he was the man who was soon to take the surname Atatürk. He remained a dictatorial ruler and moderniser of Turkey until his death from cirrhosis of the liver in November 1938. Pavlova dedicated her book to the Young Turk movement since the revolution of 1908, and to 'Progress, Liberty and Justice' as embodied by the 'grand figure' of the Ghazi.[56] He was, she wrote, 'the man of destiny' who was stamping his will on his country to its enormous benefit.[57] The better to gauge his beneficent rule, she had travelled to the new capital of Ankara. There she held lengthy and intimate interviews with most of the leading ministers, but not Atatürk. Her assessment of the new Turkey was overwhelmingly positive. Ankara was 'the most extraordinary capital in the world', a city of 'effort and work'. In every way – linguistic, cultural and economic – Kemal was rendering his people modern and united; he had, for example, legislated in favour of female 'liberation and emancipation'. With such policies, the minister of education told her, Turkey had achieved a real revolution, under 'Our Saviour', the Ghazi.[58]

Kemal and his government, she also learned in her optimistic or self-interested manner, were Francophiles. Rahmi Köken, the minister of the national economy, a Macedonian by origin (as was Atatürk) and so from Pavlova's part of the world, was sure that Turkey and France could augment their trade ties. In friendly conversation, Minister of Foreign Affairs Tevfik Rüştü Aras agreed with her that republican France stood on one side of the Mediterranean and republican Turkey on the other, each a pillar of virtuous revolution. They were natural friends and colleagues.[59] Neither raised the topic of the wartime Armenian massacres in which Aras had played a cruel leading role.

In Pavlova's mind, between the good of France and Turkey lay the evil of Italy, Fascism and Mussolini. Pavlova was too raw in her loss of Amendola not to draw negative comparisons between the Ghazi and the Duce in what she must have hoped was a withering final chapter.[60] Kemal, she pronounced, was a real moderniser whose powerful revolution was sweeping his country towards a happy future. Mussolini, by contrast, adopted the 'most worn-out ideas, the most condemned habits, the most archaic institutions'. He was an unrequited imperialist who sustained thievish ambition against every surrounding country. He had overvalued the lira to the ruin of the economy. Corruption was taking hold everywhere in his administration, she maintained, businessmen disgracefully suborned by the dictator. Italy was a 'superannuated monarchy', Turkey a republic; Mussolini was dictator for life, Kemal's position was renewed by the parliament every four years. Mussolini was a tyrant working for a party, Kemal a chief sacrificing himself for a people. The Duce had totally rejected the high ideals of 'the great martyr of the Fascist regime' – that is, Amendola, whose name she did not mention. Her dead lover had advocated 'a national consciousness springing from the inviolable and sacred consciousness of every individual'. Mussolini, by contrast, had merely opted for violence, 'defying the law, destroying *liberté*'.[61]

Amendola had been an austere, severe, intransigent man, punctilious in his devotion to work. He had been as absent as present in his final personal relationship with Pavlova, and he scarcely treated her as an intellectual equal or as a partner whose importance to him might match his memory of Eva. From the evidence available on each of his relationships, his comprehension of democracy scarcely extended to the female half of the population, who, after all, did not get the vote in Italy until 1945. Yet Amendola remained an object of worship for Nelia Pavlova, even after the realities of her life separated her from Italy and from contact with the Amendola family, and even after her son, their putative child, died.

Certainly, whenever possible, she reminded the French public about her liberal democrat saint, martyr and lover. In April 1933, she presented flowers as part of a leftist but non-communist international salute to Giovanni's tomb in Cannes. By then Giorgio was in a Fascist gaol. But the recent Nazi arrival in power in Germany, assisted by the rigidity of the Comintern's social fascist line, enhanced the number of men and women who joined in remembering Giovanni Amendola. In its report of the event, the moderate 'socialist and internationalist' Paris daily *Le Populaire* described Pavlova as 'Giovanni's faithful partner', while claiming that he had been a 'fervent republican'. Amendola, the paper added, had been as surely and vilely murdered by the Fascists as was Matteotti.[62]

Pavlova did publish one more book, which must have been her most successful since it appeared in a number of editions through the 1930s.[63] Focused on Romania, now ruled erratically by King Carol, it explored familiar themes. In the twelfth edition (1938), she drew an impressionist portrait of the country gained from a decade of visits and chats with a wide circle of the country's political and social elite. She waxed lyrical when, by now a sophisticated international journalist, who, in her work, had wracked up 676 air hours, she could look down on the blooming 'golden wheatfields' of Romania from her airplane.[64] She dedicated her study to Romanian 'peasant youth' and the country's 'intellectual elite', who, she declared, together bore the national soul in all its rich promise. She had every confidence that they were choosing to follow the path of 'democratic France' towards 'human progress, social justice and universal peace'.[65] Bucharest was, she stated in agreeable cliché, 'the most amiable, receptive and open capital city' in Central and Eastern Europe. Romania stood as 'the most advanced sentinel of western civilisation' in the East, still true to its participation on the French side in the First World War (during which it had annexed Bulgarian territory in the southern Dobruja).[66]

To be sure, there were tares in this paradise. Swarms of Italian and German businessmen were hawking their wares. The Iron Guard was a terrorist organisation, mimicking the murderousness of those blackshirts in Italy who had killed Matteotti, Amendola and the priest Don Giovanni Minzoni. Guardists had endeavoured to import Fascism, Nazism and antisemitism to a country where there were many Jews and where King Carol, despite his love of France and desire to be a constitutional monarch, had been driven to take greater power into his own hands.[67]

Pavlova did not just lob in and out of Bucharest but sought to explore the country, with her work and her private life mingling in her thoughts. In Brasov she bought a piece of local pottery to be reminded of 'the imperishable Giovanni Amendola', his tomb at Cannes and the unity of the Mediterranean.[68] In the Dobruja, she remembered her youth and the way in which the Romanians had, in 1913, begun to help deliver Bulgaria from 'the mad pride of Tsar Ferdinand de Cobourg, the sower of famine and desolation'.[69] She may have still been her father's girl (and beside the Danube she saluted Botev and the origins of Bulgarian nationalism). On her father's death in 1935 she had donated to the nation the house at Dolni Vadin, a small village near his crossing of the Danube in 1876 and where he had sometimes lived after 1907. Today, its administrative capital, Oryahovo, has a museum complex, partly dedicated to Mladen.[70]

Her Bulgarian background mattered to Nelia – a photograph exists of her dressed in Bulgarian peasant female garb in 1914 – but Amendola commanded her soul. At the beach at Costanza on her travels in 1938, she suddenly recalled: 'As for my dead love, I carry him always with me, night and day, in my solitary heart. Proudly I live through him; [I live] to serve him. My dead love is my strength, my being, my very life.'[71] Again, on her flight back to Paris, by now a little unsure whether Carol could save his country from 'the Nazi epidemic', she took comfort in the memory of her 'only love' and the France that was her 'adopted mother'.[72]

What, then, should be made of Nelia Pavlova's story in a situation where some details of her life, notably how, when and where the conception of her ill-fated son, probably Giovanni Amendola's illegitimate son, remain unknown? Was Amendola being fair, protective or just patriarchal when he told Albertini in January 1926 that 'Signora Pavlova' had no strong political commitments? After all, Amendola had never fully plumbed Eva Kühn's wide-ranging political enthusiasms, nor, despite early talk about deep mutual philosophising, did he make much attempt to build an intellectual partnership with her along his own political road. The surviving evidence indicates that, in his shorter relationship with Pavlova, he behaved in the same manner.

But, after his harrowing death, did Pavlova genuinely bear Amendola's political inheritance? The answer to this question is probably yes – and more directly than did his sons. It may be that Pavlova, although a woman of considerable analytical ability and an enemy of Mussolini, did not probe deeply into what Fascism meant, except that she knew that she must be Anti-Fascist. In that regard she did not conclude that communism was the only meaningful way of opposing Mussolini's dictatorship in the fashion that each of Amendola's legitimate sons (but not his daughter) did. Giovanni's ghost may well have applauded her opinion. Pavlova's politics remained somewhere on the moderate French Left, republican (she had reasons to bear a grudge against Victor Emmanuel III, as well as against King Ferdinand), and pleased that the 'people' were the heirs of the Great Revolution of 1789, loyal defenders of *liberté*. She gave less attention to *egalité*. As for *fraternité*, like her lover, she was a Eurocentric, if one whose attention fell on Eastern Europe and on 'modernising' Turkey (but not on imperial territories further afield).

In March 1939, again with a journalist's flare, she was staying in Prague between 18 and 23 March when Nazi forces marched in on 15 March to destroy the rump of the Czechoslovak state that had been left after the Munich conference. She wrote about their invasion at some length to Hristov, long her friend and mentor and a man who had spent his own time in Prague. She declared that she had cried her eyes out at the sight of the Nazi occupation of Czech libraries and other cultural sights. She was sure that the ghosts of 'Bismark [sic], Moltke and the philosophers, poets and jurists of great Germany' were appalled at Nazi inhumanity. It was time for democracies to toughen up, she wrote. They should 'restore hierarchies and discipline' in some version of a 'policy of National Health'. She admired the 'noble and wise' French Radical prime minister, Édouard Daladier, and approved his recent request for 'full power'. Perhaps, in her mind by then, he was the nearest figure in her circle to the somewhat authoritarian ideas of Giovanni Amendola.[73]

This was her last appearance in print. According to a Turkish source's 'guesstimate', she died in 1940, although it does not say exactly when, where or why (she was only forty-five).[74] But, unless other evidence is unearthed, it may be assumed to be true, especially since, when her mentor and friend Hristov perished from cancer in 1944, there is no last letter of condolence in their extensive correspondence nor had there been any other wartime exchange of letters.

What, then, should be concluded about the woman who was probably Giovanni Amendola's last lover? No doubt Pavlova's elite 'contacts' were an important support in her life as a journalist. Her willingness to hobnob with political chiefs and effusively report their views entailed her failing to ask critical questions about members of the ruling class in the Balkans or Turkey and their actual devotion to freedom. At times, her ready respect for strong men (but not Mussolini, of course) seemed to contradict her regard for *liberté*. Her escape was always to accept these leaders' claims that they had massive public support, without doing anything much to question their view.

Pavlova's comprehension of 'democracy' had its limits. Yet, throughout her life, Saint Giovanni, the martyr of liberal democracy, stood prominent and unchallenged in commanding her soul. As she often said, he was her all. It might be seen as shameful that the highly politically active sons of the Amendola family, and, for that matter, the numerous later historians of Fascism and Anti-Fascism, did not make, and have not made, more effort to grant her a place in resisting the Italian dictatorship.

In that regard, it is sadly typical that the standard biography, published by Alfredo Capone in 2013, to hail Giovanni Amendola as 'the founding father of Anti-Fascist liberal democracy', with a pious endorsement from President Giorgio Napolitano, a sometime client in the PCI of Giorgio, makes only one reference to Nelia.[75] Unexplained, she appears on the book's final page as 'Pavlova', attending Giovanni's deathbed at Cannes. Her first name is mistakenly given as 'Tatiana' in the index. So much for Napolitano's claims that Capone had produced 'a complete reconstruction of the figure and thought of Giovanni', one true to his positive influence on Giorgio.[76] Napolitano's and Capone's silence about Nelia Pavlova, her place in Giovanni's life, and the fate of their presumed son is deafening.

Through his life choice for communism, Giorgio Amendola was always aware, sometimes uneasily, of being *il figlio di un ministro* and not just any minister, but the murdered Giovanni, pure victim of Fascism. Under the Republic, as the years wore on, it became easier to forget Giovanni's anti-communism and the party's reciprocal dislike of the senior Amendola. Once upon a time, in his first serious article in *Stato Operaio* in 1931, Giorgio had stated that the Aventine had been merely 'a reactionary battle by classes who defended an economic system that is now visibly overcome by what has happened to capitalism' in the Depression.[77] In his new clothes as a young communist, at that time Giorgio felt a stronger filial duty to communist leader Palmiro Togliatti than he did to his own father. Eventually he papered over the division between his two 'fathers' and, throughout his life, he tried, at least verbally, to be loyal to each. Yet, during the 1930s, when it came to bearing Giovanni's liberal democrat heritage, rather simpler in her commitment (and devotion) was the Bulgarian-French journalist Nelia Pavlova.

5   Giorgio Amendola, 1907–43
True Love and Totalitarianisms (Italian-Style)

In Giorgio's memories of his bohemian early family life, books earn a major place. There were Giovanni's books, Eva's books, his books (Giorgio recalled being given a copy of the patriotic Risorgimento classic, Giuseppe Cesare Abba's *Diary*, for his eighth birthday, heavy going for a child of that age;[1] it had been posted to him by his father, absent at the front).[2] There were books everywhere, 'books shoved onto improvised book cases, the household's only riches'. They scattered across the Amendola couple's relatively modest flat at Via Paisiello 15, and Giorgio, still in elementary school, was charged by his busy and preoccupied parents first with dusting and later with cataloguing them. The Via Paisiello lay in a part of Rome already being converted into the upmarket Parioli zone of today's city. Yet, before the Great War, it retained a raffish air. The Futurist painter Giacomo Balla (1871–1958) inhabited a flat just down the road; his most celebrated work, *Dynamism of a Dog on a Leash*, was first exhibited in 1912. Italians apart, Eva cherished close connections with emigrants from the Romanov empire who washed up in Rome. Before 1917, they were likely to be self-conscious members of the intelligentsia, painters, writers, or 'old Russian princesses', living in 'asphyxiating shadow', 'whose hands', Giorgio knew, 'I had to kiss'. As his reading expanded, he learned more about their background from pages of his mother's favourite novelist, Dostoevsky; he sometimes proofread her translations.[3]

Giovanni and Eva, Giorgio and Ada had transferred to their new flat late in 1912, after years of nervy switching from one apartment to another, and from one city to another. Now Giovanni was drifting restlessly away from philosophy to political journalism.[4] The change meant a regular salary from *Il Resto del Carlino* and then *Il Corriere della Sera* and a deepening orthodoxy about his place in society – less bohemian, more bourgeois. But Eva was, if anything, growing more radical, with her past mystical religiosity morphing into a fascination with Futurism. She left the flat early each day on her own account, impervious to the respectable idea that she should stay at home and look after the

118

children. Giorgio, when still a small boy of five or six, remembered her taking him to the Caffè Aragno in the Via del Corso, until the 1950s the prime haunt of Rome's artists and intellectuals. He also accompanied Eva to the theatre and was her juvenile escort to any Futurist event being staged in the capital, no matter how unruly. Her mother-in-law and other senior Amendolas registered their disapproval. But Eva replied that 'it was good for a boy to start looking as soon as possible at whatever there was to see'.[5]

At that time, and for some years afterwards, Giorgio partially assumed the place of the frequently absent or preoccupied Giovanni in his parents' stressful marriage. In 1914–15, Eva and Giovanni did sometimes go to interventionist demonstrations together, cheering for Italy to join in the war against Austria-Hungary and Germany. Giorgio, turning seven, automatically embraced their Italian and/or Russian nationalism. Mostly it was Eva who led the way, introducing Giorgio to F. T. Marinetti, celebrated author of the *Futurist Manifesto* (1909). He was a frequent guest in the flat and, then or later, one of Eva's lovers. Giorgio also heard the orotund speechifying of Gabriele D'Annunzio, so much more traditional than the Futurists' feverishly clever wordplay. When Italy did enter the war on 24 May 1915, Eva took Giorgio to the Caffè Aragno deep into the night for flamboyant celebration, with much singing and toasting righteous victory.

Well before then, Eva's family in Vilnius had been forced by the arrival of German troops to flee to St Petersburg (Petrograd). From May 1915 both segments of the family were warring on the same side. Maybe Giovanni's role as an Allied officer restored the marriage. Eva, the two children and lots of cousins were transported to Livorno, patriotically to salute Lieutenant Amendola and his men when they marched off for initial training in March 1915 and then, in June, to the front. In that process, during May, Eva organised some days with Giovanni after he was posted to Padua. Then, as Giorgio narrates it, 'there must have been … a genuine reconciliation. In [February] 1916 Antonio was born.'[6]

When Eva had been afflicted by 'mental crisis' in 1914, Giovanni had enrolled Giorgio with English nuns at an elementary school on the Salita di San Sebastianello, between the Villa Medici and the Spanish Steps.[7] Giorgio recalls enjoying the slow trip there from the Via Paisiello in a horse-drawn carriage. He met Sergio Fenoaltea, to be his closest friend for a decade until they broke when Fenoaltea complained that Giorgio's opting for communism meant betraying Giovanni.[8] Yet some tie survived and Fenoaltea was Giorgio's partner walking up the stairs of the Propaganda Fide to find De Gasperi when the GAP bomb exploded on the Via Rasella on 23 March 1944. Fenoaltea's family were Piedmontese and so, in Giorgio's mind, 'ordered' by contrast with the '*picturesque bohème* of the Amendola house'.[9]

Suddenly, in spring 1917, Eva decided on a whim to cease renting in the Via Paisiello and, independently of Giovanni but with his acceptance of the move,[10] to take the children to Frascati, where there was a special hospital for blinded soldiers, one of her welfare passions. The family stayed for only a couple of months and then moved into a small hotel back in Rome where Giovanni joined them, so often in his war experience more a journalist than a fighting soldier. Giorgio heard whispered, anguished conversations between his parents over the near catastrophic defeat at Caporetto in October 1917 and how to save the nation thereafter. Soon the Amendolas learned of the contemporaneous Bolshevik revolution and its rejection by the great majority of Eva's family, who fled what was being rebranded Leningrad. Giorgio tried to impress each of his parents by reading *War and Peace* when still short of his tenth birthday (without knowing anything about Tolstoy's tortured views on marriage).

Meanwhile, a useful opportunity for housing was offered by the patriotic and soon Anti-Fascist Jewish mathematician Vito Volterra (although in his fifties, he had volunteered for war service in 1915). He knew of an available flat on the Via di Porta Pinciana. It was there that the final child in Eva's and Giovanni's marriage, Pietro, was born in October 1918 and there that the horror of Giovanni's confrontation with Fascism reached its first climax. It was there, too, that Giorgio entered his teens, with a memory that climbing up the six flights of stairs was hard work when he came home hungry, as he always was, from school.[11]

Giorgio had a high forehead, darkish unruly hair and big brown eyes but did not look so classically 'southern' as his father; few mistook him for an Indian god. He could appear dishevelled in a fashion to which his father never descended. Even at *liceo* Giorgio put on weight, as much fat as muscle, a process that continued in his twenties and beyond. He smiled more readily than did his father or his often pensive and self-absorbed mother; neither was much into fun.[12] As a youth, Giorgio enjoyed sport, whether football, boxing, cycling, swimming, diving, rowing or skiing, pursuits that spoke of the privilege of class and gender and that were unavailable to the vast majority of Italian workers, peasants and women.[13] His father had been too severe and reserved for sport, except that, still wearing his suit, he was often willing to give his eldest son a punch, or receive one from him, or to take him to watch boxing bouts. Much of the difference in male physical activity was generational. George Mosse, the German-American historian, recalled that his publisher father (born 1885) considered the act of breaking into a run as hideously undignified.[14] In Liberal Italy, Giovanni Amendola and his circle, let alone Benedetto Croce, were equally disapproving of athletic venture by men of their class.

In summer 1918, the heavily pregnant Eva took Giorgio on holiday to Capri. Giovanni typically stayed busy in Rome. Eva allowed the ten-year-old to run wild across the island, not yet homogenised and pasteurised by mass tourism. Giorgio remembered meeting Russian acquaintances of his mother; some defended the revolution, others deemed that it presaged the end of global civilisation. One young man, later a communist, taught him chess. But he also got to know girls and boys from working-class or fishing families on the island, gangs of whom clung to their own morality. Giorgio learned about Capri's wealthy homosexuals, 'always ready to offer boys a cake or a gelato'. He avoided them. But the Capresi boys and girls taught him about sex – in his phrasing, 'normal relations and abnormal ones' – and let him join in their 'collective masturbation'. Perhaps it is the respectable, elderly, communist author who adds quickly that it was on the island that he also first saw the nature of 'hard and even degrading' human work for poorer men, women and children. On Capri, the funicular was reserved for 'bathers and tourists'. All other goods had to be transported by hand. 'The girls who carried loads of coal made a great impression on me. Their faces were black and shining with sweat ... Every now and again they stopped to spread their thighs and piss like horses. The effort demanded of them was bestial ... The spectacle left me contemplating a confused and disturbing mixture of indecency and inhumanity.'[15]

His sense of release on Capri may have been greater because, in his first year of *scuola media* at the *ginnasio* Tasso in Rome, he failed outright, to be told in rebuke that he was a loafer who must repeat the year. To save him from such humiliation, his kind-hearted mother moved him to a Jesuit school beside the Piazza dei Cinquecento where he was tempted into contemplating the vocation and took to serving mass. His father, slow to detect what was happening to his son, was rankled by the news and forced him to transfer back to a state school. '*Basta con i preti*' (Enough of priests), he, although not especially anti-clerical, set down in chagrin as family policy.[16]

The war was coming to an end, with ambiguous and tarnished national victory declared at Vittorio Veneto on 4 November 1918. It did not bring content to the nation. D'Annunzio stood out in celebrity while maintaining that it amounted to a 'mutilated victory'. On one occasion Giorgio was charged to deliver a letter to him at the Grand Hotel, there breaching the coven of a little bald man, ensconced in a dark and smelly room and dressed in a silk gown. 'He took the letter and caressed my face with a

hand that seemed cold and wet and told me to say hello to my mother.'
Giorgio was relieved eventually to escape into the Rome sun.[17]

Over these years of the rise of Fascism, Italy was to experience a *biennio
rosso* (1919–20) and a *biennio nero* (1921–2). The Amendola parents were
anti-Marxist but divided on the best way forward. Eva now added a
young soldier patriot, Giuseppe Bottai, soon to become Mussolini's most
intellectualist (and starstruck) minister, to those special friends whom
she eagerly welcomed into the family flat.[18] But her avid ambition was to
get away to Milan, where Marinetti based himself and where, on
23 March 1919, a young ex-socialist journalist called Benito Mussolini,
whom she knew, had been proclaimed Duce of a new movement called
the Fasci di Combattimento. Giorgio and his sister, Ada, suddenly found
themselves transposed to upper-class boarding schools in Milan, where
the children of 'poor messy intellectuals, and, what was worse,
southerners', were badly received by classmates sprung from the industrial bourgeoisie or the 'Lombard provincial nobility'.[19] Eva, after a hotel
stay in central Milan proved too costly even for her, rented a house on
Lake Lugano, where she earned enough money to get by translating from
Russian.

Giorgio recalls that, most Saturdays, she showed up at his college to
drag him around town and eventually to a 'chattering and smoke-filled'
evening at Marinetti's place. She did not come on 16 November, election
day (down at Sarno, Giovanni was winning his seat in the Chamber),
when she was engaged in distributing propaganda for Mussolini's dis-
mally unsuccessful effort to enter parliament. When, immediately after
the election, Mussolini and Marinetti were (briefly) imprisoned on
the orders of Prime Minister Nitti for subversion, Eva carried a 'packet
of books and chocolates' to the pair at San Vittore gaol as 'proof of
solidarity'.[20]

In practice, Eva's politics were taking a chimerical twist, after an
accidental meeting with a local anarchist persuaded her that the path of
virtue lay with his movement's ideals. Giovanni, now an MP, did make it
to Lake Lugano for Christmas. Again, the Amendola parents reconciled,
although Eva and the children did not return to the Via di Porta Pinciana
until some months after the fall of Nitti's government and the end of
Giovanni's brief term as under-secretary for finance. For the
1920 summer holiday season, Giorgio – he had passed his exams this
time – was packed off to stay with a branch of the Donnarumma family in
a *paese* in the hills above Sarno. There he watched the 'somnolent' local
Liberal notables, every day congregated in their dingy club, 'talking
about hunting, playing endless and ruinous games of *scopa*, spending
long hours in their chairs slapping flies or recounting intricate and

imaginary stories of their conquest of females'. But he also gazed at the peasants at work, as on Capri, male and female, adults and children, but somehow less degraded than on the island. He noted in the village how they lived 'ten to a room, looking out onto dusty lanes full of animal excrement', yet they remained 'strong and generous'.[21] He was absorbing detail that could be fitted into ideology, when he could claim that Gramsci taught communism was best built on an alliance of workers, peasants and (sympathetic) intellectuals, no matter what their class.

Back in Rome, this time to stay throughout his father's years of Anti-Fascist struggle, Giorgio enrolled at the celebrated Liceo Visconti, where he encountered friends from all the (urban) classes and a 'democratic spirit' that broke down social differences. Many clouds, however, were gathering. In 1921, Eva and the children returned to Capri for an extended summer holiday, where Giorgio remembered playing with the sons of such later Fascist chiefs as Roberto Forges Davanzati and Alfredo Rocco; the latter was to take charge of creating the legal framework of the 'totalitarian state'. At that time, Giorgio also met Galeazzo Ciano, four years his senior, future husband of Edda Mussolini and, from 1936, Europe's youngest minister of foreign affairs.[22]

On 6 September 1921, Ada wrote to her father about Capri, reporting that her mother kept staring into the mirror to check if she was putting on weight and that little Pietro expected every docking boat to carry Giovanni back to the family.[23] It might have seemed humdrum news, but, in fact, Eva was in a bad way. She had decided that Luisa, Marchesa Casati, a slim figure who lived in a more opulent villa nearby, was plotting against her. The by now debt-ridden Casati was a some-time lover of D'Annunzio and a woman who had provoked fascination in the European, and especially British, artistic world. In Giorgio's memory, Eva howled through the night against her as 'the personifica-tion of evil'. The fourteen-year-old Giorgio had to step up as head of the family, until, following two days of his mother in delirium, Giovanni arrived from his work life in Rome and escorted Eva to a clinic in Naples. For the whole month of October, Giorgio was left in that city to observe his mother's health, bringing her cakes and cheer before they all reassembled in Rome, to find the capital ever more brutalised by squadrism.[24]

In the late summer of 1922, Eva was absent on her troubled trip back to Vilnius, getting back in September with the national crisis visibly deepening.[25] After her homecoming, she entered a nursing home, the Casa di Cura Santa Rosa at Viterbo.[26] During school holidays, Giorgio, who, it was feared, might have a weak heart, stayed alone – his siblings sent elsewhere – with his Uncle Mario and Aunt Palmira in Naples. Palmira, a Roman from Trastevere, had been chosen as a young woman by the local paper in an early beauty contest; she had claims to have been the first 'Miss Italy'. Giorgio's niece, Antonella, remembers how beautiful she was even when eighty years old.[27] It is not clear if Giorgio, with his own adolescent fixations, noticed. He was examined by various doctors who gave rival estimations of his health. Eventually, at the age of seventy-two, he was to die from cardiac weakness, but he lived an active life until then; in 1922, he countered negative medical rumours by energetic swims in the sea or a local thermal pool.

Once again, he had not starred at school. In July, Giovanni wrote to complain to Eva about Giorgio's latest exam failures, which had been punished by his being forced to eat alone in his room for a week.[28] Giovanni remained a cold and distant parent, banning any member of his family from making use of a ministerial car while he held the ministry of colonies under Facta, and rejecting suggestions from Donnarumma that Giorgio might learn a lot from accompanying his father on Giovanni's journey to Libya in June. Even in August 1925, at Chamonix for a while, en route to his first operation in Paris, Giovanni found time to send his eldest son a monitory letter. Giorgio, he wrote, must be disciplined into rising at 6 a.m., studying from 6.30 a.m. to 10 a.m., and in the afternoon from 3 p.m. to 6 p.m. He must be in bed by 10 p.m. Only thus could he 'consolidate the bases of his wobbling and approximate culture'. As the eldest son, he must never cease to be a guide to his siblings and keep a constant eye on his mother's comfort and condition.[29]

Late in 1922, with the gaining of power by Mussolini and his Fascist squads, change was coming for one who had often been a mother's boy. Soon, Giorgio entered a more adult role, backing his father's Anti-Fascism as it hardened and drifted leftwards while remaining patriotic, monarchist and liberal. At least in so far as the evidence inscribed in his autobiography in old age is concerned, a narrative designed to explain how he became a 'national communist', Giorgio, still only fourteen, made a personal statement on how a man-child should confront Fascism. He did so on the afternoon and evening of 31 October 1922, the day when the Fascists marched through the Italian capital in celebration of their 'revolution'. Giorgio and his friend Fenoaltea, who was five months his senior, wandered around the city streets restively watching events, noting dejectedly how the king and queen saluted the victors from the Quirinal palace balcony. The two disgusted schoolboys knew that the Fascists were *canaille who could* easily have been dispersed by a whiff of grapeshot.

What were they to do? Why not try the brothel in the Via Capo le Case, not far from the Spanish Steps, their juvenile machismo suggested? They found the place crowded, 'because the blackshirts, in homage to their festa, had won the right not to pay the fee. It was my first time. The dark-haired girl who welcomed me was particularly kind when she knew that I was not one of them: "Having had to go with so many *mascalzoni* [shits], I'm content finally to have a clean boy,"' she confided. It had been, in more than one sense, a day to remember. As Giorgio stated in his autobiography, 31 October 1922 marked the 'end of my [scatty] adolescence'.[30]

He was young to be making this sea change. But, according to his later construction of his personal history, one drastic event toppled over another. In 1923, he turned sixteen, just after the devastation of the Nitti villa and the departure of Filomena to Paris and just before his father's first major bashing. In 1924, the publication by *Il Mondo* of the Rossi memorandum occurred soon after his seventeenth birthday, followed by Mussolini's declaration of dictatorship. In the following summer came the Scorza-led death-dealing assault on his father. When his father died in Cannes in April 1926, Giorgio was eighteen; his father's friends (and family patrons) viewed him as the new head of the family, with the rights and duties that the position entailed.

Giorgio had lived his father's tragedy, acting on occasion as his junior lieutenant. After the grim beating in 1925, there were moments of intimacy. Giovanni took to regaling him with melancholy accounts of his poverty in his youth and the fact that he had not been able to buy all the books he wanted, half apologising for his 'closed and gloomy charac-ter'.[31] Throughout his life, despite the different path that he took, Giorgio never forgot that he was Giovanni's son – nor that he was Eva's. Certainly, his schooling at the Liceo Visconti shaped him, as did his class base, but family life, however unsettled, retained a deep influ-ence. Giorgio had read widely in the classics of European literature, notably in Russian and French, at least the latter in the original language. He had scanned quite a bit of Risorgimento history and was proud of his paternal and maternal grandfathers' connections to Garibaldi and Mazzini.

Yet a literary culture and a taste for history were not all that he had learned. While, in his youth, his sombre father was seeking the reli-gious or philosophical meaning of life in study or library, young Giorgio, untethered by parental control, had eagerly explored the back streets of Rome and Milan and was becoming ever more familiar with Naples. He had seen up close, perhaps too close for comfort, the heights of the Italian intelligentsia. Yet, unlike his father, he had recognised what life meant for male and female workers and peasants, and he knew of their *miseria*, family bonds and culture. When, after graduating, he did compulsory military service at Viterbo, an accommodating officer engaged him in wide-ranging political discussion and permitted him to explore the past socialism of peasant ordinary soldiers from the Po Valley, another sector of the country with which he acquired familiarity.[32] Whereas Giovanni and Eva always wrote to each other in French (Nelia Pavlova did the same) and sought to plumb the works of Dostoevsky and Tolstoy, Schopenhauer, Henry George and William James, Giorgio followed an Italian path towards maturity, a track more practical, realistic and humane than that of his parents.

In 1923, Giorgio had had to fight for his cause – or rather, his father's cause – against pro-Fascist fellow pupils or milling squadrists, assembled menacingly in the square outside the Liceo Visconti. That summer, Giovanni took his son into a small specialist shop in Rome and bought him his own version of a *manganello*, 'a fine heavy leather stick reinforced with steel'.[33] Giorgio discovered ways to use it on a number of occasions: for example, outside parliament on the morning of 3 January 1925. He was wearing a purple tie, conscious as a convinced anti-communist that it 'had nothing of proletarian red' about it. But Fascist thugs accused him of socialism and demanded that he pull it off. A running brawl resulted up and down the Rome Galleria, across the road from the Chamber of Deputies.[34] He must have been a known figure, Giovanni Amendola's sturdy son, because Carabinieri intervened, bundled him into a taxi and directed him back to the family flat.[35]

Over the next weeks, he observed his father cast down by events but 'less severe and gruff, more affectionate' with his children. That did not mean that he indulged in any favouritism, leaving Giorgio to stew through a night in the cells following his arrest when, as a member of the Unione Goliardica per la Libertà, and, as so often, in association with his friend Fenoaltea, he was caught distributing Anti-Fascist pamphlets in the city centre. In his memoirs, Giorgio added with family propriety that he behaved the same way when his own daughter, another Ada, got into trouble at demonstrations in Naples and Rome in the 1950s and 1960s.[36] Despite his many setbacks, Giovanni still campaigned against Fascism.[37] When, in spring 1925, he spoke in favour of the freedom of the press in the Chamber, on leaving the building to return home, he was surrounded by armed blackshirts but defended by Giorgio and his friends in what became another brawl. Giorgio remembered being crestfallen when the police seized and kept his steel and leather stick.[38]

By then, Giovanni's fate was sealed. Giorgio had been unable to do anything about the beating in Tuscany. The two operations in France failed to save Giovanni from his dying hours in Cannes. Giorgio heard his father's final words and absorbed his last will and testament. He listened when Albertini and other rich, generous but defeated friends of his father told him to work hard, be serious and accrue sufficient money to sustain his siblings and mother. But through 1926–8 Giorgio stiffened in his resolve to become fully independent and find his own way to be an activist Anti-Fascist. Communism beckoned.

Giorgio, who turned twenty-one at the end of 1928, had determined by then fully to break free from what he ironically called his 'super-tutors': Albertini, Croce, Fortunato and the rest. He similarly wanted to be independent of Uncle Mario, yet another new baby cousin, and his unresponsive sister Ada, sedulously devoted to her university medicine course and seemingly blind to politics.[39] In spring 1929, Giorgio fled the household on the Vomero, gaining employment that he enjoyed in a Naples bookshop.[40] Before too long he was persuaded to return to his uncle's house. But, at the end of the year, he joined the communists, without telling Mario (or Ada). Little over a year later, he deserted the family nest in a more drastic fashion than had occurred when he departed to the bookshop. Now he left for Paris and PCdI headquarters. He had set out on a path that meant loyalty to party leader, Palmiro Togliatti, who became a sort of new and communist father to him. Giorgio's move also entailed a decade of service to more or less orthodox communism, with a concomitant obedience to Stalinism.

Yet Giorgio was never a simple party cadre. To some extent, he always remained the bourgeois, athletic but bookish son of Giovanni and Eva. He may have tried loyally to 'believe, obey and fight' for international communism (to redeploy the well-known Fascist slogan), but communist totalitarianism did not fully occupy his soul. In his private life, he retained his own mind. He remained an Italian rather than a rootless cosmopolitan as a Marxist, especially as one with intellectual habits and ambitions was meant to be. When not fully engaged by party work, he happily took to the back streets of Paris as once he had done in Milan and Naples. For Giorgio, much loved Paris was for ever the city of 1789 and of the combative and victorious working class, the city of romance and passion, spiritual and physical, for ever the capital of the Revolution. In his eyes, it mattered much more than distant, unknown, cold Leningrad or Moscow could ever do.

Did he reflect that the father from whom he had turned away had been, like Robespierre, another 'sea-green incorruptible' whose liberalism had proved too pure for the people? Certainly, Giorgio, more tumultuous in his life than austere, delighted in locating squares and settings that he had read about in Duhamel, Rolland, Barbusse and the novelists of the 1920s, and that he had seen depicted by Modigliani or the impressionists.[41] He tried to avoid old and stuffy friends of his family, knowing that many were appalled by his conversion to communism. He did bump into Filomena Nitti, who was accompanied by a 'tall, strong, fair-haired young man. I realised that he was her husband'; in January 1931, she had married the Polish-Jewish communist journalist and historian Stefen Walter Freund, who had also taken sanctuary in Paris. Filomena had joined the party in 1930, but now the three acted as though they scarcely knew each other, lest some spy be watching. When Filomena walked away, Giorgio recalled, 'I was full of emotion, a whole period of my youth was definitively over,' and so was the chance for what would have been a family-blessed marriage.[42] In 1936, in unforgiving Moscow, Filomena's connubial relationship within the party broke down. She returned to Paris, working at the Institut Pasteur with Daniel Bovet, soon her second husband. Speedily she became his indispensable and brilliant scientific partner.[43]

Giorgio, handsome and ready in his memory to narrate himself as an Italian lover, claimed that he found plenty of accommodating partners among the Parisian girls of his age. Love sessions with them, he maintained, took place between equals – unlike in Naples, where class and dialect difference, and female illiteracy, left him feeling like a master having sex with slaves. 'I was always "*il signorino*" and that gave sexual relations a servile and degrading character that seemed humiliating also for me,' he mused.[44]

By summer 1931, the party had found him accommodation in a flat on the Rue Gutenberg in the fifteenth arrondissement, not far from the Seine. He loved his surroundings, rejoicing in mingling every day with workers from the nearby Citroën and Renault production lines. He was especially elated as 14 July approached. Confirming his sense of place, the local population organised night after night of popular celebrations of 'Revolution' in the Place Beaugrenelle. A succession of bands or orchestras played. On warm evenings, families consumed their food and wine on the grass. Young people met, talked and flirted. Any who wanted could dance. 'There was a sort of ceremony to invite girls whom you did not know' to join you. No doubt, he later noted with deliberate banality, 'I was an Italian and therefore not a recommendable type where relations with ladies were concerned.' But young women were generous to the tall, smiling, friendly foreigner, so happy to be in Paris. A dentist's assistant named Dominique, 'beautiful and willing', especially liked his company. For the hot evening of 12 July, they made an appointment to meet at

10 p.m.[45] However, when he stumbled among the crowd looking for her, Giorgio was disappointed. He had arrived an hour late, held up by an earnest party restaurant meal with Longo and his elders. By the time he appeared, Dominique had found other entertainment.

Giorgio searched out a substitute. 'It was then that my gaze fell on Germaine ... young, elegant, slim, a little bewildered.' With her was an older, taller, severe-looking woman, her mother, Hélène Augustine Lecocq. They had emerged from a cinema facing the square. Giorgio drew the impression that Germaine wanted to dance but her mother preferred to go home. He dashed over, automatically being *il figlio di un ministro* as he clicked his heels and bowed to Mme Lecocq, while requesting her permission for a dance with Germaine. He bought Madame a beer and plonked her down at a table so she could watch the young people. Giorgio and Germaine then joined the dancing couples of working-class Paris.

It was a fast waltz, hard for me who did not know how to turn with such a rapid rhythm. Beside me young proletarians did miracles. I was enchanted by the attraction of my partner, with her beauty not at all bold or tricked up, but reserved and modest. Her clear, clean face slowly revealed its irresistible appeal. Her hands slender and dry suggested the grace of her soul and heart. Animated as though freed from an old burden, her eyes lit by a flame, she clung to my arms with unwavering trust, her body agile and firm. It was love at first sight, not that of a cheap romance, but the very basis of our life. Forty-nine years have gone past. I write. She paints. We grow old together. But all began then on that hot evening of a popular festival.

Or so, in their mutual old age and just before their all but mutual deaths, Giorgio portrayed the meeting.

When the music of the first dance stopped, Giorgio virtuously took Germaine back to her mother. Germaine was half a head shorter than him and neither then nor later approached his girth. Photographs show her to have had naturally curly hair. Mother did not object when the two considered another dance. Worldly-wise, Giorgio slipped over to the band and gave them a tip so they could play a slower tango, which he had learned years before on Capri. Another tip, two more slow dances. He and Germaine were ever more entranced; she melted into his arms. When, in the early morning, it was finally time to leave, he, still a gentleman, escorted Germaine and her mother back to their flat, which, it turned out, lay around the corner from his own. Germaine, he learned, was two years his junior. Hélène was a war widow from Bruay-en-Artois, near the border with Flanders. Her socialist unionist miner husband, a real worker, had been killed fighting for France in the early months of the First World War. She had moved to Paris to save her son, Charles, from heavy and dangerous work underground. Currently, he was doing military service, but afterwards he made a good living as a hairdresser for women. Mme Lecocq kept the family going as a dressmaker, a family activity that Germaine shared. A purist Marxist might have defined the Lecocqs as working class with developing petit bourgeois overtones.

On the next night, after an approving signal from Hélène, Giorgio and Germaine danced again. On the Sunday afternoon, they went for a stroll together, stopping on the island in the Seine by the Pont Mirabeau. 'This time, Germaine talked, showed what she was like, I got to know her. We talked for hours and hours. We finished the evening at the *bar-tabac* in Place Mirabeau. Time slipped by without either of us noticing. When we got back to her home it was already dark and Mme Lecocq had been getting worried.'[46] But that day had ensured that her virgin working-class daughter and the sexually experienced, culturally sophisticated, bourgeois communist Giorgio were partners.

Like Giovanni (whether with Eva or Nelia), Giorgio had chosen as his companion a woman who was not Italian. It was to prove a far less intellectually and physically vexed relationship than Giovanni's. But the path of Giorgio and Germaine did not yet run smooth. Given Giorgio's political commitments, after the mutual ecstasy of their first meetings, more challenging times lay ahead for the couple as Paris and the rest of Europe in the 1930s lurched from one crisis to the next.

Giorgio was still only twenty-three but Togliatti esteemed him a prime addition to the PCdI. Even among communists, the Amendola name held cachet. Shortly before Giorgio's meeting with Germaine, Togliatti had sent him to Cambridge to meet sympathetic economist Piero Sraffa.[47] In what Giorgio in his autobiography identifies as 'July', without clarifying whether before or after the first dance with Germaine, he also travelled to Berlin on party business to do with the ambiguous role of a Sezione Alleati del Proletariato (SAP, Allies of the proletariat branch), in which he had been assigned a leading role. SAP may or may not have been pursuing leftist unity, despite the official line rejecting 'social fascism'. The Stalinist view, presumably the ruling one, was that its key purpose was in reality to divide and disconcert such non-communist Anti-Fascist bodies as the Rosselli brothers' liberal democrat Giustizia e Libertà. Giorgio also remembered, in what may have been old-age Byronic mode, somewhat contradicting his sentimental account of blooming true love with Germaine, that, when he stayed at a local *pensione*, 'the very young and attractive maid entered my room, and, without being asked, stripped naked and lay down on my bed. I did not know how I could refuse so independent and comely a girl.'[48]

In November 1931, now equipped with a false identity and proud in his clandestinity, he travelled to Turin, Pavia and Milan, contacting old friends from his student days, with the official and still ambiguous task of forging some sort of unity between his party and supporters of Giustizia e Libertà, Republicans and socialists. Realising that the Fascist secret police were on his tail, he dodged them by catching an express train to Zurich and was back in Paris by early December. There, he found a cold reception from Longo, who was a purist defender of the official 'no alliance with social fascists' line, which had such a devastating effect on European politics.[49]

Party discussions apart, Giorgio had his private life to consider. Before his November trip he went back to see Germaine (the party had moved him to the periphery of Paris, far from the Lecocq flat). Their relations remained chaste. But Germaine began to want to know who this man of hers was. Stretched out in late autumnal sunshine in the Bois de Boulogne, she asked to see his passport but was fobbed off when he told her that she was showing a lack of faith in him. Just as well, he remembered, since he was carrying a fake passport that claimed he was a building worker, married with four children. He and Germaine continued to enjoy the cinema, often with Mme Lecocq in their company. As a twosome, they walked interminably around Paris to see the famous sites, whose historical background Giorgio bookishly knew. Germaine also began to read with something like Giorgio's seriousness; he bought her novels by Balzac and Zola. 'We spent hours in cheap restaurants, each reading, one next to the other, our own books.' They went dancing. They did tourist trips to Versailles and Fontainebleau. Germaine was a working-class young woman happy to receive intellectual training from her man.

But there was a third in their relationship: the party. Giorgio was spotted at a screening of *Battleship Potemkin*. Who was the girl, comrades asked, whom he had his arm so intimately around? When he replied that their relationship was serious, censorious elders told him that it was impossible given the illegality of his presence in Paris. But, as usual, Togliatti was more indulgent, emphasising in paternal tones that, as party chief, he held no veto, but Giorgio should remember to behave responsibly, whether to the girl or to the party. Giorgio decided that it was finally time to admit to her who he was, what he did, and what he was likely to do. In telling Germaine about his real life, he was sure that he would have the backing of Mme Lecocq.[50]

In June 1932, again the party required him to cross the dangerous Italian border. Before leaving, he went to consult Mme Lecocq; Germaine was away at a cousin's wedding at their home village. He told her mother all (or almost all). He wanted to marry Germaine, he declared, but could not do so for the present. When next he came back (he claimed to be going to Brussels), he would propose and they could live together. Mme Lecoq signalled her approval and said not to worry too much about legal forms. Giorgio promised to return to Paris 'within a month'.

But would he, he wondered?[51] He was right to confess doubts. It was another two years before he and Germaine saw each other. Then they would marry and have sex for the first time on the Fascist prison island of Ponza off the coast of Naples. Mme Lecocq would join them there.

Giorgio left Paris on 3 June. He travelled via Montreux, where a meeting had been arranged with the pacifist Romain Rolland, who had written regretting Giovanni's death, although in approaching such a famous writer Giorgio may have recalled his mother and her friends. Rolland was old and sick, not fully receptive of Giorgio's earnest plea for another public manifestation of intellectual Anti-Fascism. Having drawn a blank with that tie, Giorgio crossed the border to Milan. There, on the morning of 5 June, he injudiciously made a phone call that alerted the secret police to his arrival. Later that day, he was arrested, interrogated at San Vittore prison, dumped in solitary confinement, but not tortured.

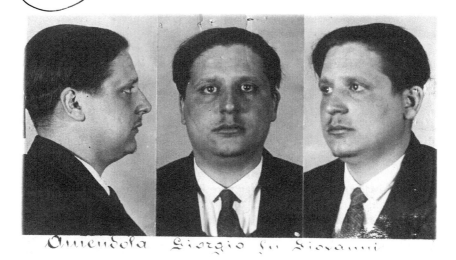

Figure 5.1 Police image of Giorgio at Poggioreale prison (1935).

He remembered that Milan prison soup was OK, better than Rome, while in Naples it was worst – a droll example of the national 'southern problem'. A priest librarian gave him access to Manzoni's *The Betrothed*, other nineteenth-century classics, the *Iliad* and *Odyssey*, and *La Gazzetta dello Sport*, but not more serious or contemporary publications. He was also allowed to write to Uncle Mario, to whom he stated he had become engaged, gave Germaine's Paris address and asked for her to be told his fate. The letter was censored but, meanwhile, the party had got the story of his arrest to Mme Lecocq. His sister, Ada, could also write to his gaol and give him family news.[52]

On 30 June, Giorgio was transferred to 'Rome and Regina Coeli prison, just behind the Palazzo Corsini, where, decades before, his grandfather had worked to establish the family in the capital. Giorgio stayed in isolation for eleven months. He was troubled by wet dreams, he recalled, but tried to keep his cell as clean as possible (and free of fleas). Now he could read travel literature, the Fascist popular, colonialist and racist writer Mario Appelius,[53] and the establishment journal *Nuova Antologia*, edited by Luigi Federzoni, who, in 1922, had succeeded Giovanni as minister of colonies. Giorgio was pent up in solitary silence but not in the vicious, death-dealing manner familiar in the USSR or as was to come in Hitler's Germany. To his dismay, Giorgio belatedly heard the news of Hitler's gaining of the chancellorship on 30 January 1933 (partially assisted by the communist 'social fascist' line of no alliances). He drew on his literary knowledge for solace, claiming with what might seem intellectual pomposity that Schiller's *Don Carlos* helped him comprehend German tyranny.[54] In Fascist imprisonment, he remained a communist and the child of parents of high culture.

For a while he was not sent before the judges of the special tribunal from whom he was expecting a sentence of twenty years. Instead, from time to time, Guido Leto, third in charge of the secret police, dropped into his cell for a chat. Flatteringly, he claimed to have read and appreciated Giorgio's first serious article as a communist, published by *Stato Operaio* in 1931 (then his hand had been guided by Togliatti, whose severity and austerity reminded him of Giovanni, and by Ruggero Grieco, who, he later wrote, had corrected his piece like a professor).[55] Giorgio recalled that Leto, as a 'well-informed, cultivated and intelligent' bureaucrat, also knew about Giorgio's essay,[56] but he was not rude enough to underline that it was markedly critical of Giovanni Amendola and the Aventine Secession.[57] Instead, Leto, while also seeking information on his friends and contacts, tartly assured Giorgio that he had chosen a losing side, since Fascism had much to be said for it and was the cause of the future.[58]

From within the family, news was sparse. Ada's dry letters gave little cheer, even though soon she graduated from her medical studies in Naples (in 1933–4) with a first-class degree and wrote brightly to Albertini about how dedicated she was to medicine. She planned to move back to Rome – 'my city' – and do the exams for a state job (for which she did not add that she would need Fascist Party membership).[59] On her own initiative, when she had almost finished her studies and Giorgio was in prison, Ada took her mother away from the nuns and, for the rest of Eva's life, she remained close to her 'mammina' (little Mummy), as she called her.[60] Ada grew into a solid and formidable-looking bourgeois woman. At the moment of her release, Eva, too, wrote to Albertini to thank him for his years of financial support. She stated that she had only learned of the death of her 'adored husband' from an article she had read in L'Illustrazione Italiana in 1930. She had 'suffered much' but now intended to live in the interests of her children, 'whose affection is my only consolation'. Ada had been a great help but 'the fate of my first born causes me much anguish', she noted. But now she could, with Ada's help, go back to work as a translator.[61]

With what may have been sisterly malice, Ada told Giorgio that Antonio and Pietro were doing much better at school than he had done but disclosed few other personal details to their much older brother. Germaine, too, wrote succinctly, even if Giorgio did maintain in his autobiography that every message from her brought a 'breath of hope'.[62] The news that he could glean from Nuova Antologia about politics in Germany and the rest of Europe was dire.

Still, something was happening. Uncle Mario, who was now living in the family villino (modest villa) in the Via Sant'Alessio on the Aventine, had obtained permission to see him. The concession disclosed much about the survival of unspoken assumptions in Fascist Italy, at least among the respectable classes. Second in charge of the secret police was Carmine Senise, a Neapolitan.[63] His father, like Giorgio's grandfather, had been a Garibaldian. They had fought together against papal troops at Mentana in 1867. It was said that Pietro Paolo Amendola had then heroically saved the life of Tommaso, Carmine's father. In Italy, one good turn deserved another, even under totalitarianism. Parcels came through from Germaine in Paris, an over-large sweater that she had knitted, some biscuits she had cooked; prison regulations, which the perpetually hungry Giorgio called cruel, allowed him to consume only one. In fact, the Roman prison diet (without outside exercise) pushed his weight up from 94 to 104 kilograms in ten months.

In March 1933, the news arrived that Giorgio did not have to face the special tribunal in person. Rather, he was to be moved to the prison island of Ponza and be 'confined' there for five years (not twenty).[64] While awaiting transfer, he was no longer kept in 'solitary' at Regina Coeli and could mix with the other prisoners. But best was the information that it seemed possible for Germaine to join him on the island and for the two to be married.

Receiving the good news in Paris, she busied herself to obtain needed permissions and papers, impressing Giorgio with her capacity for work and attention to detail. As he remarked sententiously in his autobiography: 'Love is not exclusively a physical matter but a much denser relationship, a meeting of very many matters, physical certainly but also sentimental and moral.'[65] After a brief stay at Poggioreale prison in Naples, much the worst in terms of conditions – he found it filthy, with blood from fleas all over the walls and sleep impossible – he was on a ferry to Ponza.

He had more than a year to wait for his French bride. While that time slowly passed, Giorgio took his place as just another comrade among the communists imprisoned on the island. The months allowed the longest, deepest and most direct contact Giorgio, the bohemian and bourgeois intellectual, had had, or would have, with the working class.

One of the sillier clichés of totalitarianist theorists is that such regimes utterly atomise their populations and especially their prisoners. Primo Levi, in what is the greatest book of the twentieth century, demonstrated that this was not true, even in the ultimate hell of Auschwitz. In that place of total death, love and competition lingered, as did a variety of capitalism.[66] Ponza had long been a place of imprisonment; Nero Caesar, brother of the Emperor Caligula, was executed there in 30 CE. Fascist administration could be ruthless, but, in 1933, as far as communists were concerned, its rule was loose and distant, while the chance for special deals flourished.

Communist party control was perhaps more evident than Fascist. Everyday life was decided – strictly and, in theory, collectively – by the prisoners obeying processes and behaviour that fitted the party line. Here, for Giorgio, there was no repetition of the careless family life of

his youth or even the bourgeois discipline of Uncle Mario. For a while he did try to look like a worker, by following the proletarian fashion of only shaving once per week.[67] For Italian males, the amount of stubble on a chin was a major class marker.

Class had other ramifications. In his autobiography, Giorgio tells of arriving on Ponza to be greeted by a canteen, grocery, coffee shop and barber, each in communist hands. All, he decided, illustrated the rich cooperative experiences of Tuscany and the Emilia, where pre-communist socialism had flourished before 1914. The islanders were readily persuaded by the cheap fixed prices and good quality of food or service to become customers, too. Even the police bought 'communist'.

Beyond daily consumption needs, tailors and cobblers proffered their services. So did a laundry, illustrating another tile in the complex mosaic of the 'southern problem' (and predictable sexism). Female prisoners, whether wives or companions, washed, ironed and repaired the clothes of the males. Northerner women could be relied on to press shirts or trousers tidily. The same could not be said for southerners from families where poverty had never required clothing to be trim or neat. When comrades jostled to win northern attention, the party had to intervene to prevent quarrelling. It also patrolled meal arrangements. All took turns to help the cook, while seating arrangements were strictly based on when a prisoner had reached the island. Here, at least in what may have been Giorgio's gilded memory, was the ordered little world of socialism, Ponza style.[68]

It was known that Giorgio planned to get married and so he was not at once placed into the groups of couples and singles; each had different fees to pay at the canteen. Any money that arrived from relatives in Italy was added to a common pot and distributed according to need. Giorgio was told emphatically that, as *il figlio di un ministro*, he would be dealt with rigorously and therefore by implication expected to pay rather than to take.

Yet, with a certain softness, he was given charge of the library and required to teach a course in modern Italian history, assisted by two working-class tutors, whose real role was to supervise him. The 1933 version of history, he remembered, was obliged to dismiss Mazzini and Garibaldi as 'social fascists' from the past. In 1934, following a switch in the party line, he could restore his sense of family honour by present-ing a Risorgimento with positive aspects for the people; Mazzini and Garibaldi were again national heroes. As librarian (and Eva's son), he took pains to school young communist readers in Turgenev and Tolstoy, Balzac, Victor Hugo and Dickens. He wrote to editors of journals and reviews on the mainland, requesting free copies of their publications, among them the leading historical journal, *Nuova Rivista Storica*. Most obliged, presumably impressed by being approached by an Amendola. The secret police, however, banned Croce from sending his works.

Ponza was not quite an arcadian paradise. Fascism could always decide to stiffen its control. And Giorgio, son of Giovanni, was not a man to take a step back when challenged. So, a squabble in the library with an anti-communist follower of Giustizia e Libertà – the place was meant to be open to all prisoners – caused Giorgio and four working-class comrades to be arrested and charged with assault. The matter was held over for the time being, but the authorities exploited the dispute to clamp down on communist privileges. It was time to stop comrades taking over much of the island's commercial life. As a result of such interference, the member of the communist hierarchy who had the task of observing Giorgio now instructed him to send in his name a com-plaining telegram (collectively composed) to Mussolini. The party intention was to provoke arrests and a public trial with resultant publi-city in Naples.[69]

Despite the island commandant's unsuccessful attempt to dissuade him from so quickly causing annoyance on high, Giorgio was arrested again. As planned, his comrades then protested vociferously. In punish-ment, a number of them were sent on a rough sea trip to Naples and shut in Poggioreale to await trial. In that unlovely place, strict egalitarianism was the rule. When Giorgio wrote to Germaine, using a stamp that was more costly than for local mail, he was informed that his comrades had extracted the expense from the mutually agreed sum. As a result, he had to go without food supplementary to the prison diet for a few days. Mutterings could be heard that he was 'a petit bourgeois, an individual-ist, an egoist'. In the USSR, such accusations could be lethal. However, Giorgio later reckoned that, in Naples, he won his proletarian fellows around by good-humoured reference to his size – even though he had reduced his girth preparatory to Germaine's arrival. Was he not a *grosso borghese* (fat bourgeois), he laughed?[70] He had his uses, too. Helped by eminent lawyers who had known his father and by a legal system that still functioned to some extent in a Liberal fashion, Giorgio and his friends had the case of riot against them dismissed and were sent back to Ponza. While he was in the courtroom, it was perfectly possible to salute family and old friends.

With the New Year of 1934, Giorgio heard wonderful news from Paris. Germaine, having completed the paperwork but also having had her case expedited following a friendly chat between Uncle Mario and Senise, was on her way. PCdI propaganda made her fear that she was going to Devil's Island or some other torture chamber. As Giorgio remarked in old age, 'material conditions were not too bad' on Ponza, whatever the psychological damage inflicted by imprisonment and the fitful behaviour of the regime and its officials. Poor peasant (*braccianti*) prisoners managed to send some of their meagre gaol stipend (ten lire per day, then cut to five) home to their families in deprived areas such as Puglia.[71] They were communist victims of Fascism, but also tough and resilient emigrants, who knew in their bones how to make do on a pittance, and they were committed both to party and to family.

Germaine as yet had no Italian. Perhaps the hardest part of her journey, Giorgio recalled, was a week's stay with Mario and the rest in the house on the Aventine, the heavy food and whispered malicious gossip about her as a poor, ordinary girl and a foreigner. Aunts rattled on that Giovanni had married a stranger, too, with the implication that his fate had not been a happy one. She did find sympathy from young Antonio, just eighteen and the liveliest and most independent member of the family. He went with her to Gaeta, helping to load her luggage on board the steamer to Ponza.

There, on 30 June, she finally arrived, off-puttingly under the eyes of all, Fascists and communists. Giorgio was something of an island celebrity but she looked like a 'fragile teenager'. Too aware of watching eyes, they embraced with some embarrassment; she held back tears. They had been apart for two years.

Confino was the major punishment system in Fascist Italy; in all, 12,330 were condemned to it, 700 in total on Ponza. Communists were always the main target. Its provisions could be harsh – 177 died under its rule.[72] Yet, it was never as tyrannical as were imprisonment practices in Nazi Germany or the USSR, while, by its very existence, it decreed that some parts of the nation were best avoided. Prisoners were sent south or to obscure villages or barren islands in a way that denied the key Fascist argument that they ruled over a seamlessly united nation. It is also true that Liberal Italy had 'confined' both criminals and those who endeavoured to overthrow its rule, and, after 1946, the Italian Republic did not at once abandon the practice.

Insofar as life on Ponza under Fascism was concerned, a number of privileges and opportunities survived (as did an ever present hope of amnesty). Married prisoners, for example, were allowed to rent island cottages, so long as they stood open to police inspection.[73] In the case of Giorgio and Germaine, Fascist gaze reached into their bedroom. There was an outside toilet, inaccessible at night when the doors had to be locked. But the home allotted to Giorgio boasted a magnificent view over the Tyrrhenian sea. Furthermore, for the day of their being reunited, the comrades had prepared an ample breakfast, especially good from Germaine's point of view, with fresh ripe figs and peaches. Some of the communist prisoners used their peasant arts to grow wonderful fruit and vegetables, even if they had to put up with being accused of being 'a kulak'.[74] 'We talked and talked' and the hours fled by. With the approach of evening, *militi* (Fascist militia) bawled that they could not stay together for the night since they were not married. Under Fascism, rules were rules. Or maybe not, since the blackshirts accepted a temptingly generous glass of wine, while they waited for an officer to adjudicate. Germaine became tearful at the prospect of being left alone.

Eventually the officer arrived and granted permission. The Fascists left the lovers alone. It was night. In an instant Germaine fell fast asleep and, with Giorgio lovingly watching her, did not awake until well after the sun was up. He made the first coffee; it remained his charge throughout their married life. This morning they dutifully trooped off to the canteen, where the comrades allowed them to eat together. But they added the curt warning that soon they must find their exact separate places in the male and female groupings that were decided by their date of arrival. Under communism, rules were rules. Or maybe not, since they could opt to eat together at home and avoid the collective canteen. Giorgio remembered how cheap and fresh fish and lobster were for the young couple. Maybe their fondness for elite food ensured that doubts and suspicions among ordinary communists about Giorgio lingered. Soon one was remarking sternly to Germaine: 'You come from a working-class family and are a bonny lass. But make sure you don't get led astray by your husband. He could be very useful to the party. But he must proletarianise himself. And you must help him.' Eventually, Germaine had time to read Rolland, Gide, Proust, Verlaine, Rimbaud, Baudelaire and Apollinaire, but she abstained from Marx.[75]

At their cottage, another day came and went. They talked on. Giorgio, endeavouring to be a virtuous communist, remembered in old age that he spoke with propagandist verbosity about the relationship between his political commitment and their marriage. Only the party, he said, had allowed them to meet in Paris. They were for ever its servants. Together they must accept that the workers' struggle continued. Their own fate, their own happiness, their private life must be secondary to that.

Figure 5.2 Giorgio, Germaine and little Ada on Ponza, not quite Auschwitz or Siberia (1936).

Then the third night and they had sex, 'full and shaking us to our souls'. There was a negative. Germaine began to bleed. At first they joked about how pleased southern comrades would be, after they washed and dried the sheets, at the proof of his thrust and her virginity. But she kept bleeding. They were locked down. Giorgio broke curfew to seek a doctor,

luckily not too far away. The medic gave Germaine an injection and a
sedative, and she slept. He did the same the next day and told them not
to be impatient. A week later, on 10 July, they married following state
rules at the Ponza *municipio* (town hall) with the national anthem playing.
The presiding public officials offered them a celebratory aperitif. 'For us,
the ceremony did not matter. Our attachment to each other was already
fully formed.'[76]

By autumn, despite their precautions, Germaine was pregnant, and
Mme Lecocq was en route from Paris to join them. Giorgio had invited
her for a few weeks. But she arrived with an immense trunk – she had
sold her Paris flat – and was immediately installed to be part of their
family until her old age. Giorgio admits that, at first, he was not an
enthusiast about his mother-in-law's presence. He accepted it because
he knew that further political demonstration was planned in which he was
bound to take a leading, exposed role. Germaine viewed the addition of
her mother to their little household as 'natural and inevitable' and, he
added, with a hint of regret, she always did as her mother said. Mme
Lecocq therefore ruled their domestic roost. Mme Lecocq's 'brusque'
and direct manner appealed to ordinary communists, among whom she
acquired 'great popularity'; she must have been their image of a working-
class mum.[77] And, after communist protest was renewed, Giorgio was
again dragged off to Poggioreale where he stayed for months, mewed up
with working-class comrades and living under a severely disciplined,
party-approved, 'puritan' organisation of their time from one moment
to the next.[78]

On Ponza, the news arrived that the regime was hardening in its
policies as it moved to bloody war in Ethiopia. At home, the previous
version of Fascism (Italian-style) was set aside by a greater commitment
to populism, illuminated by Mussolini's charisma. For the prisoners on
Ponza, this cruder version of Fascism brought an order to expel to their
mainland homes all wives and partners. Germaine joined a women's
demonstration against this decree and was lucky that her pregnancy
survived punches and kicks from the militia. But Giorgio's protest about
this behaviour, seconded by the eminent Parisian lawyer Count René de
Chambrun, caused the regime to back off in the case of Germaine and
her mother; marriage and residence on Ponza had made Germaine an
Italian citizen.

The couple (and Mme Lecocq) decided that Germaine should give
birth in Rome, where medical attention should be more reliable than
on Ponza. In fact, matters were not so easy. Germaine arrived a month
early to find that her sister-in-law, Ada, who had married a fellow
doctor, Mario Cecchi, on 30 January 1935, was anything but pleased.

By early the next year, Ada was to follow her husband to a medical post in Eritrea, just as the colony became the first base of brutal military attacks on Ethiopia; she had personally asked Alessandro Lessona, the Fascist under-secretary, then minister of colonies (1929–36), to secure her the post.[79] To her brother's disgust, she joined the PNF since party membership was a requirement for her employment; in a letter from Pietro to Giorgio that fell into the hands of the secret police, he tried to say that Ada was only acting out of 'family necessity'.[80] In her own old age, Ada recalled that the pay was good in the colonies.[81]

In the summer of 1935, Ada refused to house Germaine on the Aventine. Giorgio's wife was therefore forced during the last month of her pregnancy to find refuge at a modest pensione. There she was successful in fending for herself (and her mother). On 2 July, a healthy baby daughter, also confusingly named Ada, was born at an overcrowded Santo Spirito hospital. Sure in their communist atheism, the parents did not have little Ada baptised.[82]

Giorgio had stayed at Poggioreale and was soon alarmed to hear that Germaine was suffering from puerperal fever. It was checked only when she booked herself out of the hospital and back into the pensione, where an Austrian doctor managed to lower Germaine's 40° temperature with ice and gave her needed injections. Three months later, Germaine was allowed a visit to Naples. As Giorgio remembered: 'Ada had grown. She started to cry when I tried to take her into my arms and the traitor preferred to play with the buttons on the prison guard's uniform.'[83] Finally, six months later, in April 1936, Giorgio, Germaine, little Ada and Mme Lecoq were reunited on Ponza.[84] By then, the Fascist regime was within a few weeks of 'winning' the Ethiopian war, hailed as a Mussolinian and national triumph and, according to Renzo De Felice, writing in the 1970s, bringing to new heights popular 'consent' for the dictatorship, 'Mussolini's masterpiece'.[85]

Fascism may have been unnervingly victorious in the great world but Giorgio had family matters with which to cope. He always felt that he must deal with them in a manner fitting both an orthodox communist and the eldest son of the martyred Giovanni. Shortly – perhaps too shortly – after Germaine's first arrival on Ponza, Giorgio's younger brothers had arrived with special permission that, as usual, seemed far more possible for the Amendolas than for humbler party members. They interrupted Giorgio's and Germaine's happy habit of dancing through the evening to French music playing on their gramophone. The couple had ignored opposition from the *militi*, annoyed by the noise, the freedom involved or the foreign origin of the music. Giorgio's young brothers were not just there for a *'villeggiatura'* (holiday camp).[86] Antonio had good news to whisper to the head of his family: he had become a communist. A trigger had been time spent in the Croce family library and the lesson that he learned from the famous, but tedious and old, philosopher of passivity and defeat.[87]

Pietro, still only fifteen, for the moment remained a liberal loyal to his father's thought. But his Anti-Fascism soon directed him, too, to party membership (in 1937), defined by one historian as of a 'sentimental and impulsive kind'. It was followed swiftly enough by arrest, appearance in 1940 before the special tribunal and, despite his stressing his opposition to the Ribbentrop–Molotov Pact, a ten-year sentence on Ventotene, an island off Sicily. After Mussolini's sacking in July 1943, Pietro was able to leave; he became a partisan after 8 September.[88]

Figure 5.3 Antonio Amendola, *littore* (and communist) triumphant (*c.* 1937).

But what of Antonio, a young man with ideas of his own, very bright, and with a network of like-minded friends in Rome and Naples? For the moment, Giorgio was proud of his brother's conversion to communist truth. But in April 1935, there was alarming news. Antonio had entered the regime's Littoriali competition for promising youth in the field of literary criticism[89] and had been awarded first prize for an essay on the relationship between politics and literature. In this work, he used *La Voce*, the pre-eminent pre-1914 journal for aspiring intellectuals, including Giovanni Amendola and Benito Mussolini, as key evidence. In his capacity as a *littore*, he attended a congress of leading French and Italian experts on corporatism marketed as a social and economic 'third way' between capitalism and socialism. Eva's sometime friend Giuseppe Bottai, who was the regime's most committed advocate of corporatism, presided genially over it.[90]

Giorgio and Antonio could communicate only by letter, but Giorgio was cross. Antonio told him in tart response that he was becoming a silly old man who did not understand the new generation.[91] As Pietro Ingrao, later to be Giorgio's rival in the PCI leadership during the 1960s, recalled, meeting Antonio changed his life. A poet in the Littoriali events, Ingrao, the son of a landowner declined into being a minor bureaucrat (and PNF member) from the South, knew the name of Giovanni Amendola and was impressed by Antonio's independent thought; Antonio shared Ingrao's literary passion and guided him from culture to politics.[92] In summer 1936, Ingrao's first response and that of his friends to the Francoist rising in Spain was to oppose the reactionaries and the church, and therefore favour the Spanish Republic, as Antonio did. Without knowing anything much about Marx or Lenin, Stalin or Moscow, such fledgling dissidents from the Italian dictatorship were charting their own paths to communism.[93]

In 1937–8, Antonio again triumphed in the Littoriali games, held at Naples and then Palermo. He had just graduated from Rome University, achieving the Italian equivalent of a starred first from his Fascist examiners for a thesis on the governments of the *Destra* (Right) during the first two decades after the Risorgimento. Once, Giovanni had admired them. Antonio was earnest and polite enough to sign off his and his family relationship with Croce by sending the liberal philosopher a letter justifying his switch to communism while not forgetting to express his 'profound esteem and admiration' for Croce, who haughtily warned Antonio and his young friends against believing the 'magic, overexciting, formulae' of Marxism.[94] On 28 August 1938, Antonio, ignoring growing regime propaganda about what had just become their Jewish racial enemy (the regime issued its *Manifesto della Razza* on 14 July), married

Maria Lucetta Liuzzi. She was the daughter of an eminent Jewish music-ologist, Fernando Liuzzi. A daughter, Eva Paola, later to be a historian of Fascism and perhaps significantly named after Antonio's mother, was born in 1940.[95]

Shortly after Giorgio resumed life with Germaine on Ponza in the spring of 1936, Antonio had again been allowed to visit. On this occasion he spelled out in greater detail his ideas about '*fratelli in camicia nera*' (black-shirted brothers). In his plausible view, the regime was sagging. Its youth was growing ever more unconvinced by its over-loud claims to revolution and/or its deifying of the Duce, visibly undermined by the corruption and cynicism of every Fascist boss. The challenge for an Italian communist was, therefore, to work within the regime's organisa-tions but persuade young men and women that the communist revolu-tion was the real one. Knowing what was expected of a loyal communist, Giorgio passed the news back to party headquarters in Paris and won over Grieco, always his most reliable patron, and recalled with advan-tages by Giorgio a decade after Grieco's death in 1955[96] for his sympathy towards a fresh approach to Fascism. In July 1936, *Stato Operaio* sug-gested that communists and ordinary Fascists could be 'brothers in work and suffering'.[97] Pietro Amendola, by contrast, a new PCdI member and always the most orthodox and least questing among his brothers, told Giorgio that he disapproved of Antonio and his friends.[98]

Antonio pressed on regardless. Girt with the title of *littore*, earned from his Littoriali success, he published an article in the Fascist fortnightly for university students, *Gioventù Fascista* (Fascist Youth), stating, with what must have been intended ambiguity, that his fellows above all wanted 'to struggle'. A further article in *Il Meridiano di Roma* argued that criticism was just what the regime needed. This piece ignited a lively debate in the Fascist intellectual world, extending into the regime's most authoritative journal, *Critica Fascista*, edited by Bottai, now minister of education. Antonio's 'magnetic personality' had won him quite a following; cer-tainly, he had an intellectual's high forehead. Meanwhile, like his grand-father and qualifying by his class (despite it having theoretically been surpassed by Fascism), he did officers' training in Naples.

By 1940, the regime was growing less tolerant of new generation vagaries and many arrests followed, but Antonio remained at liberty in some transgression from the PCdI, given his open objection to the Ribbentrop–Molotov Pact, an attitude approved by Ingrao and some but not all of the young Rome group.[99] Helped by old family networks, Antonio obtained paid employment at the Banca Commerciale Italiana, a major bank from which the regime never eliminated an Anti-Fascist side, and moved with his wife and child to Milan. However, his mental health was deteriorating; Ingrao and his friends sadly realised that from now on they had to exclude from their meetings a comrade whom they viewed as their leader.[100] Matters took a graver turn early in 1942, just as Antonio was called up to the Soviet front. What his main biographer has called a combination of depression and nerves, always part of his excitable personality and perhaps inherited from Eva (or from his grandfather in his last days), became too much for him. His marriage fell apart.[101] He was moved to the psychiatric hospital of Santa Maria della Pietà in Rome, from which he never emerged, dying 'insane' on 20 October 1953.[102] According to a much later account by Maria Antonietta Macciocchi, Pietro's wartime wife, Antonio perished after an unsuccessful lobotomy that, she added uncharitably, left Giorgio as 'the unique, the only Amendola, alive or dead', the 'inflated emblem of faith in the party'.[103]

Within the Amendola family, before and during the war, Eva, as so often in her life, was a law unto herself. In October 1935, as many mothers of *confinati* did in a permeable system known to allow amnesties and special pleading, she wrote personally to Mussolini asking that her eldest son be freed from prison. When he learned of her initiative, Giorgio furiously rejected such cowardly dealing. But she did not reply.[104] That year, she had visited Vilnius with talk about a university post (and possible membership of the Fascist Party), although she also remained under surveillance by the secret police. For most of the time, Eva resided on the Aventine in Rome, getting back to regular work as a translator. By 1938–9, she was employed by Fascist ministries, where, now that the regime had become antisemitic, she needed to have official recognition that she was an Aryan. A polyglot, she translated from and into German, Polish, English, French and Russian, her work on one occasion being to provide foreign-language copies of the new antisemitic legislation. Her children tried in their different ways to love, safeguard and channel her, but, for the most part, she sailed on regardless.[105]

Despite Giorgio's dudgeon at his mother's attempt to make a special case of him, an effort repeated in two interviews that she sought and gained with Leto, he was indeed to receive privileged treatment. On his return to Ponza, fat and pale from his long months in Poggioreale, he found Germaine down to forty-two kilograms, her physique unable to cope with breastfeeding the large, hungry Ada. Giorgio persuaded her to stop. It was a mistake. Ada ceased growing, showed signs of dysentery, and her weight plummeted from nine kilograms to six to five. Doctors on the island offered no solution. The parents decided that Ada and Germaine (and Mme Lecocq) must move urgently to Rome, where Ada arrived in a dangerous state of dehydration. There she was brought back from the edge of disaster but she had incurred the liver damage that killed her.[106]

In Rome, family troubles were deepening. The elder Ada's marriage with Mario Cecchi did not prosper; there were no children.[107] Ada had returned from the colonies and sought a job in the Fascist welfare system. She found it at the spa not of Montecatini but Salsomaggiore, working for the Istituto Nazionale Fascista per l'Assicurazione contro gli Infortuni al Lavoro, the regime organisation to assist those injured at work. At a later date, she went back again to Eritrea and she was there when the colony was rapidly overrun by a ragtag British imperial army in 1941.[108] Three years later, she was still awaiting British military clearance to return to Italy.[109]

In Rome, in 1936, Ada, in her usual tough-minded way, had demanded Uncle Mario leave the house on the Via Sant'Alessio but again was scarcely eager to greet Germaine and little Ada. Faced with these family arguments, Giorgio, first winning party approval on Ponza and in Paris, requested special leave to sort out the difficulties and sell the property in Rome. Obligingly, the Fascist police granted him ten days' leave and a meeting with Leto, with an additional three days off for dental appointments (another bourgeois undertaking). Then, Giorgio and his family sailed back to Ponza.

They did not stay. Almost immediately, Giorgio heard that he was to be granted an amnesty of a kind. Uncle Mario could report from his own contacts that Leto and Senise had been hostile to such concession. But the police chief, Arturo Bocchini, and Mussolini were favourable. In his autobiography, Giorgio claims that they concluded that he would be easier to place under tight, daily surveillance on the mainland than on Ponza. A historian might add, noting Mussolini's efforts to give some protection to Matteotti's widow and children, that the Duce lacked the bloodiness of Stalin and other dictators in eliminating whole families of his opponents.[110] Somewhere in his soul, he may, on occasion, not have been entirely sure that Giovanni Amendola's fate had been just.

Mme Lecocq ensured that they left no scrap of their property on the island. Giorgio, in old age, judged that his years there had brought more benefit than loss in his private and his party life. 'I left [Ponza] politically stronger. I had learned to know the comrades. Through them, I had learned to know Italy in its diversity. I had studied. The balance of four years was, in sum, positive. I was now thirty years old and had become a man.'[111]

Back in Rome, Eva greeted them joyfully; sister Ada was away looking after a Fascist summer camp. Eva had hired a willing maid from nearby working-class Testaccio to look after them all in the 'big house', as

Giorgio called it. But Mme Lecocq and Eva were soon at war over Amendola extravagance. Germaine began to plead for a return to Paris and scratched her husband's face in fury over his hesitations at her suggestion. When approached shortly afterwards, Leto granted Germaine permission, mocking Giorgio over the facial evidence he gave of family fights, which had been reported by the secret agents who watched over them. Germaine, little Ada and her mother left first, with Giorgio giving his wife a secret note to party headquarters enquiring whether he should stay in Rome. In getting Germaine the right to leave, he had promised the Fascist police that he 'would not even minimally engage in politics or cause any annoyance to them'.[112] Ignoring such unlikely promise, he asked his party chiefs in Paris whether he should further pursue Antonio's line about *fratelli in camicia nera*. Were there family contacts with Ciano and Bottai that could be exploited? Or was the risk of further arrest too great? Should he urgently arrange his own expatriation? As Ingrao charitably remembered, his and Antonio's newly minted young communist friends in Rome viewed Giorgio as a hero: 'He was one who fought; he had been in *confino*; he was the son of Giovanni Amendola' and therefore personified 'the connection between the liberal tradition and communist militancy'.[113]

Giorgio did not stay long. Once Germaine passed on his questions to the PCdI leadership, Grieco sent helpful advice that he should clear out of Italy as soon as he could.[114] For some months, Giorgio lay low, cautiously renewing ties with old Anti-Fascist friends as the son of Giovanni might, and finding employment in the raffish, bourgeois cinema, with the Roman office of Paramount films, and in other cultural fields. He later recalled that Bottai and Ciano, the friends of his youth, intimated, falsely, that the dictatorship would soon liberalise.[115] Finally, a false passport came through from Paris, with a note saying that he should cross the border at Chiasso on the evening of 28 October 1937. By that hour, it could be assumed, border police had drunk deep in celebration of the March on Rome and slipping past them would be easy enough. On the Aventine, Antonio and Pietro embraced him when he left for the slow and tortuous journey north, but Eva slept through his departure.

Party counsel was right. Giorgio walked over the border, mixing with emigrant 'guest workers' in Switzerland who had spent the festival day in Italy. From Lugano, a dutiful son still, he cabled his mother with apologies for not saying goodbye. His brothers rushed this news to the police, who, a little bewildered by the brothers' apparent Fascist zeal, did not arrest them. Instead, they dull-wittedly recorded that Giorgio had 'disappeared'.[116] By the morning of 29 October, he was back with

Germaine, Ada and Mme Lecocq in Paris. There, Germaine's brother, Charles, had risen out of the working class with his successful hairdressing business. Now he owned a car and lived comfortably in a suburban house with a garden. Destiny seemed as ever to be on Giorgio's side, at least in his private life. Giorgio and Germaine took the chance to spend their first night together in a hotel before a morning appointment with the party.[117]

There, Grieco offered warm welcome and pooh-poohed the idea that Giorgio should at once depart to Spain and a fighting front in its civil war. Instead, he, the married man, should stay in Paris. Yet party life was anything but tranquil. Togliatti was in Moscow, somehow avoiding being purged along with many of the Russian and international party leadership. Longo was in Spain. Grieco was under attack, with the chief grounds being his support for the idea of *fratelli in camicia nera*; in April 1938, he was dropped as party secretary in Paris, being replaced by Giuseppe Berti as 'commissioner', with backing from Togliatti (and Stalin) in Moscow. Lapped by personal and ideological disputes and a deep sense of failure, party chiefs seemed not to know what to do with Giorgio. With marked lack of originality and implied mistrust, they put him in charge of a bookshop and library, almost as if he were back on Ponza.[118] Germaine, Giorgio, Ada and Mme Lecocq found more humble accommodation than with newly bourgeois Charles. Germaine had not fully recovered physically from Ada's birth; the couple had no further children. But, as in 1931, they did enjoy the cinema, the International Exhibition and the other sights of Paris, mostly as an intergenerational foursome.[119] They holidayed at Chambéry and, like most Europeans (including Italians), reacted with relief when the Munich crisis did not explode into war.

In his autobiographical writings of the 1970s, Giorgio is at pains to admit that, throughout these years, he was a Stalinist, accepting that the Great Man in Moscow was an infallible guide to communist utopia.[120] He made ready to fight for Stalinism. Yet, in a way that was not totally dissimilar to his avoidance of the more violent aspects of Fascist totalitarianism – he was not beaten as Giovanni had been – Giorgio experienced Stalinism from a safe distance. He never had to wipe the blood of comrades from the walls of the Lubyanka. He was never cross-examined by Vyshinsky. He never actually met the Soviet vozhd. He must have known, whether directly or indirectly, comrades from the PCdI, more than a hundred of whom disappeared into the Soviet gulag. But none was a close friend or associate.

In fact, he was traversing a path protected by the myth of his father's martyrdom; the wiser leaders of the PCdI liked having an Amendola in

their ranks. In 1939–40, he was despatched to safe and distant Tunis to run an emigrant newspaper; it had a print run of 2,000 but sold few of these.[121] There, he explained away the Ribbentrop–Molotov Pact without too much personal travail. It was, he recalled, 'a moment to prove our "unconditional" faith in the country of socialism, in the Communist Party of the USSR, in comrade Stalin'.[122] Once Italy entered the war, and especially after Germany invaded the USSR, he assumed an elevated place as a negotiator; the party was eager to use his name and the ghost of Giovanni (expurgated of his anti-communism). During this period, his four-person household had to settle and resettle as needed; Giorgio remained a clandestine resident of France between 1939 and 1943, although a later observer might be surprised at the failure of Vichy's secret police or of the Fascist occupiers of Savoy and Provence up to the gates of Marseille to spot him – Giorgio *il Grosso* – his wife, daughter and Mme Lecocq.

In 5 June 1940, they made a hasty transfer from Paris to Marseille, again weighed down by heavy baggage. For a time they stayed at a poor hotel, but Germaine, for whom it was less dangerous to walk around the streets, located a suitable apartment at the Petite Corniche, rented by an Italian immigrant. They remained there for two years, from time to time welcoming comrades without police challenge.[123] Marseille became a recognised party centre with Giorgio's role growing in seniority.

After June 1941, matters simplified to a degree. Giorgio travelled occasionally on party business to Monte Carlo, Nice, Grenoble, Toulouse and Lyons, tasked with rallying support and uniting the membership in exile. Germaine always went with him out of conjugal love and because she made his false identity documents more convincing. Mme Lecocq looked after Ada. It marked the beginning of a pattern, he recalled in 1973 in his first major autobiographical writing. During the Italian Republic after 1946, he always visited this or that city and party branch in Germaine's company. When there were exceptions, friends asked in alarm: 'But are you alone? How is Germaine?'[124] They were an inseparable couple.

By spring 1943, Giorgio was readying to cross the Italian border to organise and train fighting partisans at a time when there were still few such people. He reached Milan on the night of 18–19 April. First, he had to find a sanctuary for his family, since the bombing of Marseille was intensifying, as were police raids across the town. He and Germaine spent their spare time seeking somewhere suitable in the hinterland of Nice. Finally, they identified a place that they could afford at Gattières, the last station on the railway branch line from Vance to Grasse. They taught the reluctant Ada to say that her surname was Lecocq, not

Amendola. They transported most of their accumulated luggage. It was time for Giorgio to go; the Via Rasella was, unknown to him, on his itinerary. Amid many difficulties, Germaine, Ada and Mme Lecocq survived the war at Gattières, in deepening material discomfort. As Giorgio recalled limply: 'Germaine was practically forgotten by the comrades, especially after the Liberation [of France] in the summer of 1944. A story of bureaucratic forms in the apparatus, which occurs in every situation!'[125] Once again, he and Germaine (and Ada and Mme Lecocq) were to be separated for two years. In that time, for Giorgio, the party bulked pre-eminent over his family, and killing Fascists and Nazis mattered more than married love. Giorgio's Second World War was to be a good one, but not quite in the same fashion as the First War had pleased and seemingly elevated his father.

6   Giorgio Amendola and a National Road to Socialism and the End of History

During the two years that followed April 1943, Giorgio joined with a will in the Communist Party's participation in armed resistance. As was described in Chapter 1, the bloodiest event over which he presided was the controversial attack in the Via Rasella on 23 March 1944. Memory has still not settled in favour or against the communist ruthlessness then displayed. More generally, historians still argue over the effectiveness of a fighting resistance in its jittery alliance with the Allied armies, which began their invasion of Sicily on 9 July and thereafter moved slowly up the peninsula. Mussolini and his supporters in the RSI, lacking the will or opportunity for much genuine independence, per force stood for 'Nazi-fascism', while their country descended into a form of civil war, another event that still divides Italians. In it, three stances were possible: 'Fascist' alliance with the fanatical Nazis, resistance, or endeavouring to be neutral and wait out the bloody battles that were killing more Italians than had died in the first phase of the war from 1940 to 1943 (this last undoubtedly the choice of most Italians).[1]

Nazi-fascism did go down to total defeat. On 28 April 1945, Mussolini, who, in the company of a brigade of German soldiers, had been arrested by partisans, was shot by the communist Walter Audisio. His body and those of his last lover, Claretta Petacci, and fifteen of his most stubbornly loyal lieutenants were trucked back to Milan and exposed to public abuse in the Piazzale Loreto. By 2 September, Japan, too, had surrendered. The Second World War was won, even if the wartime alliance of the USSR and the USA and other liberal capitalist democracies was not destined to last.

How, then, had Giorgio Amendola experienced the long months of battle after he crossed back into Italy? And as Nazi-fascist totalitarianism collapsed, how was he comprehending Italian and Soviet communism? How was he managing his sense of being the titular 'son' of PCI chief Palmiro Togliatti, and at the same time being the head of the Amendola family and actual son of liberal democrat, Anti-Fascist, anti-materialist martyr Giovanni?

A first answer to these queries might appear by focusing on Giorgio when victory came. During the preparatory months of that bitter but hopeful spring of 1945, he was hiding in Turin, a party chief, but not *the* party chief. As far as he and the party were concerned, he was laying the groundwork for a popular insurrection in this key industrial city, where the proletariat may never have fully succumbed to Fascism and where, it was hoped, they would naturally rally to the PCI after 1945.[2] The situation reached its climax on 26–27 April. When, in the 1970s, he came to write his account of that time, Amendola was sure that the rising had 'illuminated the entire nation with its penetrating light'. It demonstrated 'to the whole world that Italy was thereby affirming its right to a place in the great meeting of free peoples to work together for the reconstruction and reorganisation of the world'.[3] In such recollection, he sketched a picture snugly fitting what historians have called the 'myth of the Resistance', which, from 1960 until the end of the 1980s, achieved hegemony in the public memory of Italy's Second World War.[4]

In 1945, Giorgio had transmitted a less harmonious message. As he asserted in the party daily *L'Unità* on 29 April, under the heading 'Pietà l'è morta' (No mercy any more), the battle in Turin was not yet fully won, despite partisans securing the backing of 'all the people'. Every street and piazza, deeply tarnished by dictatorship, must be combed and cleansed. Popular tribunals must execute all 'spies, provocateurs and criminals'. 'An immediate and radical purge is the first condition for commencing a new democratic life,' Amendola wrote pitilessly, 'our dead must be revenged, every one of them. The criminals must be eliminated. The Fascist plague must be wiped out. Only then shall we be able to advance. With Jacobin resolution, the knife must cut deep into the disease and the whole infection must be excised.'[5] As he added starkly a little later, it was Lenin who had defined freedom as the time when 'rifles were in the hands of workers'.[6] Giorgio may have been a patriot, still *il figlio di un ministro*, but, he seemed to pronounce, he was also a hard-line communist, ready to set the execution squads into action.

In Turin, Amendola's categorical phrases justified the lynching of local *repubblichino* boss Giuseppe Solaro, whom Giorgio vengefully remembered as having shouted down his father's last speech to the Chamber of Deputies in June 1924; Solaro was hung from a tree on the Corso Vinzaglio in the city's centre.[7] Amendola's cry of family vendetta and revolutionary victory seemed to replicate the worldviews of Stalin and Vyshinsky and to pledge totalitarian communism. His chosen surgical metaphor has a long and vicious history of killing attached to it.[8] It prompts taxing questions. Might the PCI have imposed bloody,

Stalinist-style tyranny over the whole country had the victors in the war at Yalta placed Italy in the Soviet and not in the western zone? How responsible was the PCI leadership for the killings that continued through the summer of 1945, perhaps 10,000 of them, a toll brought back into memory during the spread of 'Anti-Anti-Fascism' in the 1990s when Italy adjusted to the end of communism and the withering away of the PCI?[9]

The first question is impossible to answer since Italy was left in the West. The second is riddled with the politics of Berlusconi's Italy and the longstanding features of Italians' failure after 1945 to confront the fact that Mussolini's dictatorship had sent a million people early to their graves, about half of them in the nation's empire. What is clear is that neither Amendola, despite his stern phrases on victory, nor the PCI, once more sagely piloted by Palmiro Togliatti following his return from Moscow on 27 March 1944, four days after the events on the Via Rasella, in reality itched for a violent seizure of power. On the contrary, with Stalin's approval, on 24 April Togliatti pushed the Comitato di Liberazione Nazionale into the '*svolta di Salerno*' (U-turn at Salerno). Through that deal, all the Anti-Fascist parties, including the PCI, agreed to collaborate with the monarchy and its military prime minister, Pietro Badoglio. They should leave institutional issues and the purging of those who had culled profit from the dictatorship to the future. Italy did become a republic following a popular vote on 2 June 1946. However, any retribution for Fascist crime and corruption was further curtailed with the 'Togliatti Amnesty' of 22 June (the PCI chief then served as minister of justice), ensuring that the Republic's policy towards Fascist perpetrators was to forgive and forget, as we have already seen in regard to those responsible for the grievous fate of Giovanni Amendola.

When Togliatti imposed his *svolta* on his party, did Giorgio reflect on the fact that his dead father had once been the local parliamentary representative in Salerno and advocate of liberal democracy, not communism? Certainly, when Giorgio had re-entered Rome in the urgent days following Mussolini's overthrow on 25 July 1943, he could not escape Giovanni's ghost, nor could he ignore family assistance and duties; he arrived in the eternal city without even a spare shirt but was handed fresh clothes by a provident aunt and uncle.[10] He reached Rome by train on the afternoon of 26 July, immediately to engage in discussions with an array of 'Anti-Fascist' political figures including such armed party comrades as Antonello Trombadori and Paolo Bufalini (once a classmate of Antonio Amendola at the Liceo Visconti) and such old men from the Liberal past as Vittorio Emanuele Orlando (prime minister 1917–19), Ivanoe Bonomi (prime minister 1921–2 and 1944–5 and first head of the CLN), as well as that watcher at Giovanni's deathbed, Meuccio Ruini.

These last could not greet Giorgio without reminding him of their admiration for his father. Bonomi and Ruini had for a time supported the Unione Nazionale, Giovanni's proto-liberal party, in 1924–5. For them, whatever his current politics, Giorgio remained his father's eldest son, a communist no doubt but an acceptable ally in a shared Anti-Fascism, perhaps, as some of his own comrades feared, ready to 'defraud' the party of revolution, or anyway a young man with whom reasonable conversation was possible.[11]

Still a clandestine, Giorgio recalled stretching out on a small bed in a friend's flat on his second night back in Rome and wrestling with the contradictions in his life between party and family. 'I had found at every meeting memory of my father and the emotion that such memory sustained'. What could such personal fame mean? He claimed to have avoided his sometime 'super-tutors', but Fortunato and Albertini were dead and Croce was as usual cogitating, safe in his palace in Naples. Yet Giorgio could not forgo his duties as the eldest Amendola boy. On the morning of 28 July, he located his still nervy mother, Eva, who had taken refuge in the 'comfortable enough' Pensione Capranica, near the Pantheon. 'I found her little room stuffed with books and papers. For someone who was sixty-three, her health was fine,' as was her devotion to intellectual life. She, too, at once confessed how moved she was by the memories that were circulating of Giovanni. On the evening of 25 July, she had been persuaded by old friends to appear for toasts and applause in her old stamping ground at the Caffè Aragno, where, in his boyhood, Giorgio had been her male escort.

Giorgio even managed to see Antonio, about whose psychological woes he had been only partially informed. Just before 8 September, the three brothers were able to dine together in the house on the Aventine, where Eva now re-established herself. Pietro had just returned from his sentence of ten years' *confino* on Lipari and was soon to face personal complications of his own. Antonio could not settle. At the family dinner his nerves frayed, he did not comprehend what was going on politically and had to be escorted back to his clinic. Cousins and other relatives also demanded to see Giorgio; the family of the Amendolas may have had its tares but it had not disintegrated under Italian-style totalitarianism.[12] Germaine, Mme Lecocq and young Ada might be fending for themselves in Provence (and the flight of the king and Badoglio on 8 September quashed any idea of bringing them to Rome),[13] but Giorgio could not renounce his other private duties. He was still head of his family.

Yet, in his mind, the party (and Stalin) needed him more. The collapse of Fascist rule ensured that 'the Anti-Fascist parties [as rallied in the CLN] must take on the job of directing the national struggle'.[14] They must be united in a sort of wartime popular front – no whisper of 'social fascism' now. Through August–September 1943, German armies kept arriving. Any fighting resistance in Rome did not last long. Briefly, on 10 September, Giorgio heard 'the incessant firing of machine guns and rifles' when he walked near the Porta San Paolo and helped rescue one wounded youth. It may have been the nearest that he ever came to active battle. His greater task remained until the war's end, organisational, propagandist and political, even if, replacing Luigi Longo who moved to Milan in September 1943, he formally 'directed military work' for the party in and around Rome in association with Sandro Pertini of the Socialist Party and Riccardo Bauer of the liberal democrat Partito d'Azione (Action Party).[15] In retrospect, the PCI's wartime policies may look deeply ambiguous in their combination of Italian particularity and service to Soviet international or imperial power. Giorgio's own effortlessly friendly dealings with non-communist Anti-Fascists make him seem a model of a party always trying to look two ways.

He was, after all, still a second-rank chief, coping as best he could with the frequent squabbles between the more elevated leadership in Milan, in Rome and in Moscow or Paris. In November 1943, he was attacked by the group in Milan for arguing too forcibly for the seniority of the capital in discussions over the best party policy and being too ready to ignore policies being charted by Togliatti from the USSR.[16] On more than one occasion he rejected the charge that GAP partisans under his command were insufficiently active. The planting of bombs in the Via Rasella may have been partially prompted to show Milan how brave and efficient Roman comrades were.

But the bitterest moment for Giorgio came in May 1944 when he was transferred to Milan, greeted by Longo coldly as a 'transformist southerner', more ready nimbly to make deals with old elites than stoutly marshalling the working class to victory. Since September 1943, he was told in severe communist rebuke, he had behaved like a 'petit bourgeois'. Amendola tried to stand up for himself, but he must have thought that he was back under his father's purist lash. His fears probably mounted when Togliatti backed Longo, maintaining, with his characteristic ability to speak out of both sides of his mouth, that the *svolta di Salerno* did not mean unnatural dallying with the leftover Liberal ruling class.

Thereafter, Amendola accepted that, when it came to organising fighting resistance, he was a subordinate; he methodically followed Longo's orders to inspect communist partisans and their 'Garibaldi' brigades in

Emilia-Romagna. On one such venture on 2 August 1944, he was arrested by two SS officers in Parma and, with Fascist militia from Florence watching, gaoled for a fortnight. With the luck that was often his, a *repubblichino* was friendly and told him, if he had cash in his pocket, he could order in food. Giorgio *il Grosso* behaved in character when he arranged a 'bumper' dinner, agreeing in worldly-wise manner that he should pay a generous tip to the helpful *milite* on top of the exorbitant price of his black-market meals.

Amendola was handed cheap novels to read and left to curse his imprudence in silence while the Germans investigated his claims to be a Neapolitan lawyer, a refugee in Milan from the Anglo-American enemy. Late one night he was dragged out of his cell to be interrogated by a 'sleek, perfumed' SS officer. Again his fortune held, assisted by his class colouration. Soon, the German confessed that he, too, was a lawyer and disliked having to be a nuisance to a gentleman like him. Asked whether he had joined the Salò Republic's Partito Fascista Repubblicano (PFR, Republican Fascist Party), Amendola replied 'No' because he was a nationalist who had been appalled by the events of 25 July and the betrayal of Italy's 'German comrades and allies'. He had read his gaoler's mindset right. The SS officer, more old-fashioned German racist than Nazi-fascist ideologue, agreed that all Italian politicians were 'bragging cowards' (including, by implication, Mussolini) and escorted him back to his cell. There he stayed for another ten days, 'the longest in my life', while what must have been superficial checking of his quickly concocted story proceeded. Back in 1940, Guido Leto had passed his photograph and other personal details to the Nazis,[17] but, for some reason, he now escaped identification.

Giorgio was cheered when two working-class comrades who had been arrested when he was were released. Without letting on that they knew him, they talked loudly of their fate while they passed his cell door. Finally, on 16 August, he, too, was freed and, even though unshaven and unwashed since his arrest, managed to persuade a nearby restaurant to feed him another rich meal, outside, in the summer sun, under a pergola. That night, he hitched a slow ride to Bologna, dreaming happily, he recalled, of how he would soon see Germaine, while at once resuming his labours for the party.[18]

The next months of Giorgio's war were spent mainly on propaganda work in Milan, one issue being how active partisans should be over the 1944–5 winter after General Alexander's proclamation of 13 November ordering a pause in activity. By no means cowed by Anglo-American instruction, the party began planning its 'national insurrection', and, in January, Giorgio was moved to Turin.[19] On New Year's Eve, he and some friends in Milan had managed to greet the New Year and approaching victory together, Giorgio having received the news that Gattières, and so Germaine and his family, had been freed from Nazi-fascist rule. There was a downside to the celebration; the risotto prepared by some female comrades was a terrible sticky mess, he did not fail to recall, appetite unsatisfied.[20]

The events of 27–28 April 1945 were near, with the partisan claim that Italy thereby had 'liberated itself'. This interpretation of the last hours of Fascism was destined to become an enduring plank of the 'myth of the Resistance'. In Turin, Giorgio had time to organise the first post-Fascist celebration of May Day as the workers' festival and participate in a joint military parade on 6 May of Allied soldiers and fighting partisans. By 11 May he was in Milan awaiting orders from Togliatti, who had joined Longo there. He had not seen his 'other father' since May 1932 and thought that he was welcomed with a mixture of curiosity and irony, with his leader unsure of what to make of him. Soon, Togliatti gave Amendola, along with Pietro Secchia and Umberto Massola, the task of assembling the party's documentary history of its war. Massola had entered Italy to foster resistance as early as August 1941. Amendola had met him in Turin in April 1943. Togliatti wrote the preface of the volume, stamping it with his official imprimatur. In its account, the party maintained that only Anti-Fascist unity and its alleged mass support stopped King Victor Emmanuel from summoning 'respectable' Fascists, such as Luigi Federzoni or Dino Grandi, to head a new 'regime' when Mussolini was arrested in July 1943.[21]

Inscribing a usable past was one matter, but there were plenty of more pressing present issues. Togliatti did not take long to instruct Giorgio that he must soon move to Naples, where he was badly needed; Togliatti's unspoken assumption was that a southerner might know how to talk to southerners. Naples was a fickle site for communists; Curzio Malaparte's celebrated novel *La Pelle* (The Skin) remains a rambunctious account of the desperate poverty and unmodernised politics of the place.[22] According to an English political scientist, even in the 1970s, Neapolitans clung to alienated truisms: 'He who has bread and wine must be a Jacobin,' or, bleaker still, 'Even your best friend is a traitor.'[23]

In time, Giorgio was to expend much effort striving to 'modernise' the South and convert it to communism. Yet, in 1945, he was needed in the new government being assembled in Rome. Some months earlier, Longo had opposed such promotion. Now the Milan chief acknowledged party hierarchy and said nothing when Togliatti set out Giorgio's immediate duties in Rome.[24]

In the interim, Pietro, the youngest of the Amendola brothers, could manage the city of Naples for the PCI, where he took office from

1 August 1944,[25] respectfully elected secretary of the party's provincial congress. Pietro sloughed off local personal attacks to be re-elected in October 1945. Perhaps ingenuously, he then reported progress in party organisation and support across the region of Campania.[26] Nevertheless, on 2 June 1946, the city voted heavily (79.94 per cent) to retain the Savoy monarchy. On 1 September, Pietro was recalled to Rome with his wartime partner, the later distinguished and feisty feminist, radical politician and journalist Maria Antonietta Macciocchi. Their story may be a digression but it needs elaboration as another chapter in the Amendola chronicle.

Macciocchi had been delivered of a daughter – called Giorgina,[27] in salute to Giorgio – on 30 March 1945 at Salerno. Macciocchi had entered what she called 'The Family', but she was not destined to be a happy or obedient member of it. Her marriage with Pietro, which had been celebrated in Rome on 30 June 1944, did not long survive the end of the war. Macciocchi espoused fewer conventions than did Pietro and eventually followed the trajectory of the New Left away from the PCI.[28] In 1948, the couple, detecting a way around the fact that Italy did not permit divorce, managed to obtain a 'difficult' annulment from what must have been a friendly court at San Marino; that tiny state was run by a communist–socialist coalition from 1945 to 1957.[29] In her lengthy later memoirs, Macciocchi scornfully dismissed Pietro as a 'good man but a little boring' and not good at sex.

For quite some time, the two fought over who was to have prime responsibility for bringing up Giorgina.[30] Eventually, Giorgio and the party intervened to have the little girl live with Macciocchi, despite her being sarcastic about her brother-in-law's conventional gender attitudes and sexism. She was much more polite about Germaine.[31] Given what Macciocchi called ironically her 'Stakhanovite' devotion to work, in practice Giorgina often passed into the supervision of her father or of Giorgio, Germaine and Mme Lecocq (as she was still always called).[32] Pietro married Lara Monticini in December 1950 in what was to be a more lasting relationship and they had two daughters – Antonella, who worked in journalism, and Piera, who became a parliamentary archivist[33] – and a son, Giovanni. Born 13 April 1958, he became a successful economist. Pietro and Lara, throughout the 1950s, took responsibility for his mother, Eva, living together in a flat in the Balduina zone of suburban Rome. Even though sister Ada's political commitment was to the rightist Italian Liberal Party, she visited her communist brother (and mother) 'almost daily'; her niece, Antonella, remembers her generous presents, her habit of taking Pietro's children off to Capri and her depression at other times.[34]

Figure 6.1 Pietro preaching communism (from a prepared text).

Until the end of the 1960s, Pietro pursued an orthodox party career. In 1948, he won a seat in the Chamber of Deputies for the area of Benevento–Avellino–Salerno, with his special focus then and later being on the last, 'family', province. He represented party and local interest until he resigned on 22 July 1969, officially for health reasons but also flummoxed by local divisions deepened by the crisis of 1968 and by a renewed burst of neo-Fascism in the South. Thereafter, he worked for various institutions devoted to improving the lot and reputation of wartime partisans. He remained a tractable member of the PCI, transferring automatically into the Partito Democratico della Sinistra (PDS, Democratic Party of the Left) when, on 3 February 1991, the old communist party was dissolved after the fall of the USSR. Pietro Amendola died on the night of 7–8 December 2007, for a few months outliving his eternally 'heretical' wartime wife. He had been the most straightforwardly communist Amendola.[35]

By contrast, Macciocchi pursued a hectic life as editor of the communist magazine *Noi Donne* (We Women) and then, from 1956, *Vie Nuove* (New Paths), posts that she admits that she achieved through Giorgio's patronage. In 1962, she became the correspondent in Paris for the PCI daily *L'Unità*. She was soon immersed among the passionately trendy French intelligentsia, notably as a close friend, admirer and interpreter of Louis Althusser. In 1968, she was elected to the Chamber of Deputies for the PCI in Naples but was soon flaunting her independence from party orthodoxy. In 1971, she travelled to China, immediately convinced into being a naïve but convinced enthusiast for Mao's cultural revolution, about which she wrote an overwrought account, confident that the country had been converted into 'a society of equals', with all distinctions of rank abolished. 'The very atmosphere we breathe is [genuinely] revolutionary,' she knew the moment she had stepped from the plane.[36] Back in Europe, she swiftly transferred her main place of residence to Paris. In September 1977, she was formally expelled from the PCI, about which she was surprisingly annoyed. She tended to blame her expulsion on Giorgio and PCI secretary Enrico Berlinguer, whom she loftily viewed as even duller than Pietro Amendola.[37] She almost immediately took a seat in the European parliament in the group led by Marco Pannella, founder of a new leftist Radical Party in the 1960s; it went transnational in the European parliament in 1989, welcoming the fall of Eastern European communism.[38] In 1982, Macciocchi published a meandering, idiosyncratic and self-obsessed 'diary' of her life, updated in 2000. She died on 14 April 2007.

One of Macciocchi's more malicious and less credible charges is that Giorgio, because of his dull obedience to the party, wrote his father out of family and national history, representing himself as 'the unique, the only Amendola, alive or dead', suggesting thereby that Giorgio had imposed a personal totalitarianism on the family story.[39] Yet, in reality, there is vast evidence of Giorgio's search throughout his life for a way in which to come to grips with his father's legacy, as well as with Anti-Communist Italy's sometimes jarring memory of Giovanni. It is notable that Pietro, for all his conventionality and obedience to the party line, stuck up for his father while still Macciocchi's husband. In a polemic with Anti-Fascist Freemason and sometime syndicalist Arturo Labriola, who had accused non-communist and liberal Anti-Fascists of surrendering to Mussolini in the 1920s, he vehemently defended Giovanni's heritage, declaring his father to have been 'the last of the old southern democrats and the first of the new ... [a man] who understood too late the irreparable error of failing to connect his battle to that of all the workers'.[40] For both Pietro and Giorgio, the Amendolas never ceased to be a family, an Italian family of special virtue, framed by a history that was older and deeper than that of any ideology.

Back in April 1945, Pietro's complications apart, Giorgio had his own marital arrangements to consider. He wanted to stay long enough in Turin to commandeer a car, drive over an Alpine pass and fetch Germaine and little Ada (and Mme Lecocq). That step proved bureaucratically impossible but a British officer, the Allied equivalent of the kindly SS man in Parma, agreed to get them. He found the women readily enough and there was space in his car even for the pile of luggage that Giorgio's thrifty mother-in-law had assembled; more family property, secretly stored in Nice since 1942, was regained in November 1945.[41] But when Germaine reached Turin, Giorgio was in Milan. She and her mother then headed for Milan. Giorgio rushed to find them in Turin but they had left and so he had to turn back.

His sense of urgency and frustration may have been augmented by his fear of a difficult first conjugal meeting, since, he knew, 'friendly gossips' had apprised Germaine of his alleged 'wartime relations' with willing female comrades. But an initial coolness between husband and wife was soon overcome, Giorgio lamenting that Germaine was almost as thin as a concentration camp survivor; for once she needed food as much as he always did. He added that Mme Lecocq was 'ready to take over command of the reunited family'. His mother-in-law long remained in this office, living to a great age. Hélène Lecocq died in June 1974.[42] In his private life, for Giorgio, love (Amendola-style) was again soon conquering all.[43]

Not much later, Giorgio, Pietro, Germaine and little Ada processed through the streets of Sarno in what one local remembered was a sort of 'civil and religious rite'. Women strewed rose petals in their path as though they were 'antique conquering heroes'.[44] As Giorgio ingenuously remarked elsewhere, if you were a PCI chief (at least of his stature), you were greeted as a 'man of respect'.[45] No doubt, some cheers, out of family veneration, were also for the ghost of Giovanni Amendola. Party and family identities merged.

As noted above, rather than transferring at once to Naples and the South, from June 1945 for a time Giorgio assumed the nationally significant role of under-secretary to Ferruccio Parri, the radical Partito d'Azione prime minister, who was promising that the whole country be swept by an egalitarian 'wind from the North'. Shrewdly, Togliatti had pressed Giorgio into government. Once again, the party utilised the fact that, as the son of Giovanni, he was their most respectable face.[46] Amendola took his place in advising Parri about what might constitute a new 'democratic alliance' uniting North and South. It must aim to blend workers, peasants, petit bourgeoisie and 'progressive intellectuals'. Ideally, the coming republic, across Italy's regions, could curb capitalism, demolish the brutal, traditional power of large landowners and pave a path to urban and rural socialism.[47]

In practice, a radical 'wind from the North' soon stilled and, in December, Parri was supplanted as prime minister by the worldly-wise Christian Democrat Alcide De Gasperi (a survivor from the Aventine, as well as the man who, secure in the Vatican's Propaganda Fide college, had heard the boom from the Via Rasella attack). Amendola stayed in office. His hope that Anti-Fascist unity could survive under Catholic leadership was vividly expressed at San Carlo opera house on 11 February 1946, anniversary of the signature of the Lateran Pacts between the Vatican and Mussolini's dictatorship in 1929. Amendola was all family piety and moderation when he stated that the PCI stood 'for the democratic renewal of the Mezzogiorno'; its aim was an 'Italy aligned with the democratic aspirations of Giovanni Amendola'.[48]

Giorgio continued to stress his party's sweet reasonableness until the communists ended their participation in government on 1 July 1946. The party leaders watched over the referendum that established the Republic on 2 June but scarcely converted national political life into what they understood as popular democracy. On 11 June, right-wing demonstrators in Naples, convinced that the poll had been stolen, sacked PCI headquarters in a violent riot provoked by the belated announcement of the monarchy's fall. Giorgio had to face a fierce armed mob in what became a physical struggle. Recalling his boyhood training as a boxer, he hit out hard but was outnumbered. Hostile demonstrators tore his coat to pieces, pulled his shirt away and left his tufty hair 'looking like a porcupine'. He was briefly arrested by American military police, after Italian officers, who may not have been friends of a communist, told them that he was responsible for the fracas. Only when it was established that he was the prime minister's under-secretary was he released.[49] Two days later, De Gasperi dropped him from the government. In further proof of surviving social violence in the South, Giorgio, despite his size and physical prowess, on the night of 21 August was held up on a back road near Salerno; the thieves stole his gold watch and 25,000 lire in cash (at the pitiful exchange rate, about US$50).[50] Can he have wondered whether his grandfather's battles against southern brigands in the 1870s needed renewing?

But the party wanted him where he was. Giorgio's background might in reality have been more that of a rootless cosmopolitan (like his mother) than a Neapolitan. But he had made his life choice for communism in that city and his father had lived and died as a southern parliamentarian. Togliatti and the PCI leadership agreed that Giorgio, however distant his life experience had been from the poor of the region, was best cast as an expert on the South. From 1946 to 1953, he directed the segment of the party's central committee charged with defining communist policy there. He must work to improve party organisation, diminish the differences between North and South and prepare the way for a 'socialist country, without capitalists and without large landowners'. In that process, he must seek to open the eyes of 'workers on the land', who were 'poorly informed, divided and without faith and hope', more ready to believe in magic and the Madonna than Marxist theoretics and Gramscian formulae.[51] When it came to evoking heroes, Giorgio argued in a local version of a cult of personality that Togliatti stood out grandly as the leader of leaders, adding dubiously that the Machiavellian party chief was the cynosure of all eyes whenever he came South.[52] Rather than his boss, maybe Giorgio, with his height and bulk often towering over the locals (as photographs of such events display), looked to some of the people like a glorious saviour, a power-laden heavyweight, and not just another soft bourgeois intellectual from 'Rome', always a place of irrelevance and exploitation in their minds.[53]

When it came to preaching party gospel, Amendola in his writings and speeches was accustomed to invoke the saintly name of Antonio Gramsci, ignoring the Sardinian communist's damning of Giovanni Amendola as a 'semi-fascist' back in 1924. Gramsci, locked in a Fascist prison for a decade until just before his death on 27 April 1937 and so saved from Stalinism, had been moulded into the philosopher of a party that might appear as much Italian as Soviet and committed as much to peasants as to unionised workers.[54] Togliatti had begun to use a Gramsci myth before the outbreak of the Second World War, inserting him into a lineage of the historically virtuous that included Dante, Giordano Bruno, Galileo, Mazzini and Garibaldi. As Togliatti told Giorgio in a phrase meant to indicate that there was no possibility of doubting the official line on his legacy: 'You don't joke with Gramsci.'[55]

In December 1945, Togliatti readily argued that Gramsci's thought underpinned the *svolta di Salerno*.[56] Given the party line, Amendola keenly invoked Gramsci as the pioneer of those party methods and policies devised to detach the southern peasantry from Liberal, Catholic and neo-Fascist clientelism into a genuine acceptance of democracy (and the nation).[57] As he stated to the party congress in April 1951: 'We southern communists are engaged in working always more and always better to carry out the indications that Comrade Gramsci left us.'[58] Just how many southern peasants, who in the 1950s and 1960s slowly and erratically began emerging from their age-old illiteracy, marked, read and understood Gramsci's difficult texts might be a question worth asking. But perhaps the name mattered more than the detail.

The habit of deferential citation did not disappear. In his old age, Amendola again pushed the view that Gramsci was the key Italian thinker of the twentieth century, utterly humane and utterly revolutionary (as Giorgio hoped he had been).[59] When he was no more than a fledgling communist, he recalled romantically, had not Togliatti sent him to Piero Sraffa in Cambridge to collect a secret store of letters that Gramsci had scribbled in his prison? On return, he passed them personally to Togliatti, who, in his emotion about contact with so great a mind, fumbled with the wrapping and then swore his young comrade to complete silence about the matter.[60]

Given his preoccupation in Naples and the South, Amendola, until after the death of Stalin, played a relatively minor role while the PCI adjusted from the months of armed activity in the Resistance and crafted its policy towards the enveloping Cold War. With whatever equivocation, Togliatti steered the party towards what could be sold as 'the Italian road to socialism'. Revolution must be delayed and then delayed some more. The wartime policy of alliances with all men and women of good will must continue – and especially with the more left-leaning wing of the soon dividing socialists, led by Pietro Nenni. The party should learn how to be as tactical and subtle as was its leader. It must, for example, accept the survival of deep church influence over society through the endorsement of the Lateran Pacts in the constitution. Giorgio, with his anti-clerical training and stated atheism, was less than pleased by such a choice but deferentially bowed to Togliatti's decision.[61] Over this and other issues, Amendola endorsed Togliatti's demand that the more radical sector of PCI membership, as restlessly led by Pietro Secchia, unusual among the party leadership in being the child of a worker and peasant and not bourgeois or intellectual, should be restrained and diverted.[62]

There might not yet be revolution, but Giorgio had to believe that there was plenty of change for the better. Throughout the rest of his life, he argued that, during the immediate post-war era, the PCI had done its best for Italy. It did not squander the chance of revolution but delivered liberation, the Republic and, in 1947, a modernising and potentially highly democratic constitution to Italy. In 1946–7 Giorgio served successive commissions drafting its clauses.

Figure 6.2 Giorgio, preaching in the still very poor Salerno (but not seeming to convert one member of the new generation) (1946).

As for the rest, Giorgio almost sounded like a new Croce when he argued that, before engaging in radical action, the party needed to absorb detail about Italian life, all the more so since the leadership had been in exile or gaol for two decades (and his own acquaintance with Naples and the South after 1931 had been fleeting). The June 1946 elections for a constituent assembly facing the task of drafting a new constitution had been disappointing given that the PCI won 18.92 per cent of the vote against their socialist partners' 20.67 per cent. But, again in debate with his father's ghost but with less optimism than a few months earlier, Giorgio stressed that the Partito d'Azione had eked out only 1.45 per cent. Such a dismal tally meant that no one had been able to create 'a democratic party that had a large base in the middle classes', let alone do so in the South.[63] Worse, what was really happening, whether for the moment or over the following years, was that the bourgeoisie was managing to move 'their rifle' – that is, their economic and political control – from one 'shoulder' to another. Especially in the South, much reform was required before any genuine democracy could reach the people.[64] The hopes that Giovanni Amendola had once placed in the Unione Meridionale or the Unione Nazionale still looked bleak.

Giorgio campaigned vigorously for what he still called the 'southern democratic front' in the 1948 elections. As so often he was ready to sound nationalist on occasion – for example when, on 8 January, but without the cutting edge of Malaparte's prose about Naples, he rebuked 'the negative consequences for the Neapolitan economy and the physical and moral health of the population' of American military and naval bases established in and around the city. The result, he stated, was to corrupt Naples into a version of Singapore and 'Hong-Hong [sic]', where the only beneficiaries were 'a small nucleus of traitors and parasites who live off the protection and money of the foreign powers'. Gramsci had warned against letting 'adventurers and thieves' prosper in the ranks of local leftist parties. But, Giorgio added self-righteously, he and his comrades were determined to keep the red flag flying and stand for truth, justice and the communist way.[65] Such rhetoric might droop a little, as might another effort on 13 March to rally his Amendola inheritance, or rather that of its males, behind his campaign: 'When in one family there are Garibaldian and Republican grandfathers, patriots of the Risorgimento, a father who was an Anti-Fascist martyr and partisan, and communist sons, it is reasonable to say that this family succession followed the great lines of the national development of our country.'[66]

Did anyone listen? On 18 April, Democrazia Cristiana (DC, the Christian Democrat party), heavily backed by the Americans and the Vatican of Pope Pius XII, won 48.5 per cent of the vote and an absolute majority of seats in the Chamber of Deputies. Even if the PCI outpolled the socialists in the combined Fronte Democratico Popolare (Popular Democratic Front), that body's tally of 31 per cent represented a serious fall since 1946. The future of the Italian Republic was shaped for the rest of the Cold War; Christian Democrat-led governments did not lose office until after Amendola's death. The first non-DC prime minister, in 1981–2, was the Republican journalist and historian Giovanni Spadolini.

On 14 July, the PCI was shaken after an assassination attempt on Togliatti by a Sicilian neo-Fascist student just outside Montecitorio in Rome, where Giorgio could sadly recall battling his father's assailants. Back in Naples the next day, he noted how perturbed he had been at the sight of Togliatti, who was shot three times. In hospital, 'I saw my father', he stated.[67] Some party rank and file, with the arms that they had used in the Resistance still concealed from the authorities,[68] hoped for a communist rising in response to the assault. In the Emilia, comrades had stuck to the slogan 'When the time comes, we shall be ready [for revolution]'.[69] But Giorgio and the rest of the leadership, including Secchia, opted instead for a general strike and other demonstrations. Again there was to be no march to the Winter Palace.

Giorgio had regularly evoked Giovanni Amendola's heritage, however much he had to edit out his father's anti-communism and his superficial comprehension of the southern peasant world. In 1949, Giorgio and Pietro decided that Giovanni's ashes should be brought back from Cannes, where the commemorative inscription said that he 'lay waiting'. But the brothers could not escape Giovanni's friends. The reburial in Naples in April 1950 occurred with patriotic fanfare, in the spirit of the (non-communist) Anti-Fascist unity of the wartime CLN. An honour committee formed under the auspices of President Luigi Einaudi (a Liberal economist). Members included Bonomi, Casati, Croce, De Gasperi, Nitti, Orlando, Parri, Lussu, Ruini, Enrico De Nicola (acting president from June 1946 to January 1948 and then president until Einaudi took over in May), Giovanni Gronchi (a Christian Democrat destined to be the next president of Italy and then president of the Chamber of Deputies), Carlo Sforza (minister of foreign affairs) and Ferdinando Torgetti (a socialist who was deputy president of the Chamber).[70]

The committee arranged the publication of a commemorative volume of Giovanni's speeches from 1919 to 1924. They gave no prominence to members of the PCI at the ceremony, although, as Giovanni's heirs, the Amendola brothers took their place in the monumental, nineteenth-century Poggioreale cemetery. This choice confirmed the status of

Naples as 'Amendola City', even if Giovanni had lived most of his life and fought his key intellectual and political (and personal) battles in Rome. The cemetery stands across a main road from the Poggioreale prison, where Giorgio had spent unpleasant and noisome months when moved in and out of Ponza.

At the burial, Enrico Molè, an ex-member of the Unione Nazionale and, after 1945, an independent leftist, proclaimed sonorously that 'the great exile is back. The celebrated son re-joins his mother.' Giovanni had died a heroic victim of 'Italian wounds in a foreign land'. Naples, Molè ran on with local loyalty, may have been silent through the Fascist years but its people had never betrayed Giovanni. Now their 'professionals, workers, the official delegation, the representatives of the people, women, men and even children' offered him a heavenly crown, since 'the force of Good is always destined to defeat that of Evil'. In his own lifetime, Giovanni had been a man. In death, he was 'a symbol, a religion, an idea ... our *condottiero*'.[71]

Hallowed by such high-flown sentiments, Giovanni Amendola was solemnly laid to permanent rest, even if neither he nor Giorgio might be pleased to find that, on a current website, the tomb featured most prominently is that of Benedetto Croce.[72] Giovanni takes his place in the Quadrato degli Uomini Illustri (Square of Illustrious Men; no woman is buried there) among 156 others, who include imperialist Liberal foreign minister Pasquale Stanislao Mancini and Risorgimento-Liberal writer Luigi Settembrini. A jarring recent addition is Giovanni Leone, Christian Democrat president of the Republic from 1971 to 1978, driven to resignation by allegations of corruption, to be replaced by socialist symbol of the Resistance Sandro Pertini (when Giorgio was too old and ill to stand); Pertini was proud to take office as 'an uncompromising Anti-Fascist'.[73]

When back acting as a party chief, Giorgio, up to the next set of national elections in June 1953, managed communist policy in the South. He bitterly opposed the Cassa per il Mezzogiorno, founded under Christian Democrat auspices in June 1950 to deliver state backing for economic modernisation. Its character, he complained, was irredeemably 'colonialist'; instead, he drew upon Gramsci to demand economic reform from below and not above. The Cassa, he warned, would merely act as a vehicle for electoral corruption, preventing rather than assisting social or economic reform.[74] The South was to be left where it had been under the dictatorship (and before 1922): a place of 'carnage, corruption and ballot rigging'.[75]

When the elections approached, the most debated issue was a DC suggestion of extra reward to the party that won more than half the vote, at once labelled by its opponents the *legge truffa* (cheat law) and paralleled with Acerbo's scheme in 1923–4; Secchia charged that it meant that 'Fascism' returned.[76] Amendola piously re-invoked his father's opposition to the Acerbo law, describing how his family flat at that time had been 'besieged day and night by Fascist squads'. Those who now wanted to deny the Republic's constitution, he charged, were 'taking the path to dictatorship. You cannot turn back.' His father, he wrote, had known that, 'every twenty years', Italians were made to face the choice between 'freedom and reaction'; he then launched into a familiar narrative of his family's commitment to justice and liberty ever since the Risorgimento.[77]

The law did pass in March 1953, but the June poll results did not allow its application. They saw a considerable decline in the DC vote (down to 40.1 per cent) and a minor improvement for the PCI (22.6 per cent) and the socialists (12.7 per cent), while there were also gains by the Monarchists and neo-Fascist Movimento Sociale Italiano (MSI, Italian Social Movement), a party whose name brazenly claimed inheritance from the Repubblica Sociale Italiana of 1943–5. Perhaps the election gave slight grounds for optimism, but Amendola had scarcely presided over what, in March, he had prophesied to be a 'rebirth of the South'.[78]

Throughout the post-war years, all PCI policy had to reckon with Stalin and any observations – positive or, more likely, negative – about the Italian situation delivered by the re-organised Communist International, the Cominform. In September 1947, Longo endured severe criticism of the PCI's stance since the war during a Cominform meeting at Szklarska Poreba in Poland. The Italian party's reaction to rebuke was to pledge its obedience to Moscow but not necessarily to curtail searching for its own policies.[79] In his own backyard, Giorgio was capable of sounding like an unreconstructed follower of Stalin and the USSR. In June 1952, he damned the following won in Naples by shipping magnate Achille Lauro, an ex-Fascist, who was making himself the city's boss and served as mayor from 1952 to 1958.[80] What a contrast to this city's fate, Amendola pronounced with attempted cheer, was 'the great and victorious building of socialism in the USSR', similar socio-economic progress in China and throughout the Warsaw Pact![81] Christian Democrat rule in his nation, he added almost mechanically, offered a dismal contrast to the successive five-year plans in the Soviet Union and the 'gigantic steps forward' of the 'free Soviet peoples', whose nature was being utterly transformed under their glorious leader.[82]

On 5 March 1953, Stalin died. In the party daily *L'Unità*, the editor Pietro Ingrao, another southerner who was to move towards the New Left in the 1960s, devoutly mourned the loss of 'the man who has done the most for the liberation of humankind'.[83] Togliatti flew to Moscow for the funeral and took Amendola with him. It was Giorgio's second visit to the communist Holy Land; he and Germaine vacationed there in 1949 without his ever portraying that visit as either memorable or positive. Later, Giorgio wrote that, in 1953, he found a country in tears over the loss of their *vozhd*, but he noticed that the Soviet leadership seemed more relieved than sad. When he impertinently highlighted the matter at a dinner with Togliatti and the socialist Nenni, the latter berated him as an 'impudent iconoclast', while his own party chief remained cannily silent about his insight.[84]

In 1954–5, Togliatti ushered Amendola away from the South. He replaced Secchia as the key administrator or 'organiser' within the party hierarchy and thus, to quite a few eyes, as the party dauphin. For the next lustrum, Amendola was the man who prepared the successive party congresses and chose what words and individuals were prioritised there. Delegating much specific initiative to his younger associate, Giorgio Napolitano, he could still speak up for industrialisation projects in the South while remaining hostile to the DC's management of them.[85] Large and brusque, he aroused some trepidation (and resentment) in party comrades when they differed from him. Giorgio retained his role until early 1960, when, at the IXth Congress, he was replaced by the Sardinian (of aristocratic family) Enrico Berlinguer, born in 1922 and fifteen years his junior. Thereafter, Giorgio moved to being the party expert on the functioning of the Italian economy.

The year 1956 had brought crisis to the PCI and the communist world. The XXth Congress of the Soviet Party met in Moscow for eleven long days from 14 to 25 February. Togliatti attended for the PCI. At a closed session on the last morning, Secretary Nikita Khrushchev tabled a report 'on personality cult and its consequences'. It amounted to a devastating attack on Stalin's murderous tyranny. It took months for the story fully to leak out and Togliatti's reaction was 'deeply cautious'; his fifty-three-page report to the party leadership on his return to Rome virtually ignored the matter. Amid a swirl of rumour and scandal, Amendola undertook the job of telling Togliatti that silence was no answer, perhaps astonished to hear in response that the PCI chief had 'forgotten' the issue. Giorgio may have been whistling in the wind, but his first reaction was to hail an alleged resultant advantage to the PCI, which could now candidly pursue its ideas about an Italian road to socialism.[86]

Every day, party turmoil deepened. More than a hundred men and women from the cultural and academic worlds informed the central committee that they intended to terminate their membership, being rebuked by Giorgio with a charge of 'betrayal'.[87] Through summer and early autumn, popular disturbances in Poland and Hungary raised the issue of whether the Soviet side in the Cold War was about to collapse. On 4 November – ironically for Italians, 'Vittorio Veneto Day', marking their 'victory' in the First World War – Soviet tanks rolled into Budapest. One day later, British and French paratroopers landed beside the Suez Canal, nationalised by the Egyptian leader Gamal Abdel Nasser in July, the intention being full reassertion of Western European empire.

In such circumstances, just how independent could the PCI be? Giorgio knew his answer. Each intellectual critic of the USSR was summoned to party headquarters in the Via delle Botteghe Oscure, interviewed either by Giancarlo Pajetta, party expert on foreign affairs, in his office on the third floor, or by Amendola on the fourth, his readiness to shout at what he called 'traitors' being notably formidable.[88] As Amendola put it starkly: 'When the Red Army fights, we must be on their side.'[89] By December 1957, he was assuring a workers' assembly in Milan that the party had triumphed over 'the barking hounds of our class enemies'. By supporting the Soviets' actions in Hungary, he maintained, 'we held high the banner of revolutionary faith and international socialism', sure that 'socialist superiority' in modern science would continue to outdistance capitalism.[90] It was just as well that the USSR had the bomb, he added in January 1959, with his rhetoric at its most expansive, because the Americans had to acknowledge that, if there were another world war, it would be partially fought on US soil. But all comrades wanted peace and rejected intercontinental destruction, 'because this world is ours, the future of this world is ours, it will be communist and we do not want the communist world pushed into destruction'.[91]

During the last months of 1956 and the first of 1957, the PCI shed 200,000 members. Yet its electoral fortunes did not falter much. The leadership lay in the hands of a Togliatti–Amendola alliance, distanced from the loud critics of the USSR but also favouring an Italian path to socialism, despite the combination being viewed with grave doubts by more rigid party elements.[92] Friendly relations with Nenni's socialists in the North and a willingness to seek support without too detailed an examination of past attitudes in the South helped the party vote to hold in the April 1958 national elections.

Then and thereafter, Giorgio continued publicly to prefer Soviet civilisation to that of the West, even if he did concede that, with Italy's accelerating spurt in gross domestic product (GDP), its so-called economic miracle, the spread of washing machines and other white goods and the opportunity for ordinary families to go on holidays were to be welcomed. Yet, he remained a puritan. Sport, he complained, was being reduced to spectatorship. Planning for the Olympic Games in Rome in August–September 1960 was wasting public money on extravagant appearance. By contrast, the 'gigantic' conquests of the USSR did not corrupt men and women into individualist selfishness. Soviet invention had carried 'civilisation' to the moon. The Warsaw Pact was militarily strong but stood for world peace, in contrast to the imperialist adventuring of its opponents.[93] In Vietnam, French imperialism had exhibited its cruelty and hollowness, while, throughout the 1960s, Amendola was sure that the Vietcong could beat back the Americans.[94] In that part of the world, the Soviet line was completely 'valid', Chinese criticism of the USSR mistaken, and all should acknowledge the 'grave sacrifices' that the Soviets had selflessly made across the globe in opposing US imperialism.[95]

Earlier, the return of General Charles De Gaulle to power in France at the end of 1958 stirred Giorgio to talk about renewed fascism throughout Europe, and, for some time, he remained hostile to the European Economic Community (EEC). In March 1962, he argued in *Rinascita*, the PCI's monthly popular theoretical journal, that the six original members of the EEC had associated in order to undermine growing worker movements throughout Western Europe. The EEC was tied to NATO. It stood on the side of the USA and its global interests and opposed the USSR. Yet, he added more hopefully, now there might be a chance that European ties, among leftist parties and unions, could allow a 'rebirth of democracy' and an 'advance towards socialism'.[96]

The dilemma of the party's relationship with the USSR remained a central issue for the PCI leadership. In August 1958, Giorgio and Germaine joined Luigi Longo and his new wife on a Soviet holiday. In 1953, Longo, too, had obtained an annulment in San Marino of his longstanding marriage to Teresa Noce, who had kindly helped Giorgio's acclimatisation to the party in Paris in 1931. Never quite free of party work, during their vacation the Italians met Khrushchev, who proffered a disquieting repetition of Croce's advice in 1925–6. The PCI, the Soviet chief advised, did not have to do anything but just wait until the Soviets inevitably overtook their US rivals in material progress and military strength.[97] It was scarcely a recipe that Longo and Amendola, the latter of whom annoyed Khrushchev with rebellious mumbled objection, could disclose in Italy. There, talk of the 'Italian road to socialism' became more emphatic, while, in November 1961, Amendola insisted in a speech to his central committee that the PCI must remember that not one of Gramsci, Marx or Lenin needed to be de-Stalinised.[98] A little later, he urged that socialists and communists should jointly celebrate the first foundation of a Socialist Party in Italy in 1892, since 'we come from the same origin'.[99] As the party slogan of the 1970s put it, the PCI 'came from afar', long preceding Petrograd and 1917.

Just before the crisis over Stalinism broke, there had been a major development in Amendola's private life. On 18 February 1956, daughter Ada, aged only twenty, married Dr Camillo Martino in Rome. It was a party match, and one reaffirming family ties to the South. Martino had been born at Montesarchio in the province of Benevento on 13 March 1931. As a boy he lived in Naples, before his family fled from wartime bombing. After the Liberation, he returned to the city, soon joining the party. He earned a medical degree from Naples University. Soon afterwards, he transferred to Rome, where he found a place as one of the doctors employed at the PCI head office in the Via delle Botteghe Oscure, but he retained a family residence in Naples. At the Botteghe Oscure, a medical team joined lawyers, accountants and other professionals in providing a mini-welfare state for party leaders; 500 staff were employed in the building.[100] In 1965, Martino took a field hospital to Hanoi, working there for a time in fraternal salute to the North Vietnamese.[101]

But the marriage with Ada did not prosper. Miriam Mafai, a communist journalist a decade Ada's senior, recalled meeting her soon after the Liberation, when she was 'on the edge of adolescence, radiant, slim, beautiful'. Happiness did not last. Seeing her later on a number of occasions at the party branch in Monteverde, a bourgeois part of Rome, Mafai noted that she often became overexcited about political and private issues.[102] Maybe she found the task of embodying the party and the Amendola family too much. Maybe she carried psychic troubles inherited from Eva. She and Camillo had two daughters, Elena and Sandra, but, to Giorgio's dismay, they were divorced on 23 October 1971, in what must have been one of the first legal separations in Italy after the passage of the divorce law in December 1970. The party and Giorgio moved leadenly towards that reform, with Berlinguer convinced in June 1969 that the PCI was itself a 'vital and unique family' whose members hated any idea of divorce flooding the country.[103] Ada, who had never fully recovered physically from her infant attack of dysentery and the belated remedial attention she then received, may have used drink as a refuge from her troubles. She died from liver failure on 18 January 1974. Giorgio, it was said, could never again bring himself to walk past her Naples apartment.[104]

Not long after Ada's wedding, Giorgio opted for more straightforward family piety, in this case with regard to his mother, who turned eighty in 1960; she died on 28 November of the following year. Allegedly on her initiative, but surely on the advice of her surviving sons, Eva Amendola Kühn, as the title page put it, brought out a work entitled *Vita con Giovanni Amendola* (Life with Giovanni Amendola). More than 600 pages long, it began what was to become a massive venture in publishing Giovanni Amendola's correspondence, in this initial case making public many of the letters that he and Eva had exchanged when they were young lovers and parents; the book took 445 pages to get past the First World War. Eva provided brief and superficial commentary. There was no mention of Nelia Pavlova or her son.

Vita con Giovanni Amendola did not appear with a communist publishing house, such as Riuniti, but with Parenti in Florence, a company that began under Fascism and tended to concentrate on the literary field. Giorgio wrote a short coda where he commenced recording those childhood memories on which he was to enlarge in his autobiographical writings of the 1970s.[105] Giovanni Cerchia may exaggerate when he says that the book signalled a return in Giorgio's mind of Giovanni Amendola's heritage, taking a step away from his party 'father', Togliatti, and exhibiting a renewed sense that he himself carried the genes both of Anti-Fascist liberal democracy and of Anti-Fascist communism, going all the way back to the Risorgimento.[106] Plainly, the book demonstrated that, as far as the Amendolas were concerned, the family mattered a great deal and had been a telling microcosm of all that had been positive in Italian political and social history in the *longue durée*. As Giorgio told a journalist in December 1961, 'the older he became, the more he felt himself to be like his father'.[107]

Perhaps there was some special pleading in this statement, since Giorgio had seldom missed the opportunity to harness his family history to the cause of the party. Between 1958 and the death of Togliatti on 21 August 1964, Giorgio seemed to be cementing his place at the top of the PCI leadership and was widely beheld by friends and enemies as Togliatti's natural successor. The long-term party leader died after a stroke and cerebral haemorrhage at Yalta on the Black Sea, where he was holidaying and peering through the murk of Kremlin politics in the usual PCI combination of play and work. (In fact, Khrushchev was ousted from office by Leonid Brezhnev in October 1964 after a carefully organised party coup already being planned during the summer.) Togliatti's body was transported to Rome for a lavish funeral ceremony, while the Soviets renamed the city of Stavropol on the Volga Togliattigrad (Tolyatti) in his honour; it retains its name in post-Soviet Russia.

As far as the Italian party was concerned Togliatti had expired like a monarch in his palace. All but automatically, he was succeeded the day after his death by his deputy-secretary and titular heir apparent, Luigi Longo. In this appointment, there was no consultation with the party membership or with anyone else. Longo's elevation signalled the end of

Giorgio's ambition to lead the PCI; like his father, the call to the highest office to which he aspired never came. Longo, who was only seven years older than Giorgio, suffered a severe stroke late in 1968.

Amendola and Ingrao bumped into each other while Giorgio was striding purposefully down a corridor on the second floor of the Botteghe Oscure offices.[108] In their exchange, Giorgio, with an abruptness of manner that had become his norm, told Pietro Ingrao, the two being seen by many as rival and feuding lieutenants, that they must back out of any suggestion of their own advancement. Giorgio denied that he led any faction but he had accused Ingrao of imitating the DC in such personal rivalry.[109] Now, Giorgio announced, they must encourage the party to promote Enrico Berlinguer as Longo's deputy and chief agent. However, Berlinguer did not formally replace Longo as PCI secretary until 17 March 1972.

How, then, did Giorgio chart his course through party debates between 1958 and 1969, the decade that led to the end of his direct power within the PCI? These were years of major change in Italian society and in the political functioning of the Italian Republic. Italian GDP began to grow at an annual average of 5 per cent (higher in the North than in the South). Between 1958 and 1968, national wealth all but doubled and Italy seemed to be catching up with the larger economies of Germany, France and Britain. Italians suddenly began to eat meat, grow taller, ride Vespas or drive cars and take holidays; a few hesitant steps were even taken towards female equality. By 1987, there were credible, if short-lived, claims that the country had achieved an economic *sorpasso* of the UK. From the late 1950s, the uneven growth across the country sparked massive internal migration; four million southerners left their homes between 1951 and 1971, an increasing majority for sites within Italy.[110] If the power of organised crime remained stubbornly present in Sicily (the Mafia), Calabria (the 'Ndrangheta) and Naples (the Camorra), to some degree the ancient patterns of *miseria* were broken in many southern *paesi*. At last, more than 5 per cent of children in the South commenced high school. Some may have begun to read Gramsci.

Politically, there was a major political crisis between March and July 1960 when a DC prime minister, Fernando Tambroni, endeavoured to rule in coalition with Monarchists and the neo-Fascist MSI. To the pleased surprise of the PCI leadership, massive popular objection, especially from the trade unions, to this apparent abandonment of the 'myth of the Resistance' soon prompted Tambroni's fall, with Giorgio, after the event, congratulating his union comrades on the 'great Anti-Fascist mobilisation' and rejoicing in the 'actuality of the Resistance'.[111] In that regard, Amendola remained an advocate of unity somehow reframed across the parties of the Left and especially between the PCI and those socialists still being led by Pietro Nenni. In March 1963, during a conference at the Istituto Gramsci in Rome examining Italian capitalism, Giorgio went quite a way towards denying any lingering vulgar Marxist and catastrophist reading of the national economy, half suggesting that the communists could become part of a 'democratic alternative' that, from time to time, would take office without seeking revolution.[112] Over the years, he reiterated that his party should see itself as part of 'the governing realm' of Italy, thereby being a prophet of the 1970s' policy proclaimed by Berlinguer of a 'historic compromise' that could link the communists and the Christian Democrats in coalition in Rome, and, well before that, in many a provincial capital.[113] In July 1969, Berlinguer in fact had opposed Amendola's suggestion of searching for some way to enter government.[114]

During the first years of the 1960s, all participants in internal debates in the party sought to win Togliatti to their side, with the veteran leader opposed to any suggestion that Italian comrades should turn their back on the USSR. Giorgio, too, could not or would not go too far, late in 1964 rejecting a case made by Norberto Bobbio, a leftist philosopher, who had joined the Partito d'Azione in the Resistance and now urged that it was time for a fully refashioned Left party in Italy. For Bobbio, that step meant that the PCI should drop the 'communism' from its name and commence a new history.[115]

Amendola needed to make it clear that he was not ready for such renunciation since Ingrao and his supporters were accusing him of 'repudiating communism' and 'marching to the right'; in his own account, Ingrao remembered 'Giorgione', red in face, launch furious personal attacks on him while, 'as for me, I did not use a single bad word in reply'.[116] It was put more kindly by Giorgio Napolitano, in his turn to be president of Italy from 2006 to 2015, a bourgeois Neapolitan communist born in 1925 who rose through party ranks as Giorgio's young man and lived to embody the final domestication of the PCI. Giorgio, he recalled, then and always expressed 'political energy in its pure state'.[117] The DC was traditionally riven by shifting factions (*correnti*) and the PCI's image was too serious for such byplay. Nonetheless, the battle with Ingrao continued. Giorgio often lost his temper in discussion, but he won a partial victory at the 1966 XIth Party Congress. Neither had a final break until both lost authority with Berlinguer's appointment as vice secretary in February 1969.[118]

In practice, from 1962 to 1963 what resulted in the political world was the so-called *apertura alla sinistra* (opening to the Left). The formula of national government from then until 1976 became coalition between the DC (which kept the prime ministership) and the Socialists. It was a system that faced its own crisis in the Italian version of the European '1968', the year when angry students and angry workers, rarely in harness, assaulted their country's ruling classes and demanded the repudiation of many conservative assumptions.[119]

At that time, Amendola reacted to student demonstrations as a sixty-year-old might. It was utterly absurd, he growled, to think that angry, hedonistic juveniles were the same as the working class.[120] Throughout its history, he contended loudly in an article in *Rinascita*, the PCI had had to struggle against enemies on both its right and its left. Such prophets of the 'New Left' and its version of libertarianism as Herbert Marcuse must be understood as enemies of the working class. All good communists should stand four-square against such 'infantile' errors as 'sectarianism, schematism and extremism'. Students and their dubious counsellors were dallying with 'ancient anarchism', in no way equal in profundity and purpose to the 'patrimony of ideas that we have accumulated over decades of hard experience'.[121] The working class was for ever the working class.

To domestic 'contestation' was added a deep crisis in the Warsaw Pact; from January, the Czechoslovak communist leader Alexander Dubček welcomed a 'Prague Spring' and a policy of 'socialism with a human face', far from the rigidity of Brezhnev and the dull old men in charge of the USSR. On the night of 20–21 August 1968, the Soviets lost patience with Prague and sent in the tanks as they had done in Hungary in 1956. In those summer days, Giorgio and Germaine were on holiday in Bulgaria (no hint of reckoning there with the ghost of Nelia Pavlova), a satellite that, per force, had to offer Brezhnev's Soviets full support. Four months earlier, Amendola had written in praise of the Czechs and what he discerned was 'a rising and autonomous articulation of the [international] socialist camp'.[122] But, in August, even if he disliked military action, he adopted a 'tepid' stance on noisy criticism of the Warsaw Pact's invasion from within the party, the student movement and the New Left.[123] Following a familiar pattern in his worldview, he worried lest the Cold War turn hot and urged the PCI to further emphasise its commitment to internationalism. As a signal that his party could not simply be the Soviets' subordinate in regard to foreign affairs, in March 1969 he led a PCI delegation to Brussels. There he reversed his initial dislike of the EEC. Soon he publicly endorsed Willy Brandt, Social Democrat chancellor of West Germany (1969–74), and his *Ostpolitik*, through which the German sought calmer relations with the USSR.[124] In 1976, Giorgio solidified his presence in Strasbourg, three years later winning a seat in the first direct elections to the European parliament.

Amendola was almost ready to state that the USSR existed ultimately to provide an alternative to the USA and the market, and for no other obvious reason, even if that purpose continued to justify PCI links with Moscow. He did express his dislike of Soviet dissidents, whom he believed were always servants of the Americans.[125] He told himself that the USA spent 13 per cent of its GDP on armaments. Events in the Middle East and elsewhere intimated that capitalism was facing deepening crisis. Workers across the world no longer accepted 'a brusque deterioration in their life and work conditions', let alone high unemployment figures. What was needed, in Amendola's view, was 'education in socialism' for an eager working class, helped by an avant-garde that was 'politically conscious and organised into a revolutionary and internationalist political party' for whose members 'the political and intellectual patrimony of lived experience' included the 'grandiose times of the October Revolution'. Comrades should also remember the war and Stalingrad.[126] Opponents might call him a 'conservative' or a 'Stalinist of the right', but Amendola believed that he was a 'national communist', with both adjective and noun expressing unbreakable commitment and loyalty (and his family's traditions).[127] As he put it again in 1971–2, the USA demonstrated what it wanted in Europe by its support of dictatorship in Spain and Portugal since the war, its longstanding backing of Italian neo-Fascism, and its favouring of the new tyranny of the colonels in Greece. The Americans found Italy's steady 'democratic and socialist progress insupportable'.[128] Italian youth must be reminded every day about the Resistance and Anti-Fascism, their country's and the PCI's special history – and, by implication, the choices since the Risorgimento of the Amendola family.[129]

The 1970s were Amendola's last decade, a time when the commanding, hot-tempered politician, his time as a party chief over and the fate of the family passed into the hands of a new generation, morphed into a gentler, kinder being, if also an ample one. Through these years Giorgio continued to put on weight, eventually tipping the scales at 136 kilograms. No wonder he was known as Giorgione. His sometime sister-in-law, Maria Antonietta Macciocchi, thought cruelly that he looked like a 'large wardrobe'.[130] Germaine tried to persuade him to eat salads and other slimming food. But he would sneak into a friendly nearby *rosticceria* and fill up there first before going home.[131] No wonder Germaine noisily berated him on occasion. But, despite such squabbles, she and Giorgio retained what Camillo Martino labelled a 'living, completely united, symbiosis',[132] with Giorgio known to all comrades as 'the most faithful' of husbands.[133] During their last decade they lived in a party-owned new

migliorish .

apartment complex out on the Via Cristoforo Colombo; it led to the model Fascist suburb of EUR (in fact finished by the Christian Democrats).[134] Relaxing at home, Giorgio was said to enjoy watching downmarket variety programmes on Italian state television – something that, in his more intellectual youth, he might have disliked. He was pleased to be a friend of Raffaella Carrà, sexy host of the celebrated programme *Canzonissima*; according to Wikipedia, Carrà, to tut-tutting from the Vatican, was the first television personality to display her belly button on camera.[135] By now, he and Germaine possessed a retreat at Velletri in the Alban Hills, almost a Roman version of a Soviet *dacha*, where, mellow at last, he could do some gardening or read Simenon's 'realist' murder stories, while Germaine could paint her nature scenes without interruption.[136]

Figure 6.3 Giorgio in old age at his place at Velletri, in friendly talk with Gillo Pontecorvo, in his time a Jewish Anti-Fascist and communist, who separated from the party in 1956 but did not renounce Marxism.

Germaine had taken to art in a serious manner. Commencing at Avezzano in 1972, her work was exhibited in some major Italian cities, including Bologna (1973), Milan (1974), Salerno (1975) and Rome (1977). Her exhibitions were endorsed by a number of famous Italian painters and art critics, most either members or friends of the PCI. Among them was Renato Guttuso, who maintained that surveying her canvases provoked 'intense emotion', all the more so since he knew of her and Giorgio's rich contribution to the Italian people. When it came to her artwork, Guttuso judged that she possessed force and natural-ness, while defending 'chastity and purity'. Perhaps a more obvious feature of her subjects is a love of nature and what might be a serene or melancholy vision. In the catalogue of her exhibition at the Galleria La Barcaccia in Rome, of the thirty-three paintings displayed only one includes a human being. It is of a young woman in a white dress that may be a bridal gown. Her face is blank.[137] Maybe there is some reflection of Germaine's sorrow and that of Giorgio at the early death of their daughter, Ada.

While Germaine sketched, Giorgio wrote. He had always been a wordsmith, whether of speeches or pungent articles in *Rinascita* and other party-approved journals. Works of that kind continued to appear – they even did so during the first years after his death. During the 1970s, he joined the fashionable activity of giving serious publishable interviews, whether on the nature of Anti-Fascism or on the party's efforts to renew itself in the 1950s.[138] In 1985, the American cultural historian T. J. Jackson Lears sardonically described Gramsci as 'the Marxist whom you can take home to mother'.[139] Already, in the previous decade, Giorgio had all but assumed a role as a western communist of whom any nice mother might approve. Although he never mastered English, his attitudes reached the pages of the self-consciously radical *New Left Review*, where he explained that the PCI envisaged a long, long 'transi-tion' to socialism; 'You cannot make a revolution against the wishes of the majority,' he avowed with propriety. But there was hope in Rome, since Italy had become 'the most advanced country in Western Europe' from a 'democratic standpoint'.[140]

While contemporaries pondered the place of the PCI in domestic and international theory and practice, Giorgio, warned by his doctors of his deteriorating heart condition,[141] turned his hand to autobiography. First came his *Lettere a Milano: ricordi e documenti 1939–1945* (Letters to Milan: Memoirs and Documents). Weighing in at more than 750 pages, it was published by the PCI house of Riuniti in 1973 and narrated a tale of war and resistance that might live for ever. It placed on record Giorgio's version of his and the party's virtue and dedication in defeating

Nazi-fascist evil through those years. Despite lingering *parti pris*, it won the prestigious 1974 Premio Viareggio for narrative.

Later, there was a shift into shorter, more deeply individual, memoirs, *Una scelta di vita* (1976) (A Life Choice)[142] and *Un'isola* (1980) (An Island)[143]. Each was published by the commercial Rizzoli. Now the political became the personal, while Giorgio, with a humour and humanity that make the volumes the best Italian memoirs for centuries, fused his love story with Germaine and his complex ties with his father and the rest of the Amendolas into his communist life. Rizzoli commissioned Germaine to provide an image for the cover of *Un'isola* (which is dedicated to her).[144] It is of a green island in a blue sea beneath a mutedly blue sky. A scattering of white houses can be detected on the hillside. But there are no people.

For the party, the decade of the 1970s seemed to be leading to triumph. A national election in 1972 offered a predictable result (PCI 27 per cent versus DC 38 per cent) but a referendum on the divorce legislation on 12 May 1974 constituted a massive defeat for the Right (divorce upheld by 59.3 per cent to 40.7 per cent). In the aftermath of the referendum, the party made major gains in regional elections, and, through the months before the June 1976 national poll, there were suggestions of a *sorpasso* in which the communists and their leftist allies could win more than 50 per cent of the vote. In his 1975 interview on Anti-Fascism, Giorgio was hopeful that such a victory might be imminent.[145]

In reality, on 20 June 1976, the PCI reached a summit of 34.4 per cent (the DC got 38.7 per cent); with the socialists and some dissidents of the New Left, the Left's total passed 46 per cent. Berlinguer had enunciated the '*compromesso storico*' (historic compromise) back in 1973; the PCI stated its support for a coalition – fitting memory as enshrined in the myth of the Resistance over what had happened in 1944–5 – with democratic and civilised elements in the country, embracing many in the DC. All could join in government. Italy, Berlinguer advised, could thereby avoid outraging the USA, where Henry Kissinger openly rejected any toleration of the PCI.[146] The Americans had recently backed a violent military coup against the 'Marxists' of Chile, headed by Salvador Allende. In his careful line, the Resistance and the thought of Gramsci were his lodestones, Berlinguer maintained.[147]

Berlinguer distanced his party ever further from the USSR with what was called 'Eurocommunism'. He told a journalist from *Il Corriere della Sera* that he and his comrades felt safer on the NATO side of the Cold War and that détente was best preserved by the Italian presence there.[148] Following the elections, on 10 August 1976, he announced, with Italian subtlety, that the party would not oppose the new government led by Christian Democrat Giulio Andreotti (*sfiducia*), nor would the communists back it (*fiducia*); rather, they would opt for *non-sfiducia* (non-opposition).[149]

The peak of 1976 was soon followed by a fall. In the June 1979 elections, the PCI vote declined to just over 30 per cent, and, after Giorgio's death, it continued to dribble away; Berlinguer renounced the *compromesso storico*, perhaps appropriately in a speech at Salerno, on 28 November 1980. He died, widely esteemed a tragic figure, on 11 June 1984. The PCI share of the vote had almost held in the 1983 elections, but by 1987 it waned to 26.6 per cent. After the collapse of the USSR, the party split. The mainstream group, now calling itself the Partito Democratico della Sinistra (Democratic Party of the Left), secured 16 per cent of the vote in the 1992 elections, when the more traditionalist, Rifondazione Comunista (RC, Re-founded Communists) earned 5.6 per cent. The party was over.

The 1970s had constituted '*gli anni di piombo*' (the years of lead) in Italy, when rightist and leftist terrorists took a heavy toll. The climax occurred on 16 March 1978 when members of the Brigate Rosse (BR, Red Brigades), boasting that they embodied the 'living traditions' of the 'armed Resistance',[150] kidnapped DC secretary Aldo Moro from the streets of Rome; they held him in a 'people's prison' until they murdered him on 9 May. During the fruitless search for the kidnappers and their victim, the PCI stood firmly against some deal with the BR, emphasising, in principled manner, that five police officers had been shot when Moro was seized. The Italian state could not remain credible if it surrendered in any way to their murderers. Moro's corpse was driven through central Rome and deposited in the Via Caetani, often said to be halfway between the Botteghe Oscure and DC headquarters in the Piazza del Gesù. It was more emblematic that they parked their Renault 4 outside the Biblioteca di Storia Moderna e Contemporanea (Library of Modern and Contemporary History). The terrorists were crudely announcing their dissatisfaction with national history. For Amendola, in particular, a positive line had begun with the Mazzinians and Garibaldians of his family through to Giovanni and on to the PCI. All rubbish, the BR said, and murdered with a smile. As a student radical who was not in the BR put it with what might be read as menace in November 1975, Giorgio and his ilk had engaged in 'a pitiful attempt to remake history for their own use and consumption' and the sad tactics of Eurocommunism and historic compromise were the result.[151]

How did Giorgio, during his last decade, cope with the new course for the PCI to 1976 and then the travails of party and nation during his last years of life? His stance on terrorism was clear from start to finish and sprang from what he had already decided about dissenting students in 1968, who, he reiterated, must never be confused with the working class. Like the maximalists of the *biennio rosso*, they lacked self-discipline and, when they indulged in terrorist acts, they simply transmuted into Fascists. As he underlined on a number of occasions before the Moro murder, the BR were 'catastrophists' with a fatuous reading of history, a repetition of attitudes that had ushered the Nazis into power[152] or had made some Italians fight for the Salò Republic. Every Italian had to agree that, under the Republic since 1946, they had become prosperous as never before.[153] It might be that some terrorists were, in a merciful phrase of the moment, 'young men in error', but, both then and now, they were enemies whom the Resistance had shot.[154] Giorgio did, however, reject the suggestion by Republican Ugo La Malfa (a youthful admirer of Giovanni) that the death penalty needed to be restored. The US model, Giorgio typically maintained, showed the damage capital punishment inflicted on society.[155]

With what sounded like a glimmer of memory of boyhood home life, he again warned the party against preferring intellectuals to their real worker and union base. 'With intellectuals, there is a greater risk of squabbles, of emotional responses, of less self-control, of meagre continuity of work, of a lack of respect for undertakings, of failing to meet the demands of the political calendar.'[156] Communists stood not merely for determinist economics but also for human justice, freedom and dignity. They did not need flighty intellectuals to keep them up to the mark. Their deep and long history led them to virtue.[157]

Insofar as international relations were concerned, Giorgio had warmed to Europe, even if he still hoped that the West and East of the continent, which, he believed, ran as far as the Urals, should be organised and united through their working classes.[158] Given that all had staffed the Resistance in the war against Nazi-fascism, they could steer away from the endless and dangerous conflict between the USA and the USSR.[159] The result could be general disarmament, the withdrawal of all foreign armed forces from various states, and the opening up of deep dialogue with the developing world, without always running into US imperialist interference.[160] Then, planning, technological exchange, better environmental policies and greater opportunities for women could progress further towards the genuine democracy that he and the PCI had always wanted.[161]

Shortly before his death, Amendola was one of the few in his party not to oppose the Soviet invasion of Afghanistan. In January 1980, he wondered out loud whether he should resign from the leadership group over the issue. In taking this stance, he did not know the appalling fate of Afghanistan through to the present, the rent between fundamentalists, initially armed and financed by the US and its allies, and more moderate elements, with the country's peasants left in *miseria*. Rather, he again feared that the Cold War might turn hot; he had no inkling yet of American total victory in it.[162] A month earlier, he had read the economic future just as poorly when he predicted that Thatcherite neoliberalism could not prosper. Rather, he argued doggedly, with no hint of comprehending the eventual penetration of Trumpian populism into our contemporary democracies and in what might be read as his final message: 'If we want to gain the faith of Italians, we must tell the truth, the whole truth.'[163]

On 5 June 1980, a final heart attack took Giorgio's life. He was being tended in room 229 on the first floor of the Villa Gina, a clinic in the Via della Sierra Nevada, located amid the (fine) Fascist architecture of EUR. Germaine was present and stayed in his room that evening, after his body was removed. Her son-in-law, Camillo Martino, divorced from Ada but still a member of the family and the party, was there to watch over her. Martino gave Germaine a sedative but she woke in the early hours of the morning of 6 June with a heart attack of her own; shortly afterwards, she died peacefully. By 11.55 a.m., the surviving Amendola brother, Pietro, was sorrowfully announcing her death. Giorgio's and Germaine's granddaughters, Elena and Sandra, who joined the salute, stated that their grandparents had always said that they would die together; they were too close for one to outlive the other.[164] It was a romantic, beautiful ending to forty-nine years of partnership, begun in momentous times and continued unbroken near the centre of national Italian politics.

The two received a respectful state funeral at Rome's main cemetery, Campo Verano, where a common sacred area had long been reserved for PCI leaders.[165] In burial, party and family fused eternally, as Giorgio doubtless wanted. During the speechifying of this event, the shrewd Catholic Giulio Andreotti maintained that the atheist Giorgio had been a Christian without knowing it, devoting himself to resolving the problems of the earth. Eugenio Scalfari, the editor of the independent leftist paper *La Repubblica*, suggested that Giorgio was 'almost a reincarnation, even physically' of Giovanni, each 'a revolutionary and a conservative'. From Strasbourg, his comrade Giancarlo Pajetta, with greater orthodoxy, urged that Giorgio be recalled as 'a patriot, a partisan commander' and a member of the PCI.[166]

Like his father, Giorgio composed a final testament. Unlike his father, Giorgio did not range widely in it. After all, his only child was dead and he had less reason to moralise to surviving family than Giovanni had.

Moreover, no Nelia Pavlova needed blanking from his story. There was, of course, his 'life choice' for the party. But that, too, at least according to Martino's memoirs, was absent from his last thoughts, to the stifled displeasure of Berlinguer and the PCI leadership. Instead, Giorgio focused on Germaine and their deep mutual love.[167] In their private life together, Giorgio and Germaine – the massive bourgeois, cosmopolitan, 'national' communist and the fragile working-class Paris girl – had lived a love story that, it might be hoped, will never fade.[168] That inscription into national memory was certainly Giorgio's last hope.

Conclusion

The year 1980 was one of dying on the political Left in Italy. Apart from Giorgio and Germaine, among those who passed away were Pietro Nenni (1 January), Luigi Longo (16 October), his sometime wife Teresa Noce (22 January), and Giorgio's sister, Ada, who died from breast cancer in Sardinia on 31 January. Not just individuals but a whole society, a whole way of reading past, present and future were perishing in the dawning, durable era of neoliberalism. Not for nothing would American political scientist Francis Fukuyama become a celebrity before the decade was out by diagnosing a global 'end of history'.[1]

In this process, which has continued into our own times, Giorgio was a loser on almost every count. Over the following years, there came the demise of many causes and institutions that had framed his life choice. The invasion of Afghanistan did not disseminate socialist civilisation to that country's complex society; rather, it spread mayhem, enhanced religious fanaticism, and led to the eventual bloody defeat of Soviet armies. Mikhail Gorbachev may have sounded like a convert to Eurocommunism when he became Soviet general secretary in March 1985 and hypothesised a 'common European home' for his country. But his attempt at a liberal (or social democrat) turn in the Soviet empire did not prosper. In 1989–90, Warsaw Pact and communist Eastern Europe withered away, to be followed in August 1991 by the USSR, in the aftermath of an abortive, hard-line, 'Stalinist' coup. Ten years after Giorgio Amendola's death, the USA had won the Cold War, while Russia's unlovely subsequent fate was to adapt into a corrupt and authoritarian empire, ruled in dictatorial manner by an ex-KGB officer, Vladimir Putin.

In the Italian sideshow of these global events, the PCI surrendered its name and purpose. The last party congress (ironically, the XXth) on 31 January 1991 assented to dissolution. Palmiro Togliatti may long have acted as a second father to Giorgio. But now even his ghost was dead and conservative historians readily found evidence of his pusillanimous collaboration in Stalinist evil.[2] During these years, there was much talk of

187

Con Luigi Longo (1952)

Figure C.1 Giorgio *il Grosso* with PCI dauphin Luigi Longo (1952).

the disintegration of the 'First Italian Republic', the 'regime' that had
been forged in the constitution of 1947, at least in Giorgio's mind,
through the democratic sacrifice and brave purpose of the Resistance.
All the parties of the post-war era collapsed or switched nomenclature;
many Italians damned the First Republic precisely for being a '*partito-
crazia*', a system where liberty and equality were not furthered by parties
and their ideological debate, rather being frustrated and corrupted.
Thereafter, for almost two decades, the leading politician of the
'Second Republic' became the rich and perhaps corrupt businessman

Silvio Berlusconi. His populism was expressed in his party name, Forza Italia (Go, Italy), with no basis in formal ideology, its origins springing from the football field.[3] As I write in 2022, Italy is governed by a transformist coalition, headed by the 'technocrat' banker Mario Draghi; none of its members admits a heritage carried from the thought or practice of the PCI. Its largest grouping pledges loyalty of a kind to an anti-party called M5S (Movimento Cinque Stelle, the Five Star Movement), whose name disdains all previous politics.

At a more general level, since 1980 Italy and the world have watched the death of the social forces that Giorgio treasured. Five months after Giorgio's death, Ronald Reagan was elected president of the USA to embody the global power of neoliberal ideals. As his gospel preached: 'Government is not the solution to our problems, government is the problem' and 'the nine most terrifying words in the English language are: "I'm from the government, and I'm here to help."'[4] From 1980, with Reagan and Thatcher in the van, across the world governments laid waste union power and privatised state agencies. No doubt global free trade brought greater wealth to many. But the accompanying industrial and technological revolutions rendered work precarious rather than life-long. Any Left unity that may have remained during the 1970s frag-mented. Talk of collectivity, except, often perversely, where nationalism (or racism) could be exploited as making 'us' great again, was spurned. Giorgio's belief that capitalism was to be replaced by socialism as the world's economic system now looked inane or antique.

'Identity politics' became and remained the key to most political association and dissonance. Class subsided into an all but meaningless term compared with gender, colour, ethnic identity, sexual preference and even religion. Giorgio had doubtless expressed sympathy for 'developing societies', but he had little inkling of the migration and environmental issues that torment the current world. Even before his death, peasants had disappeared from much of Western Europe and were ever harder to find in the Italian South. Gramsci's formula, so regularly evoked by Giorgio, of the democratic and socialist bonding of workers, peasants and enlightened intellectuals lost traction. Some recalled Gramsci's exploration of hegemony, but more often in conservative than revolutionary vein.[5] Once, Giorgio, however blinkered his eyes were by communism, sought to perceive and unveil the 'real' and not the 'fake' truth to his listeners; not for him the privatised and social media view, now omnipresent, that individual opinion and belief outweigh societal expertise and science.

Giorgio's life story had steered its path through the two versions of 'totalitarianism' – Fascism and communism – although, in the Italian case, every sensible observer must add that they were 'Italian-style'. In his interview on Anti-Fascism, Giorgio stressed that the Mussolini dictatorship should not be confused with Adolf Hitler's Nazi rule in Germany; Fascism's initial squadrist violence, he argued, was mostly modified into state violence (and, he did not add, into corruption and patron–client dealings) of a kind familiar under the Liberal Giolitti.[6] Yet, Giorgio was only too ready to believe that fascist 'contagion' lingered after 1945, and therefore he, too, overused the word when he might have been better persuaded that Nazism or neo-Nazism should replace it as the descriptor of today's racist Far Right.[7] However, he never did accept the parallel use of the word 'totalitarian', which may mean something when addressed to state practice in the pitiless 'communist' monarchy of North Korea but, elsewhere, is easier to trumpet than accurately to define. Stalin may have committed terrible crimes, but, in Giorgio's mind, they never matched those of Hitler.[8]

Given the four decades of neoliberal mastery, a wry historian by now might suggest that we should talk instead about contemporary consumerist market totalitarianism; there are plenty of politicians and economists convinced that all should be for the market, nothing should be outside the market, and no one should be against the market. Has the thesis 'I shop, therefore I am' become a global civic religion? In the current world, there may be endless invocation of individual freedom and 'democracy', but always set under market rules, backed by widespread policing from global agencies, and with an unshakeable belief in neo-Darwinian victory for the strongest and the richest; as Boris Johnson half remembered in March 2021, the certainty that 'greed is good' rules OK.[9] It is a worldview that did not figure even in Giorgio's nightmares, and neither did the arrival of Vladimir Putin as a bloody tyrant in our contemporary Russia, one who may on occasion mouth Soviet slogans but one who has actually accepted, like the neoliberals, that we live in a Darwinian world where 'might is right'.

What these developments mean is that, when it comes to tracing historical ghosts in Italy, it is easier to find Giovanni than Giorgio. The son chose communism, which is dead and buried in the serious world, except in its idiosyncratic Chinese manifestation of state-run, authoritarian and nationalist neoliberalism. Giovanni stood for 'freedom' (somehow defined). When, in the post-war era, liberal (and imperialist) philosopher-historian Benedetto Croce was trying to argue that Fascism had been a 'parenthesis' in national history, discounting sin in Liberal Italy, he sneeringly dismissed Giorgio as 'the exact type of a sporty Fascist' whom he had never seen 'with a book in his hand'.[10] Croce's intimation was that, although Giorgio may have thought his life choice was to fight fascism, he carried its totalitarian evil in his heart. Since he was not a liberal, Croce suggested, Giorgio could not carry a positive message into history.

Could Croce be right? Certainly, today, Giovanni is the Amendola who visibly counts. One way to plumb historical influence in Italy is through streetscapes. Across the country, street names record those who have left their political or cultural mark on the nation, with much repetition. Can there by any town without a Via or Piazza Garibaldi? The exception to authorised urban memory is that, since 1945, the numerous names that once hailed the Fascist regime's chiefs or alleged achievements have almost always been purged.

Three heirs or successors of the Duce, two granddaughters (the half-sisters Alessandra and Rachele) and a great-grandson (Caio Giulio Cesare) may currently sell their Mussolini name brand to the electorate,[11] but public record is muted. So, in Rome, the Piazza Montecitorio outside the parliament had been named for Costanzo Ciano, father of Galeazzo, corrupt boss of Livorno,[12] major figure in the 1920s (and uncharitable witness to Carlo Scorza's wedding in Lucca). In 1945 it returned to its old designation. The Foro Mussolini, the sports complex on the Tiber to the north, was prudently converted into the Foro Italico (although its celebratory Fascist mosaics were left intact).[13] Perhaps the dictatorship's most egregious naming was in the area around the Ostiense station during the German Führer's visit to Rome in May 1938. There, the Piazzale Adolfo Hitler was amended after Rome's liberation in 1944 to the Piazzale dei Partigiani (Partisans' Square) and the Viale Adolfo Hitler to the Viale delle Cave Ardeatine (Ardeatine Caves Street). No mention of Giorgio Amendola in this part of Rome, but hints linger of the ceaseless debates whether the bloody *gappisti* attack at the Via Rasella was justified.

So, instead, let us ask what happens when Vie or Piazze Giorgio or Giovanni Amendola are mapped across the country? Is there direct urban recollection of Giorgio? Zealous search can locate a short street invoking his name on the far eastern periphery of Rome. Such memory surfaces with similar bashfulness of positioning in Naples and Turin, if there the roads are a little longer. In Milan, Giorgio is relegated to Segrate outside the city limits. In the 'Amendola province' of Salerno, he does have streets commemorating him in the smallish centres of Agropoli, Nocera Inferiore and Siano, while, at Sarno, the 'provincial road' out of town bears his name. Similarly, in the province of Palermo, a street salutes him at Bagheria, but not outside the splendid Museo Guttuso, which exhibits many of the paintings of the sometime communist patron of Germaine.

If tracking Giorgio's municipal evocations leads down side alleys, Giovanni, by contrast, finds a central place in almost every city streetscape. In Rome, the Via Giovanni Amendola lies a couple of blocks down from the city's Stazione Termini (the main station housed in a modernist building planned from 1939, altered after 1944, and completed in 1950). Cheeringly for Giovanni's ghost, this Via Amendola runs past streets commending such Risorgimento heroes as Cavour and Gioberti before switching into being the Via Filippo Turati, summoning remembrance of the moderate socialist who was another Aventine Secessionist. Less happily, it runs parallel with the (longer) Via Giolitti. For a brief period Amendola had earned a greater posthumous victory over Liberal Italy's ghosts when the Via Regina Elena, running down from the Piazza Barberini towards Montecitorio, was renamed for him. Perhaps the fact that it lay parallel to the Via Rasella suggested that it soon become the Via del Tritone after Bernini's statue of the sea god in the Piazza Barberini and not after the father of a communist perpetrator.[14]

Other cityscapes pay homage to Giovanni Amendola all over Italy, at Turin, Bologna, Salerno, Palermo and many other places, large and small. In Milan, there is a Metro station hailing him as a '*martire*' (martyr) of Anti-Fascism, while the square outside elevates him to a '*statista*' (statesman). His liberal democracy is given an economic veneer that might have surprised him since the Metro stop is called Amendola Fiera (opened 1964), because of the large international commercial site for a time planned nearby. In Naples, a Piazza Giovanni Amendola lies not far from the beautiful, waterfront, Riviera di Chiaia. In Bari, one of the roads out of the *centro storico* carries his name. At Sarno, the Corso Giovanni Amendola is the main street in the old town; it runs past a Donnarumma pharmacy, still belonging to the family of Giovanni's sometime faithful secretary and helpmeet in 1925. A state school pays tribute to him, boasting a 'tree of [Giovanni] Amendola's ideas' in its library; they must be assumed to grow eternally.[15] In Salerno, Giovanni stands erect and suited in a statue on a main street. His presence lingers everywhere in Italy, although my favourite example is situated in the small Sicilian coastal town of Marsala, where the Via Giovanni Amendola runs from the Piazza Matteotti (almost) as far as the Corso Gramsci.

Giorgio does have a foundation in his honour. It is based in Turin and tightly linked to the Associazione Lucana Carlo Levi. The latter body celebrates the author of *Christ Stopped at Eboli*, with his compelling portrait of ancient rather than specifically Fascist tyranny. A joint website exhibits a Carlo Levi painting of his red-headed self proselytising attentive southern peasants, with a bronze bust of Giorgio standing at his side.[16] Giorgio's fine biographer, Giovanni Cerchia, presides over the foundation's research work, which ranges widely as an active and progressive social force, while not forgetting on occasion to celebrate Giorgio's moderation, good sense and acceptance of Italy's European destiny.[17]

There is no equivalent Giovanni Amendola Foundation. But the father has been publicly remembered over and over again through the decades since 1945, even if his resuscitation did take time. The first major historical study about him under the Republic was by the Marxist Giampiero Carocci, and, to the dismay of liberals, argued that Giovanni was a belated and partial opponent of Fascist dictatorship.[18] When Carocci's book appeared in 1956, already some of Giovanni's speeches and writings had been republished and, over the next years, there was a smattering of memoir reference.

However, it was during the 1970s, that crucial time of threatened drastic change in Italian politics, that he came into his own as a liberal champion, whether in academic historiography or in more public celebration. Not for nothing did Giovanni Spadolini, a man who combined historical writing with Republican – that is, moderate liberal – politics, suggest that 1976 be named the 'Amendola year', with a polite, canny double reference to Giovanni and to Giorgio's *Una scelta di vita*.[19] It was the year of the PCI's narrow failure to achieve a political '*sorpasso*' and the fiftieth anniversary of Giovanni's death in Cannes.

As far as Giovanni Amendola was concerned, further republications of his works with flattering introductions now appeared; one from De Felice argued characteristically that final assessment must be delayed until fuller documentation was available.[20] During 1976, two major conferences examined Amendola's legacy, and the liberal Einaudi Foundation published a book of essays about him.

The first event was held at Sarno between 7 and 11 April 1976 (before the crucial June elections), under the auspices of the *comune* and the region of Campania. An eventual book recorded, in print and photographs, the celebrations in the halls, schools and streets of the town. Giorgio, Pietro and their sister, Ada, were all present. Eva was remembered as having been an 'exceptional woman';[21] there was no mention of Nelia Pavlova. Spokespeople came from across the non-fascist political spectrum. Giulio Andreotti sent his apologies for the opening but offered a short paper stressing that Giovanni and his own mentor and patron, Alcide De Gasperi, shared a 'rigorous intransigence' in their affirmation of democracy.[22] Carlo Galante Garrone, in his youth near to Partito d'Azione chief Ferruccio Parri, but by 1976 an 'independent of the Left' senator (that is, one elected with PCI backing), gave official welcome, sure that Giovanni's blend of high morality, 'severe intransigence' and permanent willingness to engage in democratic debate made him an eternal prophet of Anti-Fascist leftist unity.[23] At a subsequent round table, participants agreed that Giovanni was 'still alive'.[24]

A second and more academic conference was held under the auspices of the region of Emilia-Romagna in Bologna from 3 to 5 December. This region had a leftist administration, headed by the socialist Silvano Armaroli; the local president was the communist Sergio Cavina. Giovanni Spadolini, that man for all seasons, opened discussion, focused on Giovanni's 'battle for democracy'. When its proceedings were published, Spadolini provided the approving preface. There, he took care to endorse the 'authenticity' of Giorgio's family memories of 'an authoritative, not really authoritarian, father' but one who admittedly operated a 'fair way' apart from ordinary family life. Giovanni, he explained mildly, was all but totally 'immersed in his political and civil battle'. His prime aim, Spadolini argued in a later speech, was to construct a new 'ruling class' that would be free from the evils and tyranny of Fascism. All in all, Spadolini asserted, Giovanni Amendola was 'the heir and key interpreter' of a liberal philosophy, originating in the Risorgimento and the first Destra (rightist) governments of the 1860s. They had never yielded to the snares of *trasformismo*, Giolitti or 'Italietta' (disappointingly little Italy) – and, he did not add, of socialism.[25]

A range of other speakers amplified this picture but offered debate rather than a single interpretation of Amendola's ideas and purpose. Elio D'Auria, preparing his decades-long devotion to his meticulous, six-volume edition of Amendola's correspondence, led the way. No fellow traveller of the PCI, D'Auria was sure that Amendola's fundamental aim was to preserve liberalism and prepare democracy happily integrated into a modern liberal state.[26] Other participants highlighted Giovanni's deep interest in religion, his eschewing of Marxism and his hope that entering the First World War could allow Italy to demonstrate that it was 'a serious and civilised country'.[27] There were some mild criticisms. Paolo Spriano, the major historian of the PCI, suggested that Amendola's severity made it hard for him to win many to his side.[28] Leo Valiani, another in 1945 close to Parri, argued that the Aventine Secession had not worked well and complained that Giovanni had preserved a trust in King Victor Emmanuel III for far too long.[29]

More painstaking in tone and emphasis was the Einaudi volume, edited by the conservative patriotic diplomatic historian Ruggero

Moscati (born in Salerno in 1908). In his preface, Moscati underlined his admiration for Giovanni's 'totally pure' thought and action. He insisted that his message from the 1920s had 'surprising analogies and parallels for our cultural and political life', a coded warning against too much truck with totalitarian communism.[30] Among the book's contributors were D'Auria and Capone, two younger historians destined to produce many works on Giovanni. Each, then and later, was sure that Giovanni's liberalism kept its meaning fresh. They never doubted that his desire to convert the soul of the people to the nation was a fully democratic and modern project.[31] Salvatore Valitutti, a historian and Liberal member of parliament, seconded such praise; in his eyes, Giovanni aimed to create a modern state and 'a grand peasant democracy', which would disavow 'parties' as the corrupt vehicle of personal self-interest and a drag on the needed 'spiritual growth of Italian consciousness'.[32] As Leone Cattani, another but more radical Liberal, added, such profound and lasting ambitions explained why Giovanni Amendola was Mussolini's chief opponent, why he died and why his message was eternal.[33] In 1976, then, Giovanni Amendola mattered but the meaning of his legacy was being politely disputed between observers connected with the PCI (and his communist sons) and those who were overtly anti-communist and believed that Giovanni's ghost belonged to them.

It was a dispute that shed much of its meaning over the next years as communism (and the PCI) faded away. The next major commemoration of Giovanni Amendola was inspired by the fiftieth anniversary of the creation of the Republic and the framing of its constitution, but also by the seventieth anniversary of his death. From 25 to 27 October 1996, a conference met at Montecatini Terme, promising an analysis of Giovanni's world 'between the ethical and the political'. Some of its debates were hosted at the Grand Hotel e La Pace, which had been so rudely invaded by Scorza's squadrists in July 1925. D'Auria and Capone were the first two speakers. D'Auria repeated his stock view that Amendola laboured righteously to defend the Italian state as 'enemy number one of the regime'. Capone focused instead on Amendola's intellectuality, conceding that there might have been something enigmatic about his philosophy.[34] Among other speakers, Giorgio Spini, himself a Waldensian and another ex-backer of the Partito d'Azione, examined Amendola's religiosity, stressing how devoted Giovanni was to the idea that the Italians must experience 'religious rebirth', not through some tired connection with the Vatican nor, perish the thought, via Fascist totalitarians, but as benignly believing members of the Italian nation.[35]

What was most novel about this event was its presentation of local documents tracking the Fascist attack in 1926 on Giovanni in its remorseless barbarity. After an exhibition of this material was opened by a local archivist, Pietro Amendola gave his family blessing, and a memorial plaque to Giovanni was inaugurated at the Montecatini council chambers. Pietro's second daughter, Antonella, spoke later, expressing a positive memory of her grandmother, Eva Kühn, who, she reported reverentially, in old age was given to staring at a portrait of Giovanni ('Vanya'), her 'hero, always a boy, whom evil did not succeed in bending'. Antonella dwelt on Eva's pleasure over the publication in 1960 of *Vita con Giovanni Amendola*, a book that, she maintained, was 'the first and most precious contribution for all students of the thought and work of Amendola'.[36] In weighing up the documents, the local historian Umberto Sereni gave proceedings a more 'Anti-Anti-Anti-Fascist' character, not as effusive as Giorgio would once have been about the Resistance, but still deeply opposed to any legitimation of Fascism within Italy.[37]

More years passed. Giovanni Amendola won still greater fame on the ninetieth anniversary of his death in yet another conference, this one assembling on 25–26 November 2016 in the Sala della Lupa (where the Aventine Secessionists had first assembled) at the Campidoglio in Rome in the presence of the president of the Republic, the Sicilian Sergio Mattarella, a Catholic lawyer, academic and politician. Elio D'Auria formally initiated pious recollection of 'a life in defence of freedom' by lauding Giovanni as the representative of 'Anti-Fascism in its most noble dimension'.[38] In a longer paper he again pushed the case for Giovanni as a 'martyr for freedom and democracy', as well as the first to provide a serious diagnosis of totalitarianism.[39] Mario Pendinelli, a left liberal from the South, added that Giovanni was 'not only a martyr of Anti-Fascism but also a great liberal reformer', a 'politician-intellectual of European dimension'.[40]

Other contributors were less effusive. But there could be no doubt that, by this time, Giovanni had been moulded into a '*Padre della Patria*', a father of the Fatherland, a figure whom all Italians should admire and respect. There was no need for anyone to worry whether his desire for a strong state was compatible with contemporary neoliberal privileging of the market nor whether Giovanni much understood economics, banking and finance or was particularly interested in how capitalism should best flourish. Nor should it be asked whether southern peasants in the 1920s were near to becoming democratic citizens of a modern nation or whether Giovanni, for all his politicking in the South, made any serious attempt to comprehend them – and, anyway, now they have vanished.

Equally, there was no need to ponder the extent to which Giovanni's ideas about a national religious faith becoming the prime identity for all Italians went even further than Fascist ambitions to impose a 'civic religion' on the people.[41] What Giovanni might have thought about the end of European and Italian empire and of Italian emigration to the wider world, with its replacement by global immigrants, quite a few from ex-colonies, could readily be left obscure. So, too, his understanding of modern women, where the tares in his relationship with his wife, it seemed, troubled only critical feminist historians (and Nelia Pavlova remained unmentionable). Historical doubts and complications slipped away. It may be assumed that, on the centenary of his beating and death in 2025–6, Giovanni Amendola doubtless will stand below Giuseppe Garibaldi in the pantheon of Italian heroes but he may well hold the place that Mussolini assigned to him as the country's leading Anti-Fascist. On what medievalists call the wheel of fortune, Giovanni the father stands in reputation and legacy ever higher, Giorgio, the son, ever lower.

There is one counter to this story of a posthumous victory for Giovanni the liberal. Throughout my account of an ideological wrangle between liberalism, communism (and fascism), the family has been ever present. The more naïve commentators on totalitarianism, a term of which Giovanni was the likely inventor in 1923, if then without its full later meaning, are convinced that its pressure on ordinary citizens is so devastating that they are reduced into atomised individuals. Under the yoke of totalitarianism, men, women and children blindly worship and obey their regime's leader and are ever ready to fight murderously for him. Can the idiosyncratic Asiatic totalitarian monarchy of North Korea be like that? Perhaps. But, certainly, Mussolini's Italian dictatorship and any PCI regime that Giorgio's party might have imagined lacked such overweening intention. For all their political passion and hard work, Giovanni and Giorgio, Eva and Ada (senior), Antonio and Pietro never forgot that they belonged to the Amendola family, gained profit from it and had duties to it. Giorgio, Antonio and Pietro may have sounded at times like loyal Stalinists. But some qualification always lurked in the fact that they were still Amendolas.

Similarly, in the inscription since Giorgio's death of the activities of father and son across the century from 1880 to 1980 into history, this family identity has survived. It has been assisted by a younger generation who have avoided too much direct politicking but have prompted efforts by professional commentators to reunite the Amendolas in death. I am too much of an outsider to participate in that process. Yet, while I have used the lives of Giovanni and Giorgio Amendola to illuminate a century of Italian history and the fierce ideological conflict through those years, I have had to concede that, when it came to deep belief, often enough family surpassed political ideology. Giovanni may have been a liberal of some sort; Giorgio a communist, ditto. Each may have dreamed of converting all Italians to their (rival) causes. But neither ever stopped being an Amendola.

Afterword

It has brought me a great pleasure putting together in 2020–2 this study of the Amendolas, father (liberal democrat, Anti-Fascist, saint and martyr) and son (communist). In my narration I have remained an '*indipendente di sinistra*' (Australian-Oxfordian or rootless cosmopolitan-style). I have never renounced an Anti-Fascism of my own slant. In my research for this book, I have been helped by email contact with the liberals Elio D'Auria and Antonella Amendola, who may well end up wondering if Rosario Romeo was not right about me and 'Botany Bay'. Giovanni Cerchia, from further to current Left and the academic director of the Fondazione Giorgio Amendola, together with Prospero Cerabona, the foundation's president, have also generously assisted me, both in my research and, importantly, in obtaining quality reproductions of many of the photographs that illustrate this text, whether sourced directly from the foundation or from the Istituto Gramsci in Rome.

When it came to the intriguing Bulgarian face of Giovanni Amendola's life and his relationship with Nelia Pavlova, I am in debt to Maria Todorova of the University of Illinois Urbana-Champaign and her contacts in the Sofia archives (where are located quite a few photographic images of Pavlova). I was further assisted by Yavor Siderov, once of the University of Western Australia and now of Sofia. John Pollard has kept Mike's and my locked-down spirits up by blending food and history conversations. Paul Corner has been ready to receive news of Afghanistan's cricket successes (and failures), while in Italy patiently awaiting a jab. Patty Rizzo, Nerida Newbigin and Ros Pesman sent through details about *Altro polo* that I had forgotten. Gianfranco Cresciani, Rob Stuart and David Laven have been subeditors extraordinaire. David also found for me Nelia Pavlova's Paris address. My book is dedicated to David, in a similar spirit of gratitude and inadequacy that I once had with my frequent teaching partner, Tony Cahill, at the University of Sydney.[1] Many academic people say to me, with implied deep doubts over my activities, 'Richard, you write so much' (even in lockdown). I know. I can't stop. But I do deeply admire colleagues who

199

know so much more than I ever shall and who are much better at not writing all the time.

As ever, Michal has put up with me retreating to my study, putting on one opera or another as blot-out-music, writing and writing some more (and making bad jokes about '2020 vision'). March 2022 signals the sixtieth anniversary of when we met in Ernest Bramsted's second-year History Honours Class at the University of Sydney; I think the Jewish, Social Democrat refugee from Nazism may have mentioned Mazzini in his course on nineteenth-century Europe but I don't recall other Italian names. Down the road in present-day Oxford, there is also our criminologist daughter, Mary, her art historian husband, Anthony Gerbino, and two clever, beautiful, granddaughters, Ella and Sophia. Frequently on the phone has been our banker son, Edmund. We Bosworths have held up through the barren weeks and months of pandemic in a way that shows 'family' means something to us, too.

How wonderful it has also been, with the assistance of Michael Watson and Liz Friend-Smith, and their two perceptive manuscript readers, to be publishing what surely must be my last book and doing it with Cambridge University Press, the elegant and scholarly publishers of my first, *Italy, the Least of the Great Powers*. A tiny reference to Giovanni Amendola can be found in its pages. It has also been a delight to be assisted in the familiar publication processes by Judith Forshaw, Divya Arjunan and Stephanie Taylor, with their highly honed professional skills. I, and they, were duly dependent on Diana Volpe for the book's New Model index. While surviving that process, I have been regularly enlightened by old-age colleagues at Jesus College. I am also especially grateful for the help I have received from Prospero Cerabona and Giovanni Cerchia, President and Director, respectively, of the Fondazione Giorgio Amendola in Turin. All the photographs are reproduced with the permission of the Fondazione and the Istituto Gramsci in Rome, with the exception of Figure 4.1, which is reproduced with permission of the Central Bulgarian State Archives in Sofia, where it can be found in the Hristov papers.

I trust, in this current work, those who are scanning these pages have enjoyed pondering the lights and shadows in the Amendolas' lives more fully and perceiving the extent to which they illuminate the human condition, even in a world where (social) democracy often seems so permanently trumped.[2]

Notes

Preface

1 For my youthful account on return, see R. J. B. Bosworth, 'Why watermelons belong on the left: the Italian general elections of 1976', *Australian Outlook*, 31, 1977.

2 The English-language version is Denis Mack Smith, *Mussolini's Roman Empire* (London: Longman, 1976).

3 See R. J. B. Bosworth, 'In the green corner, Denis Mack Smith, in the red? black? corner, Renzo De Felice: an account of the 1976 contest in the historiography of Italian Fascism', *Teaching History*, 11, 1977. In 1976, there was still much debate over Renzo De Felice, *Mussolini il duce: gli anni del consenso 1929–1936* (Turin: Einaudi, 1974). My copy had reached me in Australia in September 1975. I was a speedier reader of Renzo De Felice, *Intervista sul fascismo* (ed. Michael A. Ledeen) (Bari: Laterza, 1975), in which the American rightist editor, whose politics I deeply disliked, tried to clarify De Felice's tangled thought.

4 See Giorgio Amendola, *Intervista sull'antifascismo* (ed. Piero Melograni) (Bari: Laterza, 1976).

5 See, with a terrible pun (Echo Point is a major tourist site in the Blue Mountains), R. J. B. Bosworth, 'The point of Eco', *Australian Book Review*, 51, 1983.

6 See https://nuovoteatromadeinitaly.sciami.com/en/la-gaia-scienza-en/ (accessed 19 March 2021).

7 He died in 1988, but YouTube has a performance reading of the kind he did in Sydney: 'Aviation/Aviateur (Poesia vocale di Adriano Spatola)'. See www.youtube.com/watch?v=GnBehkXHX00 (accessed 19 August 2022).

8 For one resultant assessment, see Enrico Serra, 'Richard J. B. Bosworth e l'Italia', *Rivista di Studi Politici Internazionali*, LXVII, 2000.

9 See, as one tardy result (but then some of our academic contributors were very slow to produce), R. J. B. Bosworth and Sergio Romano (eds), *La politica estera italiana 1860–1985* (Bologna: Il Mulino, 1991).

10 See also notes 98 and 121 in Chapter 2.

11 Can it be that I owe him thanks for the rapid decision of the PCI house Riuniti to translate my Cambridge University Press book on pre-1914 foreign policy?

201

See R. J. B. Bosworth, *La politica estera dell'Italia giolittiana* (Rome: Riuniti, 1985).

12 See further Gianfranco Cresciani and Bruno Mascitelli (eds), *Australia and Italy: an asymmetrical relationship* (Ballarat: Connor Court Publishing, 2014), pp. 39–80.

13 See R. J. B. Bosworth and Gianfranco Cresciani (eds), *Altro polo: a volume of Italian studies* (Sydney: Frederick May Foundation, 1979); R. J. B. Bosworth and Gino Rizzo (eds), *Altro polo: a study of intellectuals and ideas in contemporary Italy* (Sydney: Frederick May Foundation, 1983). The latter included my chapter 'Italian foreign policy and its historiography', where I tried wryly to rebut a hostile review of *Italy, the Least of the Great Powers* by acerbic patriotic Liberal historian Rosario Romeo (whom I tried but failed to tempt to Australia). Romeo detected that I was an 'Italy hater'. When Italians talked about *romanità*, he surmised, such commentary might 'steal from Boswarth [sic] that peace of mind to which democratic descendants of Botany Bay can legitimately aspire' (p. 65). Australians were so often racist about Italian immigrants that it was nice to find an Italian intellectual being racist about an Australian.

14 See, for example, Silvio Trambaiolo and Nerida Newbigin (eds), *Altro polo: a volume of Italian studies* (Sydney: Frederick May Foundation, 1978); Raffaele Perrotta (ed.), *Altro polo: Italian poetry today: a critical anthology* (Sydney: Frederick May Foundation, 1980); Conal Condren and Ros Pesman (eds), *Altro polo: a volume of Italian Renaissance studies* (Sydney: Frederick May Foundation, 1982); Peter Groenewegen and Joseph Halevi (eds), *Altro polo: Italian economics past and present* (Sydney: Frederick May Foundation, 1983); Anne Reynolds (ed.), *Altro polo: the classical continuum in Italian thought and letters* (Sydney: Frederick May Foundation, 1984); Camilla Bettoni (ed.), *Altro polo: Italian abroad: studies on language contact in English-speaking countries* (Sydney: Frederick May Foundation, 1986); Ian Grosart and Silvio Trambaiolo (eds), *Altro polo: studies of contemporary Italy* (Sydney: Frederick May Foundation, 1988): Tim Fitzpatrick (ed.), *Altro polo: performance: from product to process* (Sydney: Frederick May Foundation, 1989); Suzanne Kiernan (ed.), *Altro polo: Italian studies in memory of Frederick May* (Sydney: Frederick May Foundation, 1996).

Introduction

1 The Italian communist party was the PCdI until 1943 and then the Partito Comunista Italiano (PCI).

Chapter 1

1 Eva Kühn Amendola, *Vita con Giovanni Amendola* (Florence: Parenti, 1960), p. 600.

2 Bruno Casinelli, *Giovanni Amendola: l'uomo – il pensatore – il filosofo – ciò che la morte ha impedito* (Rome: Labor, 1926), p. 11; Simona Colarizi, *I democratici*

all'opposizione: Giovanni Amendola e l'Unione Nazionale (1922–1926) (Bologna: Il Mulino, 1973), p. 30.

3 See Susan Zucotti, *Under His Very Windows: The Vatican and the Holocaust in Italy* (New Haven: Yale University Press, 2002).

4 It has recently been restored. See www.lacittadisalerno.it/cronaca/parte-il-restauro-della-statua-di-giovan-battista-amendola-1.1931728 (accessed 23 October 2020).

5 Giampietro Carocci, *Giovanni Amendola nella crisi dello stato italiano 1911–1925* (Milan: Feltrinelli, 1956), p. 9.

6 Mario Vinciguerra, 'Introduzione' in Giovanni Amendola, *Etica e biografia* (Milan: Riccardo Ricciardi Editore, 1953), p. x.

7 Giorgio Amendola, *Una scelta di vita* (Milan: Rizzoli, 1976), p. 14.

8 *Ibid.*, pp. 50–1.

9 He was proud that two of his football mates graduated to the Italian national team. Loris Dadam (ed.), *Giorgio Amendola nella storia d'Italia: antologia critica degli scritti* (Turin: Cerabona Editore, 2007), p. 22.

10 Vittoria Sgambati, 'La formazione politica e culturale di Giorgio Amendola', *Studi Storici*, 32, 1991, p. 734. In 1916, Mussolini chose that name for his own eldest (legitimate) son.

11 See Giorgio Amendola, *Una scelta di vita*, pp. 55–8 for that trip and the fate of the family.

12 See Giovanni Amendola, *Carteggio 1923–1924* (ed. Elio D'Auria) (Manduria: Piero Lacaita, 2006), p. 147.

13 For brief historical background to the order, see www.villagiuseppina.it/villa-giuseppina/la-struttura/la-storia (accessed 23 October 2020). Perhaps ironically, their psychiatric centre moved to the Viale Prospero Colonna, on the other side of the Tiber, in 1960. More ironically for the modernist Amendola family, the order had been founded by the virulently anti-modernist Pope Pius X in 1910.

14 For the spate of complications in Mussolini's sex life, see R. J. B. Bosworth, *Claretta: Mussolini's Last Lover* (London: Yale University Press, 2017).

15 Giorgio Amendola, *Una scelta di vita*, pp. 79–80.

16 Those doubtful if Nitti or Amendola much understood the peasantry in such a region will be strengthened in their views by reading the two classic accounts of the region: Norman Douglas, *Old Calabria* (London: Secker and Warburg, 1955 [1915]); Carlo Levi, *Christ Stopped at Eboli: The Story of a Year* (New York: Farrar, Straus and Giroux, 1947).

17 Giorgio Amendola, *Una scelta di vita*, pp. 77–8. I owe the details about Ada's and Eva's lack of interest in kitchen activities to Antonella Amendola.

18 See, for example, his denunciation of the French employment of 'barbarous' African troops in their occupation of the Rhineland. Francesco Saverio Nitti, *La decadenza dell'Europa: le vie della ricostruzione* (Florence: Bemporad, 1922), p. 141; Francesco Saverio Nitti, *La tragedia dell'Europa: che farà l'America* (Turin: Piero Gobetti Editore, 1924), pp. 38–9.

19 Giorgio Amendola, *Una scelta di vita*, pp. 79–80.

20 Giovanni Amendola, *Carteggio 1923–1924*, p. 149 n. 2.

21 Alfredo Capone, *Giovanni Amendola* (Rome: Salerno Editrice, 2013), pp. 290–1.

22 See, for example, Guglielmo Policastro, *Crispi e Mussolini* (Mantua: Edizioni Paladino, 1928).

23 Alceste De Ambris, *Amendola: fatti e documenti*, revised edition (Sala Bolognese: Arnaldo Forni Editore, 1976), p. 33.

24 *Ibid.*, p. 23; Giorgio Amendola, *Una scelta di vita*, p. 81.

25 Mimmo Franzinelli, *I tentacoli dell'OVRA: agenti, collaboratori e vittime della polizia politica fascista* (Turin: Bollati Boringhieri, 1999), p. 39.

26 Goffredo Locatelli, *Il deputato dei 27 voti: la storia vera e mai scritta di Giovanni Amendola* (Milan: Mursia, 2014), p. 277.

27 *Ibid.*, p. 287.

28 Giuseppe Prezzolini (ed.), *Amendola e 'La Voce'* (Florence: Sansoni, 1973), p. 25.

29 Giorgio Amendola, *Una scelta di vita*, p. 82.

30 Giovanni Amendola, *Carteggio 1923–1924*, pp. 154–77.

31 Roberto Pertici (ed.), *Carteggio Croce-Amendola* (Naples: Istituto Italiano per gli Studi Storici, 1982), p. 789.

32 Luigi Albertini, *Epistolario 1911–1926*, 4 volumes (ed. Ottavio Bariè) (Milan: Mondadori, 1968), vol. IV, p. 1769.

33 Giovanni Amendola, *La nuova democrazia* (Naples: Riccardo Ricciardi Editore, 1951), pp. 197–208.

34 Giorgio Amendola, *Una scelta di vita*, pp. 86–7.

35 For his own account well after the event, see Amerigo Dumini, *Diciassette colpi* (Milan: Longanesi, 1958).

36 Carocci, *Giovanni Amendola nella crisi dello stato italiano*, p. 112.

37 See further R. J. B. Bosworth, *Mussolini and the Eclipse of Italian Fascism: From Dictatorship to Populism* (London: Yale University Press, 2021); Valentina Zaghi, '"Con Matteotti si mangiava": simboli e valori nella genesi di un mito popolare', *Rivista di Storia Contemporanea*, 19, 1990, pp. 432–46.

38 For a detailed account of the kidnapping and murder, see Mauro Canali, *Il delitto Matteotti* (Bologna: Il Mulino, 2004).

39 Renzo De Felice, *Mussolini il fascista. I: La conquista del potere 1921–1925* (Turin: Einaudi, 1966), pp. 686–8, 701.

40 *Ibid.*, p. 633. Gramsci put the Catholic Partito Popolare chief, Don Luigi Sturzo, and reformist socialist, Filippo Turati, in the same category.

41 Benito Mussolini, *Opera Omnia*, 36 volumes (eds Edoardo Susmel and Duilio Susmel) (Florence: La Fenice, 1951–63), vol. XXI, pp. 235–41.

42 Giorgio Amendola, *Carteggio 1925–1926* (ed. Elio D'Auria) (Soveria Mannelli: Rubbettino, 2016), pp. 16–19.

43 Still the best introduction to this period is Alberto Aquarone, *L'organizzazione dello stato totalitario* (Turin: Einaudi, 1965).

44 Giorgio Amendola, *Carteggio 1925–1926*, pp. 31–2.

45 *Ibid.*, pp. 36, 58.

46 *Ibid.*, p. 80.

47 *Ibid.*, pp. 81–2.

48 *Ibid.*, pp. 146–7.

49 *Ibid.*, p. 167.
50 Mussolini, *Opera Omnia*, vol. XXXIX, p. 462.
51 It still exists. See www.grandhotellapace.it/en/ (accessed 27 October 2020).
52 Giovanni Amendola, *Carteggio 1925–1926*, p. 184.
53 Giorgio Amendola, *Una scelta di vita*, pp. 125–6.
54 See the finely detailed account, Umberto Sereni, 'Un'azione fascista: l'aggressione a Giovanni Amendola. Montecatini 20 luglio 1925' in *Giovanni Amendola tra etica e politica: atti del convegno di studio Montecatini Terme 25–26–27 ottobre 1996* (Pistoia: CRT, 1999), p. 196.
55 See Umberto Sereni, 'Carlo Scorza e il fascismo "stile camorra"' in Paolo Giovannini and Marco Palla (eds), *Il fascismo dalle mani sporche: dittatura, corruzione, affarismo* (Rome: Laterza, 2019), pp. 190–217.
56 For an inadequate and forgiving biography, see Carlo Rastrelli, *Carlo Scorza: l'ultimo gerarca* (Milan: Mursia, 2010). Rastrelli is proud to be the grandson of one of Carlo's squadrists.
57 *The Times*, 24 June 1992.
58 Sereni, 'Un'azione fascista', pp. 181–92.
59 *Ibid.*, p. 174.
60 Marco Francini and Fabio Giannelli, 'Appendici' in *Giovanni Amendola tra etica e politica*, pp. 277–8.
61 *Ibid.*, pp. 287–8.
62 See Sereni, 'Un'azione fascista', pp. 214–15; Francini and Giannelli, 'Appendici', pp. 277–90; Giorgio Amendola, *Una scelta di vita*, pp. 127–30.
63 Giorgio Amendola, *Una scelta di vita*, p. 128.
64 Francini and Giannelli, 'Appendici', p. 280.
65 Among those who did not write was Giuseppe Volpi, by then minister of finance but earlier governor of Tripolitania under Giovanni as minister of colonies. See Giovanni Amendola, *Carteggio 1925–1926*, p. 285. Prezzolini, Papini and Ojetti did send their regrets (pp. 267, 277–8).
66 See obituary in *The Times*, 8 April 1926.
67 Giorgio Amendola, *Una scelta di vita*, pp. 130–1.
68 Rastrelli, *Carlo Scorza*, p. 212. Scorza also soon took the opportunity to publish a positive account of the role in the March on Rome of his followers. See Carlo Scorza, *Bagliori d'epopea* (Lucca: Edizione La Lecchesia, 1926).
69 For his grovelling, see Carlo Scorza, *Brevi note sul fascismo: sui capi, sui gregari* (Florence: Bemporad, 1930); Carlo Scorza, *Il segreto di Mussolini* (Lanciano: Gino Carabba Editore, 1933).
70 Sereni, 'Un'azione fascista', pp. 225–9.
71 Rastrelli, *Carlo Scorza*, pp. 206–9.
72 Kühn Amendola, *Vita con Giovanni Amendola*, pp. 447–8.
73 On that day in Rome, the Irish aristocrat Violet Gibson narrowly failed to kill Mussolini as he emerged from speaking fulsomely to an international surgeons' conference. For an English-language description, see Frances Stonor Saunders, *The Woman Who Shot Mussolini* (London: Faber and Faber, 2010).
74 *Il Corriere della Sera*, 8 April 1926. A not totally negative obituary (on 7 April) called Giovanni a man of 'firm and severe spirit, with more of a thinker's temperament than that of a politician'.

75 De Ambris, *Amendola*, pp. 51–3. De Ambris denied that Giovanni had in fact made an effort at peace.

76 Benito Mussolini, *Opera Omnia: Appendici* (eds Edoardo Susmel and Duilio Susmel) (Rome: Giovanni Volpe Editore, 1980), vol. VIII, p. 46.

77 Giorgio Amendola, *Una scelta di vita*, pp. 138–40.

78 Giovanni Amendola, 'Testamento' in *Giovanni Amendola nel cinquantenario della morte 1926–1976* (Rome: Fondazione Luigi Einaudi per Studi di Politica ed Economia, 1976), pp. 333–7.

79 Giorgio Amendola, *Una scelta di vita*, pp. 140–2.

80 For background, see Albertina Vittoria, *Intellettuali e politica alla fine degli anni '30: Antonio Amendola e la formazione del gruppo comunista romano* (Milan: Franco Angeli, 1985), pp. 12–15.

81 Mario Rossi-Doria, 'Prefazione' in Giovanni Amendola, *Carteggio 1897–1909* (ed. Elio D'Auria) (Bari: Laterza, 1986), p. vii.

82 See Giovanni Cerchia (ed.), 'Luigi Albertini e la famiglia di Giovanni Amendola (1922–1936)', *Mondo Contemporaneo*, 2009, pp. 123–5.

83 In 1915, disgusted by Mussolini's 'betrayal' of socialism for war, he had fought an extended duel against him. See R. J. B. Bosworth, *Mussolini*, revised edition (London: Bloomsbury, 2010), p. 109.

84 Giorgio Amendola, *Fascismo e movimento operaio* (Rome: Riuniti, 1975), p. 82.

85 Giorgio Amendola, *Una scelta di vita*, pp. 168–71.

86 *Ibid.*, pp. 153–4.

87 *Ibid.*, pp. 260–5.

88 Giovanni Cerchia, *Giorgio Amendola: un comunista nazionale* (Soveria Mannelli: Rubbettino, 2004), p. 212.

89 Giorgio Amendola, *Un'isola* (Milan: Rizzoli, 1980), pp. 11–15.

90 Giorgio Amendola, *Una scelta di vita*, p. 126.

91 *Ibid.*, pp. 236–7; Giovanni Cerchia, *Giorgio Amendola: gli anni della Repubblica (1945–1980)* (Turin: Cerabona Editore, 2009), p. 266. In 1938, Giorgio did attend a demonstration in Cannes at his father's tomb.

92 Giorgio Amendola, *Una scelta di vita*, pp. 227–8.

93 Cerchia, *Giorgio Amendola: un comunista nazionale*, pp. 331–8.

94 Giorgio Amendola, *Lettere a Milano: ricordi e documenti 1943–1945* (Rome: Riuniti, 1973), pp. 6–7.

95 *Ibid.*, p. 10.

96 Dadam (ed.), *Giorgio Amendola*, p. 84.

97 Giorgio Amendola (ed.), *Il comunismo italiano nella seconda guerra mondiale: relazione e documenti presentati dalla direzione del partito al V Congresso del Partito comunista italiano* (Rome: Riuniti, 1963), pp. 160–2, 179–81.

98 *Ibid.*, p. 195.

99 Giorgio Amendola, *Lettere a Milano*, p. 227.

100 Cerchia, *Giorgio Amendola: un comunista nazionale*, pp. 390–6.

101 Giorgio Amendola (ed.), *Il comunismo italiano nella seconda guerra mondiale*, pp. 217–19.

102 Perhaps a convenient concatenation, since the attack was first planned to occur on 21 March. See Alessandro Portelli, *The Order Has Been Carried*

Out: History, Memory and Meaning of a Nazi Massacre in Rome (New York: Palgrave Macmillan, 2003), p. 134.

103 Giorgio Amendola, *Lettere a Milano*, p. 291.

104 Dadam (ed.), *Giorgio Amendola*, pp. 107–8.

105 Portelli, *The Order Has Been Carried Out*, p. 166.

106 Roberto Bentivegna and Cesare De Simone, *Operazione Via Rasella: verità e menzogne* (Rome: Riuniti, 1996), p. 22; cf. Franco Calamandrei, *La vita indivisibile: diario 1941–1947* (eds Romano Bilenchi and Ottavio Cecchi) (Rome: Riuniti, 1984), pp. 154–9.

107 Portelli, *The Order Has Been Carried Out*, pp. 142–3.

108 For their background, most often bourgeois and intellectual, see Bentivegna and De Simone, *Operazione Via Rasella*, pp. 56–67.

109 *Ibid.*, pp. 21–2.

110 Calamandrei, *La vita indivisibile*, pp. 153–65. When at home, Calamandrei was spending his time translating Diderot and reading theoretical works by J. Stalin.

111 Giorgio Amendola, *Lettere a Milano*, pp. 291–2.

112 Bentivegna and De Simone, *Operazione Via Rasella*, pp. 23–36.

113 Portelli, *The Order Has Been Carried Out*, p. 6; cf. Robert Katz, *Death in Rome* (London: Jonathan Cape, 1967); Robert Katz, *Fatal Silence: the Pope, the Resistance and the German Occupation of Rome* (London: Weidenfeld and Nicolson, 2003), especially pp. 209–36; R. J. B. Bosworth, *Whispering City: Rome and Its Histories* (London: Yale University Press), pp. 232–5.

114 Portelli, *The Order Has Been Carried Out*, p. 2.

115 Pietro Ingrao in 2004 had not the slightest doubt about the attack and the party's response thereafter. See Pietro Ingrao, *Volevo la luna* (Turin: Einaudi, 2004), pp. 139–40.

116 Giorgio Amendola (ed.), *Il comunismo italiano nella seconda guerra mondiale*, pp. 57–61.

117 See, for example, Dadam (ed.), *Giorgio Amendola*, p. 11; Giorgio Amendola, *Tra passione e ragione: discorsi a Milano dal 1957 al 1977* (Milan: Rizzoli, 1982), pp. 139–40.

118 See editorial of *L'Unità*, 30 March 1944 with that view. Giorgio Amendola (ed.), *Il comunismo italiano nella seconda guerra mondiale*, p. 219.

Chapter 2

1 Giovanni Amendola, *Carteggio 1913–1918* (ed. Elio D'Auria) (Manduria: Piero Lacaita, 1999), p. 146.

2 For solid analysis, see Carmine Pinto, *Le guerra per il Mezzogiorno: italiani, borbonici e briganti* (Bari: Laterza, 2019); cf. Eugenio Di Rienzo, *Il brigantaggio post-unitario come problema storiografico* (Nocera Superiore: D'Amico Editore, 2020).

3 See, for example, Giovanni Amendola, *Carteggio 1910–1912* (ed. Elio D'Auria) (Bari: Laterza, 1987), p. 264.

4 On Pietro Paolo's death in 1908, Giovanni told Croce that he was then fifty-eight, therefore born in either 1850 or 1849. See Giovanni Amendola, *Carteggio 1897–1909* (ed. Elio D'Auria) (Bari: Laterza, 1986), p. 434.

5 Alfredo Capone, *Giovanni Amendola e la cultura italiana del Novecento (1909–1914) alle origini della 'nuova democrazia'* (Rome: Editrice Elia, 1974), pp. 19–20.

6 Giorgio Amendola, *Una scelta di vita* (Milan: Rizzoli, 1976), pp. 11–12.

7 *Ibid., pp. 12–13.*

8 *Ibid.,* pp. 10–11.

9 For massive account, see Aldo A. Mola, *Storia della Massoneria italiana dall'Unità alla Repubblica* (Milan: Bompiani, 1976). Mola rightly notes, however, that Freemasonry created as much division as unity.

10 Capone, *Giovanni Amendola e la cultura italiana*, pp. 20–2.

11 *Ibid.,* p. 37; Roberto Pertici, 'Giovanni Amendola: l'esperienza socialista e teosofica (1898–1905)', *Belfagor*, 35, 1980, pp. 185–8.

12 Pertici, 'Giovanni Amendola', p. 191.

13 Giovanni Amendola, *Carteggio 1897–1909*, p. 22. For further background, see Alfredo Capone, *Giovanni Amendola* (Rome: Salerno Editrice, 2013), pp. 40–5.

14 Anne Taylor, *Annie Besant* (Oxford: Oxford University Press, 1992). p. 4. This standard biography pays no attention to her movement's role in Italy.

15 Pertici, 'Giovanni Amendola', pp. 186–7.

16 Federico Guazzini, 'Giovanni Amendola ministro delle colonie. "Lasciate mi solo davanti agli arabi"' in Elio D'Auria (ed.), *Giovanni Amendola: una vita in difesa della libertà. Atti del convegno di studi per il 90 anniversario della morte (1882–1926)* (Soveria Mannelli: Rubbettino, 2018), p. 204.

17 Giovanni Amendola, *Carteggio 1897–1909*, p. 17.

18 Capone, *Giovanni Amendola e la cultura italiana*, p. 18. In 1903–4, he did compulsory military training, naturally as a young officer. But his main letter on the subject to Vincenzo complained about how awful the food was. Giovanni Amendola, *Carteggio 1897–1909*, p. 47.

19 See, for example, Giovanni Amendola, *Carteggio 1913–1918*, pp. 56–7, 100–1.

20 Capone, *Giovanni Amendola e la cultura italiana*, p. 40.

21 Raffaello Franchini, 'Amendola e la filosofia del suo tempo' in *Giovanni Amendola: una battaglia per democrazia: atti del convegno di studi con il patrimonio della Regione Emila-Romagna* (Bologna: Arnaldo Forni Editore, 1978), pp. 36–7; Capone, *Giovanni Amendola*, p. 36.

22 Italian sources say that, in December 1899, he heard and met a visiting guru called Roy Chatterji, who gave five lectures in Rome. See Capone, *Giovanni Amendola e la cultura italiana*, pp. 28–31, 42–3.

23 *Onoranze a Giovanni Amendola nel cinquantenario della morte 1926–1976* (Salerno: Arti Grafiche Boccia for Regione Campania and Comune di Sarno, 1977), pp. 87–8.

24 Capone, *Giovanni Amendola e la cultura italiana*, p. 49.

25 Giovanni Amendola, *Carteggio 1897–1909*, p. 86.

26 Pertici, 'Giovanni Amendola', pp. 193–4.

27 Antonietta G. Paulino, 'Eva Kühn Amendola: ovvero dell'insostenibile tragicità del vivere' in Giovanni Cerchia (ed.), *La famiglia Amendola: una scelta di vita per l'Italia* (Turin: Cerabona Editore, 2011), pp. 93–4; cf. Eva Kühn Amendola, *Vita con Giovanni Amendola* (Florence: Parenti, 1960).

28 Antonella Amendola, 'Intervista' in *Giovanni Amendola tra etica e politica: atti del convegno di studio Montecatini Terme 25–26–27 ottobre 1996* (Pistoia: CRT, 1999), p. 103.

29 Paulino, 'Eva Kühn Amendola', p. 95.

30 For some background, see Dale Jacquette (ed.), *Schopenhauer, Philosophy and the Arts* (Cambridge: Cambridge University Press, 2007).

31 Giovanni Amendola, *Carteggio 1897–1909*, p. 60. The date was 26 December, a day of ill omen for Giovanni.

32 *Ibid.*, p. 61.

33 *Ibid.*, pp. 62–5.

34 *Ibid.*, pp. 66–7.

35 Antonella Amendola, 'Intervista', p. 104.

36 Annie Besant, *Thought Power, Its Control and Culture* (London: Theosophical Publishing Society, 1901).

37 Giovanni Amendola, *Carteggio 1897–1909*, p. 74.

38 *Ibid.*, p. 88.

39 *Ibid.*, pp. 77–8.

40 *Ibid.*, pp. 83–8.

41 *Ibid.*, pp. 88, 95–6.

42 *Ibid.*, p. 96.

43 Capone, *Giovanni Amendola*, pp. 46–9.

44 Giovanni Amendola, *Carteggio 1897–1909*, p. 106.

45 *Ibid.*, pp. 108–11.

46 *Ibid.*, pp. 112–13.

47 *Ibid.*, pp. 119, 123–5; Paulino, 'Eva Kühn Amendola', pp. 95–6.

48 Goffredo Locatelli, *Il deputato dei 27 voti: la storia vera e mai scritta di Giovanni Amendola* (Milan: Mursia, 2014), p. 11.

49 Paulino, 'Eva Kühn Amendola', pp. 95–6; cf. Capone, *Giovanni Amendola e la cultura italiana*, pp. 59–61, 70–2.

50 Lucia Re, 'Women at war: Eva Kühn Amendola (Magamal) – Interventionist, Futurist, Fascist', *Annali d'Italianistica*, 33, 2015, p. 281.

51 Giovanni Amendola, *Carteggio 1897–1909*, p. 170.

52 Capone, *Giovanni Amendola e la cultura italiana*, p. 265.

53 For background, see, for example, Walter Adamson, *Avant-garde Florence from Modernism to Fascism* (Cambridge, MA: Harvard University Press, 1993); Emilio Gentile, *La Grande Italia: ascesa e declina del mito della nazione nel ventesimo secolo* (Milan: Mondadori, 1997); and many other such studies.

54 Adamson, *Avant-garde Florence*, pp. 13, 83.

55 For a detailed and respectful survey of Amendola's pre-war philosophical divagations, see Capone, *Giovanni Amendola*, pp. 58–133.

56 Giovanni Amendola, *Carteggio 1897–1909*, pp. 141–3, 155, 158.

57 *Ibid.*, p. 171.

58 Eva Kühn Amendola, *Vita con Giovanni Amendola*, p. 39.

59 Giovanni Amendola, *Carteggio 1897–1909*, pp. 180–3.
60 *Ibid.*, pp. 185–9, 192–5.
61 *Ibid.*, p. 204.
62 *Ibid.*, pp. 197–8.
63 *Ibid.*, p. 214.
64 *Ibid.*, p. 224.
65 *Ibid.*, p. 237.
66 *Ibid.*, pp. 240–1, 254, 273, 269–71.
67 *Ibid.*, p. 275.

68 Pietro Paolo died on 14 July 1908, after a sudden decline into what the family labelled 'madness'. See *ibid.*, pp. 433–4.
69 Giovanni Cerchia, *Giorgio Amendola: un comunista nazionale. Dall'infanzia alla guerra partigiana (1907–1945)* (Soveria Mannelli: Rubbettino, 2004), p. 3.
70 Mauro Pendinelli, 'L'ingresso nel giornalismo: la corrispondenza politica del "Resto del Carlino" e del "Corriere della Sera"' in D'Auria (ed.), *Giovanni Amendola: una vita in difesa della libertà*, p. 110.
71 Giovanni Amendola, *Carteggio 1897–1909*, pp. 572–3. Eva herself had gone to Vilnius with the toddler, Giorgio, in July–August (pp. 523–4).
72 *Ibid.*, pp. 278, 391–2.
73 Giovanni Amendola, *Carteggio 1913–1918*, pp. 37–8.
74 Luigi Albertini, *Epistolario 1911–1926* (ed. Ottavio Bariè) (Milan: Mondadori, 1968), vol. III, pp. 1174–6.
75 Giuseppe Prezzolini (ed.), *Amendola e 'La Voce'* (Florence: Sansoni, 1973), p. 10.
76 Giovanni Amendola, *Carteggio 1910–1912*, pp. 279, 290.
77 *Ibid.*, pp. 420, 425–7, 437.
78 Alexander De Grand, *The Hunchback's tailor: Giovanni Giolitti and Liberal Italy from the Challenge of Mass Politics to the Rise of Fascism, 1882–1922* (Westport, CT: Praeger, 2001), p. 1.
79 Bruno Casinelli, *Giovanni Amendola: l'uomo – il pensatore – il filosofo – ciò che la morte ha impedito* (Rome: Labor, 1926), p. 19.
80 Capone, *Giovanni Amendola e la cultura italiana*, p. 314.
81 Alfredo Capone, 'Moderatismo e democrazia nel pensiero di Giovanni Amendola' in *Giovanni Amendola nel cinquantenario della morte 1926–1976* (Rome: Fondazione Luigi Einaudi per Studi di Politica ed Economia, 1976), p. 110.
82 Prezzolini (ed.), *Amendola e 'La Voce'*, p. 212.
83 Gentile, *La Grande Italia*, p. 99.
84 Capone, *Giovanni Amendola e la cultura italiana*, p. 269.
85 Giampiero Carocci, *Giovanni Amendola nella crisi dello Stato italiano 1911–1925* (Milan: Feltrinelli, 1956), p. 19; Prezzolini (ed.), *Amendola e 'La Voce'*, p. 13.
86 Capone, 'Moderatismo e democrazia nel pensiero di Giovanni Amendola', p. 108.
87 Carocci, *Giovanni Amendola nella crisi dello Stato italiano*, p. 26.
88 Capone, *Giovanni Amendola*, p. 167.

89 Giovanni Amendola, *Carteggio 1910–1912*, p. 14.

90 Cerchia, *Giorgio Amendola: un comunista nazionale*, p. 10.

91 Giovanni Amendola, *Carteggio 1910–1912*, pp. 104–5.

92 *Ibid.*, pp. 35, 174–5.

93 Her Italian translation of his novel, *The Adolescent*, was republished by Einaudi in 2013. For a list of her translations and (not always accurate) biographical information on her and her family, see www.russinitalia.it/dettaglio.php?id=442 (accessed 18 February 2021).

94 Giovanni Amendola, *Carteggio 1910–1912*, pp. 481–2.

95 Re, 'Women at war: Eva Kühn Amendola (Magamal)', p. 283.

96 *Ibid.*, pp. 283–5.

97 Giorgio Amendola, *Una scelta di vita*, p. 19. Typically, in his eulogistic biography, Capone makes no mention of her and she does not appear in the volumes of Giovanni's correspondence.

98 Giorgio Spini, *Italia liberale e protestante* (Turin: Claudiana Editore, 2002), pp. 308–9.

99 Re, 'Women at war: Eva Kühn Amendola (Magamal)', pp. 286–9; Paulino, 'Eva Kühn Amendola', pp. 97–8.

100 Giovanni Amendola, *Carteggio 1913–1918*, p. 144; Giorgio Amendola, *Una scelta di vita*, pp. 21–2.

101 Giovanni Matteoli (ed.), *Giorgio Amendola: comunista riformista* (Soveria Mannelli: Rubbettino, 2001), p. 119.

102 Giovanni Amendola, 'La philosophie italienne contemporaine', *Revue Métaphysique et de Morale*, 16, 1908, pp. 635–65.

103 See Mario Vinciguerra, 'Introduzione' in Giovanni Amendola, *Etica e biografia* (Milan: Riccardo Ricciardi Editore, 1953), pp. xi–xii.

104 Giovanni Amendola, *Etica e biografia*, p. 85.

105 Casinelli, *Giovanni Amendola*, p. 7.

106 Capone, *Giovanni Amendola e la cultura italiana*, p. 170.

107 Giovanni Amendola, *Etica e biografia*, p. 32.

108 See https://r.unitn.it/it/lett/circe/lanima (accessed 26 November 2020).

109 Giovanni Amendola, *Carteggio 1913–1918*, pp. 80–2; Capone, *Giovanni Amendola e la cultura italiana*, pp. 239–40.

110 Roberto Pertici (ed.), 'Introduzione' in *Carteggio Croce–Amendola* (Naples: Istituto Italiano per gli Studi Storici, 1982), p. ix.

111 Giovanni Amendola, *Carteggio 1913–1918*, pp. 110–11.

112 Giovanni had been in appreciative contact with him since at least 1911. See Giovanni Amendola, *Carteggio 1910–1912*, p. 267.

113 For background, see David D. Roberts, *Historicism and Fascism in Modern Italy* (Toronto: University of Toronto Press, 2007), among many other works.

114 Giovanni Amendola, *Carteggio 1913–1918*, p. 117.

115 Cerchia, *Giorgio Amendola: un comunista nazionale*, p. 26.

116 Giovanni Amendola, *Carteggio 1913–1918*, p. 183.

117 In 1909, when, after his father's death, the family needed to move house, Amendola asked Casati for a 300 lire loan in assistance. See Giovanni Amendola, *Carteggio 1897–1909*, p. 471.

118 See www.bibliotecasalaborsa.it/cronologia/bologna/1909/gli_agrari_acquisis cono_il_resto_del_carlino (accessed 28 November 2020). At the end of 1913, Filippo Naldi became its co-editor. After Mussolini walked away from socialism in October 1914 to favour Italian entry in the war, Naldi helped him financially to found *Il Popolo d'Italia* and then located further funds from the French secret service. See R. J. B. Bosworth, *Mussolini*, revised edition (London: Bloomsbury, 2010), pp. 89–90.

119 Giovanni Amendola, *Carteggio 1910–1912*, p. 468.

120 Prezzolini (ed.), *Amendola e 'La Voce'*, pp. 8–15, 23.

121 See Spini, *Italia liberale e protestante*, pp. 310–11.

122 For an introduction, see Richard Bosworth and Giuseppe Finaldi, 'The Italian empire' in Robert Gerwarth and Erez Manela (eds), *Empires at War 1911–1923* (Oxford: Oxford University Press, 2014), pp. 34–43.

123 For background on the colonial war, see R. J. B. Bosworth, *Italy, the Least of the Great Powers: Italian Foreign Policy before the First World War* (Cambridge: Cambridge University Press, 1979); for Federzoni, cf. R. J. B. Bosworth, *Mussolini and the Eclipse of Italian Fascism* (London: Yale University Press, 2021), pp. 71–5.

124 Giovanni Amendola, *Carteggio 1913–1918*, p. 61.

125 Capone, *Giovanni Amendola*, pp. 138–9.

126 Capone, *Giovanni Amendola e la cultura italiana*, pp. 271–5.

127 Capone, 'Moderatismo e democrazia nel pensiero di Giovanni Amendola', p. 127.

128 Giovanni Amendola, *La crisi dello stato liberale* (ed. Elio D'Auria) (Rome: Newton Compton, 1974), p. 17.

129 Giovanni Amendola, *Carteggio 1913–1918*, pp. 14–6; cf. Cesira Filesi, 'La Tripolitania nella politica coloniale di Giovanni Amendola', *Africa: Rivista Trimestrale*, 32, 1977, pp. 519–20.

130 Carocci, *Giovanni Amendola nella crisi dello Stato italiano*, pp. 32–3.

131 Michelangelo Buonarroti (ed. Giovanni Amendola) *Poesia* (Lanciano: R. Carabba Editore, 1911).

132 Elena Papadia, 'I vecchi e i giovani: liberal-conservatori e nazionalisti a confronto nell'Italia giolittiana', *Contemporanea*, 5, 2002, pp. 664–5.

133 See Gaetano Salvemini, *Come siamo andati in Libia e altri scritti dal 1900 al 1915* (ed. Augusto Torre) (Milan: Feltrinelli, 1963).

134 Eva Kühn Amendola, *Vita con Giovanni Amendola*, pp. 295–7, 300–2.

135 Giovanni Amendola, *Carteggio 1910–1912*, pp. 334–6, 340–1, 350–1.

136 Giovanni Amendola, *La crisi dello stato liberale*, p. 53.

137 *Ibid.*, p. 68.

138 See Denis Mack Smith, *Storia di cento anni di vita italiana visti attraverso il Corriere della Sera* (Milan: Rizzoli, 1978). It is typical of the paper's history that they should choose the most famous foreign historian of the country to write this work.

139 Luigi Albertini, *I giorni di un liberale: diari 1907–1923* (ed. Luciano Monzali) (Bologna: Il Mulino, 2000), p. 150.

140 Giovanni Amendola, *Carteggio 1913–1918*, pp. 96–8, 112–13.

141 Giovanni Amendola, *La crisi dello stato liberale*, p. 89.

142 Casinelli, *Giovanni Amendola*, p. 10.
143 Papadia, 'I vecchi e i giovani', p. 675.
144 Mack Smith, *Storia di cento anni di vita italiana*, p. 191.
145 For further detail, see Giovanni Amendola, *Carteggio 1913–1918*.
146 Casinelli, *Giovanni Amendola*, p. 10.
147 Albertini, *Epistolario 1911–1926*, vol. I, p. 260.
148 *Ibid.*, vol. II, pp. 411–12. See also Giovanni Amendola, *Carteggio 1913–1918*, pp. 188–90.
149 Casinelli, *Giovanni Amendola*, p. 11.
150 Giovanni Amendola, *Carteggio 1913–1918*, p. 213. His youngest sister, Maria, had just died in Rome from typhus, still a recurrent disease in the national capital.
151 *Ibid.*, pp. 225–8.
152 *Ibid.*, pp. 326–8.
153 *Ibid.*, p. 334.
154 *Ibid.*, pp. 338, 375 (he told his wife proudly that he would not accept a bronze – but he did).
155 Olindo Malagodi, *Conversazioni della guerra 1914–1919* (ed. Brunello Vigezzi) (Milan: Riccardo Ricciardi Editore, 1960), vol. I, pp. 221–2.
156 Albertini, *Epistolario 1911–1926*, vol. II, pp. 488–92.
157 Locatelli, *Il deputato dei 27 voti*, p. 316. There is no reference in Amendola's correspondence to such a meeting.
158 See https://commons.wikimedia.org/wiki/File:Mladen_Pavlov_home_with_memorial_plaque,_104_Evlogi_i_Hristo_Georgievi_Blvd.,_Sofia.jpg (accessed 3 February 2021).
159 Mladen Pavlov, *МЕМОАРИ КРАТКИ БЕЛЕЖКИ ИЗ☒ МОβ ЖИВОТ☒* [*Memoirs, Brief Notes from My Life*] (Sofia: Cooperative Printing House 'Franklin', 1928).
160 For a Bulgarian biography, mainly focused on his early revolutionary years, see Anton Petrov, *Kozloduiskoto daskalche* (Moravitsa: ANPET Publishing, 1996). I owe the last two references to Yavor Siderov.
161 John D. Bell, *Peasants in Power: Alexander Stamboliski and the Bulgarian National Union 1899–1923* (Princeton, NJ: Princeton University Press, 1977), pp. 95–6.
162 *Paris Soir*, 14 June 1926.
163 Bulgarian archives, Sofia, 131K, оп., a.e. 314. I owe this reference to Professor Maria Todorova of the University of Illinois. Hristov's political course was not dissimilar to Nelia's and he had good connections with the Italian cultural world. He also spent much time outside his country. See further https://bnr.bg/en/post/101306082/writer-kiril-hristov-lyrical-master-and-collector-of-memories (accessed 5 February 2021).
164 *Paris Soir*, 14 June 1926.
165 See, for example, Giovanni Amendola, *Carteggio 1913–1918*, p. 194.
166 *Ibid.*, pp. 177–8, 197–8.
167 See, for example, *ibid.*, p. 283.
168 *Ibid.*, pp. 322, 326.
169 *Ibid.*, pp. 352–4.

170 For this, see especially the account in Re, 'Women at war: Eva Kühn Amendola (Magamal)', pp. 275–91.

171 Capone, *Giovanni Amendola*, pp. 187–9.

172 From the song '*Se otto ore*', campaigning for an eight-hour day. See www .youtube.com/watch?v=xih-NDc-168 (accessed 30 November 2020). For the text, see Giuseppe Vettori (ed.), *Canzoni italiane di protesta 1794–1974 dalla Rivoluzione Francese alla repression cilena* (Rome: Newton Compton ·Editori, 1974), pp. 133–4.

173 Giovanni Amendola, *La crisi dello stato liberale*, pp. 226–30.

174 Albertini, *Epistolario 1911–1926*, vol. II, p. 930.

175 Malagodi, *Conversazioni della guerra*, vol. I, pp. 182–4.

176 Albertini, *I giorni di un liberale*, pp. 156, 174.

177 Malagodi, *Conversazioni della guerra*, vol. I, p. 177.

178 Albertini, *Epistolario 1911–1926*, vol. II, pp. 873–5; Giovanni Amendola, *La crisi dello stato liberale*, p. 198; Casinelli, *Giovanni Amendola*, p. 11.

179 Giovanni Amendola, *La crisi dello stato liberale*, pp. 133, 229.

180 *Ibid.*, pp. 226–7.

181 Giovanni Amendola, Giuseppe A. Borgese, Ugo Ojetti and Andrea Torre, *Il patto di Roma* (Rome: Quaderni della Voce, 1919), p. 8.

182 *Ibid.*, pp. 10–11.

183 For a comparison of the two, see Casinelli, *Giovanni Amendola*, p. 14.

184 For my survey of the situation, see R. J. B. Bosworth, *Italy and the Wider World 1860–1960* (London: Routledge, 1996).

185 See, for example, Albertini, *Epistolario 1911–1926*, vol. II, pp. 748, 890–1.

186 Malagodi, *Conversazioni della guerra*, vol. I, pp. 260–1.

187 Albertini, *Epistolario 1911–1926*, vol. II, p. 946.

188 For splendid case study, see Christopher Clark, *The Sleepwalkers: How Europe Went to War in 1914* (London: Allen Lane, 2012), pp. 3–64.

189 Giovanni Amendola et al., *Il patto di Roma*, p. 20.

190 See Benito Mussolini, *Opera Omnia*, 36 volumes (eds Edoardo Susmel and Duilio Susmel) (Florence: La Fenice, 1951–63), vol. X, p. 450.

191 Giovanni Amendola et al., *Il patto di Roma*, pp. 29–37.

192 For a fine recent study of complications from below, see Dominique Kirchner Reill, *The Fiume Crisis: Life in the Wake of the Habsburg Empire* (Cambridge, MA: Belknap Press of Harvard University Press, 2020).

193 For more detail, see Capone, *Giovanni Amendola*, pp. 179–208.

194 Giovanni Amendola, *Carteggio 1913–1918*, pp. 407–8, 529.

195 Giovanni Amendola, *La crisi dello stato liberale*, pp. 267–73.

196 Giovanni Amendola, *Carteggio 1913–1918*, pp. 551–2.

Chapter 3

1 Valeria Sgambati, 'La formazione politica e culturale di Giorgio Amendola', *Studi Storici*, 32, 1991, p. 738.

2 See Paolo Ardali, *San Francesco e Mussolini* (Mantua: Edizioni Paladino, nd [1927]); cf. also his parallel between Duce and Pope: Paolo Ardali, *Mussolini e Pio XI* (Mantua: Edizioni Paladino, nd [1926]). Ardali was a priest.

3 This is the most useful theme of Christopher Duggan, *Fascist Voices: An Intimate History of Mussolini's Italy* (London: Bodley Head, 2012).

4 Renzo De Felice, *Mussolini il fascista. 1: La conquista del potere 1921–1925* (Turin: Einaudi, 1966), pp. 359–64.

5 Alfredo Capone, *Giovanni Amendola* (Rome: Salerno Editrice, 2013), pp. 209–34.

6 Giovanni Amendola, *Carteggio 1925–1926* (ed. Elio D'Auria) (Soveria Mannelli: Rubbettino, 2016), pp. 536–8.

7 Rachele Mussolini, *The Real Mussolini (as told to A. Zarca)* (Farnborough: Saxon House, 1973), p. 66.

8 Giovanni Amendola, *Carteggio 1919–1922* (ed. Elio D'Auria) (Bari: Laterza, 2003), p. 84. It was another ironical parallel with 'Professor Mussolini'.

9 See Renzo De Felice (ed.), *Utopia: rivista quindicinale del socialismo rivoluzionario italiano, direttore Benito Mussolini* (Milan: Feltrinelli, 1976).

10 See www.mussolinibenito.it/fogliomatricolare.htm (accessed 8 December 2020).

11 Giovanni Cerchia, *Giorgio Amendola: un comunista nazionale. Dall'infanzia alla guerra partigiana (1907–1945)* (Soveria Mannelli: Rubbettino, 2004), pp. 37–8.

12 See, for example, Benito Mussolini, *Il mio diario di guerra 1915–1917* (Imperia: Casa Editrice del Partito Nazionale Fascista, 1923). It can also be found in Benito Mussolini, *Opera Omnia*, 36 volumes (eds Edoardo Susmel and Duilio Susmel) (Florence: La Fenice, 1951–63), vol. XXXIV.

13 Giovanni Amendola, *Carteggio 1919–1922*, p. 75.

14 Paolo Soave, *Una vittoria mutilata? L'Italia e la Conferenza di Pace di Parigi* (Soveria Mannelli: Rubbettino, 2020), p. 50.

15 Luigi Albertini, *Epistolario 1911–1926* (ed. Ottavio Bariè) (Milan: Mondadori, 1968), vol. III, p. 1142.

16 Giovanni Amendola, *Carteggio 1919–1922*, pp. 51–2, 55.

17 *Ibid.*, p. 33.

18 *Ibid.*, pp. 46–8.

19 *Ibid.*, p. 85.

20 *Ibid.*, p. 104.

21 This matter was commonly explored by anthropologists after 1945. For some commentary, see R. J. B. Bosworth, *Mussolini and the Eclipse of Italian Fascism: From Dictatorship to Populism* (London: Yale University Press, 2021), pp. 161–70.

22 Giovanni Amendola, *La nuova democrazia* (Naples: Riccardo Ricciardi Editore, 1951), p. 25.

23 Luigi Albertini, *I giorni di un liberale: diari 1907–1923* (ed. Luciano Monzali) (Bologna: Il Mulino, 2000), p. 130.

24 See Benito Mussolini, *Opera Omnia*, vol. XII, pp. 22–4. An article of 22 November 1918 attacked the 'mad imperialism' of the Yugoslavs, against which the 'gentlemanly' behaviour of Italian Liberals could get nowhere. At this stage, Mussolini, like Giovanni, retained hopes in the 'Empire of Wilson', which, he reckoned, had no borders but carried the hopes and faith of

humanity; it should allow post-war justice to triumph (article of 5 January 1919, pp. 110–2).

25 Giovanni Amendola, *Carteggio 1919–1922*, pp. 10–1.

26 *Ibid.*, p. 101.

27 Giovanni Amendola, *La crisi dello stato liberale* (ed. Elio D'Auria) (Rome: Newton Compton, 1974), pp. 323–5. For further background on the confused efforts of Nitti and his government to favour civilian 'squads' against 'revolutionary' strikers, see Matteo Millan, 'From "state protection" to "private defence": strikebreaking, civilian armed mobilisation and the rise of Italian fascism' in Matteo Millan and Alessandro Saluppo (eds), *Corporate Policing, Yellow Unionism and Strikebreaking 1890–1930; In Defence of Freedom* (Abingdon: Routledge, 2021), pp. 242–58.

28 Giovanni Amendola, *Carteggio 1919–1922*, p. 139.

29 Albertini, *Epistolario 1911–1926*, vol. III, p. 1286.

30 Giovanni Amendola, *La nuova democrazia*, pp. 61–73. For massive detail, see Francesco Lefebvre D'Ovidio, *L'Italia e il sistema internazionale dalla formazione del governo Mussolini alla Grande Depressione (1922–1929)* (Rome: Edizioni di Storia e Letteratura, 2016). Grandi was under-secretary of foreign affairs 1925–9 and then minister to 1932.

31 Giovanni Amendola, *Carteggio 1919–1922*, p. 23.

32 Lucia Re, 'Women at war: Eva Kühn Amendola (Magamal) – Interventionist, Futurist, Fascist', *Annali d'Italianistica*, 33, 2015, p. 286.

33 Giovanni Amendola, *Carteggio 1919–1922*, pp. 145, 150.

34 *Ibid.*, p. 210.

35 *Ibid.*, p. 204.

36 Giovanni Amendola, *La nuova democrazia*, pp. 3–18.

37 For background, see R. J. B. Bosworth, *Mussolini* (London: Bloomsbury, 2010), pp. 133–7; in fuller detail, David R. Forsyth, *The Crisis of Liberal Italy: Monetary and Financial Policy 1914–1922* (Cambridge: Cambridge University Press, 1993).

38 Giovanni Amendola, *Carteggio 1919–1922*, pp. 246–7. One of the droller virtual histories of Italy is to imagine Il Comandante running a budget, if he had been put in charge of the Italian nation, as quite a few rightists wanted.

39 *Ibid.*, p. 248.

40 See their many personal letters, in Giovanni Amendola, *Carteggio 1913–1918* (ed. Elio D'Auria) (Manduria: Piero Lacaita, 1999).

41 See, for example, Francesco Saverio Nitti, *Peacelesss Europe* (London: Cassell, 1922); *La decadenza dell'Europa: le vie della ricostruzione* (Florence: Bemporad, 1922); *La tragedia dell'Europa: che farà l'America* (Turin: Piero Gobetti Editore, 1924).

42 Giovanni Amendola, *Carteggio 1919–1922*, pp. 427–8.

43 For background, see Bosworth, *Mussolini*, pp. 128–34.

44 Giovanni Amendola, *Carteggio 1919–1922*, pp. 255–6.

45 *Ibid.*, pp. 376–7.

46 Albertini, *Epistolario 1911–1926*, vol. III, p. 1461.

47 Giovanni Amendola, *Carteggio 1919–1922*, pp. 372–3.

48 *Ibid.*, p. 313.

49 *Ibid.*, pp. 324–5.
50 Giovanni Amendola, *La nuova democrazia*, p. 4.
51 Giovanni Amendola, *Carteggio 1919–1922*, pp. 359–60.
52 *Ibid.*, pp. 257–9.
53 *Ibid.*, p. 278.
54 *Ibid.*, pp. 288–9.
55 *Ibid.*, p. 445.
56 Goffredo Locatelli, *Il deputato dei 27 voti: la storia vera e mai scritta di Giovanni Amendola* (Milan: Mursia, 2014), p. 152.
57 Giovanni Amendola, *Carteggio 1919–1922*, p. 406; cf. Albertini, *Epistolario 1911–1926*, vol. III, p. 1430.
58 Albertini, *Epistolario 1911–1926*, vol. III, p. 1453.
59 Giovanni Amendola, *Una battaglia liberale: discorsi politici 1919–1923* (Turin: Piero Gobetti Editore, 1924), pp. 7–10. The dictatorship was soon embracing the language of war and claiming that all its policies were 'battles', again with striking parallels to the Anti-Fascist Amendola.
60 Giovanni Amendola, *Carteggio 1919–1922*, pp. 415–17.
61 *Ibid.*, pp. 427–8.
62 *Ibid.*, p. 425.
63 Giovanni Amendola, *La nuova democrazia*, pp. 89–94.
64 De Felice, *Mussolini il fascista. 1: La conquista del potere*, p. 246.
65 Bruno Casinelli, *Giovanni Amendola: l'uomo – il pensatore – il filosofo – ciò che la morte ha impedito* (Rome: Labor, 1926), p. 22.
66 For background, see Bosworth, *Mussolini and the Eclipse of Italian Fascism*, pp. 117–20.
67 Richard Bosworth and Giuseppe Finaldi, 'The Italian Empire' in Robert Gerwarth and Erez Manela (eds), *Empires at War 1911–1923* (Oxford: Oxford University Press, 2014), pp. 50–1.
68 Federica Guazzini, 'Giovanni Amendola ministro delle Colonie: "Lasciatemi solo davanti agli arabi"' in Elio D'Auria (ed), *Giovanni Amendola: una vita in difesa della libertà. Atti del convegno di studi per il 90 anniversario della morte (1882–1926)* (Soveria Mannelli: Rubbettino, 2018), p. 202.
69 Naturally, Alfredo Capone sees him as behaving 'democratically' there. Capone, *Giovanni Amendola*, pp. 258–75.
70 R. J. B. Bosworth, *Italy, the Least of the Great Powers: Italian Foreign Policy before the First World War* (Cambridge: Cambridge University Press, 1979), pp. 36–7.
71 For more detail on his career, see R. J. B. Bosworth, *Italian Venice: A History* (London: Yale University Press, 2014).
72 Cesira Filesi, 'La Tripolitania nella politica coloniale di Giovanni Amendola', *Africa: Rivista Trimestrale*, 32, 1977, p. 524.
73 Giovanni Amendola, *Carteggio 1919–1922*, pp. 459–60.
74 Eileen Ryan, *Religion as Resistance: Negotiating Authority in Italian Libya* (Oxford: Oxford University Press, 2018), pp. 129–30.
75 Giovanni Amendola, *La nuova democrazia*, p. 100.
76 Giampiero Carocci, *Giovanni Amendola nella crisi dello Stato italiano 1911–1925* (Milan: Feltrinelli, 1956), p. 160.

77 Filesi, 'La Tripolitania nella politica coloniale di Giovanni Amendola', p. 541. Less critical but admitting carry-over to the Fascist years is Guazzini, 'Giovanni Amendola ministro delle Colonie', pp. 223–31.

78 *Ibid.*, pp. 246–52.

79 Giovanni Amendola, *La nuova democrazia*, pp. 115–16; cf. Bosworth, *Mussolini and the eclipse of Italian Fascism*, p. 242.

80 Filesi, 'La Tripolitania nella politica coloniale di Giovanni Amendola', pp. 536–7.

81 Giovanni Amendola, *La nuova democrazia*, p. 133.

82 Giovanni Amendola, *Una battaglia liberale*, pp. 229–30.

83 Nitti, *La decadenza dell'Europa*, p. 145.

84 Guazzini, 'Giovanni Amendola ministro delle Colonie', p. 207.

85 For background, see Antonio Sarubbi, *'Il Mondo' di Amendola e Cianca e il crollo delle istituzioni liberali (1922–1926)* (Milan: Franco Angeli, 1986); cf. Gerardo Nicolosi, '"Il Mondo" di Giovanni Amendola: una scuola di vita e di democrazia. Proprietà, formula giornalistica, eredità' in D'Auria (ed.), *Giovanni Amendola*, pp. 165–82. Capone, *Giovanni Amendola*, pp. 242–5 deems the Democratic Party a genuine party in the making.

86 See Lucio D'Angelo, 'Meuccio Ruini, Giovanni Amendola e il "partito democratico"' in D'Auria (ed.), *Giovanni Amendola*, p. 282.

87 Giovanni Amendola, *Carteggio 1919–1922*, pp. 517, 550.

88 De Felice, *Mussolini il fascista. 1: La conquista del potere*, pp. 283–4; Cerchia, *Giorgio Amendola*, pp. 79–80.

89 Giovanni Amendola, *La democrazia dopo il VI aprile MCMXXIV* (Milan: Corbaccio, 1924), pp. 5–6.

90 *Ibid.*, p. 14; cf. Carocci, *Giovanni Amendola nella crisi dello Stato italiano*, p. 160.

91 Giovanni Amendola, *La democrazia dopo il VI aprile MCMXXIV*, pp. 23–5.

92 *Ibid.*, pp. 27–30.

93 Emilio Gentile is the leading theorist in this regard. See, for example, Emilio Gentile, *E fu subito regime: il fascismo e la Marcia su Roma* (Rome: Laterza, 2012). I have long been unconvinced. For my fullest account why, see R. J. B. Bosworth, *The Italian Dictatorship: Problems and Perspectives in the Interpretation of Mussolini and Fascism* (London: Arnold, 1998).

94 Giovanni Amendola, *La democrazia dopo il VI aprile MCMXXIV*, p. 46.

95 De Felice, *Mussolini il fascista. 1: La conquista del potere*, pp. 346–87.

96 Giovanni Amendola, *La democrazia dopo il VI aprile MCMXXIV*, p. 60.

97 *Ibid.*, pp. 62–3.

98 Giorgio Amendola, *Una scelta di vita* (Milan: Rizzoli, 1976), pp. 63–4. The exact timing of these events is disputed.

99 Giovanni Amendola, *Carteggio 1919–1922*, pp. 177–8.

100 Giovanni Amendola, *La democrazia dopo il VI aprile MCMXXIV*, pp. 67–9.

101 For a notably intelligent study of how much Amendola shared Fascist ideas, see Giuseppe Bedeschi, 'L'analisi del fascismo in Giovanni Amendola' in D'Auria (ed.), *Giovanni Amendola*, pp. 301–14.

102 Giovanni Amendola, *Carteggio 1919–1922*, p. 608.

103 *Ibid.*, pp. 612–13.

219

104 Giovanni Amendola, *La crisi dello stato liberale*, p. 342.
105 Giovanni Amendola, *La democrazia dopo il VI aprile MCMXXIV*, pp. 81–6.
106 *Ibid.*, pp. 91–2.
107 *Ibid.*, pp. 102–6; cf. Giovanni Amendola, *La crisi dello stato liberale*, pp. 344–6. For further description, see Elio D'Auria, 'Giovanni Amendola: martire della libertà e della democrazia' in D'Auria (ed.), *Giovanni Amendola*, pp. 26–7.
108 Giovanni Amendola, *La democrazia dopo il VI aprile MCMXXIV*, pp. 115–17.
109 *Ibid.*, pp. 125–8.
110 *Ibid.*, pp. 98–101.
111 *Ibid.*, pp. 202–6.
112 *Ibid.*, pp. 207–8.
113 *Ibid.*, pp. 288–93.
114 *Ibid.*, pp. 305–7.
115 *Ibid.*, pp. 110–14.
116 Carocci, *Giovanni Amendola nella crisi dello Stato italiano*, pp. 137–8; Giovanni Amendola, *La democrazia dopo il VI aprile MCMXXIV*, pp. 168–9, 178–80.
117 Carocci, *Giovanni Amendola nella crisi dello Stato italiano*, pp. 103–5. Ironically, in August 1921, Amendola had told Nitti that Acerbo was 'a boy with a good ideal', who might yet push Fascism in a positive direction. Giovanni Amendola, *Carteggio 1919–1922*, pp. 396–7; for Acerbo's background, cf. Bosworth, *Mussolini and the Eclipse of Italian Fascism*, p. 48.
118 Giovanni Amendola, *La nuova democrazia*, pp. 155–77, 129–30.
119 Giampiero, *Giovanni Amendola nella crisi dello Stato italiano*, pp. 103–6.
120 Giovanni Amendola, *La democrazia dopo il VI aprile MCMXXIV*, pp. 164–6.
121 Giovanni Amendola, *Carteggio 1923–1924* (ed. Elio D'Auria) (Manduria: Piero Lacaita Editore, 2006), pp. 63–4.
122 Giovanni Amendola, *La democrazia dopo il VI aprile MCMXXIV*, pp. 193–4.
123 *Ibid.*, pp. 198–201.
124 *Ibid.*, pp. 212–14.
125 *Ibid.*, pp. 231–4.
126 Giovanni Amendola, *Carteggio 1923–1924*, pp. 72, 84, 121.
127 See Piero Meldini, *Sposa e madre esemplare: ideologia e politica della donna e della famiglia durante il fascismo* (Florence: Guaraldi, 1975).
128 Giovanni Amendola, *La democrazia dopo il VI aprile MCMXXIV*, p. 216.
129 Giovanni Amendola, *Carteggio 1923–1924*, pp. 184, 197; Albertini, *Epistolario 1911–1926*, vol. IV, p. 1772.
130 Giovanni Amendola, *Carteggio 1923–1924*, pp. 193–4.
131 Giampiero Carocci, *Giovanni Amendola nella crisi dello Stato italiano*, p. 82.
132 *Ibid.*, p. 109.
133 Giovanni Amendola, *Carteggio 1923–1924*, p. 401.
134 Giovanni Amendola, *La democrazia dopo il VI aprile MCMXXIV*, pp. 149–69.
135 Giovanni Amendola, *Carteggio 1923–1924*, p. 355.
136 *Ibid.*, pp. 374, 387, 477.

137 *Ibid.*, pp. 497–8.
138 *Ibid.*, pp. 407–8.
139 *Ibid.*, pp. 416–17.
140 *Ibid.*, pp. 438–40.
141 *Ibid.*, p. 459.
142 Simona Colarizi, *I democratici all'opposizione: Giovanni Amendola e l'Unione Nazionale (1922–1926)* (Bologna: Il Mulino, 1973), p. 51.
143 *Ibid.*, p. 107. Even Alfredo Capone acknowledges that it never possessed the lineaments of a modern party. Capone, *Giovanni Amendola*, pp. 320–4.
144 Paolo Spriano, 'Tra dopoguerra e fascismo: Amendola, Gobetti, Gramsci' in *Giovanni Amendola: una battaglia per democrazia: atti del convegno di studi con il patrimonio della Regione Emila-Romagna* (Bologna: Arnaldo Forni Editore, 1978), p. 317.
145 See Cerchia, *Giorgio Amendola*, pp. 112–16. He details the uneasy relationship between Gobetti and the adolescent Giorgio Amendola.
146 Elio D'Auria, 'Ringraziamenti' in Giovanni Amendola, *Carteggio 1925–1926*, pp. 3–4; cf. in greater detail, the defence in Capone, *Giovanni Amendola*, pp. 300–20.
147 Giuseppe Prezzolini (ed.) *Amendola e 'La Voce'* (Florence: Sansoni, 1973), pp. 272–80.
148 Alessandro Lessona, *Un ministro di Mussolini racconta* (Milan: Edizioni Nazionali, 1973), pp. 25–7; cf. Bosworth, *Mussolini and the Eclipse of Italian Fascism*, pp. 127, 206.
149 Capone, *Giovanni Amendola*, pp. 329–34.
150 Giovanni Amendola, *Carteggio 1925–1926*, p. 57.
151 See Giovanni Amendola, *Carteggio 1923–1924*, pp. 486–8. When Prezzolini defended Pirandello's choice to join the PNF, Amendola damned him too. Ironically, Pirandello's novel *Il fu Mattia Pascal*, which marked a major breakthrough in his career, satirized theosophists in Rome and the deep philosophising that had attracted the young Giovanni. See Luigi Pirandello, *The Late Mattia Pascal* (Sawtry: Dedalus, 1987), pp. 116–70.
152 See Renzo De Felice (ed.), *Autobiografia del fascismo: antologia di testi fascisti 1919–1945* (Turin: Einaudi, 2019); cf. Emilio R. Papa, *Storia di due manifesti* (Milan: Feltrinelli, 1958).
153 Giovanni Amendola, *Carteggio 1925–1926*, p. 88.
154 Eugenio Di Rienzo, 'Le scelte di un liberale conservatore: Benedetto Croce e il fascismo. Una rilettura', *Nuova Rivista Storica*, CIV, 2020, p. 30; cf. pp. 102–10 for his rejection of the Aventine.
155 For an account of the survival of some legal forms from Liberal times, cf. Paul Garfinkel, *Criminal Law in Liberal and Fascist Italy* (Cambridge: Cambridge University Press, 2016).
156 Giovanni Amendola, *L'Aventino contro il Fascismo: scritti politici (1924–1926)* (ed. Sabato Visco) (Milan: Riccardo Ricciardi Editore, 1976), p. 313.
157 Giovanni Amendola, *Carteggio 1925–1926*, pp. 177–8.
158 *The Times*, 8 April 1926; Locatelli, *Il deputato dei 27 voti*, pp. 341–6.
159 Giovanni Amendola, *Carteggio 1925–1926*, p. 277.
160 *Ibid.*, pp. 315–17.

161 *Ibid.*, pp. 324–5.
162 *Ibid.*, pp. 328, 333, 335–6.
163 *Ibid.*, pp. 340–2.
164 *Ibid.*, p. 350.
165 *Ibid.*, p. 351.
166 *Ibid.*, p. 352.
167 *Ibid.*, pp. 338–9, 342, 353–5, 365–6, 372–3, 378.
168 Giorgio Amendola, *Un scelta di vita*, p. 137.
169 Giovanni Amendola, *Carteggio 1925–1926*, p. 367.
170 *Ibid*, pp. 373–4, 381–2, 384–5.
171 *Ibid.*, pp. 380–1, 386–7.
172 *Ibid.*, p. 382.
173 See Stanislao Pugliese, *Carlo Rosselli: Socialist Heretic and Antifascist Exile* (Cambridge MA: Harvard University Press, 2001). It is significant that Pugliese's collection on the Resistance omits any writing by Amendola. Stanislao Pugliese, *Italian Fascism and Antifascism: A Critical Anthology* (Manchester: Manchester University Press, 2001). See also, more recently, Isabelle Richet, *Women, Antifascism and Mussolini's Italy: The Life of Marion Cave Rosselli* (London: I. B. Taurus, 2018), p. 75. Richet notes the Rosselli couple's sadness at Amendola's death and Marion Cave's approval of his political line in 1924.
174 Sandro Rogari, 'Immagine e mito di Giovanni Amendola nell'emigrazione antifascista' in *Giovanni Amendola tra etica e politica: atti del convegno di studio Montecatini Terme 25–26–27 ottobre 1996* (Pistoia: CRT, 1999), p. 238.
175 Gaetano Arfè, 'L'eredità politica e morale di Giovanni Amendola' in *Giovanni Amendola tra etica e politica*, p. 254.
176 Leo Valiani, 'L'eredità politica di Giovanni Amendola', *Nord e Sud*, 23, 1977, p. 16. Valiani was inclined to add the British and US participation in the Second World War as springing from a similar ideal base.
177 Eugenio Di Rienzo, *Benedetto Croce: gli anni di scontento 1943–1948* (Soveria Mannelli: Rubbettino, 2019), p. 23.
178 For a still useful (partial) critique, see Denis Mack Smith, 'Benedetto Croce: History and Politics', *Journal of Contemporary History*, 8, 1973, pp. 41–61.
179 Giovanni Amendola, *La democrazia italiana contro il fascismo 1922–1924* (Milan: Riccardo Ricciardi Editore, 1960), p. x.
180 Max Salvadori, *Ricordo di Giovanni Amendola* (Sala Bolognese: Arnaldo Forni Editore, 1976), pp. 3–4.
181 Salvatore Valitutti, 'Lo Stato nel pensiero di Giovanni Amendola' in *Giovanni Amendola nel cinquantenario della morte 1926–1976* (Rome: Fondazione Luigi Einaudi per Studi di Politica ed Economia, 1976), p. 239. Giovanni Amendola, *L'Aventino contro il Fascismo*, pp. 257–61.

Chapter 4

1 Goffredo Locatelli, *Il deputato dei 27 voti: la storia vera e mai scritta di Giovanni Amendola* (Milan: Mursia, 2014), pp. 316–17.

i Amendola, *Carteggio 1923–1924* (ed. Elio D'Auria) (Manduria: ~aita Editore, 2006), p. 323.

Il deputato dei 27 voti, p. 318.

Amendola, *Carteggio 1923–1924*, p. 320.

_ ᴜ. Bell, *Peasants in Power: Alexander Stamboliski and the Bulgarian National Union 1899–1923* (Princeton NJ: Princeton University Press, 1977), pp. 120–1, 131–51.

6 Locatelli, *Il deputato dei 27 voti*, pp. 315–19.

7 Bulgarian archives, Sofia, Hristov papers, letter Nelia Pavlova to Hristov, 12 April 1922. I owe such references to Professor Maria Todorova and her researchers in Sofia.

8 Borghese was the diplomat brother of Scipione Borghese, whose greatest claim to fame was to have had the most comfortable ride in the team of three Italians who won the Peking to Paris car race in 1907. See the delightful Luigi Barzini, *Peking to Paris: Prince Borghese's Journey across Two Continents in 1907* (London: Alcove Press, 1907). Livio was also the father of Junio Valerio Borghese, a fanatical Fascist to the bitter end and beyond, leader of an attempted neo-fascist coup in Rome in December 1970, which, had it succeeded, may have quickly got rid of Giorgio Amendola.

9 *Bulletin Périodique de la Presse Bulgare*, 53, 20 June 1922.

10 For useful background, see Joseph Rothschild, *East Central Europe between the Wars* (Seattle: University of Washington Press, 1974), pp. 324–41.

11 Richard J. Crampton, *A Short History of Bulgaria* (Cambridge: Cambridge University Press, 2005), pp. 147–53.

12 *Annuaire général des lettres*, 1932.

13 In this case, see *Notre Temps*, July 1939 and an extended interview with the foreign minister, Dragiša Cvetković. It is her last traceable commentary.

14 Giovanni Amendola, *Carteggio 1925–1926* (ed. Elio D'Auria) (Soveria Mannelli: Rubbettino, 2016), pp. 496–7.

15 *Ibid.*, pp. 501–3.

16 The Italian literature is all but completely silent about this child. In his racy piece of 'faction', Goffredo Locatelli does mention a pregnancy in '1925' but suggests the child was born after Giovanni's death, a timing that does not fit these letters or the further evidence from the Bulgarian archives. See Locatelli, *Il deputato dei 27 voti*, p. 319.

17 Giovanni Amendola, *Carteggio 1925–1926*, p. 503.

18 *Ibid.*, pp. 504–5.

19 See Mimmo Franzinelli, *I tentacoli dell'Ovra: agenti, collaboratori e vittime della polizia politica fascista* (Turin: Bollati Boringhieri, 1999), pp. 127–8; Mauro Canali, *Le spie del regime* (Bologna: Il Mulino, 2004), pp. 53–4. Garibaldi was soon to try to win over Anti-Fascist exiles to a false plot against the regime, with the intention of getting them expelled from France.

20 Giovanni Amendola, *Carteggio 1925–1926*, pp. 505–6.

21 *Ibid.*, pp. 507–8.

22 *Ibid.*, pp. 508–9.

23 In this letter, unusually she calls Giovanni *vous* not *tu*. Maybe, therefore, it should be dated earlier. *Ibid.*, p. 509.

24 *Ibid.*, p. 512.

25 *Ibid.*, pp. 515–16. She was writing in Paris to Armand Massard, an ex-socialist turned nationalist. He edited *La Presse* and *La Patrie*.

26 This claim is repeated in the only Bulgarian biography of Mladen Pavlov. See Angel Petrov, *Kozloduiskoto daskalche* (Moravitsa: ANPET Publishing, 1996), p. 96. She does seem to have used it for local consumption, given her dislike in Paris of being viewed as Giovanni's widow. No doubt it made her single motherhood easier to explain. Cf. note 41 below.

27 Bulgarian archives, Hristov papers, letter of 24 June 1930, Nelia Pavlova to Hristov.

28 Bulgarian archives, Hristov papers, letter of 22 August 1928, Nelia Pavlova to Hristov.

29 Locatelli, *Il deputato dei 27 voti*, p. 359.

30 Giovanni Cerchia (ed.), 'Luigi Albertini e la famiglia di Giovanni Amendola (1922–1936)', *Mondo Contemporaneo*, 3, 2009, p. 118, letter from Giovanni Amendola to Albertini, 23 January 1926.

31 *Ibid.*, p. 120, letter from Giovanni Amendola to Albertini, 3 February 1926. Also in Giovanni Amendola, *Carteggio 1925–1926*, p. 366.

32 Giorgio Amendola, *Una scelta di vita* (Milan: Rizzoli, 1976), p. 131.

33 Giovanni Amendola, 'Testamento' in *Giovanni Amendola nel cinquantenario della morte 1926–1976* (Rome: Fondazione Luigi Einaudi per Studi di Politica ed Economia, 1976), pp. 333–7.

34 Loris Dadam (ed.), *Giorgio Amendola nella storia d'Italia: antologia critica degli scritti* (Turin: Cerabona Editore, 2007), p. 38.

35 Giorgio Amendola, *Una scelta di vita*, p. 140.

36 *Paris Soir*, 14 June 1926.

37 *La Lanterne*, 13 November 1926.

38 *Le Rappel*, 7 November 1926.

39 *Le Quotidien*, 14 June 1927.

40 Cerchia, 'Luigi Albertini e la famiglia di Giovanni Amendola (1922–1936)', pp. 123–5.

41 They included *Les fleurs du mon printemps* (poems) (Paris: Les Éditions de la Sirene, nd) and *Vagabondages littéraires parisiens* (Milan: Studio Editoriale, nd). Neither book is held in the national libraries of France, Italy or the UK. More readily available is Nelia Pavlova, *Au Pays du Ghazi: Monde d'Aujourd'hui* (Paris: Éditions de la Revue Mondiale, 1930).

42 Giorgio Amendola, *Una scelta di vita*, p. 160.

43 *Ibid.*, pp. 191–2.

44 *Ibid.*, p. 161.

45 *Le Cri des Peuples*, 6 May 1928.

46 *Le Gaulois*, 18 August 1928.

47 *Le Petit Parisien*, 16 and 21 August 1928.

48 *L'Oeuvre*, 19 March 1929.

49 *Le Petit Parisien*, 29 June 1929.

50 *Le Petit Journal*, 27 April 1934. For the background to the Gömbös nomination, see R. J. B. Bosworth, *Mussolini and the Eclipse of Italian Fascism* (London: Yale University Press, 2021), pp. 34, 132.

51 *Le Quotidien*, 30 July 1936.
52 *L'Oeil de Paris*, 10 April 1933.
53 *Le Populaire*, 18 May 1937.
54 *L'Oeil de Paris*, 1 August 1930.
55 See https://ivaveleva.wixsite.com/womenshistory/galeriya?lightbox=dataItem-iy5x8bri (accessed 5 February 2021).
56 Pavlova, *Au Pays du Ghazi*, p. 9. Ghazi is an Arabic term for military leader, not far in meaning from the Italian Duce.
57 *Ibid.*, p. 13.
58 *Ibid.*, pp. 23–4, 49–50, 61, 74–6.
59 *Ibid.*, pp. 134, 141, 154, 160, 171–82.
60 For some of the positive Fascist paralleling of Atatürk's Turkey and Mussolini's regime, see Bosworth, *Mussolini and the Eclipse of Italian Fascism*, pp. 5, 28, 56, 107, 115, 136. A Turkish edition of Pavlova's book appeared in 1985. Nelia Pavlova, *Gazi'nin Ülkesinde* (Denizli: Sanayi Odası Yayınlar, 1985).
61 Pavlova, *Au Pays du Ghazi*, pp. 210–23.
62 *Le Populaire*, 10 April 1933.
63 Nelia Pavlova, *Au pays du maïs et des blés d'or (La Roumanie)* (Paris: Notre Temps, 1938).
64 *Ibid.*, p. 9.
65 *Ibid.*, p. 7.
66 *Ibid.*, pp. 10–15.
67 *Ibid.*, pp. 64–71. She recalled having interviewed Romanian Prime Minister Ion Duca for *Era Nouvelle*, 7 December 1932. The Iron Guard assassinated him on 29 December 1933.
68 *Ibid.*, p. 149.
69 *Ibid.*, p. 158.
70 See www.tulipfoundation.net/en/news/the-community-of-dolni-vadin-village-opened-mladen-pavlov-ethnographical-house-4-august-2007-349/ (accessed 3 February 2021); www.guide-bulgaria.com/nw/vratsa/oryahovo/dolni_vadin (accessed 3 February 2021). The Bulgarian archives, notably in the Hristov papers, contain a number of other photographic images of her.
71 Pavlova, *Au pays du maïs et des blés d'or*, p. 166.
72 *Ibid.*, pp. 249–51.
73 See Bulgarian archives, Hristov papers, 18–23 March 1939, Nelia Pavlova to Hristov.
74 See http://kutuphane.ankaraka.org.tr/upload/dokumandosya/97.pdf (accessed 6 April 2021). The source wrongly declares her to have been born in 1890.
75 It was also approved by Antonella Amendola. See *La Repubblica*, 15 March 2014, https://ricerca.repubblica.it/repubblica/archivio/repubblica/2014/03/15/amendola-impegno-politico-la-lezione-morale.html (accessed 16 March 2021).
76 Alfredo Capone, *Giovanni Amendola* (Rome: Salerno Editrice, 2013), pp. 370, 430. For Napolitano, see p. 7.

77 Sandro Rogari, 'Immagine e mito di Giovanni Amendola nell'emigrazione antifascista' in *Giovanni Amendola tra etica e politica: atti del convegno di studio Montecatini Terme 25–26–27 ottobre 1996* (Pistoia: CRT, 1999), p. 233.

Chapter 5

1 It is available in English. Giuseppe Cesare Abba, *The Diary of One of Garibaldi's Thousand* (London: Oxford University Press, 1962).

2 Giovanni Cerchia, *Giorgio Amendola: un comunista nazionale. Dall'infanzia alla guerra partigiana (1907–1945)* (Soveria Mannelli: Rubbettino, 2004), p. 27.

3 Giorgio Amendola, *Una scelta di vita* (Milan: Rizzoli, 1976), pp. 22–3, 50.

4 *Ibid.*, pp. 7–10.

5 *Ibid.*, p. 18.

6 *Ibid.*, p. 26.

7 Giovanni Amendola, *Carteggio 1913–1918* (ed. Elio D'Auria) (Manduria: Pietro Lacaita, 1999), p. 144.

8 Giorgio Amendola, *Una scelta di vita*, pp. 259–60.

9 *Ibid.*, p. 16.

10 Giovanni Amendola, *Carteggio 1913–1918*, pp. 329–31.

11 Giorgio Amendola, *Una scelta di vita*, pp. 27–31.

12 Goffredo Locatelli, *Il deputato dei 27 voti: la storia vera e mai scritta di Giovanni Amendola* (Milan: Mursia, 2014), p. 10.

13 Giorgio Amendola, *Una scelta di vita*, pp. 174, 177. In Naples, under severe training at an elite club, his rowing weight fell to seventy-eight kilograms.

14 See George Mosse, *Confronting History: A Memoir* (Madison: University of Wisconsin Press, 2000), p. 4.

15 Giorgio Amendola, *Una scelta di vita*, pp. 33–4.

16 *Ibid.*, pp. 37–8.

17 *Ibid.*, p. 40.

18 For what seemed like Bottai's crush on Mussolini, see R. J. B. Bosworth, *Mussolini* (London: Bloomsbury, 2010), pp. 156–7.

19 Giorgio Amendola, *Una scelta di vita*, pp. 39–41.

20 *Ibid.*, pp. 42–4; cf. Renzo De Felice, *Mussolini il rivoluzionario 1883–1920* (Turin: Einaudi, 1965), pp. 573–7.

21 Giorgio Amendola, *Una scelta di vita*, pp. 45–8. Giorgio's image of the class gap between town notables and the peasantry is similar to Carlo Levi's brilliant account of such division in 1935–6 when he was sent to *confino* in the Basilicata. See Carlo Levi, *Christ Stopped at Eboli: The Story of a Year* (New York: Farrar, Straus and Giroux, 1947).

22 Giorgio Amendola, *Una scelta di vita*, pp. 97–9.

23 Giovanni Amendola, *Carteggio 1919–1922* (ed. Elio D'Auria) (Bari: Laterza, 2003), p. 402.

24 Giorgio Amendola, *Una scelta di vita*, pp. 51–5. For Casati, see Scot Ryersson and Michael Yaccarino, *Infinite Variety: The Life and Legend of Marchesa Casati* (Minneapolis: University of Minnesota Press, 1999).

25 Giovanni Amendola, *Carteggio 1919–1922*, p. 538.

26 It still exists. See https://ospedaliere.it/index.php (accessed 9 November 2020).

27 Antonella Amendola, letter to me, 16 March 2021.
28 Giovanni Amendola, *Carteggio 1919–1922*, p. 503.
29 Cerchia, *Giorgio Amendola: un comunista nazionale*, p. 126.
30 Giorgio Amendola, *Una scelta di vita*, p. 65.
31 *Ibid.*, p. 100.
32 *Ibid.*, pp. 178–80.
33 *Ibid.*, p. 74.
34 Giovanni Amendola, *Carteggio 1925–1926* (ed. Elio D'Auria) (Soveria Mannelli: Rubbettino, 2016), p. 16.
35 Giorgio Amendola, *Una scelta di vita*, pp. 106–7.
36 *Ibid.*, pp. 111–12.
37 See Giovanni Amendola, *L'Aventino contro il Fascismo: scritti politici (1924–1926)* (ed. Sabato Visco) (Milan: Riccardo Ricciardi Editore, 1976).
38 Giorgio Amendola, *Una scelta di vita*, pp. 115–16.
39 *Ibid.*, pp. 159–62.
40 *Ibid.*, pp. 206–7, 241–8.
41 Giorgio Amendola, *Un'isola* (Milan: Rizzoli, 1980), pp. 28–30. In 1986, Carlo Lizzani made a three-part film version for television, boosting the prominence and independence of Germaine.
42 *Ibid.*, p. 30.
43 For her biography, see www.treccani.it/enciclopedia/filomena-nitti_(Dizionario-Biografico)/ (accessed 10 November 2020); cf. Marco Ciardi and Miriam Focaccia, 'Filomena Nitti Bovet (1909–1994)' in Jan Apotheker and Livia Simon Sarkadi (eds), *European Women in Chemistry* (Weinheim: Wiley-VCH, 2011), pp. 187–90.
44 Giorgio Amendola, *Un'isola*, pp. 9–10.
45 *Ibid.*, pp. 41–3.
46 *Ibid.*, pp. 42–7.
47 *Ibid.*, pp. 31–3.
48 *Ibid.*, pp. 52–3.
49 *Ibid.*, pp. 56–67. For his effort to be an objective historian of the period rather than a memoirist, see Giorgio Amendola, *Storia del Partito Comunista Italiano 1921–1943* (Rome: Riuniti, 1978), pp. 196–205.
50 Giorgio Amendola, *Un'isola*, pp. 75–9.
51 *Ibid.*, p. 85.
52 *Ibid.*, pp. 83–93.
53 See Livio Sposito, *Mal d'avventura. La storia di Mario Appelius, viaggiatore irrequieto, giornalista e avventuriero, fascista per caso* (Milan: Sperling e Kupfer, 2002).
54 For this period of his life, see Giorgio Amendola, *Un'isola*, pp. 98–104.
55 Giorgio Amendola, *Intervista sull'antifascismo* (ed. Pietro Melograni) (Bari: Laterza, 1976), p. 112.
56 Giorgio Amendola, *Un'isola*, p. 95.
57 For the piece, see Giorgio Amendola, 'Con il proletariato o contro il proletariato? Discorrendo con gli intellettuali della mia generazione', *Stato Operaio*, June 1931.

58 Giorgio Amendola, *Un'isola*, pp. 95–9. The Leto story is telling about one level of Fascist policing. See Guido Leto, *Ovra: fascismo, antifascismo* (Bologna: Cappelli, 1951); cf. the career of Guido's son, the filmmaker Marco. His 1973 *La villeggiatura* (The Holiday Camp), which is about a prison island like Ponza and the experiences there of a young gentlemanly liberal, more Fenoaltea than Giorgio, is the subtlest of all cinema representations of Italian Fascism.

59 Giovanni Cerchia (ed.) 'Luigi Albertini e la famiglia di Giovanni Amendola (1922–1936)', *Mondo Contemporaneo*, 2009, p. 128.

60 I owe this reference to Antonella Amendola.

61 Cerchia (ed.), 'Luigi Albertini e la famiglia di Giovanni Amendola', p. 130. For a list of Eva's translations, see www.russinitalia.it/dettaglio.php?id=442 (accessed 19 November 2020).

62 Giorgio Amendola, *Un'isola*, pp. 102–3.

63 For his autobiography and belated Anti-Fascism, see Carmine Senise, *Quando ero Capo della Polizia 1940–1943* (Rome: Ruffolo Editore, 1946).

64 Giorgio Amendola, *Un'isola*, pp. 104–5.

65 *Ibid.*, p. 105.

66 Primo Levi, *If This Is a Man* [and] *The Truce* (Harmondsworth: Penguin, 1979). The binding together of the work on Auschwitz with Levi's memory of his trip from there back to Italy, much of it through Stalin's USSR, where confusion and misapprehension reigned at least as much as totalitarian tyranny, is brilliant.

67 Piero Garofalo, Elizabeth Leake and Dana Renga, *Internal Exile in Fascist Italy: History and Representations of* Confino (Manchester: Manchester University Press, 2019), p. 124.

68 Giorgio Amendola, *Un'isola*, pp. 112–15.

69 *Ibid.*, pp. 119–27.

70 *Ibid.*, p. 127.

71 *Ibid.*, pp. 130–1.

72 For the fullest detail, see Adriana Dal Pont and Simonetta Carolini, *L'Italia al confino: le ordinanze di assegnazione al confino emesse dalle Commissioni provinciali dal novembre 1926 al luglio 1943*, 4 volumes (Milan: La Pietra, 1983).

73 The major English-language study of *confino* is Michael R. Ebner, *Ordinary Violence in Mussolini's Italy* (Cambridge: Cambridge University Press, 2011). It takes the totalitarianist line in reviewing what Ebner calls the 'archipelago' of imprisonment with implied but excessive parallel with the USSR. On p. 124 he finds Giorgio's account of Ponza as over-cosy.

74 Giorgio Amendola, *Un'isola*, p. 113.

75 *Ibid.*, p. 142.

76 *Ibid.*, pp. 135–40.

77 *Ibid.*, pp. 146–8.

78 *Ibid.*, pp. 150–3, where Giorgio also philosophised about masturbation and the need to avoid homosexual ties in prison.

79 For Lessona's disappointment at not acquiring a noble title in Eritrea, see R. J. B. Bosworth, *Mussolini and the Eclipse of Italian Fascism: From Dictatorship to Populism* (London: Yale University Press, 2021), p. 51.

80 Archivio Centrale dello Stato, DGPS, UCP, 23, 24 May 1936, Pietro Amendola to Giorgio.

81 Letter, Antonella Amendola to me, 16 March 2021.

82 Giovanni Cerchia, 'Note del Curatore' in Giovanni Cerchia (ed.), *La famiglia Amendola: una scelta di vita per l'Italia* (Turin: Cerabona Editore, 2011), p. 18.

83 Giorgio Amendola, *Un'isola*, pp. 159–62.

84 Cerchia, *Giorgio Amendola: un comunista nazionale*, pp. 295–6.

85 See Renzo De Felice, *Mussolini il duce. 1: Gli anni del consenso 1929–1936* (Turin: Einaudi, 1974).

86 This word earned notoriety in Italian memories of Fascism when Berlusconi used it to downplay the dictatorship's punishment system. For able response, see Silverio Corvisieri, *La villeggiatura di Mussolini: il confino da Bocchini a Berlusconi* (Milan: Baldini, Castoldi, Dalai, 2004). Corvisieri often refers to Giorgio's account to illustrate prisoner protests and tough reaction to them.

87 Giorgio Amendola, *Un'isola*, pp. 143–6.

88 Massimilliano Marzillo, 'Pietro Amendola' in Cerchia (ed,), *La famiglia Amendola*, pp. 162–5.

89 For the Littoriali, where the cream of the Italian intelligentsia after 1945 cut their teeth, see Aldo Grandi, *I giovani di Mussolini: Fascisti convinti, fascisti pentiti, antifascisti* (Milan: Baldini and Castoldi, 2001); cf. Christopher Duggan, *Fascist Voices: An Intimate History of Mussolini's Italy* (London: Bodley Head, 2013), pp. 293–5.

90 See Laura Cerasi, 'Intellectuals in the mirror of fascist corporatism at the turning-point of the mid-thirties' in António Costa Pinto and Federico Finchelstein (eds), *Authoritarianism and Corporatism in Europe and Latin America: Crossing Borders* (Abingdon: Routledge, 2019), p. 28.

91 Giorgio Amendola, *Un'isola*, pp. 162–3.

92 Pietro Ingrao, *Le cose impossibili: un'autobiografia raccontata e discussa con Nicola Tranfaglia* (Rome: Aliberti, 2011), p. 19.

93 Pietro Ingrao, *Volevo la luna* (Turin: Einaudi, 2006), pp. 44–6, 60–1.

94 Sergio Bertelli, *Il Gruppo: la formazione del gruppo dirigente del PCI 1936–1948* (Milan: Rizzoli, 1980), pp. 22–4.

95 See, notably, her two-volume contribution to an illustrated history of Fascism from below, published by Riuniti, the PCI's serious publishing house, just as it was dissolving in the 1990s. See Eva Paola Amendola, *La nascita del fascismo 1919–1925* (Rome: Riuniti, 1998); Eva Paola Amendola and Pasquale Iaccio, *Gli anni del regime 1925–1939* (Rome: Riuniti, 1998).

96 Giorgio Amendola, *Comunismo antifascismo e Resistenza* (Rome: Riuniti, 1967), pp. 33–89.

97 Giorgio Amendola, *Un'isola*, p. 163; Bertelli, *Il Gruppo*, pp. 43–5.

98 Giorgio Amendola, *Un'isola*, pp. 173–4.

99 Bertelli, *Il Gruppo*, pp. 116–18; Ingrao, *Volevo la luna*, pp. 68–9.

100 Ingrao, *Volevo la luna*, pp. 84–5. After the war, Ingrao did look Antonio up in his asylum but found him detached from any comprehension or memory of reality.

101 Giorgio Amendola, *Lettere a Milano: ricordi e documenti 1943–1945* (Rome: Riuniti, 1973), pp. 121–2.

102 For more detail, see Albertina Vittoria, 'La breve vita di Antonio Amendola' in Cerchia (ed.), *La famiglia Amendola*, pp. 119–60; Albertina Vittoria, *Intellettuali e politica alla fine degli anni '30: Antonio Amendola e la formazione del gruppo comunista romano* (Milan: Franco Angeli, 1985). For the hospital, now closed and converted into a memory site, see www.cartedalegare.san .beniculturali.it/fileadmin/redazione/inventari/Roma_OspedalePsichiatrico_ SMP.pdf (accessed 16 November 2020).

103 Maria Antonietta Macciocchi, *Due mila anni di felicità: diario di un'eretica* (Milan: Il Saggiatore, 2000), pp. 72–3.

104 Giorgio Amendola, *Un'isola*, pp. 163–4.

105 For the most useful summary, see Antonietta G. Paolino, 'Eva Kühn Amendola' in Cerchia (ed.), *La famiglia Amendola*, pp. 93–118.

106 Giorgio Amendola, *Un'isola*, pp. 168–70.

107 They did not divorce. He died from a road accident on 16 June 1958, aged fifty-three. After 1945, Ada had a relationship with Franz Lisi, a rich Puglian businessman with contacts to the Egyptian royal family (and a wife whom he could not divorce). When they separated, Lisi generously passed money to Ada to assist in the maintenance of Eva. Letter, Antonella Amendola to me, 16 March 2021.

108 Giorgio Amendola, *Lettere a Milano*, p. 121.

109 Letter, Antonella Amendola to me, 16 March 2021.

110 See R. J. B. Bosworth, *Mussolini's Italy: Life under the Dictatorship* (London: Allen Lane, 2005), p. 340.

111 Giorgio Amendola, *Un'isola*, p. 185.

112 ACS, DGPS, UCP, 23, Amendola to ministry of the interior, 4 August 1937.

113 Ingrao, *Le cose impossibili*, p. 25.

114 Giorgio Amendola, *Un'isola*, pp. 191–203.

115 Giorgio Amendola, *Storia del Partito Comunista Italiano*, p. 271.

116 ACS, DGPS, UCP 23, 25 October 1937, ministry of the interior to the questura.

117 Giorgio Amendola, *Un'isola*, pp. 215–18, 223–4.

118 *Ibid.*, pp. 225–37.

119 *Ibid.*, pp. 241–2.

120 For clear analysis, see Cerchia, *Giorgio Amendola: un comunista nazionale*, pp. 317–22.

121 Giorgio Amendola, *Intervista sull'antifascismo*, p. 132.

122 Giorgio Amendola, *Lettere a Milano*, pp. 6–7.

123 *Ibid.*, pp. 27–30.

124 *Ibid.*, p. 46.

125 *Ibid.*, p. 80.

Chapter 6

1 For background, see R. J. B. Bosworth, *Mussolini* (London: Bloomsbury, 2010), pp. 16–33, 324–31. The major Italian study of these months is

Claudio Pavone, *Una Guerra civile: saggio storico sulla moralità nella Resistenza* (Turin: Bollati Boringhieri, 1991).

2 For a key local study, see Luisa Passerini, *Fascism in Popular Memory: The Cultural Memory of the Turin Working Class* (Cambridge: Cambridge University Press, 1987).

3 Giorgio Amendola, *Lettere a Milano* (Rome: Riuniti, 1974), p. 571.

4 See R. J. B. Bosworth, *The Italian Dictatorship: Problems and Perspectives in the Interpretation of Mussolini and Fascism* (London: Arnold, 1998), pp. 15–16, 180–204.

5 Giorgio Amendola, *Lettere a Milano*, pp. 573–5.

6 Loris Dadam (ed.), *Giorgio Amendola nella storia d'Italia: antologia critica degli scritti* (Turin: Cerabona Editore, 2007), p. 117.

7 *Ibid.*, pp. 115–16.

8 For broad exploration, see Antonio Ferrara, 'Beyond genocide and ethnic cleansing: demographic surgery as a new way to understand mass violence', *Journal of Genocide Research*, 17, 2015, pp. 1–20.

9 In this regard, see the reiterated claims of the journalist Giampaolo Pansa, notably in his *Il sangue dei vinti* (Milan: Sperling and Kupfer, 2003). By this revised edition, he maintained that the book had sold 350,000 copies in Italy (p. xiii).

10 Dadam (ed.), *Giorgio Amendola nella storia d'Italia*, p. 101.

11 Sergio Bertelli, *Il gruppo: la formazione del gruppo dirigente del PCI 1936–1948* (Milan: Rizzoli, 1980), p. 10.

12 Giorgio Amendola, *Lettere a Milano*, pp. 119–22.

13 *Ibid.*, pp. 159–60.

14 *Ibid.*, pp. 161–2.

15 *Ibid.*, p. 174.

16 *Ibid.*, pp. 179–226; cf. Giovanni Cerchia, *Giorgio Amendola: un comunista nazionale. Dall'infanzia alla guerra partigiana (1907–1945)* (Soveria Mannelli: Rubbettino, 2004), pp. 390–6.

17 Mimmo Franzinelli, *I tentacoli dell'Ovra: agenti, collaboratori e vittime della polizia politica fascista* (Turin: Bollati Boringhieri, 1999), p. 382.

18 Giorgio Amendola, *Lettere a Milano*, pp. 372–81.

19 Cerchia, *Giorgio Amendola: un comunista nazionale*, pp. 406–14.

20 Giorgio Amendola, *Lettere a Milano*, p. 495.

21 Giorgio Amendola (ed.), *Il comunismo italiano nella seconda guerra mondiale: relazione e documenti presentati dalla direzione del partito al V Congresso del Partito comunista italiano* (Rome: Riuniti, 1963), p. 28.

22 See Curzio Malaparte, *The Skin* (London: Alvin Redman, 1952). Malaparte was traversing his idiosyncratic course from fevered Fascism to Anti-Fascism to the PCI to Maoism.

23 Percy Allum, *Politics and Society in Post-War Naples* (Cambridge: Cambridge University Press, 1973), pp. 50, 93.

24 Giorgio Amendola, *Lettere a Milano*, pp. 582–3.

25 For a scabrous portrait of the city, far from communism, in that month, see John Horne Burns, *The Gallery* (London: Harborough Publishing, 1948).

26 Massimiliano Marzillo, 'Pietro Amendola: passione civile, politica e coerente idealismo' in Giovanni Cerchia (ed.), *La famiglia Amendola: una scelta di vita*

per *l'Italia* (Turin: Cerabona Editore, 2011), pp. 166–7. This book was, naturally enough, launched by Massimo D'Alema, the ex-member of the PCI who became Italian prime minister (1998–2000). For the YouTube record, see www.youtube.com/watch?v=nYy1RmViUTc.

27 She was another competent Amendola. For her work on science education, see Giorgina Amendola, Fulvio Balata and Paola Migliorini, *Quale tecnica* (Florence: La Nuova Italia, 1985).

28 See, notably, Maria Antonietta Macciocchi, *Lettere dall'interno del PCI a Louis Althusser* (Milan: Feltrinelli, 1969). For a brief biography composed by her Resistance friends, see www.anpi.it/donne-e-uomini/1417/maria-antonietta-macciocchi (accessed 26 January 2021); cf. www.treccani.it/enciclopedia/maria-antonietta-macciocchi/ (accessed 26 January 2021). *The Guardian* gave her a positive obituary after her death on 15 April 2007, stating that she had been Pietro's companion, not his wife, and so omitting the San Marino annulment. See www.theguardian.com/news/2007/may/21/guardianobituaries.italy (accessed 26 January 2021).

29 For this detail, see Marzillo, 'Pietro Amendola', p. 175. Maria Antonietta was pregnant when they married.

30 Maria Antonietta Macciocchi, *Due mila anni di felicità: diario di un'eretica* (Milan: Il Saggiatore, 2000), pp. 126–7, 144–5, 235. Despite her feminism, Macciocchi makes no reference to Nelia Pavlova.

31 See, for example, *ibid.*, pp. 73, 125–6, 234–5.

32 *Il Corriere della Sera*, 10 August 2010.

33 See https://siusa.archivi.beniculturali.it/cgi-bin/pagina.pl?TipoPag=prodpersona&Chiave=53621&RicLin=it (accessed 25 February 2021).

34 Letter, Antonella Amendola to me, 16 March 2021.

35 Macciocchi, *Due mila anni di felicità*, pp. 168–70.

36 Maria Antonietta Macciocchi, *Dalla Cina: dopo la rivoluzione culturale* (Milan: Feltrinelli, 1971); in rapid English translation, Maria Antonietta Macciocchi, *Daily Life in Revolutionary China* (New York: Monthly Review Press, 1972), pp. 26–7.

37 Macciocchi, *Due mila anni di felicità*, p. 407.

38 Later in the decade she became a fan of populist Pope John Paul II, claiming that, when in February 1988 he held in his hands her head in blessing, it felt like an electric shock passing through her. *Ibid.*, pp. 724–7; cf. Maria Antonietta Macciocchi, *Le donne secondo Wojtyla. Ventinove chiavi di lettura della Mulieris dignitatem* (Milan: Edizioni Paoline, 1992).

39 Macciocchi, *Due mila anni di felicità*, p. 86.

40 Marzillo, 'Pietro Amendola', p. 168.

41 Giovanni Cerchia, *Giorgio Amendola: gli anni della Repubblica (1945–1980)* (Turin: Cerabona Editore, 2009), p. 83.

42 I thank Antonella Amendola for this detail.

43 Giorgio Amendola, *Lettere a Milano*, p. 384.

44 Abdon Alinovi, 'Ricordi e testimonianze' in Cerchia (ed.), *La famiglia Amendola*, pp. 317–8.

45 Giorgio Amendola, *Il rinnovamento del PCI: intervista di Renato Nicolai* (Rome: Riuniti, 1978), p. 168.

46 Cerchia, *Giorgio Amendola: gli anni della Repubblica*, p. 46.
47 Francesco Barbagallo, 'Il PCI, i ceti medi e la democrazia nel Mezzogiorno 1943–1947', *Studi Storici*, 26, 1985, pp. 524–6.
48 Cerchia, *Giorgio Amendola: gli anni della Repubblica*, p. 91 note 150.
49 *Ibid.*, pp. 93–6.
50 *Ibid.*, p. 106 note 25.
51 Giorgio Amendola, *La democrazia nel Mezzogiorno* (Rome: Riuniti, 1957), pp. v–vii.
52 *Ibid.*, pp. 46–51.
53 For examples of such images, see the photographs in Dadam (ed.), *Giorgio Amendola nella storia d'Italia*.
54 For a fine study of this process, see Guido Liguori, *Gramsci conteso: storia di un dibattito 1922–1996* (Rome: Riuniti, 1996).
55 Giorgio Amendola, *Comunismo antifascismo e Resistenza* (Rome: Riuniti, 1967), p. 156.
56 Giorgio Amendola, *La democrazia nel Mezzogiorno*, pp. 19, 28.
57 See, for example, *ibid.*, pp. 23, 46.
58 *Ibid.*, p. 229.
59 Cf. the sardonic review of his and especially Togliatti's use of the myth of Gramsci for party ends in Maria Antonietta Macciocchi, *Per Gramsci* (Bologna: Il Mulino, 1974), pp. 45–57. Giorgio's ex-sister-in-law viewed Gramsci instead as a prophet of continuing radical change, as, for example, in Chairman Mao's cultural revolution.
60 Giorgio Amendola, *Antonio Gramsci nella vita culturale e politica italiana* (Naples: Guida Editore, 1978), pp. 53–4. For that event, cf. also Giorgio Amendola, *Un'isola* (Milan: Rizzoli, 1980), pp. 31–4.
61 Cerchia, *Giorgio Amendola: gli anni della Repubblica*, pp. 123–4.
62 See Luigi Cortesi, 'Pietro Secchia da Livorno alla Resistenza', *Belfagor*, 41, 1986, pp. 633–55.
63 Giorgio Amendola, 'Riflessioni su una esperienza di governo del PCI (1944–1947)', *Storia Contemporanea*, 5, 1974, pp. 701–35.
64 *Ibid.*, p. 726.
65 Giorgio Amendola, *La democrazia nel Mezzogiorno*, pp. 185–205.
66 Cerchia, *Giorgio Amendola: gli anni della Repubblica*, pp. 138–9.
67 *Ibid.*, pp. 144–5.
68 For microcosmic detail in Bologna, see Luca Alessandrini and Angela Maria Politi, 'Nuove fonti sui processi contro i partigiani 1948–1953: contesto politico e organizzazione della difesa', *Italia Contemporanea*, 178, 1990, pp. 46–7.
69 Giorgio Amendola, *Il rinnovamento del PCI*, p. 22.
70 Preface to Giovanni Amendola, *La nuova democrazia* (Naples: Riccardo Ricciardi Editore, 1951), pp. vii–viii.
71 Preface to Giovanni Amendola, *La democrazia italiana contro il fascismo 1922–1924* (Milan: Riccardo Ricciardi Editore, 1960), pp. xiii–xiv.
72 See www.espressonapoletano.it/persone-famose-sepolte-a-napoli-piccola-guida/ (accessed 27 January 2021).

73 *L'Espresso*, 9 July 1978. Giorgio's name had gone forward during the first votes in the Chamber.

74 Giorgio Amendola, *La democrazia nel Mezzogiorno*, pp. 265–99.

75 *Ibid.*, p. 262.

76 Pietro Secchia, *La Resistenza accusa 1945–1973* (Milan: Mazzotta, 1973), pp. 172–4.

77 Giorgio Amendola, *La democrazia nel Mezzogiorno*, pp. 347–91.

78 *Ibid.*, p. 29.

79 Cerchia, *Giorgio Amendola: gli anni della Repubblica*, pp. 127–31.

80 For background, see Allum, *Politics and Society in Post-War Naples*, pp. 93–111, 275–300.

81 Giorgio Amendola, *La democrazia nel Mezzogiorno*, pp. 113–30.

82 *Ibid.*, pp. 313–46.

83 Pietro Ingrao, *Le cose impossibili: un'autobiografia raccontata e discussa con Nicola Tranfaglia* (Rome: Aliberti Editore, 2011), p. xxxvii.

84 Giorgio Amendola, *Il rinnovamento del PCI*, pp. 120–3, 129; cf. Cerchia, *Giorgio Amendola: gli anni della Repubblica*, pp. 182–4.

85 For a useful case study, see Onofrio Bellefemine, 'Antimonopolitismo e sviluppo del Mezzogiorno: il PCI e la nascita del quarto centro siderugico di Taranto 1955–1959', *Nuova Rivista Storica*, CV, 2021, pp. 1–32.

86 Cerchia, *Giorgio Amendola: gli anni della Repubblica*, pp. 213–25.

87 *Ibid.*, p. 227.

88 Miriam Mafai, *Botteghe oscure addio. Com'erevamo comunisti* (Milan: Mondadori, 1996), pp. 113–14.

89 Cerchia, *Giorgio Amendola: gli anni della Repubblica*, p. 229.

90 Giovanni Amendola, *Tra passione e ragione: discorsi a Milano dal 1957 al 1977* (Milan: Rizzoli, 1982), p. 13.

91 *Ibid.*, p. 43.

92 Cerchia, *Giorgio Amendola: gli anni della Repubblica*, pp. 234–44.

93 Giorgio Amendola and Arrigo Morandi, *Un forte ed esteso movimento associativo per lo sviluppo di una vasta azione di educazione democratica: documenti del convegno promosso dalla direzione del PCI e della FGCI* (Rome, 28–29 November 1959), pp. 28–31, 90–1.

94 Giorgio Amendola, *L'affare Sifar: discorso e dichiarazione di voto pronuniciati alla Camera dei deputati nei giorni 30 gennaio e 1 febbraio 1968* (Rome: Sezione Centrale Stampa e Propaganda del PCI, nd [1968]), p. 48; *Classe operaia e programmazione democratica* (Rome: Riuniti, 1966), pp. 13–14, 138–40.

95 Giorgio Amendola, *La classe operaia italiana* (Rome: Riuniti, 1968), pp. 138–40.

96 Giorgio Amendola, *Classe operaia e programmazione democratica*, pp. 253–4; *Il rinnovamento del PCI*, p. 196.

97 Cerchia, *Giorgio Amendola: gli anni della Repubblica*, pp. 253–4.

98 Giorgio Amendola, *Polemiche fuori tempo* (ed. Giulio Goria) (Rome: Riuniti, 1982), p. 5.

99 Cerchia, *Giorgio Amendola: gli anni della Repubblica*, pp. 269–70.

100 Mafai, *Botteghe oscure addio*, p. 19.

101 See www.eletteedeletti.it/diaristi/camillo-martino/ (accessed 3 February 2021). Evidence from Camillo Martino, 'La vita a Botteghe Oscure al tempo dei comunisti'.

102 Mafai, *Botteghe oscure addio*, pp. 92, 96–7.

103 Fiammetta Balestracci, 'Il PCI, il divorzio e il mutamento dei valori nell'Italia degli anni sessanta e settanta', *Studi Storici*, 54, 2013, p. 1016.

104 I owe this information to Giovanni Cerchia.

105 See Eva Amendola Kühn, *Vita con Giovanni Amendola* (Florence: Parenti, 1960).

106 Cerchia, *Giorgio Amendola: gli anni della Repubblica*, pp. 263–70.

107 *Ibid.*, p. 267.

108 Ingrao, *Le cose impossibili*, p. 181; Mafai, *Botteghe oscure addio*, p. 138.

109 Giorgio Amendola, *Polemiche fuori tempo*, pp. 13, 69–72.

110 Zeffiro Ciuffoletti and Maurizio Degl'Innocenti, *L'emigrazione nella storia d'Italia 1868–1975* (Florence: Vallecchi, 1978), vol. II, p. 282.

111 Giorgio Amendola, *La classe operaia italiana*, pp. 130, 154.

112 Cerchia, *Giorgio Amendola: gli anni della Repubblica*, pp. 284–90.

113 Giorgio Amendola, *Fascismo e Mezzogiorno* (Rome: Riuniti, 1973), p. 12.

114 Cerchia, *Giorgio Amendola: gli anni della Repubblica*, pp. 368–9.

115 See Giorgio Amendola, *Polemiche fuori tempo*, pp. 41–51.

116 Pietro Ingrao, *Volevo la luna* (Turin: Einaudi, 2006), pp. 312–13.

117 Giorgio Napolitano, *Dal PCI al socialismo europeo: un'autobiografia politica* (Bari: Laterza, 2005), p. 14.

118 Cerchia, *Giorgio Amendola: gli anni della Repubblica*, pp. 320–6.

119 For background, see Ben Mercer, *Student Revolt in 1968: France, Italy and West Germany* (Cambridge: Cambridge University Press, 2020).

120 Giorgio Amendola, *Gli anni della Repubblica* (Rome: Riuniti, 1976), p. 254.

121 Giorgio Amendola, *Polemiche fuori tempo*, pp. 87–95.

122 Giorgio Amendola, *La classe operaia italiana*, p. 15.

123 Cerchia, *Giorgio Amendola: gli anni della Repubblica*, pp. 351–2.

124 *Ibid.*, pp. 357–63.

125 Giorgio Amendola and Alfonso Leonetti, 'La svolta del 1930 e il problema dello stalinismo', *Belfagor*, 32, 1977, p. 90.

126 Giorgio Amendola, *La classe operaia italiana*, pp. 77–83, 105–18.

127 Cerchia, *Giorgio Amendola: gli anni della Repubblica*, p. 351 note 162.

128 Giorgio Amendola, *La crisi italiana* (Rome: Riuniti, 1971), pp. 12, 68.

129 Giorgio Amendola, *Fascismo e Mezzogiorno*, pp. 172–4.

130 Macciocchi, *Due mila anni di felicità*, p. 86.

131 See www.eletteedeletti.it/estratti/giorgione-amendola/ (accessed 3 February 2021).

132 *Il Corriere della Sera*, 10 August 2010.

133 Mafai, *Botteghe oscure addio*, p. 80.

134 For the ambiguity of its post-Fascist naming, see R. J. B. Bosworth, *Whispering City: Rome and Its Histories* (London: Yale University Press, 2011), p. 252.

135 See https://en.wikipedia.org/wiki/Raffaella_Carr%C3%A0 (accessed 26 February 2021).

136 Cerchia, *Giorgio Amendola: gli anni della Repubblica*, p. 336.
137 *Germaine Lecocq: testimonianze* (Montecatini: Galleria d'Arte La Barcaccia, 1977). Its pages are unnumbered but include the cited letter from Guttuso and other endorsements. The main La Barcaccia office was at Montecatini, where this collection had also been exhibited.
138 Giorgio Amendola, *Intervista sull'antifascismo* (ed. Pietro Melograni) (Bari: Laterza, 1976); *Il rinnovamento del PCI*.
139 T. J. Jackson Lears, 'The concept of cultural hegemony: problems and possibilities', *American Historical Review*, 90, 1985, p. 567. Cf. eleven years earlier, Eric Hobsbawm, 'The great Gramsci', *New York Review of Books*, XXI, 18 April 1974, pp. 39–44.
140 Giorgio Amendola, 'The Italian road to socialism', *New Left Review*, 106, 1977, pp. 39, 42.
141 Cerchia, *Giorgio Amendola: gli anni della Repubblica*, p. 419.
142 Giorgio Amendola, *Una scelta di vita* (Milan: Rizzoli, 1978).
143 Giorgio Amendola, *Un'isola*.
144 With a different meaningfulness, *Una scelta di vita* has on the cover a painting of Liberal gentlemen on the Pincio by Armando Spadini, another of Giovanni's and Eva's artistic friends.
145 Giorgio Amendola, *Intervista sull'antifascismo*, p. x.
146 Valentine Lomellini, 'The PCI and the USA: rehearsal of a difficult dialogue in the era of détente', *Journal of Modern Italian Studies*, 20, 2015, p. 346.
147 David Sassoon (ed.), *The Italian Communists Speak for Themselves* (Nottingham: Spokesman, 1978), pp. 89–90, 141–3.
148 Enrico Berlinguer, *La grande avanzata comunista: discorsi e interviste della campagna per le elezioni politiche del 20 giugno 1976* (Rome: Sarmi, 1976), p. 20.
149 Giacomo Sani, 'The PCI on the threshold', *Problems of Communism*, 25, 1976, p. 27.
150 Giancarlo Caselli and Donatella Della Porta, 'La storia delle Brigate Rosse: strutture organizzative e strategia d'azione' in Donatella Della Porta (ed.), *Terrorismi in Italia* (Bologna: Il Mulino, 1984), p. 184.
151 Salvatore Toscano, *A partire dal 1968* (Milan: Mazzotta, 1978), p. 177.
152 Giorgio Amendola, *Tra passione e ragione*, p. 302.
153 Giorgio Amendola, *Intervista sull'antifascismo*, p. 1.
154 Cerchia, *Giorgio Amendola: gli anni della Repubblica*, p. 447.
155 Giorgio Amendola, *Polemiche fuori tempo*, p. 153.
156 Giorgio Amendola, *Il rinnovamento del PCI*, p. 67.
157 Giorgio Amendola, *Polemiche fuori tempo*, p. 5.
158 Giorgio Amendola, *I comunisti e le elezioni europee* (Rome: Riuniti, 1979), pp. 9–10.
159 *Ibid.*, p. 43.
160 *Ibid.*, pp. 68–9.
161 *Ibid.*, pp. 74, 96–102.
162 Napolitano, *Dal PCI al socialismo europeo*, pp. 174–5.
163 Giorgio Amendola, *Polemiche fuori tempo*, pp. 181–91.
164 *Il Corriere della Sera*, 5, 6 and 7 June 1980.

165 Mafai, *Botteghe oscure addio*, p. 35. For a newsreel image of the funeral, see www.youtube.com/watch?v=Fx9Scy2pyiw (accessed 1 March 2021).
166 Cerchia, *Giorgio Amendola: gli anni della Repubblica*, pp. 470–2.
167 *Il Corriere della Sera*, 10 August 2010.
168 Should I really be so certain? After all, Giorgio knew, as I do, that democratic history must always be an argument without end. Cf. Simona Colarizi, 'La storiografia' in Cerchia (ed.), *La famiglia Amendola*, p. 274.

Conclusion

1 Francis Fukuyama, 'The end of history?', *The National Interest*, 18, 1989–90; and, more fully, Francis Fukuyama, *The End of History and the Last Man* (London: Hamish Hamilton, 1992). For my response, see R. J. B. Bosworth, *Explaining Auschwitz and Hiroshima: History Writing and the Second World War 1945–1990* (London: Routledge, 1993).
2 See, for example, Elena Aga Rossi and Victor Zaslavsky, *Togliatti e Stalin: il PCI e la politica estera staliniana negli archivi di Mosca* (Bologna: Il Mulino, 1997).
3 See Paul Ginsborg, *Silvio Berlusconi: Television, Power and Patrimony* (London: Verso, 2004) for a leftist attempt to depict him as a proto-fascist.
4 See www.reaganfoundation.org/ronald-reagan/reagan-quotes-speeches/inaug ural-address-2/ (accessed 2 March 2021). This website asks users to donate further to the neoliberal cause.
5 See, for example, Michael Gove in pushing a rightist side of the 'culture war' in the UK. See www.theguardian.com/education/2013/feb/05/michael-gove-inspirations-jade-goody (accessed 2 March 2021).
6 Giorgio Amendola, *Intervista sull'antifascismo* (ed. Pietro Melograni) (Bari: Laterza, 1976), pp. 8, 12–13.
7 This is a major theme of R. J. B. Bosworth, *Mussolini and the Eclipse of Fascism: From Dictatorship to Populism* (London: Yale University Press, 2021).
8 Giorgio Amendola and Alfonso Leonetti, 'La svolta del 1930 e il problema dello stalinismo', *Belfagor*, 32, 1977, p. 89.
9 *Guardian*, 24 March 2021.
10 Eugenio Di Rienzo, *Benedetto Croce: gli anni dello scontento 1943–1945* (Soveria Mannelli: Rubbettino, 2019), pp. 109–10.
11 See Bosworth, *Mussolini and the Eclipse of Italian Fascism*, p. 8.
12 For the corruption, see Matteo Mazzoni, 'Costanzo Ciano e famiglia, i grandi ricchi del regime' in Paolo Giovannini and Marco Palla (eds), *Il fascismo dalle mani sporche: dittatura, corruzione, affarismo* (Rome: Laterza, 2019), pp. 49–70.
13 For some description, see R. J. B. Bosworth, *Whispering City: Rome and Its Histories* (London: Yale University Press, 2011), pp. 242–7.
14 For a splendidly full account of renaming, see www.rerumromanarum.com/2015/10/roma-strade-che-hanno-cambiato-nome-dopo-il-fascismo.html (accessed 4 November 2020).
15 See www.scuolamendolasarno.gov.it/wp-content/uploads/2015/01/giornalera gazzi.pdf (accessed 2 March 2021).

16 See https://upload.wikimedia.org/wikipedia/commons/3/32/Giovanni_Amen
    dola_statua.JPG (accessed 2 March 2021).

17 See, for example, the conference of 2 December 2021 on 'Comunisti e
    riformisti: l'eredità del Giorgio Amendola nella storia del PCI', www
    .fondazioneamendola.it/2021/11/25/convegno-comunisti-e-riformisti-lere
    dita-di-giorgio-amendola-nella-storia-del-pci/ (accessed 2 December 2021).

18 Giampiero Carocci, *Giovanni Amendola nella crisi dello Stato italiano
    1911–1925* (Milan: Feltrinelli, 1956); cf. the largely positive review by
    Raffaele Colapietra, 'Giovanni Amendola nella crisi dello Stato italiano
    1911–1925', *Belfagor*, 11, 1956, pp. 606–704.

19 Giovanni Spadolini, 'Prefazione' in *Giovanni Amendola: una battaglia per
    democrazia: atti del convegno di studi con il patrimonio della Regione Emila-
    Romagna* (Bologna: Arnaldo Forni Editore, 1978), p. 9.

20 Renzo De Felice, 'Presentazione' in Giovanni Amendola, *La crisi dello stato
    liberale* (ed. Elio D'Auria) (Rome: Newton Compton, 1974), pp. vii–viii. Elio
    D'Auria began a lifelong devotion to Giovanni studies in his 100-page
    'Introduzione', where he argued staunchly that, through the First World
    War, Giovanni was modernising Italian liberalism. Cf. also Giovanni
    Amendola, *L'Aventino contro il fascismo: scritti politici (1924–1926)* (ed.
    Sabato Visco) (Milan: Riccardo Ricciardi Editore, 1976).

21 *Onoranze a Giovanni Amendola nel cinquantenario della morte 1926–1976*
    (Salerno: Arti Grafiche Boccia for Regione Campania and Comune di
    Sarno, 1977), p. 12.

22 Giulio Andreotti, 'Amendola e De Gasperi' in *Onoranze a Giovanni Amendola
    nel cinquantenario della morte*, pp. 53–4.

23 Carlo Galante Garrone, 'Giovanni Amendola' in *ibid.*, pp. 10–17.

24 'Democrazia e socialità nel pensiero di Giovanni Amendola' in *ibid.*,
    pp. 24–42.

25 Spadolini, 'Prefazione', pp. 9–10; Giovanni Spadolini, 'Prolusione' in
    *Giovanni Amendola: una battaglia per democrazia: atti del convegno di studi con
    il patrimonio della Regione Emila-Romagna* (Bologna: Arnaldo Forni Editore,
    1978), pp. 19–25.

26 Elio D'Auria, 'Giovanni Amendola, il partito nuovo e l'opposizione al fas-
    cismo' in *ibid.*, pp. 221–33.

27 See Raffaello Franchini, 'Amendola e la filosofia del suo tempo' in *ibid.*,
    pp. 33–40; Alfredo Capone, 'Etica e politica in Giovanni Amendola' in *ibid.*,
    pp. 41–60; Sandro Rogari, 'Formazione e pensiero religioso di Amendola' in
    ibid., pp. 79–106; Massimo Mazzetti, 'L'intervento di Amendola' in *ibid.*,
    pp. 149–60.

28 Paolo Spriano, 'Tra dopoguerra e fascismo: Amendola, Gobetti, Gramsci' in
    ibid., pp. 215–20. For his work on the PCI, see Paolo Spriano, *Storia del
    partito comunista italiano* (5 volume) (Turin: Einaudi, 1967–75); cf. Paolo
    Spriano, *Intervista sulla storia del PCI* (ed. Simona Colarizi) (Bari: Laterza,
    1979). In this last, he noted that Gramsci had still not been properly pub-
    lished in the USSR (p. 181).

29 Leo Valiani, 'L'eredità politica di Giovanni Amendola' in *Giovanni Amendola:
    una battaglia per democrazia*, pp. 245–59.

30 Ruggero Moscati, 'Questo volume' in *Giovanni Amendola nel cinquantenario della morte 1926–1976* (Rome: Fondazione Luigi Einaudi per Studi di Politica ed Economia, 1976), pp. v–xv.

31 See Elio D'Auria, 'Gli studi amendoliani nel cinquantenario della morte' in *ibid.*, pp. 5–92; Alfredo Capone, 'Moderatismo e democrazia nel pensiero di Giovanni Amendola' in *ibid.*, pp. 93–144.

32 Salvatore Valitutti, 'Lo Stato nel pensiero di Giovanni Amendola' in *ibid.*, pp. 197–244.

33 Leone Cattani, 'Amendola e i giovani' in *ibid.*, pp. 245–54.

34 Alfredo Capone, 'Giovanni Amendola: filosofia e politica'; Elio D'Auria, 'Amendola e lo Stato' in *Giovanni Amendola tra etica e politica: atti del convegno di studio Montecatini Terme 25–26–27 ottobre 1996* (Pistoia: CRT, 1999), pp. 23–56.

35 Giorgio Spini, 'Filosofia e religiosità in Giovanni Amendola' in *ibid.*, pp. 67–84; cf. Giorgio Spini, *Italia liberale e protestante* (Turin: Claudiana Editore, 2002).

36 *Giovanni Amendola tra etica e politica*, pp. 61–2 (Pietro), 103–6 (Antonella).

37 Umberto Sereni, 'Un'azione fascista: l'aggressione a Giovanni Amendola: Montecatini 20 luglio 1925' in *ibid.*, pp. 171–229; cf. Marco Francini and Fabio Giannelli (eds), 'Appendici' in *ibid.*, pp. 271–305 for the documents.

38 Elio D'Auria, 'Presentazione' in *Giovanni Amendola: una vita in difesa della libertà. Atti del convegno di studi per il 90 anniversario della morte (1882–1926)* (ed. Elio D'Auria) (Soveria Mannelli: Rubbettino, 2018), p. 7.

39 Elio D'Auria, 'Giovanni Amendola: martire della libertà e della democrazia' in *ibid.*, pp. 26–7.

40 Mario Pendinelli, 'L'ingresso nel giornalismo: la corrispondenza del "Resto del Carlino" e del "Corriere della Sera"' in *ibid.*, p. 105.

41 No doubt he was scarcely consistent on the matter but, in December 1934, Mussolini denied that his regime had any intention of intruding into religious affairs. See Benito Mussolini, *Opera Omnia*, 36 volumes (eds Edoardo Susmel and Duilio Susmel) (Florence: La Fenice, 1951–63) vol. XXVI, pp. 399–400.

Afterword

1 See R. J. B. Bosworth, *Explaining Auschwitz and Hiroshima: History Writing and the Second World War 1945–1990* (London: Routledge, 1993).

2 I trust that I have not used the words jab or roll-out in my text.

Select Bibliography

Primary Sources

Albertini, Luigi, *Epistolario 1911–1926*, 4 volumes (ed. Ottavio Bariè) (Milan: Mondadori, 1968).

Albertini, Luigi, *I giorni di un liberale: diari 1907–1923* (ed. Luciano Monzali) (Bologna: Il Mulino, 2000).

Amendola, Antonella, 'Intervento' in *Giovanni Amendola tra etica e politica: atti del convegno di studio Montecatini Terme 25–26–27 ottobre 1996* (Pistoia: CRT, 1999).

Amendola, Eva Paola, *La nascita del fascismo 1919–1925* (Rome: Riuniti, 1998).

Amendola, Eva Paola and Pasquale Iaccio, *Gli anni del regime 1925–1939* (Rome: Riuniti, 1998).

Amendola, Giorgio, *La democrazia nel Mezzogiorno* (Rome: Riuniti, 1957).

Amendola, Giorgio, *Lotta di classe e sviluppo economico dopo la liberazione* (Rome: Riuniti, 1962).

Amendola, Giorgio (ed.), *Il comunismo italiano nella seconda guerra mondiale: relazione e documenti presentati dalla direzione del partito al V Congresso del partito comunista italiano* (Rome: Riuniti, 1963).

Amendola, Giorgio, *Classe operaia e programmazione democratica* (Rome: Riuniti, 1966).

Amendola, Giorgio, 'L'alternativa di centro-sinistra' in Giorgio Amendola et al., *Classe operaia, partiti politici e socialismo nella prospettiva italiana* (Milan: Feltrinelli, 1966).

Amendola, Giorgio, *Comunismo antifascismo e Resistenza* (Rome: Riuniti, 1967).

Amendola, Giorgio, *La classe operaia italiana* (Rome: Riuniti, 1968).

Amendola, Giorgio, *L'affare Sifar: discorso e dichiarazione di voto pronuniciati alla Camera dei deputati nei giorni 30 gennaio e 1 febbraio 1968* (Rome: Sezione Centrale Stampa e Propaganda del PCI, 1968).

Amendola, Giorgio, *I comunisti e l'Europa* (Rome: Riuniti, 1971).

Amendola, Giorgio, *La crisi italiana* (Rome: Riuniti, 1971).

Amendola, Giorgio, *Fascismo e Mezzogiorno* (Rome: Riuniti, 1973).

Amendola, Giorgio, *Lettere a Milano: ricordi e documenti 1943–1945* (Rome: Riuniti, 1973).

Amendola, Giorgio, 'Riflessioni su una esperienza di governo del PCI (1944–1947)', *Storia Contemporanea*, 5, 1974.

Amendola, Giorgio, *Fascismo e movimento operaio* (Rome: Riuniti, 1975).

Amendola, Giorgio, *Intervista sull'antifascismo* (ed. Piero Melograni) (Bari: Laterza, 1976).

Amendola, Giorgio, *Una scelta di vita* (Milan: Rizzoli, 1976).

Amendola, Giorgio, *Gli anni della Repubblica* (Rome: Riuniti, 1976).

Amendola, Giorgio, 'La grande crisi, il partito comunista italiano e la ripresa antifascista', *Studi Storici*, 18, 1977.

Amendola, Giorgio, 'The Italian road to socialism', *New Left Review*, 106, 1977.

Amendola, Giorgio, *Storia del partito comunista italiano 1921–1943* (Rome: Riuniti, 1978).

Amendola, Giorgio, *Antonio Gramsci nella vita culturale e politica italiana* (Naples: Guida Editore, 1978).

Amendola, Giorgio, *Il rinnovamento del PCI: intervista di Renato Nicolai* (Rome: Riuniti, 1978).

Amendola, Giorgio, *I comunisti e le elezioni europee* (Rome: Riuniti, 1979).

Amendola, Giorgio, *Un'isola* (Milan: Rizzoli, 1980).

Amendola, Giorgio, *Tra passione e ragione: discorsi a Milano dal 1957 al 1977* (Milan: Rizzoli, 1982).

Amendola, Giorgio, *Polemiche fuori tempo* (ed. Giulio Goria) (Rome: Riuniti, 1982).

Amendola, Giorgio and Arrigo Morandi, *Un forte ed esteso movimento associativo per lo sviluppo di una vasta azione di educazione democratica: documenti del convegno promosso dalla direzione del PCI e della FGCI (Rome, 28–29 novembre 1959)* (Publisher unknown, nd [1959]).

Amendola, Giorgio and Alfonso Leonetti, 'La svolta del 1930 e il problema dello stalinismo', *Belfagor*, 32, 1977.

Amendola, Giovanni, 'La philosophie italienne contemporaine', *Revue de Métaphysique et de Morale*, 16, 1908.

Amendola, Giovanni, 'Il patto di Londra', *Quaderni della Voce*, September 1919.

Amendola, Giovanni, *Una battaglia liberale: discorsi politici 1919–1923* (Turin: Piero Gobetti Editore, 1924).

Amendola, Giovanni, *La democrazia dopo il VI aprile MCMXXIV* (Milan: Corbaccio, 1924).

Amendola, Giovanni, *La nuova democrazia* (Naples: Riccardo Ricciardi Editore, 1951).

Amendola, Giovanni, *Etica e biografia* (Milan: Riccardo Ricciardi Editore, 1953).

Amendola, Giovanni, *La democrazia italiana contro il fascismo 1922–1924* (Milan: Riccardo Ricciardi Editore, 1960).

Amendola, Giovanni, *La crisi dello stato liberale* (ed. Elio D'Auria) (Rome: Newton Compton, 1974).

Amendola, Giovanni, *L'Aventino contro il Fascismo: scritti politici (1924–1926)* (ed. Sabato Visco) (Milan: Riccardo Ricciardi Editore, 1976).

Amendola, Giovanni, *Carteggio 1897–1909* (ed. Elio D'Auria) (Bari: Laterza, 1986).

Amendola, Giovanni, *Carteggio 1910–1912* (ed. Elio D'Auria) (Bari: Laterza, 1987).

Amendola, Giovanni, *Carteggio 1913–1918* (ed. Elio D'Auria) (Manduria: Piero Lacaita, 1999).

Amendola, Giovanni, *Carteggio 1919–1922* (ed. Elio D'Auria) (Manduria: Piero Lacaita, 2003).

Amendola, Giovanni, *Carteggio 1923–1924* (ed. Elio D'Auria) (Manduria: Piero Lacaita, 2006).

Amendola, Giovanni, *Carteggio 1925–1926* (ed. Elio D'Auria) (Soveria Mannelli: Rubbettino, 2016).

Amendola, Giovanni, Giuseppe A. Borgese, Ugo Ojetti and Andrea Torre, 'Il patto di Roma', *Quaderni della Voce*, 15 September 1919.

Amendola Kühn, Eva, *Vita con Giovanni Amendola* (Florence: Parenti, 1960).

Berlinguer, Enrico, *La grande avanzata comunista: discorsi e interviste della campagna per le elezioni politiche del 20 giugno 1976* (Rome: Sarmi, 1976).

Bisiach, Gianni, *Pertini racconta: gli anni 1915–1945* (Milan: Mondadori, 1983).

Bordiga, Amadeo, *Scritti scelti* (ed. Franco Livorsi) (Milan: Feltrinelli, 1975).

Bottai, Giuseppe, *Quaderni giovanili* (Missaglia: Fondazione Arnaldo e Alberto Mondadori, 1996).

Bottai, Giuseppe, *Vent'anni e un giorno (24 luglio 1943)* (Milan: BUR, 2008).

Buonarroti, Michangelo, *Poesie* (ed. Giovanni Amendola) (Lanciano: R. Carabba Editore, 1911).

Calamandrei, Franco, *La vita indivisibile: diario 1941–1947* (eds Romano Bilenchi and Ottavio Cecchi) (Rome: Riuniti, 1984).

Ceretti, Giulio, *Con Togliatti e Thorez: quarant'anni di lotte politiche* (Milan: Feltrinelli, 1973).

Douglas, Norman, *Old Calabria* (London: Secker and Warburg, 1955 [1915]).

Gobetti, Piero, *On Liberal Revolution* (ed. Nadia Urbanati) (New Haven CT: Yale University Press, 2000).

Gramsci, Antonio, *Passato e presente* (ed. Vittorio Gerratana) (Rome: Riuniti, 1975).

Gramsci, Antonio, *Gli intellettuali e l'organizzazione della cultura* (ed. Vittorio Gerratana) (Rome: Riuniti, 1975).

Gramsci, Antonio, *Note sul Machiavelli, sulla politica e sullo stato moderno* (ed. Vittorio Gerratana) (Rome: Riuniti, 1975).

Gramsci, Antonio, *Le opere*, 6 volumes (ed. Valentino Gerratana) (Rome: Riuniti, 1977).

Gray, Ezio Maria, *Noi e Tunisi: come perdemmo Tunisi. Come costruimmo la Tunisia* (Milan: Mondadori, 1939).

Grifone, Pietro, *Il capitale finanziario in Italia* (Turin: Einaudi, 1971).

Ingrao, Pietro, *Volevo la luna* (Turin: Einaudi, 2006).

Ingrao, Pietro, *Le cose impossibili: un'autobiografia raccontata e discussa con Nicola Tranfaglia* (Rome: Aliberti Editore, 2011).

Labriola, Arturo, *Polemica antifascista* (Naples: Ceccoli, 1925).

Lecocq [Amendola], Germaine, *Testimonianze* (Montecatini Terme: Galleria d'Arte La Barcaccia, nd [1976]).

Levi, Carlo, *Christ Stopped at Eboli: The Story of a Year* (New York: Farrar, Straus and Giroux, 1947).

Longo, Luigi, *Un popolo alla macchia* (Rome: Riuniti, 1965).

Longo, Luigi, *Sulla via dell'insurrezione nazionale* (Rome: Riuniti, 1976).

Lussu, Emilio, *Enter Mussolini: Observations and Adventures of an Anti-Fascist* (London: Methuen, 1936).

Macciocchi, Maria Antonietta, *Lettere dall'interno del PCI a Louis Althusser* (Milan: Feltrinelli, 1969).

Macciocchi, Maria Antonietta, *Dalla Cina: dopo la rivoluzione culturale* (Milan: Feltrinelli, 1971).

Macciocchi, Maria Antonietta, *Per Gramsci* (Bologna: Il Mulino, 1974).

Macciocchi, Maria Antonietta, *Le donne secondo Wojtyla. Ventinove chiavi di lettura della Mulieris dignitatem* (Milan: Edizioni Paoline, 1992).

Macciocchi, Maria Antonietta, *Due mila anni di felicità: diario di un'eretica* (Milan: Il Saggiatore, 2000).

Mafai, Miriam, *Botteghe oscure addio: com'eravamo comunisti* (Milan: Mondadori, 1996).

Malagodi, Olindo, *Conversazioni della Guerra 1914–1919*, 2 volumes (ed. Brunello Vigezzi) (Milan: Riccardo Ricciardi Editore, 1960).

Marinetti, Filippo Tommaso, *Taccuini 1915–1921* (ed. Alberto Bertoni) (Bologna: Il Mulino, 1987).

Martini, Ferdinando, *Diario 1914–1918* (ed. Gabriele De Rosa) (Milan: Mondadori, 1966).

Massola, Umberto and Girolamo Li Causi, *Gli scioperi 1943–1944: la classe operaia in lotta contro il fascismo e l'occupante* (Rome: Società Editrice L'Unità, 1945).

Matteotti, Giacomo, *The Fascisti Exposed: A Year of Fascist Domination* (New York: H. Fertig, 1969).

Matteotti, Giacomo, *Scritti e discorsi scelti* (ed. Fondazione Giacomo Matteotti) (Parma: Guanda, 1974).

Mezzasoma, Fernando, *Essenza del GUF* (Cremona: GUF, 1937).

Mussolini, Benito, *Opera Omnia*, 36 volumes (eds Edoardo Susmel and Duilio Susmel) (Florence: La Fenice, 1951–63).

Mussolini, Benito, *Opera Omnia: Appendici*, volumes 37–44 (eds Edoardo Susmel and Duilio Susmel) (Florence: Giovanni Volpe Editore, 1978–80).

Mussolini, Vittorio (ed.), *Anno XIII – Ludi Iuvenalis* (Rome: Tipografia Luzzatti, 1935).

Napolitano, Giorgio, *Dal PCI al socialismo europeo: un'autobiografia politica* (Bari: Laterza, 2005).

Nenni, Pietro, *Ten Years of Tyranny in Italy* (London: George Allen and Unwin, 1932).

Nenni, Pietro, *Intervista sul socialismo italiano* (ed. Giuseppe Tamburrano) (Bari: Laterza, 1977).

Nenni, Pietro, *La battaglia socialista contro il fascismo 1922–1944* (ed. Domenico Zucarò) (Milan: Mursia, 1977).

Nitti, Francesco Fausto, *Escape: The Personal Narrative of a Political Prisoner Who Was Rescued from Lipari, the Fascist 'Devil's Island'* (New York: G. P. Putman's, 1930).

Nitti, Francesco Saverio, *Peaceless Europe* (London: Cassell, 1922).

Nitti, Francesco Saverio, *La decadenza dell'Europa: le vie della ricostruzione* (Florence: Bemporad, 1922).

Nitti, Francesco Saverio, *La tragedia dell'Europa: che farà l'America* (Turin: Piero Gobetti Editore, 1924).

Pajetta, Giancarlo, *Lettere di antifascisti dal carcere e dal confino*, 2 volumes (Rome: Riuniti, 1962–3).

Pajetta, Giancarlo, *Il ragazzo rosso va alla guerra* (Milan: Mondadori, 1986).

Pajetta, Giuliano, *Douce France: diario 1941–1942* (Rome: Riuniti, 1971).

Pavlov, Mladen, МЕМОАРИ КРАТКИ БЕЛЕЖКИ ИЗЪ МОβ ЖИВОТЪ *[Memoirs, Brief Notes from My Life]* (Sofia: Cooperative Printing House 'Franklin', 1928).

Pavlova, Nelia, *Au Pays du Ghazi* (Paris: Le Monde d'Aujourd'hui and Éditions de la Revue Mondiale, 1930).

Pavlova, Nelia, *Au pays du maïs et des blés d'or (La Roumanie)* (Paris: Notre Temps, 1938).

Pertici, Roberto (ed.), *Carteggio Croce–Amendola* (Naples: Istituto Italiano per gli Studi Storici, 1982).

Pertini, Sandro, *Sei condanne, due evasioni* (ed. Vico Faggi) (Milan: Mondadori,1978).

Pesce, Giovanni, *And No Quarter: An Italian Partisan in World War II* (Athens: Ohio University Press, 1972).

Prezzolini, Giuseppe (ed.), *Amendola e 'La Voce'* (Florence: Sansoni, 1973).

Prezzolini, Giuseppe, *L'italiano inutile* (Milan: Rusconi, 1986).

Ravera, Camilla, *Diario di trent'anni 1913–1943* (Rome: Riuniti, 1973).

Rocca, Massimo [Libero Tancredi], *Come il fascismo divenne una dittatura* (Milan: ELI, 1952).

Rossi, Cesare, *Trentatre vicende mussoliniane* (Milan: Casa Editrice Ceschina, 1958).

Salvadori, Max, *Ricordo di Giovanni Amendola* (Sala Bolognese: Arnaldo Forni Editore, 1976).

Salvemini, Gaetano, *The Fascist Dictatorship in Italy* (New York: H. Holt, 1927).

Salvemini, Gaetano, *Under the Axe of Fascism* (London: Gollancz, 1936).

Scorza, Carlo, *Bagliori d'epopea* (Lucca: Edizione La Lecchesia, 1926).

Scorza, Carlo, *Brevi note sul fascismo: sui capi, sui gregari* (Florence: Bemporad, 1930).

Scorza, Carlo, *Il segreto di Mussolini* (Lanciano: Gino Carabba Editore, 1933).

Scorza, Carlo, *Tipi … tipi … tipi* (Florence: Vallecchi, 1942).

Scorza, Carlo, *La notte del Gran Consiglio* (Milan: Palazzi Editore, 1968).

Secchia, Pietro, *La Resistenza accusa 1945–1973* (Milan: Mazzotta, 1973).

Senise, Camillo, *Quando ero Capo della Polizia 1940–1943* (Rome: Ruffolo Editore, 1946).

Terracini, Umberto, *Sulla svolta: carteggio clandestino dal carcere 1930–2* (Milan: La Pietra, 1975).

Trentin, Silvio, *Dieci anni di fascismo totalitario in Italia: dall'istituzione del Tribunale speciale alla proclamazione dell'impero (1926–1936)* (Rome: Riuniti, 1975).

Troisio, Armando, *Roma sotto il terrore Nazi-Fascista (8 settembre 1943–4 giugno 1944): documentario* (Rome: Editore Francesco Mondini, 1944).

Zangrandi, Ruggero, *Il lungo viaggio attraverso il fascismo* (Milan: Feltrinelli, 1962).

Secondary Sources

Giovanni Amendola nel cinquantenario della morte 1926–1976 (Rome: Fondazione Luigi Einaudi per Studi di Politica ed Economia, 1976).

Onoranze a Giovanni Amendola nel cinquantenario della morte 1926–1976 (Salerno: Arti Grafiche Boccia for Regione Campania and Comune di Sarno, 1977).

Giovanni Amendola: una battaglia per democrazia: atti del convegno di studi con il patrimonio della Regione Emilia-Romagna (Bologna: Arnaldo Forni Editore, 1978).

Giovanni Amendola tra etica e politica: atti del convegno di studio Montecatini Terme 25–26–27 ottobre 1996 (Pistoia: CRT, 1999).

Giovanni Amendola: una vita in difesa della libertà. Atti del convegno di studi per il 90 anniversario della morte (1882–1926) (ed. Elio D'Auria) (Soveria Mannelli: Rubbettino, 2018).

Adamson, Walter, 'Modernism and Fascism: the politics of culture in Italy 1903–1922', *American Historical Review*, 95, 1990.

Adamson, Walter, *Avant-garde Florence from Modernism to Fascism* (Cambridge MA: Harvard University Press, 1993).

Adamson, Walter, 'Fascism and political religion in Italy: a re-assessment', *Contemporary European History*, 23, 2014.

Aga Rossi, Elena and Victor Zaslavsky, *Togliatti e Stalin: il PCI e la politica estera staliniana negli archivi di Mosca* (Bologna: Il Mulino, 1997).

Agosti, Aldo, *Palmiro Togliatti* (Turin: UTET, 1996).

Amatangelo, Susan, *Italian Women at War: Sisters in Arms from the Unification to the Twentieth Century* (Madison WI: Fairleigh Dickinson University Press, 2016).

Apotheker, Jan and Livia Simon Sarkadi (eds), *European Women in Charity* (Weinheim: Wiley-VCH Varley, 2011).

Argenteri, Letizia, 'Pirandello e il Fascismo', *Ricerche Storiche*, 24, 1994.

Balestracci, Fiammetta, 'Il PCI, il divorzio e il mutamento dei valori nell'Italia degli anni sessanta e settanta', *Studi Storici*, 54, 2013.

Barbagallo, Francesco, 'Il PCI, i ceti medi e la democrazia nel Mezzogiorno 1943–1947', *Studi Storici*, 26, 1985.

Barié, Ottavo, 'Luigi Albertini, il "Corriere della Sera" e la politica delle nazionalità 1917–1919', *Storia e Politica*, 8, 1969.

Barié, Ottavo, 'Luigi Albertini, il "Corriere della Sera" e la crisi dello stato liberale', *Storia e Politica*, 9, 1970.

Battaglia, Roberto, *Storia della Resistenza italiana (8 settembre 1943–25 aprile 1945)* (Turin: Einaudi, 1953).

Bentivegna, Roberto and Cesare De Simone, *Operazione Via Rasella: verità e menzogne* (Rome: Riuniti, 1996).

Benzoni, Alberto and Elisa Benzoni, *Attentato e rappresaglia: il PCI e Via Rasella* (Venice: Marsilio, 1999).

Bertelli, Sergio, *Il Gruppo: la formazione del gruppo dirigente del PCI 1936–1948* (Milan: Rizzoli, 1980).

Betti, Daniela, 'Il partito editore: libri e lettori nella politica culturale del PCI 1945–53', *Italia Contemporanea*, 175, 1989.

Bosworth, R. J. B., *Mussolini's Italy: Life under the Dictatorship 1915–1945* (London: Allen Lane, 2005).

Bosworth, R. J. B. (ed.), *The Oxford Handbook of Fascism* (Oxford: Oxford University Press, 2009).

Bosworth, R. J. B., *Mussolini* (London: Bloomsbury, 2010).

Bosworth, R. J. B., *Mussolini and the Eclipse of Italian Fascism: From Dictatorship to Populism* (London: Yale University Press, 2021).

Buchignani, Paolo, *Ribelli d'Italia: il sogno della rivoluzione da Mazzini alle Brigate Rosse* (Venice: Marsiglio, 2017).

Caccavale, Romolo, *La speranza Stalin: tragedia dell'antifascismo italiano nell'URSS* (Rome: V. Levi Editore, 1989).

Caccavale, Romolo, *Comunisti italiani in Unione Sovietica: proscritti da Mussolini, soppressi da Stalin* (Milan: Mursia, 1995).

Canali, Mauro, *Il delitto Matteotti: affarismo e politica nel primo governo Mussolini* (Bologna: Il Mulino, 1997).

Capone, Alfredo, *Giovanni Amendola e la cultura italiana del Novecento (1909–1914) alle origini della 'nuova democrazia'* (Rome: Editrice Elia, 1974).

Capone, Alfredo, *Giovanni Amendola* (Rome: Salerno Editrice, 2013).

Caretti, Stefano (ed.), *Sandro Pertini dal confino alla Resistenza: lettere 1935–1945* (Manduria: Piero Lacaita, 2007).

Carocci, Giampiero, *Giovanni Amendola nella crisi dello Stato italiano 1911–1925* (Milan: Feltrinelli, 1956).

Casinelli, Bruno, *Giovanni Amendola: l'uomo – il pensatore – il filosofo – ciò che la morte ha impedito* (Rome: Labor, 1926).

Cerchia, Giovanni, *Giorgio Amendola: un comunista nazionale. Dall'infanzia alla guerra partigiana (1907–1945)* (Soveria Mannelli: Rubbettino, 2004).

Cerchia, Giovanni, *Giorgio Amendola: gli anni della Repubblica (1945–1980)* (Turin: Cerabona Editore, 2009).

Cerchia, Giovanni (ed.), 'Luigi Albertini e la famiglia di Giovanni Amendola (1922–1936)' *Mondo Contemporaneo*, III, 2009.

Cerchia, Giovanni (ed.), *La famiglia Amendola: una scelta di vita per l'Italia* (Turin: Cerabona Editore, 2011).

Colapietra, Raffaele, 'Giovanni Amendola nella crisi dello Stato italiano 1911–1925', *Belfagor*, 11, 1956.

Colarizi, Simona, *I democratici all'opposizione: Giovanni Amendola e l'Unione Nazionale (1922–1926)* (Bologna: Il Mulino, 1973).

Cooke, Philip (ed.), *The Italian Resistance: An Anthology* (Manchester: Manchester University Press, 1997).

Cooke, Philip, *The Legacy of the Italian Resistance* (Houndmills: Palgrave Macmillan, 2011).

Cortesi, Luigi, 'Pietro Secchia da Livorno alla Resistenza', *Belfagor*, 41, 1986.

Crainz, Guido, 'Secchia, Amendola, Longo e il dibattito sulla "svolta di Salerno"', *Rivista di Storia Contemporanea*, 3, 1974.

Dadam, Loris (ed.), *Giorgio Amendola nella storia d'Italia: antologia critica degli scritti* (Turin: Cerabona Editore, 2007).

D'Auria, Elio, 'Liberalismo e democrazia nell'esperienza politica di Giovanni Amendola', *Nord e Sud*, 24, 1977.

De Ambris, Alceste, *Amendola: fatti e documenti* (Sala Bolognese: Arnaldo Forni Editore, 1976).

De Felice, Renzo, *Mussolini*, 7 volumes (Turin: Einaudi, 1965–97).

De Felice, Renzo, *Intervista sul fascismo* (ed. Michael Ledeen) (Bari: Laterza, 1997).

De Grand, Alexander, *In Stalin's Shadow: Angelo Tasca and the Crisis of the Left in Italy and France 1910–1945* (DeKalb: Northern Illinois University Press, 1986).

De Grand, Alexander, *The Hunchback's Tailor: Giovanni Giolitti and Liberal Italy from the Challenge of Mass Politics to the Rise of Fascism, 1882–1922* (Westport CT: Praeger, 2001).

De Grand, Alexander, '"To learn nothing and forget nothing": Italian socialism and the experience of exile politics 1935–1945', *Contemporary European History*, 14, 2005.

De La Pierre, Sergio, 'La "via italiana al socialismo" nell'analisi del PCI dal 1956 al 1962', *Rivista di Storia Contemporanea*, 4, 1975.

Del Boca, Angelo, *Gli italiani in Libia: Tripoli bel suol d'amore* (Bari: Laterza, 1986).

Delzell, Charles, *Mussolini's Enemies: The Italian Anti-Fascist Resistance* (Princeton NJ: Princeton University Press, 1961).

Di Rienzo, Eugenio, *Benedetto Croce: gli anni dello scontento 1943–1945* (Soveria Mannelli: Rubbettino, 2019).

Di Rienzo, Eugenio, 'Le scelte di un liberale conservatore: Benedetto Croce e il fascismo. Una rilettura', *Nuova Rivista Storica*, CIV, 2020.

Dondi, Mirco, 'Division and conflict in the partisan resistance', *Modern Italy*, 12, 2007.

Duggan, Christopher, *Fascist Voices: An Intimate History of Mussolini's Italy* (London: Bodley Head, 2012).

Filesi, Cesira, 'La Tripolitania nella politica coloniale di Giovanni Amendola', *Africa: Rivista Trimestrale*, 32, 1977.

Focardi, Filippo, *La guerra della memoria: la Resistenza nel dibattito politico italiano dal 1945 a oggi* (Bari: Laterza, 2005).

Foot, John, 'Via Rasella, 1944: memory, truth, and history', *Historical Journal*, 43, 2000.

Foot, John, *Fratture d'Italia* (Milan: Rizzoli, 2009).

Franzinelli, Mimmo, *L'Amnestia Togliatti 22 giugno 1946: colpo di spugna sui crimini fascisti* (Milan: Mondadori, 2006).

Gallico, Loris, 'Fascismo e movimento nazionale in Tunisia', *Studi Storici*, 19, 1978.

Gallo, Patrick, *For Love and Country: The Italian Resistance* (Lanham MD: University Press of America, 2003).

Gentile, Emilio, *Il culto del littorio: la sacralizzazione della politica nell'Italia fascista* (Bari: Laterza, 1993).

Gentile, Emilio, *La via italiana al totalitarismo: il partito, lo stato nel regime fascista* (Rome: La Nuova Italia Scientifica, 1995).

Gentile, Emilio, *La Grande Italia: ascesa e declino del mito della nazione nel ventesimo secolo* (Milan: Mondadori, 1997).

Gentile, Emilio, *The Struggle for Modernity: Nationalism, Futurism, and Fascism* (Westport CT: Praeger, 2003).

Gentile, Emilio, 'Fascism, totalitarianism and political religion: definitions and critical reflection on criticism of an interpretation', *Totalitarian Movements and Political Religions*, 5, 2004.

Gentile, Emilio, *Contro Cesare: cristianesimo e totalitarismo nell'epoca dei fascismi* (Milan: Feltrinelli, 2010).

Gentile, Emilio, *Italiani senza padre: intervista sul Risorgimento* (ed. Simonetta Fiori) (Bari: Laterza, 2011).

Ginsborg, Paul, *A History of Contemporary Italy: Society and Politics 1943–1988* (Harmondsworth: Penguin, 1990).

Ginsborg, Paul, *Family Politics: Domestic Life, Devastation and Survival 1900–1950* (New Haven CT: Yale University Press, 2014).

Giovannini, Paolo and Marco Palla (eds), *Il fascismo delle mani sporche: dittatura, corruzione, affarismo* (Rome: Laterza, 2019).

Gobetti, Ada, *Camilla Ravera: vita in carcere e al confino con lettere e documenti* (Parma: Guanda, 1969).

Katz, Robert, *Death in Rome* (London: Jonathan Cape, 1967).

La Rovere, Luca, *Storia dei Guf: organizzazione, politica e miti della gioventù universitaria fascista 1919–1943* (Turin: Bollati Boringhieri, 2003).

La Rovere, Luca, *L'eredità del fascismo: intellettuali, i giovani e la transizione al postfascismo 1943–1948* (Turin: Bollati Boringhieri, 2008).

Liguori, Guido, *Gramsci conteso: storia di un dibattito 1922–1996* (Rome: Riuniti, 1996).

Locatelli, Goffredo, *Il deputato dei 27 voti: la storia vera e mai scritta di Giovanni Amendola* (Milan: Mursia, 2014).

Lomellini, Valentine, 'The PCI and the USA: rehearsal of a difficult dialogue in the era of détente', *Journal of Modern Italian Studies*, 20, 2015.

Matteoli, Giovanni (ed.), *Giorgio Amendola: comunista riformista* (Soveria Mannelli: Rubbettino, 2001).

Melograni, Piero, *Fascismo, comunismo e rivoluzione industriale* (Bari: Laterza, 1984).

Melograni, Piero, *La modernità e i suoi nemici* (Milan: Mondadori, 1996).

Mercer, Ben, *Student Revolt in 1968: France, Italy and West Germany* (Cambridge: Cambridge University Press, 2020).

Millan, Matteo, *Squadrismo e squadristi nella dittatura fascista* (Rome: Viella, 2014).

Millan, Matteo, 'From "state protection" to "private defence": strikebreaking, civilian armed mobilisation and the rise of Italian fascism' in Matteo Millan and Alessandro Saluppo (eds), *Corporate Policing, Yellow Unionism and Strikebreaking 1890–1930; in Defence of Freedom* (Abingdon: Routledge, 2021).

Moorehead, Caroline, *A Bold and Dangerous Family: The Rossellis and the Fight against Mussolini* (London: Chatto and Windus, 2017).

Moorehead, Caroline, *A House in the Mountains: The Women Who Liberated Italy from Fascism* (London: Chatto and Windus, 2019).

Napolitano, Giorgio, *Intervista sul PCI* (ed. Eric Hobsbawm) (Bari: Laterza, 1976).

Natoli, Aldo, 'La "svolta" del 1929–30: il contrasto Longo–Terracini', *Rivista di Storia Contemporanea*, 5, 1976.

Natoli, Aldo, 'La storia del partito comunista di Amendola', *Rivista di Storia Contemporanea*, 7, 1978.

Natoli, Claudio, 'La sinistra del PCI negli anni sessanta', *Studi Storici*, 55, 2014.

Naumov, Vladimir, *Il PCI visto da Mosca* (Milan: Teti, 1978).

Neglie, Pietro, *Fratelli in camicia nera: comunisti e fascisti dal corporativismo alla CGIL (1928–1948)* (Bologna: Il Mulino, 1996).

Papadia, Elena, 'I vecchi e i giovani: liberal-conservatori e nazionalisti a confronto nell'Italia giolittiana', *Contemporanea*, 5, 2002.

Parlato, Giuseppe, *La sinistra fascista: storia di un progetto mancato* (Bologna: Il Mulino, 2000).

Passerini, Luisa, *Fascism in Popular Memory: The Cultural Memory of the Turin Working Class* (Cambridge: Cambridge University Press, 1987).

Pavone, Claudio, *Una guerra civile: saggio storico sulla moralità nella Resistenza* (Turin: Bollati Boringhieri, 1991).

Pertici, Roberto, 'Giovanni Amendola: l'esperienza socialista e teosofica (1898–1905)', *Belfagor*, 35, 1980.

Petrov, Angel, *Kozloduiskoto daskalche* (Moravitsa: ANPET Publishing, 1996).

Piffer, Tommaso, *Gli alleati e la Resistenza italiana* (Bologna: Il Mulino, 2010).

Pisanò, Giorgio, *Sangue chiama sangue* (Milan: Pidola, 1962).

Piscetelli, Enzo, *Storia della resistenza romana* (Bari: Laterza, 1965).

Pompeo D'Alessandro, Leonardo, 'Per la salvezza d'Italia: comunisti italiani, il problema del Fronte Popolare e l'appello ai "Fratelli in Camicia Nera"', *Studi Storici*, 54, 2013.

Portelli, Alessandro, *The Order Has Been Carried Out: History, Memory and Meaning of a Nazi Massacre in Rome* (New York: Palgrave Macmillan, 2003).

Portelli, Alessandro, 'Perché ci ammazzono? Ambiguità e contraddizioni nella memoria dei bombardamenti', *Roma Moderna e Contemporanea*, 11, 2003.

Portelli, Alessandro, 'Myth and morality in the history of the Italian Resistance: the hero of Polidoro', *History Workshop*, 74, 2012.

Pugliese, Stanislao, *Italian Fascism and Antifascism: A Critical Anthology* (Manchester: Manchester University Press, 2001).

Pugliese, Stanislao, *Fascism, Anti-Fascism and the Resistance in Italy: 1919 to the Present* (Lanham MD: Rowman and Littlefield, 2004).

Rastrelli, Carlo, *Carlo Scorza: l'ultimo gerarca* (Milan: Mursia, 2010).

Re, Lucia, 'Women at war: Eva Kühn Amendola (Magamal) – Interventionist, Futurist, Fascist', *Annali d'Italianistica*, 33, 2015.

Resta, Giorgio and Vincenzo Zeno-Zencovich, 'Judicial "truth" and historical "truth": the case of the Ardeatine Caves massacre', *Law and History Review*, 31, 2013.

Riaz, Fabio Fernando, *Benedetto Croce and Italian Fascism* (Toronto: University of Toronto Press, 2003).

Riaz, Fabio Fernando, *Benedetto Croce and the Birth of the Italian Republic 1943–1952* (Toronto: University of Toronto Press, 2019).

Roberts, David D., *Historicism and Fascism in Modern Italy* (Toronto: University of Toronto Press, 2007).

Sbarberi, Franco, 'Il dibattito sulla transizione nel comunismo italiano degli anni trenta', *Rivista di Storia Contemporanea*, 6, 1977.

Sgambati, Valeria, 'La formazione politica e culturale di Giorgio Amendola', *Studi Storici*, 32, 1991.

Soddu, Paolo, 'Sulla formazione di Ugo La Malfa', *Studi Storici*, 26, 1985.

Spadolini, Giovanni, *Il partito della democrazia: per una storia della 'terza forza' da Giovanni Amendola ad oggi* (Florence: Passigli, 1983).

Spini, Giorgio, *Italia liberale e protestante* (Turin: Claudiana Editore, 2002).

Spriano, Paolo, *Storia del partito comunista italiano*, 5 volumes (Turin: Einaudi, 1978).

Spriano, Paolo, *Intervista sulla storia del PCI* (ed. Simona Colarizi) (Bari: Laterza, 1979).

Spriano, Paolo, *Antonio Gramsci and the Party: The Prison Years* (London: Lawrence and Wishart, 1979).

Spriano, Paolo, *I comunisti europei e Stalin* (Turin: Einaudi, 1983).

Staron, Joachim, *Fosse Ardeatine e Marzabotto: storia e memoria di due stragi tedesche* (Bologna: Il Mulino, 2007).

Taylor, Anne, *Annie Besant* (Oxford: Oxford University Press, 1992).

Tranfaglia, Nicola, 'Socialisti e comunisti nell'Italia repubblicana: un dialogo sempre difficile', *Studi Storici*, 33, 1992.

Valiani, Leo, 'L'eredità politica di Giovanni Amendola', *Nord e Sud*, 23, 1977.

Vittoria, Albertina, *Intellettuali e politica alla fine degli anni '30: Antonio Amendola e la formazione del gruppo comunista romano* (Milan: Franco Angeli, 1985).

Vittoria, Albertina, 'La commissione culturale del PCI dal 1948 al 1956', *Studi Storici*, 31, 1990.

Zaghi, Valentino, '"Con Matteotti si mangiava": simboli e valori nella genesi di un mito popolare', *Rivista di Storia Contemporanea*, 19, 1990.

Index